THE INTERNATIONAL STEEL CARTEL

BASIC STRUCTURE OF THE INTERNATIONAL STEEL CARTEL

I. GENERAL POLICY-DETERMINING GROUPS

> International Steel Cartel

> European Steel Cartel

> Entente Internationale de l'Acier

II. NATIONAL GROUPS

a. Founders of the EIA

France	Belgium
Germany	Luxemburg

b. Associated with the EIA

Poland
Czechoslovakia

c. Coordinated with the EIA

Great Britain
United States

III. EXPORT SALES COMPTOIRS

a. Subordinated to the EIA

Semi-finished steel | Structural shapes | Merchant bars | Thick plates — Medium plates | Universal steel

b. Closely connected with the EIA

Wire rods | Hot rolled bands | Cold rolled bands | Wide flanged beams | Sheet piling

c. Connected with the ESC

Black sheets — Galvanized sheets

d. Policies coordinated with the ISC

Rails | Wire products

e. Policies loosely coordinated with the ISC

Tubes | Tin plates | Scrap

KEY

Jointly administered comptoirs | Buying comptoirs | Relatively unimportant comptoirs

THE
INTERNATIONAL
STEEL CARTEL

BY

Ervin Hexner, S.J.D., D.Pol.Sci.

ASSOCIATE PROFESSOR AT THE UNIVERSITY
OF NORTH CAROLINA

CHAPEL HILL : 1943

The University of North Carolina Press

Abbreviations

ISC   International Steel Cartel

ESC   European Steel Cartel

EIA   Entente Internationale de l'Acier

IRMA   International Rail Makers' Association

IWECO   International Wire Export Company

TNEC   Temporary National Economic Committee of the United States Congress

F.o.b.   Free on board

C.i.f.   Quoted price includes cost, insurance, and freight to the port specified.

ICTR   Iron & Coal Trade Review (London)

May Report Report of the Import Duties Advisory Committee on the Present Position and Future Development of the Iron and Steel Industry, Presented by the President of the Board of Trade to Parliament by Command of His Majesty, July, 1937 (Cmd. 5507).

Preface

THIS STUDY is mainly concerned with a description of the structure of the International Steel Cartel (ISC) and with some of its methods of operation, during the period of its most extensive development. In its prime (1938-1939) the ISC included all important exporting producers of steel throughout the world and embraced the export markets of all of the major steel commodities. Although even at that stage the organization was incomplete, there was every reason to believe that if the Second World War had not prompted its disintegration it would have been relatively perfected within a few years.

The investigation and evaluation of the ISC and of its principal activities may be regarded as important, whether considered from an economic or from a political point of view.[1] Both in times of peaceful development and of conflict, steel has been regarded as a key commodity of rapidly mounting significance, supplying the fundamental necessities of peaceful life and of warfare; and the ISC has been justly considered the organization completely controlling the world steel export market. The international trade in steel has extensively influenced the economic life of countries importing steel because of inadequate steel-producing facilities, as well as the domestic economy of a majority of the steel-exporting countries.[2] In the case of the United States, the export trade in steel did not greatly influence domestic economy. Before the outbreak of the Second World War United States producers did not participate in world steel exports to an extent

---

[1] "They represent, in their organization *inter se*, a unique type of political experiment, and their membership, organization, agreements, and sanctions all deserve the attention of students of politics." William Yandell Elliott and Others, *International Control in the Non-Ferrous Metals* (New York, 1937), p. 17.

[2] ". . . some of the countries in Europe are dependent upon, must have, export trade [in steel] or die." Temporary National Economic Committee (TNEC), *Hearings,* Part 20, p. 10924.

justified by their production and capacity. Their comparatively slight participation may be attributed largely to the fact that export prices of steel were not particularly attractive.[3] An analysis of the ISC discloses to the student of international politics and economics a wealth of material on the beclouded issue of modern industrial Malthusianism.

Although this study is focused on the development of one single marketing control, the author has no intention of avoiding deviations to more general discussions which might shed some light, even indirectly, upon the subject. One of the most relevant detours to be made in this connection deals, however briefly, with the discussion of recent developments in the conception of that economic pattern conventionally designated as a cartel. A discussion of the cartel concept must indicate the many political and social connotations ascribed to it, as well as the passionate controversies engendered by it. In many instances even such voluntarily restricted competition as is implicit in the classical cartel concept is viewed as endangering the development of a government in the democratic direction.[4] And the concentration of economic power in private hands, even when not actually abused, is viewed as a potential menace to the agencies legitimately exercising political control. In this connection it is illuminating to read the utterances of politicians, steel producers and steel consumers, trade unions, communists, and fascists, accompanying the establishment of the ISC in 1926. This huge cartel connoted for some governments and some politicians a landmark in the peaceful coöperation of nations, for steel exporters a means of mastering overproduction and eliminating "deadly" competition on the world steel market, for steel consumers a potential rise of domestic steel prices, for socialists a pillar on which a new Marxian economy could be built, for communists the establishment of a mighty power structure combatting labor, for many fascists

---

[3] TNEC, *Hearings*, Part 19, p. 10470.

[4] See e.g. Kemper Simpson, *Big Business, Efficiency and Fascism* (New York, 1941), p. 4. Thurman W. Arnold, *The Bottlenecks of Business* (New York, 1940), pp. 79, 106-107, 110, 292 ff. Henry Simons, *A Positive Program for Laissez-Faire* (Chicago, 1934), *passim*.

"It may be naïve to speak of cartelization as a cause of fascism; yet experience has shown it to be a ready instrument of those forces which seek to establish a fascist state." . . . "Cartelization involves such danger to democratic processes that we may well exclude it as a possible technique." A. H. Feller, "Public Policy of Industrial Control," p. 138 in C. J. Friedrich and E. S. Mason, *Public Policy*, Cambridge, 1940.

"We wish to preserve the freedom of enterprise and the incentives to individual effort which are both the motives and the accompaniments of our representative democracy." National Association of Manufacturers, *Limited Government and Personal Freedom* (New York, 1941), p. 24.

a bulwark of decadent democratic capitalism against the economic tendencies of strongly nationalistic doctrines.

There is little doubt that, in wartime, economic competition in the traditional sense is either unattainable or not particularly desirable, that almost nobody advocates flexible prices, and that the conception of marketing control by combinations of entrepreneurs takes an entirely different form and evaluation from the usual one.[5] Extreme scarcity in domestic and foreign supply, along with the necessary administration of production, distribution, and consumption for the purpose of national defense, make a specific form of marketing control (including pooling of production and rational distribution of demand) essential. Even the issue of concentration of economic power in private hands recedes into the background in wartime.

Economic doctrine in totalitarian states, even before the outbreak of the present hostilities, readily solved problems revolving about the conception of restriction of economic competition, industrial combinations, and concentration of private economic power. The totalitarian axiom that there is not (and must not be) major political, economic, and social tension, either between private entrepreneurs and the community, or among private individuals themselves, implies that all are subjected to service in the common interest according to a division of labor scheme. Thereupon, the problem is easily transmuted into simple statements more or less sincerely panegyrizing the body politic which authoritatively determines economic tools and objectives. State-

---

[5] "Under war conditions the entire process is reversed. . . . Competitors must become co-operators in order to meet the very minimum demand for shortage items. Control of this co-operation rests in government." Richard H. Hippelheuser, in Bernard M. Baruch, *American Industry in the War* (New York, 1941), p. 382. See also Thurman W. Arnold, *The Bottlenecks of Business*, p. 67. However, according to a report of the *New York Times*, Jan. 20, 1942, p. 13, Thurman W. Arnold told the House Small Business Committee in Jan. 1942, that "the defense program had disclosed a great tendency of established business to keep competition out of the defense field." He attacked "many types of conspiracy" developed on the basis of price-ceiling regulations. See also *Oriental Economist* (Tokyo), Sept. 1941, pp. 458 ff.

Walter Lippmann, analyzing in his column "Today and Tomorrow" (Mar. 1, 1942) the failure of the different political and economic classes to adjust themselves fast enough to the exigencies of the war, writes about American industry: ". . . the reason why industry was so slow in enlisting for the war and the reason why today— though great progress has been made—there is still no complete pooling of resources, is that the separate corporations are thinking of their competitors and are seeking to keep as intact as possible for the post-war period their normal business organizations." See also the list of wartime combinations attached to "Suspension of Antitrust Laws, etc.," *Hearing before a Subcommittee of the Committee on the Judiciary, United States Senate* (S. 2431), May 28, 1942.

ments about economic competition and about industrial combinations (as conducted in modern totalitarian regimes) lose their most attractive problematical elements if they cannot premise entrepreneurs as self-centered units, in the proper sense, striving for their own economic sake, besides their membership in a social community.[6]

Recent political and economic treatises have often juxtaposed contrasting elements of totalitarian and non-totalitarian economic structures. They accentuate rightly that whereas in non-totalitarian economies the entrepreneur primarily strives (legitimately) for economic profit, while only secondarily professing his paramount interest in the community of which he is a member unit, in totalitarian economies the situation is reversed, at least ostensibly. Such juxtapositions often disregard the fact that in an international economic structure where two such divergent types of economy co-exist the threatening attitude of the totalitarian one imposes several concepts and patterns of its own political and economic scheme, particularly the patterns of its industrial organizations, on the other non-totalitarian economies which these have to accept in order to avoid actual political conflicts and to prepare for impending conflicts.

One of the most striking and impressive recent examples of the tendency to reduce political tension by adjusting domestic economy in a democratic country according to conceptions advocated by a totalitarian nation exists in the negotiations during the twilight months of early 1939, between the two central associations of industries in Great Britain and Germany (under government auspices) to "replace destructive competition by constructive coöperation" on world markets, through the creation of a comprehensive network of international cartel agreements, and even more, through complete domestic cartelization. This significant accord, intending to superimpose a sym-

---

[6] Karl Pribram, *Cartel Problems* (Washington, 1935), p. 184, writes: "The authoritative policy shifts emphasis entirely away from the rights of individuals to free action in trading. It equally removes from monopoly all invidious meaning as bearing upon the restriction of the freedom of individuals. The tests of policy no longer derive from individualistic habits of thought." Concerning democracy within the internal government of cartels, see *ibid.*, footnote 41. Economic competition seems to be something desirable even with totalitarian economists. The editor of the *Wirtschaftskurve* (published by the *Frankfurter Zeitung*), Aug. 1939, p. 239, praises the system of compulsory prices based on authoritatively "recognized" costs (as contrasted to "real" costs) as "exercising in a certain sense the same effect as the market in free competition does." According to Thurman Arnold and J. Sterling Livingston, "The ease with which private commercial agreements could be used to wage war has been fully understood and appreciated by the Hitler government." ("Antitrust War Policy and Full Production," *Harvard Business Review*, Spring, 1942, p. 266.)

metrical system of mechanical principles upon all industries of the world, was signed in Düsseldorf, by the British Federation of Industries and the *Reichsgruppe Industrie,* the day after the invasion of Prague, on March 16, 1939.[7]

In the House of Commons a few days after signing the agreement, both the British Prime Minister and the president of the Board of Trade expressed regrets that political considerations had killed the Düsseldorf accord, though, in the opinion of Mr. Stanley, the president of the Board of Trade, the agreement was "a valuable piece of work which might have served as a basis on which the individual industries of the manufacturing countries of the world could have solved a great many of their difficulties." It was not the first nor the last time that the squeezing of industries into an imposed national and international "cartel" structure was regarded as the skeleton on which the economic coöperation of nations and "world peace" might be based.[8] *The Economist* censured the Düsseldorf agreement with admirable courage and intellectual honesty, marking by its criticism the transition in the British political mind from the nervous shortsightedness of the thirties to (for Britain) a significant long-term soberness. According to *The Economist* this accord was not in the interests of the British community as a whole, either on short terms or long. "That issue is, in a word, that the agreement proposed to compound a commercial felony . . . instead of securing from the Germans an abandonment of their unfair methods," wrote *The Economist,* "the British negotiators seem to have swallowed them lock, stock, and barrel."[9] It would be unjust to charge the British negotiators or British industries specifically with furthering the realization of the German

---

[7] *World Economic Survey, 1938-39,* published by the Economic Intelligence Service of the League of Nations (Geneva, 1939), p. 190. Prime Minister Neville Chamberlain informed the House of Commons, Mar. 15, 1939 (the day of the German invasion of Prague), that "These discussions are still proceeding and I believe are proceeding in a satisfactory manner." Cf. Neville Chamberlain, *In Search of Peace* (New York, 1939), p. 264.

[8] See e.g. the project advocated by Mr. Neville Chamberlain in the *Journal of the Monetary and Economic Conference of London,* June 15, 1933, No. 5, page 25. The Brüning-Laval accord of 1931, agreeing on an Economic Committee, which had to establish "industrial ententes" first between German and French industries, was based on similar ideas. About fifty "ententes" were born according to that pact. However, only one of them, that for electric material, became permanent. The rest of them were solely concerned with the limitation of German imports to France and disintegrated after a short while. Cf. Laurence Ballande, *Essai d'étude monographique et statistique sur les ententes internationales* (Diss., Paris, 1936), pp. 364-365.

[9] "An Obnoxious Agreement," *The Economist,* Mar. 25, 1939, p. 607.

conception of world economy. The Düsseldorf agreement of March 16, 1939, was just one incident within the avalanche of political appeasement, emphasized here not as characteristic, but as exceptional for British economic thinking. The responsibility of the negotiators and their supporters may be reduced owing to the psychosis from which the western democracies suffered at that time.[10]

To the best knowledge of this author, only one attempt has been made, a short time preceding the Second World War, to induce large international combinations to coöperate in the framework of a common organization. There is no doubt that the field on which such private collaboration is conceivable is very narrow and vague. Dr. Clemens Lammers, a German cartel expert, recommended early in 1938 the establishment of a common agency of large international marketing controls, attached to the International Chamber of Commerce. As a result of the efforts of Dr. Lammers the *Bureau of International Cartels* was established in Paris in the summer of 1938. According to the by-laws of this organization its object was, besides studying international marketing controls and publishing results of these studies, "to discuss questions of common interest" and "to support international organizations, which already exist or are in process of formation, by lending them material or other suitable collaboration."[11] Though the ISC was a member of this Bureau and was represented on its board of directors, this new agency did not try to influence ISC policies in the slightest way. The same is true in regard to other big international cartels.

Considering the significance of the position which those men held who were in control of the ISC and its most important agencies, it would be engagingly provocative to discuss fully their pertinent personal opinions and the personal relationship of these individuals to each other.[12] Though such an extension of this study might reveal

---

[10] As an illustration of the extraordinary mass-psychosis of the prewar period penetrating the western democracies the following sentence from an article of Godfrey Wynn, in the *Sunday Express* (London), Sept. 25, 1938, in connection with the Chamberlain-Hitler negotiations, may be quoted here. "Praise be to God and to Chamberlain. I find no sacrilege, no pathos, in coupling those two names." (Quoted in Charles Madge and Tom Harrisson, *Britain by Mass Observation*, Penguin Edition, 1939, p. 82.)

[11] See the by-laws of the *Bureau of International Cartels* in Appendix II. The official journal of the Bureau, *International Cartels*, contained reliable information about the structure of international combinations obtained from official sources. Only two issues of the Journal appeared.

[12] Fritz Redlich, *History of American Business Leaders*, Vol. I (Ann Arbor, 1940),

many interesting points for the economist and political scientist, the author does not feel competent to make that extension. Only one question should be touched on briefly in this connection. Were general economic doctrines brought up in the workings of the ISC and did such doctrines influence its policies? The answer is decidedly in the negative. There was a deliberate tendency to maintain the framework of dull routine, icy soberness, crude empiricism, and to avoid all issues which were not "practical" and "factual" in the strictest sense. In this regard there was no difference between the British-American and continental European groups.[13] A brief anecdote may illustrate this point. After a business meeting of the ISC a small private circle spoke about the feasibility of limiting international business fluctuations by maintaining inflexible prices on export markets. One of the industrialists ventured to question why the cartel policies of large industrial groups were so little influenced by considerations of economic doctrine. An aged participant in the discussion, recalling his university studies of many decades ago, answered the question with gentle cynicism by referring to J. E. Cairnes' famous characterization of political economy. He spoke approvingly of Cairnes' opinion that political economy is essentially detached from all "practical" ends, and quoted nearly by heart Cairnes' analogy, "What Astronomy does for the phenomena of heavenly bodies . . . that Political Economy does for the phenomena of wealth: it expounds the laws according to which those phenomena co-exist with or succeed each other; that

---

contains interesting details about American and German business leaders in the steel industry; however, this study has no relation to problems of the ISC.

[13] John Stuart Mill regarded Americans and Englishmen as more inclined to adopt the pattern of an "Economic man" and as concentrating more on "money-getting" in business negotiations than European continental people do. "An English political economist, like his countrymen in general," wrote Mill, "has seldom learned that it is possible that men, in conducting the business of selling their goods over the counter, should care more about their ease or their vanity than about their pecuniary gain. Yet those who know the habits of the Continent of Europe are aware how apparently small a motive often outweighs the desire of money-getting, even in the operations which have money-getting for their direct object." The differences discussed by Mill were not apparent in the workings of national groups within the ISC. There is another distinction made by the famous utilitarian, which obviously has disappeared during the last decades. J. S. Mill attributed to British-American political economists peculiar properties, contrasting them to economists of other countries. "In political economy for instance," writes Mill, "empirical laws of human nature are tacitly assumed by English thinkers, which are calculated only for Great Britain and the United States. Among other things an intensity of competition is constantly supposed, which, as a general mercantile fact, exists in no country in the world except these two." *System of Logic* (Longmans, London, 1936), VI, 591.

is to say, it expounds the laws of the phenomena of wealth."[14] Deliberately exaggerating, he added to Cairnes' analogy with a shade of contempt in his voice: "We are similar to those heavenly bodies, we are moving along within given physical and social limitations, our movements being observed and interpreted by economic doctrine, but mark you, no heavenly body moves in obedience to those registered rules of astronomy." The men directing the work of the ISC maintained a somewhat similar attitude to legal problems. Whereas they regarded it as natural that each national group abide by its national laws, it was tacitly assumed that legal problems did not belong in the sphere of ISC discussions.[15] To imply, however, that the men who influenced world steel policies were wholly devoid of an interest in economic, legal, and political doctrine, is to misconstrue their point of view. The ISC was administered solely according to business principles, omitting all which could complicate that relationship or enlarge the plane of possible issues. There was no desire to gain public recognition and approval of the policies of the ISC. However, there was a strong tendency to avoid positive disapproval of ISC policies by governments and by representatives of public opinion.

While many people, inside and outside the ISC, were cognizant of the significant structure of the ISC and understood the chief methods of its operation, there were few who knew the whole network comprehensively and minutely. Even the participants in the work of the ISC generally perceived in detail only those organizations and facts that directly concerned them; or, rather, they were satisfied in knowing only those things they needed in order to collaborate. There existed many miraculous subtleties of color and inflection in the interpretation of written and oral accords, tacit understandings, and

---

[14] Cf. J. E. Cairnes, *The Character and Logical Method of Political Economy* (New York, 1875), pp. 34-35. See also A. C. Pigou, *Economics in Practice* (London, 1935), p. 107. Joseph A. Schumpeter asks ". . . do not some of our hopes for the future turn on a belief that, like so many things in life, Economic Warfare will increasingly be rationalized in time? And if so, is it not the duty of science to try to precede practice rather than follow it?" (Preface to F. Zeuthen, *Problems of Monopoly and Economic Warfare,* London, 1930, p. xiii). J. W. F. Rowe, discussing practices in international cartels, writes: "The gulf between what is in practice and what should be in theory, is thus seen to be extremely wide." (W. Y. Elliott and Others, *International Control of Non-Ferrous Metals,* p. 84.) See also Henry Demarest Lloyd, *Lords of Industry* (New York, 1910), p. 47.

[15] Mr. Aloyse Meyer, the chairman of the European continental steel cartel, explained impressively why legal problems should be omitted in cartel discussions. *World Trade,* IX, No. 6, p. 63.

practices, known only to the men directly concerned and to the members of the brain-trust of the European continental steel cartel (EIA). This varying scale of information was only partly due to the secrecy surrounding certain matters; it was caused mainly by the inherent complexity of the control schemes of the steel export market. As a matter of fact, British and American representatives did not show any ambition to penetrate problems that seemingly were the concern of continental European members. This study does not discuss the intricacies known only to a few, but is rather concerned with the main structure of the ISC and its chief methods of operation, the greater part of which may be procured from published material. Only a small part of the information used in this study was derived from sources not generally accessible. Unfortunately even some published material was unobtainable because of difficulties attendant upon receiving literature from Europe, which accounts for several conjectural statements.

The author participated as one of the representatives of the Czechoslovakian national group in the transactions of the ISC during that period on which this study focuses. Though personal observation of the working of the ISC, the perusal of original documents and statistics, participation in those meetings to which smaller national groups were invited, and acquaintance (often only perfunctory) with persons who played major and minor roles in the ISC were helpful in interpreting facts and in writing this manuscript, this personal advantage should not be overestimated. In the first place, it was not the intention of the author to write what is called an "inside story" of the ISC. In addition, by the time work on the manuscript was actually begun, authentic information and important unpublished source material were no longer at the disposal of the author.

There are no recent comprehensive treatises on the ISC. The earlier period of the cartel was a frequent subject for French and German doctoral dissertations. Incidental information about recent developments may be found in books treating steel policies of particular countries.[16] Several general publications about industrial combinations discuss earlier periods of the ISC.[17] British and American

---

[16] See e.g. D. L. Burn, *The Economic History of Steel Making* (1867-1939), Cambridge (England), 1940, pp. 402-515; C. S. Richards, *The Iron and Steel Industry in South Africa* (Johannesburg, 1940), pp. 186-261 and *passim*.

[17] See e.g. Alfred Plummer, *International Combines in Modern Industry* (London, 1938), *passim*, and Eugene Staley, *Raw Materials in Peace and War* (New York, 1937), pp. 298 ff.

government publications contain much valuable material.[18] Although works on other international commodity controls exist, the fact that in no language is there a recent comprehensive discussion of the structure and activities of the ISC is striking.[19] The present study does not claim to bridge this conspicuous gap in economic and political literature, but attempts merely to suggest its existence and to give an incentive to others to complete the study.

The writer of a study such as this is to a great extent dependent on factual information, advice, criticism and suggestions from other persons. It is a pleasant duty for this author to acknowledge the great debt he owes to Professor Gottfried Haberler of Harvard University who read the whole typescript in its final form and gave the writer the benefit of his criticism, and saved him from several egregious displays of ignorance. My thanks are also due to Professor Rex Winslow of the University of North Carolina who read the first two chapters of the manuscript in its first shape. The American Iron and Steel Institute readily gave me statistical information. Dr. Harold Van Vechten Fay of the United States Tariff Commission, and Dr. René T. Harf, Attorney at the Superior Court in Luxemburg, now in New York, gave me information in regard to special problems. Mr. George H. Hobard, of Chapel Hill, translated the Merchant Bar Agreement which is attached to this book as an appendix. Miss Georgia H. Faison, reference librarian, and Mrs. Robert P. Weed, assistant reference librarian of the University of North Carolina, fully coöperated in procuring necessary literature, even from obscure corners. The editors of *Steel* gave me permission to reproduce published dates about the international steel trade. The editors of the *Southern Economic Journal* permitted the reproduction of the major part of my article about "American Participation in the International Steel Cartel," which was published in the July 1941 issue of that magazine. Mrs.

---

[18] Among British government publications the best known is the *Report of the Import Duties Advisory Committee on the Present Situation and the Future Development of the Iron and Steel Industry,* presented by the Board of Trade to Parliament, by command of his Majesty, July, 1937, Cmd. 5507, London, H.M.S.O. *(May Report).* Among American government publications the most important discussion of the ISC up to the end of 1937 is contained in *Iron and Steel,* Report 128 (Second Series) of the U. S. Tariff Commission, Washington, 1938. Several bulletins of the Bureau of Foreign and Domestic Commerce discuss the early history of the cartel. Important recent material may be found in Part 20 of the *Hearings* of the TNEC.

[19] ". . . there was a vast and comparatively neglected field of international relations in the efforts being made by the national groups of producers of basic commodities to reach international agreements with respect to quotas for annual production." W. Y. Elliott and Others, *International Control in the Non-Ferrous Metals,* p. 3.

George E. Mowry collaborated in putting the study into its first shape, and Mr. Allan R. Richards read the proofs and helped in making the index. Last but not least Mrs. Milton A. Abernethy coöperated in editing the whole manuscript. Her advice was of great assistance.

E. H.

The University of North Carolina,
Chapel Hill, N. C.

Contents

THE INTERNATIONAL STEEL CARTEL

CHAPTER ONE

General Considerations

I

EXPORTING STEEL PRODUCERS grouped in and represented by national steel cartels united in an association, commonly referred to as the International Steel Cartel, for the principal purpose of controlling the export market of steel commodities throughout the world. These entrepreneurs and their organizations were held together in the framework of the ISC through a network of economic mechanisms, established and maintained by an intricate web of formulated and expressly sanctioned rules, by rules not formally sanctioned, by tacit understandings, by customs, by mere loyalties, and, last but not least, by threats of retribution.

The exporter-producer (mostly represented by his national steel cartel) was the simplest entity within the organization. "Pure" exporters, who did not produce the steel commodities they exported, did not participate as full-fledged sub-entities in the ISC, though ISC rules did not contain any express restriction in this respect. The mere fact that national steel cartels did not, according to their autonomous regulations, admit to membership "pure" exporters determined this point for the ISC and its filial organizations. Distributors and distributor organizations played a very important role within the ISC. However, they did not participate in policy-determining functions. They were subject to those policies which in general did not disregard the interests of the distributors.[1]

The student of the constitution of the International Steel Cartel is necessarily confronted with problems similar to those of one who

---

[1] The fact that many of the important distributors were subsidiaries of one or more steel exporter-producers, as will be pointed out later in a separate chapter, made the situation somewhat intricate.

would seek definite statements regarding the constitution of the British Commonwealth of Nations.[2] In the latter case, the existence of an extensive body of literature and the particular Statute of Westminster form a basis for consideration of the problem. In the case of the ISC, however, such bases for study are lacking. The fact that the ISC was a young organization, that in its comparatively brief history its form had changed frequently, that there was no particular tendency on the part of its central agencies to formulate and record its structural plan, its policies and procedures, contributes to the difficulty in describing the organization precisely. The reticence of the organization to record the formulation of its structure increased even more after English-speaking countries entered the ISC. The British and American steel groups were loath to commit themselves to comprehensive written rules in cartel agreements. Whereas the national steel exporting groups and the specific commodity cartels within the ISC were based on rather explicit written agreements, there existed no comprehensive document organizing the actual main structure of the ISC, especially after the admittance of Great Britain in 1935. Other than the agreement organizing the continental European steel cartel (EIA) and the very brief documents establishing the membership of Great Britain and the United States there were only hazy records and conventions composing what may be called the constitution of the ISC. Although it is possible that in the process of time this lack of an embodiment of fundamental principles of central organization might have been partially eliminated, the fact remains that there was no tendency to create a comprehensive written document embracing the rules according to which this mighty organization operated. It would be easy to explain the lack of such a document on the basis of the inadequacies of private international law, or on the basis of the offensive implications carried by such structures as cartels. However, there were other fundamental reasons which enhanced the inclination to work in the atmosphere of perfect flexibil-

---

[2] The Foreign Secretary of Great Britain, Austen Chamberlain, put it thus: "More than once at the gatherings of Ministers of the British Empire we have considered whether we might not, whether we ought not, endeavour to put into black and white the Constitution of the British Empire . . . and every time, and with unanimity, representatives of those different governments have decided that, in the very elasticity which our want of logic and our want of precise definition afforded us, lay the secret of our unity and our concord. . . . It has been our practice, therefore, to eschew these large declarations of general principles, to avoid attempting to define exactly what should be done in every possible contingency that we can contemplate. . . ." (*Verbatim Record of the Sixth Assembly of the League of Nations,* Fifth Plenary Meeting, Sept. 10, 1925.) For a brilliant criticism of the peculiar British reluctance to make "commitments," see Professor Gilbert Murray's statement in *The Fortnightly* (London), Oct. 1941, p. 331.

ity permitted by the absence of comprehensive clear-cut documents. One of these reasons was the possibility that the interpretation of formulated rules might become a source of potential misunderstandings. Because of the extraordinary political and economic circumstances of the 1930's, new political developments were expected to occur which could not be anticipated by a written constitution. It is highly significant that the chairman of the continental European steel cartel, Mr. Aloyse Meyer, wrote that the "ideal entente" should have no written regulation at all. It should be governed "by a chart setting up the general principles of the agreement."[3]

It is difficult for a student of modern business administration to believe that the world steel export market could be controlled by so simple and ostensibly so weak a machine. The simplicity and the informality of the organization of the ISC detracted neither from its comprehensiveness nor from its great effectiveness. Juristic thinking and strict procedure which would have made similar operations intricate and would have resulted in a bureaucratic machine with red tape were entirely unknown in the realm of the ISC. Its most important meetings resembled a gathering of inconspicuous businessmen, while steel agreements and records of world-wide economic importance were so simple that they resembled understandings of far less significance. Jurisdictions were not precisely allotted, and there was no doctrine of the separation of powers, nor a system of checks and balances to impede the facility and speed that characterized the functioning of this group. The whole structure of the ISC resembled a machine of wheels revolving within wheels, in which the central agencies of the ISC were the master wheel around which all other wheels revolved. These other wheels were the national cartels, the cartels controlling the markets of particular steel commodities, and organizations of distributors. The seeming mystery of how such a machine could work so smoothly without a large coördinating bureaucracy is readily solved by the knowledge that the same individuals who established the policy of the ISC directed as well those sub-entities within the ISC.[4] Directors of large steel concerns represented their national groups not only in general policy-determining agencies but in important specific international steel commodity cartels as well. The professional agents of the national steel cartels (including the London representative of the American group) were further connecting links in this respect. The

---

[3] "Cartels and Trade Fluctuations," *World Trade*, IV, No. 6, pp. 62, 63.
[4] This personal union is responsible for the gradual growth of relatively independent single steel commodity cartels into one large organization.

success of the ISC in avoiding minor conflicts was largely due to the fact that the participants knew that stubborn opposition in minor disagreements would disrupt the entire structure. For this reason a regime of arbitration and a system of deposits did not actually operate even in those instances where they were formally established.

In discussing the ISC and its component entities, terms have often been used indiscriminately. This is not the place to clarify all pertinent terminological problems. Such an attempt would require a separate extended study. However, it would be well to explain a few of the basic terms which were most subject to misunderstanding. "International Steel Cartel" is not an official name. It was and is a name "by general repute" as contrasted to a name "formally" borne by a social entity claiming a "legitimacy" to its exclusive use. It has been conventionally used to designate the network of institutions composing a collective marketing control of steel commodities designed to direct the world export market in steel. Most of the misunderstandings arose because one large unit within the framework of the International Steel Cartel—the European continental steel cartel—bore the name Entente Internationale de l'Acier (EIA), and this name has often been translated into English as International Steel Cartel.[5] The identification of the EIA with the ISC was justified until 1935 because until the entrance of Great Britain into a general agreement with the EIA there was no special reason for differentiating between the EIA and the ISC.[6] After Great Britain entered the cartel, the EIA became one part, and the British group another of the European Steel Cartel (ESC). At that time the European Steel Cartel may be considered the ISC. After America entered the cartel, at the begining of 1938, the ISC included three overlapping units, the EIA, comprising the continental European producers, the EIA and the British group, com-

---

[5] To demonstrate the confusion in literature of terms and names used in this connection the reader is referred to Robert Liefmann's *Cartels, Concerns and Trusts* (New York, 1933), p. 156, in which he calls the EIA in English "West-European Steel Ingot Association," and in French "Entente cordiale [*sic*] de l'acier." Dr. Liefmann called the EIA, in the eighth German edition of his book *Kartelle, Konzerne und Trusts* (Stuttgart, 1930, p. 193), "Westeuropäische Rohstahlgemeinschaft," attaching to this name in quotation marks "Entente cordiale de l'acier." Dr. T. W. Stadler in *Kartelle und Schutzzoll* (Berlin, 1933), p. 65, uses the French name "Entente Cordiale de l'Acier" too.

[6] The official German name for the continental European steel cartel was originally "Internationale Rohstahlgemeinschaft" (IRG). After 1933, adapting its name to the changes in its structure, it became "Internationale Rohstahl-Export-Gemeinschaft" (IREG). However, German literature often called the EIA "Festländische Rohstahlgemeinschaft," emphasizing that it embraced the continental steel industries only.

posing the European Steel Cartel, and the EIA, the British group, and American group, all of them composing the comprehensive ISC. Another reason for the confusion between EIA and the ISC was caused by the fact that the EIA often functioned in many agreements and actions as a trustee for the whole ISC without indicating that fact.

The expression "international" in the name of the ISC contrasted this organization with national steel cartels.[7]

The word "steel" in the expression ISC designated by a common denominator the commodity groups whose export market the ISC intended to control, thus distinguishing them from pig iron, iron alloys, special steels, and commodities made of steel.[8] Only rolled steel was regarded as within the jurisdiction of the ISC. Broadly speaking, semifinished steel, structural shapes, broad-flanged beams, merchant bars and sections, thick plates (3/16 inch and up), medium plates (1/8 inch and less than 3/16 inch), large flats or universals (6 inch and up), cold and hot-rolled bands and strips, wire rods, wire products, heavy rails, sheets less than 1/8 inch (black and galvanized), tinplates, sheet piling, and tubular products were direct and indirect objects of the ISC agreements.[9]

In the broadest sense even the International Scrap Convention belonged in the ISC framework, though this was a buying and not a selling cartel.

The word "cartel" was generally used in the name of the ISC

---

[7] Concerning national groups as units in "supernational economic coöperation" see William Yandell Elliott and Others, *International Control in the Non-Ferrous Metals*, pp. 22-23.

[8] An up-to-date definition of the term "steel" may be found in the recently issued *Steel Product Manual*, published by the American Iron and Steel Institute. Abraham Berglund and Philip G. Wright (*The Tariff on Iron and Steel*, Washington, 1929, p. 15) adopted the definition of the term "steel" as submitted by a special committee to the Sixth Congress of the International Association for Testing Materials in New York City, 1912. Though this definition had significant influence on modern nomenclature it has never been generally adopted and today falls short of covering the field. See *Sixth Congress of the International Association for Testing Materials*, Section A (Metals), p. 147, Vienna, 1912. Concerning new German nomenclature see Leopold Scheer, *Was ist Stahl* (Berlin, 1938), p. 1.

[9] Concerning production processes and trade terms for steel products see C. R. Daughterty, M. G. De Chazeau, and S. S. Stratton, *The Economics of the Iron and Steel Industry*, Vol. I, *passim*. The *Steel Product Manual*, published by the American Iron and Steel Institute, and the *Federal Standard Stock Catalog*, published by the Government Printing Office, contain definitions of current trade terms. A distinction between bars, plates, strips, and sheets is included in Federal Specification, Section IV, Part 5, QQ-S-636 (June 20, 1941). The expression "sheet piling" is used for steel piles forming a continuous wall, employed in the constuction of sea walls, bridges, and other similar structures.

because, according to its traditional meaning, "cartel" designates a voluntary organization of legally and economically independent entrepreneurs, or entrepreneur groups, collectively controlling the market of a commodity. A separate chapter of this study is devoted to the discussion of recent developments in the cartel concept. That chapter is concerned with the question of why the expression "cartel" was not used officially in designating the particular entities of the ISC. As a matter of fact, all national groups and single commodity cartels substituted for the expression "cartel" less significant terms such as association, federation, bureau, company, entente, convention, comptoir.[10] For many the word "cartel" carried the unfavorable connotation of anti-social and illegal activity. Although it seems incredible, the mere avoidance of the term "cartel" saved those bodies from much adverse criticism. A brief quotation may illustrate this point. A few years ago, C. Nattan-Larrier, in discussing how public opinion regarded the establishment of the EIA, noted with a certain indignation that the French public falsely called the EIA "Le Cartel de l'Acier." Although the EIA, according to Nattan-Larrier, was "only an entente," the use of the word "cartel" prejudiced the sentiments of French economic and political circles against the EIA.[11] The expression "cartel" in the name of the ISC did not originate in "official" circles, because, as mentioned above, the ISC had no "official" name.

The ISC was chiefly built upon two sets of agencies: national groups, on the one hand, and export sales comptoirs for specific commodities, on the other. The expression "national groups" denotes the organizations of steel producer-exporters in various countries which negotiated general policies for the steel exports of their respective countries. They assumed responsibility in the cartel sense for a coordinated policy concerning these exports. Within the export sales

---

[10] J. Tchernoff, *Ententes Economiques et Financières* (Paris, 1933, pp. 55-56) states that the expression "comptoir" implies (in this connection) an organization endowed with legal personality. According to him, comptoirs work in the form of regular commercial companies. However, a majority of the comptoirs within the ISC (e.g. those for merchant bars, wire rods, bands and strips, plates) were not commercial companies and had no legal personality. Frederic Benham designates comptoirs, rightly, as cartels. ("The Iron and Steel Industry of Germany, France, Belgium and the Saar," *London and Cambridge Economic Service,* Oct. 1934, Special Memorandum No. 39, p. 34.)

[11] See C. Nattan-Larrier, *La Production Sidérurgique de l'Europe Continentale et l'Entente Internationale de l'Acier* (Paris, 1929), p. 301. As to the United States, it is sufficient to quote the unfavorable criticism of private collectivisms which become concealed cartel systems after the European model, by President F. D. Roosevelt in his message to Congress of Apr. 20, 1938.

comptoirs, the national groups covered only particular commodities.[12] The expression "national group" was applied to collectives of producer-exporters within the export sales comptoirs even though these national groups did not particularly belong to the eight national groups participating in the formulation of the general policy of the ISC. Thus, for example, Italy, without participating in the formulation of the general policy of the ISC, joined the export sales comptoir known as the International Rail Makers' Association, with a share of less than one per cent, and thus was called a "national group."

The expression "export sales comptoir" referred to individual international cartel organizations which embraced specific commodities (e.g., merchant bars, structural shapes, wire rods, rails). Tradition and agreements determined to what extent the ISC and its agencies interfered with the policies of an export sales comptoir. Some comptoirs were subordinate to the paternal organization; others were fairly independent. Some of the comptoirs actually existed even at the time when the EIA was in the process of distintegration (between 1931 and 1933); others even before the establishment of the ISC. The expression "comptoir" often has been used as an abbreviation for "export sales comptoir."

For several reasons the International Steel Cartel did not concern itself with the marketing control of iron ore and pig iron. The marketing system for these materials did not fit into the marketing scheme for steel. No proper conditions existed for the development of an international marketing control scheme in iron ore. Large international steel concerns produced their own iron ores or frequently bought iron ores on long-term contracts from other entrepreneurs according to prices agreed upon on the basis of general conditions on the steel market. Naturally, prices and availability of scrap iron and steel greatly influenced the "market" for iron ores. Generally speaking there was a great conservatism in buying iron ores. Business relations were not easily severed between sellers and buyers of iron ores, even if a somewhat higher price was demanded than that of another mine whose ores the steel plant did not customarily use. However, the relatively satisfactory operation of the International Scrap Convention made ISC members consider a buying organization for iron ores.[13] In many respects the pig iron market remained a com-

---

[12] There were a few comptoirs in which entrepreneurs acted in their own name, besides being represented by national groups, or even without being represented by national groups. [13] *ICTR*, March 24, 1939, p. 551.

petitive market up to 1939, although many separate international cartel agreements existed (e.g. the Franco-Belgian-Luxemburg pig iron cartel and the one involving Holland, Germany, and Czechoslovakia).[14] Though the discussion of the reasons for that situation would be interesting, it would enlarge this paper considerably. It need only be indicated that often the lack of adequate tariff protection in regard to pig iron and iron ore made large international cartel agreements difficult. It happened that entrepreneurs and countries strongly connected by cartels in the market of steel exports competed in the market of pig iron.

The comprehensiveness and depth of the ISC organization changed continually. Several of its parts had a transient or rudimentary character; however, there existed a distinct, rather permanent organized collectivity, with a recognizable articulate volition, expressed according to more or less definite rules of procedure, and there was even gradually developing what is called institutional inertia. Therefore, the ISC may be (and has been) regarded as an entity in international economy, when viewed from other than legal aspects. The question of whether the character of entities in the legal sense ("a legal right- and duty-bearing unit") may be attributed to the ISC as a whole, on the one hand, and to its governing organization (as distinguished from the filial organizations), on the other, needs further consideration. Such consideration would have to take into account the fact that legal systems may arbitrarily determine under what conditions aggregates of people, operating according to known procedure to attain a common objective, are to be considered "right- and duty-bearing," or legal units. Furthermore, the recognition of a social structure as a legal unit may carry different consequences in the various legal systems in existence. From the point of view of one or more national legal systems, the question regarding the legal status of an organization such as the ISC, although involved, would not be insurmountably difficult to answer. However, in this study the question must be considered principally from an international point of view. There is no answer in what is called international private law to the question of what elements constitute international "personality" status.

---

[14] The pig iron prices fixed by the Franco-Belgian-Luxemburg pig iron cartel were the following in 1938, in Belgian francs, per metric ton: January 800, February 650, July 450, September 500. The Belgian National Bank called attention to the relative inflexibility of prices of commodities controlled by the ISC as contrasted with fluctuations in pig iron prices. *Bulletin d'Information et de Documentation,* "La Situation Economique de la Belgique en 1938," p. 35.

Within the hazy structure of international private (and public) law
the section concerning private international economic entities and their
personality status has been particularly dark and undeveloped.[15] As
will be pointed out later in this study, after May 1935, when Great
Britain joined the cartel, the ISC as a whole, and its central policy-
determining agency, were bodies without a fixed domicile, without a
permanent chairman, without an official business agency, and without
tangible or intangible property in the conventional sense, though they
were distinct from their component members and were supposed to
carry out an agenda differing from that of their member units. Thus
the ISC might be regarded as an "itinerant international association."
The legal status of itinerant international associations has been considered in the literature of international law, but only in regard to
so-called nonprofit organizations.[16] Although the ISC in itself was

---

[15] A very brief but comprehensive survey of modern treatises on international cartel
law is contained in Dr. Heinrich Friedländer, *Die Rechtspraxis der Kartelle und Konzerne in Europa* (Zürich, 1938), pp. 307 ff. No pertinent material on this topic can
be found in the usual textbooks on private international law. See e.g. G. E. Cheshire,
Private International Law (Oxford, 1935), *passim*. The League of Nations devoted a
special study to a *Review of the Legal Aspects of Industrial Agreements* (Geneva,
1930), prepared by Henri Decugis (France), Robert E. Olds (United States), and
Siegfried Tschierschky (Germany). "Private international law has only recently dealt
with these problems," wrote the authors, "and the conclusion has been reached that
the question is one of such difficulty that certain of the problems raised appear almost
insoluble." (p. 18.) Legal forms assumed by cartels are viewed on the basis of
national legal systems. "These international contractual organizations represent simply
a grouping of interests, and do not generally possess individual juridical personality.
They are not . . . associations or companies capable of possessing personal property or
of concluding contracts with third parties, since the members of these cartels have not
as yet renounced in favour of a joint body their right to sell or purchase direct. Such
cartels, however, constitute as between their members, unions or corporate groups,
which can hardly operate in any permanent sense without fairly strict discipline and
an internal administrative organization to direct their activities and enforce the clauses
of the contract as against members of the cartels." (pp. 6-7.)

[16] Cf. André Normandin, *Du Statut Juridique des Associations Internationales*
(Paris, 1926), p. 57. A Belgian statute (*Moniteur Belge,* November 5, 1919, pp. 5872-
74) regulates the "civil status" of international associations pursuing scientific objectives. The *Institut de Droit International* adopted a proposal of an international convention concerning the "legal" position of international associations "in order to enhance
the development of international associations which do not pursue profit-making objectives." (Both the Belgian law and the proposal of the convention of 1912 are published
as appendices in André Normandin, *op. cit.,* pp. 191-195, 199-217.) The League of
Nations periodically published *Handbook of International Organizations* and a (quarterly) *Bulletin of Information on the Work of International Organizations,* including in
these lists of international trade associations of industries. No attempt was made to
include lists of international commodity controls. The Introduction to the *Handbook*
of 1937 states that "The Handbook ignores international organizations which are run
solely for profit. . . ."

a nonprofit association, its purpose was to increase the profits of its member units. Even the consideration of nonprofit entities in international law did not result in very conclusive definitions of personality status. As far as concepts of international private associations are operative in international law, they imply the existence of a definite domicile[17] for the association and its recognition by at least one national legal system as a legal unit, thus having "a standing in the courts."[18] This conception corresponds to the traditional doctrine that, in principle, only states are entities in international law, while private persons (physical and artificial) can be obligated and authorized only by mediation of states. The ISC controlled the world export market of steel without a corporate charter from, or any other recognition as a legal unit by, any politically established public authority.

All international bureaux and all commissions for the regulation of matters of international interest, established after the Covenant of the League of Nations went into effect, were compulsorily placed under the direction of the League in Article 24 of the Covenant. Although the definition of "international bureaux" is not clarified in the Covenant, it might be assumed that large international cartels and their agencies are not excluded from it and that the activity of such an organization as the ISC is a matter of "international interest." However, the article was interpreted by the League Council and by students of international law as applying only to those international organizations which were created by collective diplomatic conven-

---

[17] International private law distinguishes between nationality and domicile of legal entities. Legal entities are presumed to have a domicile. A dual civil domicile is "impossible." See G. C. Cheshire, *op. cit.*, p. 131. See also, Barbosa de Magalhaes, "La doctrine du Domicile," in *Recueil des Cours, Académie de Droit International,* 1928, III, *passim.*

[18] "Personality is the capacity to enjoy legal rights and to have a standing in the courts." (Joseph H. Beale, *A Treatise on the Conflict of Laws,* II, 652, New York, 1935.) Frederic Hallis, *Corporate Personality* (London, 1930), p. 242, writes: "The existence of a corporate person will not be the result of a creative act of the state. It will have its foundation in social fact and its origin in the initiative of its living members." However, in the next paragraph he limits this statement somewhat by expounding: "In order that an organization of individuals may have legal personality, that is, be a legal right- and duty-bearing unit, it must have a directing idea, a definite aim which gives it a *'local habitation* and a name.'" [my italics.] The concept of corporations as defined by Chief Justice John Marshall is highly significant for the problem under discussion. "A Corporation is an artificial being, invisible, intangible, and existing only in contemplation of law. Being a mere creature of law, it possesses only those properties which the charter of its creation confers upon it, either expressly or as incidental to its very existence." (*Dartmouth College v. Woodward, 4 Wheat. 518, 636,* [1819].) See also Alexander Nékám, *The Personality Conception of the Legal Entity* (Cambridge, 1938), *passim.*

tions.[19] Thus the restricted interpretation of the Covenant article excluded private international organizations of huge public interest, such as the ISC, although the text of the Covenant did not warrant their exclusion. This is not to say that the possible "direction" of the League could have resulted in the actual determination of the price policy of large international cartels, but the authority of the League (the French text speaks of *"seront placé sous l'autorité de la Société"*) might have resulted in the much-desired public supervision of large international commodity controls, and in measures necessary to adjust cartel policies to international public interest, if a politically efficient League could have agreed upon the substance and formulation of international public interest.[20]

Though the ISC did not regard itself subject to any single national government, it was in a certain sense tolerated by those national governments which did not object to their national steel cartels joining the ISC or which permitted other activities of the ISC on their territory. The ISC created and enforced business rules embracing important marketing regulations, leaving it to participants to adjust their conduct in harmony with national legal rules.[21] National steel cartels and their members, composing the pillars on which the ISC as a whole and its policy-determining agencies rested, were subject to domestic legal regulations, both in their internal organization and in their position within the ISC. It may even be stated, though not without reservations, that those international organizations and agen-

---

[19] See e.g. Jean Ray, *Commentaire du Pacte de la Société des Nations* (Paris, 1930), pp. 667 ff. Mr. Ray quotes on page 670 the resolution of the Council of the League (1921) concerning the restriction of the application of the article to "international economic organisations which are concerned with general economics and created by collective diplomatic conventions." He further quotes the resolution of the Council of 1928, according to which this provision relates to "official" organizations only, and not to private institutions. The extent of authority conferred upon the League in placing international bureaux under its direction is discussed on pp. 671 ff. See also the four supplements to Ray's work, Paris, 1931-1935. Literature of international law often discussed the marked discrepancy between the English and French version of the covenant article. See Hans Kelsen, *Legal Technique in International Law* (Geneva, 1939), pp. 170 ff.

[20] This directing power might have been used to support international economic sanctions by a politically strong League.

[21] Dr. Heinrich Friedländer, in discussing the position of international cartels in international private law, indicates that basic principles are gradually developing for an "international law of particular industries," embracing the regulation of business conditions, marketing orders for jobbers, consumers, and so on. He quotes the international steel market as an example. (*Op. cit.*, p. 309.) Such regulations may be effective and may even be enforced; however, calling them "legal" would require further elucidation going to the very roots of what is called "law" and "legal."

cies within the framework of the ISC which had a distinct domicile were subject to legal regulations of the country of their domicile. Thus, the International Rail Makers' Association with headquarters in London, or the International Wire Export Company in Brussels were constituted according to legal forms and performed their local activities according to the legal regulations of England and Belgium respectively.

It is highly improbable that problems in regard to the status of international cartels may be answered according to what we call international law today. Thus those international cartels which have no domicile, although they have an external organization, may get along as *de facto* entities in a legal vacuum, somewhat resembling people whose citizenship is not recognized by any state, but who can nevertheless be sentenced if and when a national court autonomously determines facts establishing its own jurisdiction.[22]

II

Typical ISC activities as culled from the terms of its agreements, from a knowledge of its practices, and of the effects of its operations, are as follows: first, the establishment of a general marketing scheme for the steel export market, and the establishment of agencies to administer that scheme and to amend it if necessary; second, the establishment of national organizations of steel exporters who controlled the steel exports of their countries; third, the establishment of marketing schemes for particular steel commodities and of agencies to administer them; fourth, the establishment of quota systems determining the sharing of markets of particular steel commodities by national exporting groups; fifth, the establishment of uniform pricing systems, and the restriction of nonprice competition; sixth, the coördination of price policies among the different controlled steel products; seventh, the establishment of uniform selling conditions; eighth, the allocation of markets and customers; ninth, the stabilization of export prices within rather narrow limits throughout periods of business fluctuations; tenth, the organization of merchandising functions in impor-

---

[22] According to a modern view international law is primitive law. From this point of view, disputant states themselves may determine the facts to which international law attaches legal consequences. "Unlike the technically developed national law, it does not institute special organs authorized to establish in a legal procedure the existence of concrete facts as determined by the law in order that the consequences also prescribed by the law may be attached to these facts." (Hans Kelsen, "Recognition in International Law," *American Journal of International Law*, Oct., 1941, p. 607.)

tant importing countries; eleventh, the protection of the domestic market of the adherents; twelfth, the conclusion of "penetration agreements" with steel producers of non-member countries, fixing conditions under which the ISC penetrated the markets of producers who shared their domestic steel markets with the ISC; thirteenth, fighting or moderating outside competition; and fourteenth, the establishment of coördinated propaganda to promote the use of steel.[23]

It may be asked if the cartel agreements or conventions provided for the exchange of technical experience. Significantly, unlike marketing controls in several other industries, those of steel were not based on an administered or secret technical knowledge. Viscount Greenwood of Holbourne, who had an equally important role in British politics and in the British steel industry, said: "Our industry is more than national, it is supremely international. No industry in the world pools its knowledge and its friendships more regularly than the steel industry."[24] The chairman of the German national steel cartel, Dr. Ernst Poensgen, emphasized, "We have visited each others' works, and been shown their progress, and if at any time there was in our family a naughty boy who would prefer to keep something in the dark because he believed himself to be cleverer than his brothers, the latter have soon shown him that they could do it, and make it still better than he."[25] Even though these emphatic statements of friendship may be minimized it should be noted that the particular form in which the marketing control of national and international steel industries developed was conditioned by the fact that in the steel industry the necessity of artificially pooling patents and technical experiences did not exist to the same extent and in the same manner that led to the formation of combinations of the corporate type in certain chemical industries.[26] As a matter of fact, in the last two decades a tremendous

---

[23] The so-called charter groups (Belgium, France, Germany, Luxemburg) participated in all of the principal activities of the organization, whereas the associated national groups (Czechoslovakia and Poland) and the coördinated national groups (Great Britain and America) did not take part in all of them.

[24] *Journal of the Iron and Steel Institute,* CXXXV (1939), 30P. There is little doubt that Lord Greenwood meant an unrestricted exchange of knowledge and technical experience, as contrasted with pooling, which is restricted to a closed group and accompanied by the exclusion of nonmembers of the group.

[25] *Ibid.,* p. 34P.

[26] The late Sir Alfred Mond (Lord Melchett), one of the leaders of the chemical industry of the world, discussed the advantages of industrial combinations of the corporate type as contrasted to cartels. To secure a free exchange of information of a technical character, according to Sir Alfred Mond, "There must be more than a temporary armistice; there must be permanent peace. The cartel or combination which

rate of technical improvement occurred in the steel industry. Neither national nor international cartel ties slowed up this development. The ISC did not regulate capacity, thus it was not concerned with limiting the main effect of technical progress. But even in those national cartels where enlargement of plants was subject to domestic cartel restrictions, these provisions did not hamper the introduction of improved processing methods. The relatively slow introduction of continuous strip mills to Europe was mainly due to lack of capital and to timidity as to absorption of large quantities of sheets.[27] No accusations were ever made against international steel industries for glaring abuses of patents or processing secrets. Steel commodity controls, especially geographic limitations of markets, were not based on such mechanisms.

III

There is no specific work on the early history of national and international collective marketing controls in steel. Comprehensive treatments of the development of industrial combinations in general contain some accounts, but in a rather unsatisfactory form.[28] In the country often referred to as the mother of steel production,[29] several centuries

---

exists only for a limited number of years is in reality nothing more than an armistice in industrial warfare; and people are not going to hand over arms and methods of warfare to those who in a few years may be fighting them again." *Industry and Politics* (London, 1928), p. 236. Apparently these views were not held by those organizing marketing controls in the steel industry. However, Dr. Hjalmar Schacht, many decades ago, admonished the German industry to drop the cartel pattern of organization in favor of the "American" pattern of combinations of the corporate type, to combat foreign competition more efficiently. See Roman Piotrowski, *Cartels and Trusts* (London, 1933), p. 55 n.

[27] The fixing of prices on the material made by the patented continuous mill process was in reasonable limits and had nothing to do with ISC regulations. See TNEC, *Hearings,* Part 19, pp. 10391 ff. Certain patents for the production of special construction steel and special alloy steel were rather exceptional and did not touch on ISC policies. See e.g. TNEC, *Hearings,* Part 19, p. 10500.

[28] Even Jacob Strieder (*Studien zur Geschichte kapitalistischer Organisationsformen,* München, 1925), devoted relatively little space to iron and steel combinations. In his monograph, *Die Deutsche Montan- und Metall-Industrie im Zeitalter der Fugger,* Berlin (VDI Verlag), 1931, he almost completely omitted any discussion of the iron and steel industry. Only on page 226 is there a general remark related to the 16th century, stating that even at the end of the Middle Ages metal-producing entrepreneurs joined in "modern" combinations, like fusions and cartels. The *Kartell Rundschau,* 1926, p. 216, mentions a German steel-wire cartel of Altona in the 18th century. This cartel was formed in 1764, often renewed, and finally dissolved by public authorities in 1810. (Quoted from Piotrowski, *op. cit.,* p. 352.) Piotrowski (*op. cit.,* p. 356-357) mentions a government-sponsored Swedish iron cartel of 1745.

[29] "English technical experts were our great teachers during the establishment of the German iron industry." Dr. Ernst Poensgen, "The Economic Relations Between the

ago market controls in steel were regularly based on the coöperation
of several entrepreneurs, in contrast to the marketing controls exercised by large, single, integrated economic units. Even at the time
when Edward, Lord Dudley, and later his son, Dud Dudley, exercised
their "monopolies" concerning "the mistery, way, art, and means of
melting of iron ore with sea-coals, or pit-coals, and of making the same
into cast works or bars as aforesaid, and the same iron so cast and
made to utter and sell in gross or retail or otherwise . . ." there was
coöperation in the English steel market on the part of many of his
rivals who in joint effort destroyed his tools and ejected him by
violence from his plant because by means of his new process he was
able to sell pig iron for four pounds sterling instead of for the usual
price of seven, and bars for twelve pounds sterling instead of for the
usual price of fifteen to eighteen.[30] T. S. Ashton, in discussing early
"combinations of capitalists" in the iron and steel industry, rightly
criticizes that interpretation of economic history "according to which
an original system of free competition has been metamorphosed into a
new system of industrial monopoly. . . ."[31] There is sufficient literature concerning domestic steel combinations in the second part of the
nineteenth century.[32] Alfred Marshall's discussion of the combination

English and Continental Iron and Steel Industries," *Stahl und Eisen,* Sept. 17, 1936,
pp. 1063 ff.

[30] W. H. Price, *The English Patents of Monopoly* (Boston, 1906), pp. 109 and 194.
The industrial romance of Dud Dudley as discussed in his *Metallum Martis* (1665),
and even the fact that he produced a moderate quality of steel with mineral fuel, has
been subject to much discussion. See for example, T. S. Ashton, *Iron and Steel in the
Industrial Revolution* (Manchester, 1924), pp. 10-12, 19. The texts of patents "for
making iron without spoyle of wood" are reprinted in R. H. Tawney and E. Power,
Tudor Economic Documents, Vol. II, London, 1924. Dudley's steel patent was expressly
exempted from the Statute of Monopolies (1623-24). Concerning the concept of a
"monopolizer," Sir Edward Coke, the famous English jurist, said he was the kind of
man who would "never thrive or prosper" and who "engrosseth to himself what should
be free for all men. . . ." Speech in the House of Commons, March 1, 1620; cf.
Cobbett's *Parliamentary History of England* (London, 1806), I, 1198.

[31] T. S. Ashton, *op. cit.,* p. 185. Alfred Fell (*The Early Iron Industry of Furness
and District,* Ulverston, England, 1908, p. 254) notes an agreement of iron-masters,
made in 1757, "that no bar iron at home be sold under £19.—, at Liverpool £17.—
per ton." Harry Scrivenor's *History of the Iron Trades from the Earliest Records to
the Present Period,* new ed., London, 1854, contains significant material in this respect.
E. Benjamin Andrews, "Trusts According to Official Investigations," *Quarterly Journal
of Economics,* III (1888/89), 120-21, says that industrial combinations, essentially the
same as they existed in 1888, "have existed for centuries, being, in fact, among the
oldest institutions of which history speaks." He regarded only the magnitude of the
movement of recent origin.

[32] See e.g., D. L. Burn, *The Economic History of Steelmaking 1867-1939,* Cambridge (England), 1940. Arthur Klotzbach, *Der Roheisenverband,* Düsseldorf, 1926,

movement, in a book published in 1879, shows that there existed a widespread cartel organization in England in the 1870's.[33] R. Piotrowski's attack on German and Austrian cartel literature which insisted that the economic pattern of cartels was born on May 9, 1873, in Vienna (Austria) coming "down like a bolt from the blue" seems well founded.[34]

The first modern international steel cartels were probably the convention concluded between British and German gas pipe exporter-producers, agreed upon November 9, 1881, and the agreement among British, German, and Belgian exporter-producers of boiler tubes, both agreements coming into effect simultaneously.[35] The year 1883 marks the establishment of the most successful, most permanent, and best organized single steel commodity cartel, which is often referred to as having paved the way for the ISC. In that year British, Belgian, and German producer-exporters of heavy rails restricted the sharp competition in the export market of heavy rails by establishing the International Association of Rail Makers (I.A.S.R.M.). The accord was kept secret. Around 1890 this cartel disintegrated[36] and was reëstablished by British, German, Belgian, and Luxemburg exporter-producers in 1904. Americans soon joined this cartel[37] and special agreements with Aus-

---

passim; Tchernoff, *op. cit., passim.* Klotzbach (p. 3) speaks of a German pig iron cartel of 1845 and a German rail cartel of 1868. Francis Walker, "The German Steel Syndicats," *Quarterly Journal of Economics,* May, 1906, pp. 360 ff., discussed German iron and steel cartels of the nineteenth century.

[33] Cf. Alfred Marshall and Mary Paley Marshall, *The Economics of Industry* (London, 1879), pp. 180 ff. The contemporary American situation is well illustrated in E. Benjamin Andrews, "Trusts According to Official Investigations," *Quarterly Journal of Economics,* III (1888/89), 117 ff.

[34] *Op. cit.,* pp. 21 ff.

[35] Cf. Dr. Ernst Poensgen, "The Economic Relations between the English and Continental Iron and Steel Industries," *Stahl und Eisen,* p. 1063 ff. Robert Liefmann (*Die Unternehmerverbände, Konventionen, Kartelle,* Freiburg i. Br., 1897) listed 40 international cartels, established, though partly dissolved, up to 1896. Among them there are those for rails, tubular products, gas pipes, wire rods, needles, and screws. Professor Liefmann discussed this subject again in his article "Internationale Kartelle," *Weltwirtschaftliches Archiv,* Vol. XXV (1927, I), pp. 266 ff. Numerous early international steel agreements are discussed by Francis Walker, *op. cit.,* pp. 395 ff.

[36] Dr. Ernst Poensgen, *op. cit. Iron and Steel* (a report of the U. S. Tariff Commission, p. 386) puts the date of dissolution of the rail cartel at 1886.

[37] The first domestic American steel rail pool was established in 1887. It was managed by a Board of Control consisting of three members with comprehensive powers. There was a penalty of $1.50 to $2.50 per ton for excess production. See Lewis H. Haney, *Business Organization and Combination* (New York, 1934), p. 195. This agreement was discussed by Charles M. Schwab in *Report of the Industrial Commission on Trusts and Industrial Combinations* (Washington, 1901), XIII, 474. This domestic agreement was probably requisite to the conclusion of an international accord. The

trian, Russian, and Italian steel works eliminated potential disturbances on the export market by smaller competitors. Even at the time when no well-organized international rail cartel existed, pooling agreements and other accords in respect to large transactions softened sharp competition.[38] During the first decade of the twentieth century several international steel cartels, all relating to single steel commodities, such as tubular products and wire, operated along with the renewed rail agreement. However, no attempt was made before the First World War to establish a general international steel export organization similar to those established in 1926 and later.

IV

The complaint has frequently been made in economic and political literature that access to source material about large commodity controls is rather difficult. Indeed, it was often stated that big international cartels have been shrouded in mystery, and that their organization conceals an arcanum. This is not the place to analyze to what extent the alleged mystery could be penetrated by greater systematic effort in the collection and arrangement of the available material. No doubt, in former decades the structure and operation of many large international cartels were kept secret for commercial reasons and because of legal, political, and economic antipathies toward combinations. "Publicity for this type of international relations is even less sought by the interests concerned than it is by Foreign offices" writes W. Y. Elliott.[39] After the First World War several large cartels partly lifted former restrictions, often under pressure of national governments and public opinion.[40] A British governmental publication emphasized the importance of publicity in respect to these agreements.[41] So did the League of Nations.[42] Several governments required the registration

---

secrecy surrounding the American participation in the international rail cartel is discussed by Francis Walker, *op. cit.*, pp. 396 ff.

[38] Ernst Poensgen *(op. cit.)* rightly emphasized that the establishment of a German domestic steel cartel embracing heavy rails (in 1904) greatly promoted the reëstablishment of the international rail cartel.

[39] William Y. Elliott, *International Control*, p. 28.

[40] An American official report acknowledged the "extensive publicity given to the operations of the European Steel Syndicate." *Trade Information Bulletin*, No. 484, p. 23. However, this report relates to the initial stage of the ISC only.

[41] *Final Report of the Committee on Industry and Trade* (presented to Parliament), Cmd. 3282, London, H.M.S.O., 1929, p. 189.

[42] See the last paragraph of the fourth Resolution of the World Economic Conference, 1927, concerning industrial cartels.

of cartels and similar agreements.[43]   According to the Report of the U. S. Tariff Commission, *Iron and Steel,* published in 1938, "The very nature of these international business organizations prevents any comprehensive analysis of their scope and effectiveness, since many of the agreements and operations are wholly or partially secret.   However, it has been possible to enumerate the adherents and to describe the chief characteristics of the more important cartels."[44]   Despite this modest admission of the Commission, its report is the best monograph on the subject and is in itself proof that by considerable research the main activities of large cartels may be pieced together.   However, publicity, voluntary or if necessary compulsory, is a prerequisite for a sound national and international public economic policy in regard to collective marketing controls.   Ultimately publicity also helps to reduce passions and prejudices attached to cartel discussions.[45]

The ISC involved a maze of organizations, agreements, and policies, yet there was considerable, though not full, publicity about them.   Some of the agreements which set up important entities within the ISC were published *in extenso.*   Even those which were not immediately made publicly available could, for the most part, be reconstructed from intermittently published facts.   Although the meetings and all intercourse between the entities composing the ISC were private, the reports of trade journals[46] and of daily newspapers[47] on the

---

[43] See e.g. the Czechoslovakian Cartel Law.

[44] *Op. cit.,* p. 378.   There is no doubt that the Federal Trade Commission could make inquiries according to Section 5 of the Webb-Pomerene Act as far as American export cartels and their internal and external relations were concerned.

[45] John Maynard Keynes emphasized the importance of publicity about business facts, *The End of Laissez-Faire* (London, 1926), p. 48.   The League of Nations Economic Committee distributed mimeographed documents compiled annually containing reports about international cartelization.   The first document in this series dealt with events which had occurred since July 1, 1934.   (Geneva, Apr. 15, 1935, E890.)   The last of the series was dated Mar. 15, 1939, E1067.   ISC problems were included in these reports.   Considering the high level of most of the League's economic reporting its international cartel reports are rather unsystematic and incomplete.

[46] The *Iron & Coal Trade Review* (London) carried the most extensive and comprehensive reports about the ISC.   Among the trade journals of the U. S., *Steel* and *Iron Age* in particular discussed the current policies of the ISC.   Two fortnightly mimeographed trade journals published in German were mainly devoted to ISC policies and were written in steel cartel jargon.   The better known of them, the *Westeuropäische Wirtschaftskorrespondenz,* appeared in The Hague; the other, the *Deutscher Montan Dienst,* in Düsseldorf.   *Stahl und Eisen* (Düsseldorf) and the *Weltwirtschaftliches Archiv* (Kiel) often carried comprehensive reports about the ISC, whereas current events were reported in the *Kartell Rundschau* (Berlin).

[47] Among the English daily newspapers, *The Times* (London), among the French, the *Journée Industrielle* (Paris), and among the German, the *Deutsche Bergwerks-*

important points of those meetings may be regarded as generally reliable. Comprehensive surveys of the ISC were included in the reports of the Belgian National Bank.[48] Participants and cartel agencies were rarely subject to limitations in informing the press, and no national group was ever required to withhold even confidential information from its government. Official communiques regarding the meetings of the ISC and its entities were rarely issued. The greater part of the information given to the press and to outside observers was presented by national groups. The chairman and the administrative office of the European continental steel cartel published several official reports about the cartel organization.[49]

The ISC and its agencies collected and sent to their participants excellent statistical information. Part of this information was published by trade journals. The British, French, and German national groups published comprehensive statistical bulletins, while the statistical publications of the American Iron and Steel Institute are well known. These statistical publications contained officially collected data concerning general steel exports and were not particularly related to cartel matters.[50]

There are numerous difficulties in obtaining precise figures and comparisons about the steel export market. These difficulties relate both to quantities and prices of steel exports. The first difficulty arises because steel statistics have been published in metric tons, gross tons, and net tons. Though this is a minor problem in the coöperation of nations in the economic field, a reluctance to adopt a common system of weights and measures still exists. This conservatism may indicate a psychological reluctance to accept common standards in more serious fields of international economy.[51] Furthermore, it is

Zeitung and the *Frankfurter Zeitung,* may be mentioned as devoting great attention to the current affairs of the ISC.

[48] Banque Nationale de Belgique, *Bulletin d'Information et de Documentation.* Valuable information may be found also in the *Bulletins* of the Institute des Sciences Economiques de l'Université de Louvain. See especially Aimé Wibail, "La sidérurgie belgo-luxembourgeoise en 1933," *Bulletin,* Feb., 1934.

[49] The best known of these reports, including an historical introduction, is included in a document prepared for the Berlin Congress of the International Chamber of Commerce, *International Ententes,* Paris, 1937. Further official communications concerning the external structure of the ISC were published in 1939 in the recently established journal of the Bureau of International Cartels, *International Cartels* (Nos. I and II, English version) in Paris.

[50] Cf. annual and monthly statistical reports of the British Iron and Steel Federation, monthly reports of the *Comité des Forges* in Paris, and annual statistical reports of the *Stahlwerks-Verband,* last published for 1938.

[51] The author of this study used figures in gross tons (2240 pounds), net tons

difficult to study steel prices because they are listed in gold livre ster-lings, in paper livre sterlings, in dollars and other currencies. Statistics of steel prices seldom indicate whether so-called "official" prices or prices fixed for individual transactions, or, very rarely, actually attained prices, or a combination of these are shown. A major difficulty in analyzing steel export statistics arises from the fact that many sources do not isolate the exports of so-called steel commodities. Whereas isolated steel production statistics are readily avaliable (except those of Japan, which ceased publishing steel statistics after 1936) in the general registering of production figures of steel ingots and castings, rolled steel commodity exports are mostly included with figures for iron commodities. The valuable statistical material published by the League of Nations followed the directions of the League Committee of Statistical Experts which based its instructions on the International Customs Nomenclature drawn up by the Economic Committee of the League. Both the League and the Imperial Institute in Lon-don published, besides joint figures on exports of iron and steel, separate statistics concerning exports of semifinished steel and scrap.[52] It is true that these joint figures (for iron and steel) relate pre-ponderantly to steel, but it is impossible to distinguish between them.

V

Steel exports played an important role in international trade. Ac-cording to an estimate of the American Iron and Steel Institute, based

(2000 pounds), and metric tons (2205 pounds), in the text and appendices of this study and contributed in this regard to the general confusion. This was done because the computing of all figures into a common denominator would have required con-siderable time which was not at his disposal. The American Iron and Steel Institute has shifted to a general system of publishing steel statistics in net tons during the last few years. The general adoption of the metric system would furnish a solution of the problem. However, the great reluctance in English-speaking countries to adopt the metric system may be seen from F. A. Halsey, *The Metric Fallacy* (New York, 1920), *passim.*

[52] Cf. the following publications of the Economic Intelligence Service of the League of Nations: *International Trade Statistics*, Geneva, 1939, *International Trade in Certain Raw Materials and Foodstuffs, 1938*, Geneva, 1939, *Raw Materials and Foodstuffs, Production by Countries*, Geneva, 1939, *Statistical Year-Book of the League of Nations, 1939-40*, Geneva, 1941, and *Europe's Trade*, Geneva, 1941. Cf. also *The Mineral Industry of the British Empire and Foreign Countries*, statistical summary (Production, Imports and Exports), latest volume 1936-1938, London, Imperial Institute, 1939. The annual *Foreign Commerce Yearbook*, U. S. Department of Commerce, also lists the quantity and dollar value of international steel exports. A survey of domestic and export markets is contained in *Metal Statistics 1941* (New York, 1942), published by *American Metal Market.*

on statistics of the British Iron and Steel Federation, the annual average of world exports of steel in recent years was about 14,000,000 gross tons.[53] Though the United States represents about one-half the steel-producing capacity of the world, its average ratio of the 14 million tons did not exceed 15 per cent, whereas more than 80 per cent was exported from the Western and Central European steel region (Great Britain, France, Belgium, Luxemburg, Germany, Poland, and Czechoslovakia). Iron and steel exports (semifinished steel and scrap excluded) between 1929 and 1936 comprised approximately 5 per cent (4.67 per cent in 1929, 4.35 in 1932, 5.13 in 1934, 4.92 in 1935, 4.84 in 1936) of the value of all exports of the world. This estimate of 5 per cent is based on figures contained in official German statistics.[54] There is no estimate for steel alone. However, it may safely be assumed that semifinished steel, excluded from this 5 per cent, balanced the iron exports included in this figure. The ISC exercised a controlling influence on these exports, especially after Great Britain and the United States entered the cartel. The ISC controlled the export market of semifinished steel also and influenced the buying policy of the International Scrap convention.

The bare figures of steel capacity and output are among the most important factors in the economic and political "Who's Who" of nations. Such figures show that at present the United States contains not much less than half the capacity of the world steel industry, leaving the Axis countries, including the invaded and economically dominated territories, far behind. The United States had at the beginning of 1942 a rated steel capacity of 88.5 million net tons. Germany proper had a capacity of approximately 24 million net tons, while the rated capacity of Italy is estimated at 3, Austria 0.8, France 10.8, Belgium 4.5, Luxemburg 3, Czechoslovakia 2.5, Poland 1.8, Hungary 0.9, Rumania 0.3, Yugoslavia 0.3, and Holland 0.2 million net tons. Sweden's steel capacity is estimated at 1.3, and that of Spain at 1 mil-

---

[53] *Steel Facts*, October, 1939, pp. 1-2.

[54] Cf. Annex "Internationale Übersichten," p. 161, to the *Statistisches Jahrbuch für das Deutsche Reich*, 1938. A comparison between steel exports and imports on the one hand and the total exports and imports of particular countries on the other hand is shown through 1938 in the official publication of the German national steel cartel, *Statistisches Jahrbuch für die Eisen- und Stahlindustrie*, Düsseldorf, 1938. Value and quantity of world trade is summarized in *Review of World Trade*, 1938, published by the Economic Intelligence Service of the League of Nations, Geneva, 1939, pp. 8 ff. (See former issues also.) Concerning the scope and methods of these statistics see *ibid.*, pp. 58 ff. It is regrettable to say that no precise figures about world steel exports are available. Discrepancies among various published estimates are rather striking.

lion net tons. The steel capacity of Great Britain and the British
Dominions and dependencies may be estimated at 20.5 million net
tons. The steel capacity of the Soviet Union, disregarding the impact
of the German invasion, may be estimated at 22 million net tons. The
steel-making capacity of Japan, including Manchuria, may be estimated
at 7.2 million net tons. It is difficult to say how far the steel output
of Germany and other Axis and Axis-dominated countries has been
curtailed due to damaged steel plants, and owing to shortages of raw
materials and to transportation difficulties. It is equally difficult to
estimate the present steel situation in the Soviet Union. The United
States reached a peak production of 35,000,000 net tons in 1913, before
the First World War, increasing its output to 50,500,000 tons in 1917,
and in 1942 probably exceeding 85,000,000 net tons of steel.

It may be useful to introduce two or three general characteristics
of the steel export market. (Steel commodities are produced only on
specified orders, which indicate qualities, sizes, and quantities. Even
steel commodities bought by warehouses of importing countries are
produced according to specified orders and only exceptionally delivered from stocks of steel producers.) These steel warehouses, purchasing many kinds of steel products and stocking them in considerable
quantities, did not play a notable role in the international steel trade.
Though the great advantage of being situated near the buyer and of
delivering goods on short notice is obvious, the maintenance of a well-
assorted stock of steel commodities was difficult and costly. Larger
consumers preferred to order steel commodities from producers (contract sales), which were then considerably cheaper than if bought from
warehouse stocks. Producers of steel maintain only small stocks on
hand; they do not produce large stocks in periods lacking orders.
Thus sellers' pressure on the steel market, unlike that of many other
markets, is not exercised by the presence of large stocks. The concept
of "excess supply" as applied to finished steel products connotes an
"excess" preparedness to produce and, after production, to deliver.
Steel demand is rarely directed toward existing commodities—but
regularly to the ability and preparedness to produce. Because of the
absence of stocks a period of from six weeks to three months normally
elapses before the demand for products can be supplied. In periods
of price fluctuation this delay sometimes causes difficulty. In a majority of cases the producer-exporter of steel is advised who the consumer
of his steel commodities is to be, unless a warehouse is the consumer.
An inquiry concerning steel prices, in order to be taken seriously, has
to contain details in respect to the product's ultimate destination. The

refusal to deal with anonymous inquiries and orders is often in the interest of buyers in that a knowledge of the precise use to which a steel product is to be put is often necessary for the production of a satisfactory product. This insistence upon information regarding the ultimate destination of steel products was, however, a means of maintaining the operation of the cartel's rigid delivered-price system. In addition, knowledge of the ultimate destination and consumer facilitated the control of the market by the cartel and was an efficient weapon against clandestine competition of national groups within the cartel and against open or hidden competition from outsiders.

Another significant characteristic of the steel export market was the degree of its interrelationship with the domestic markets of exporting countries. A decrease in the domestic demand for steel acted as an incentive for seeking export markets. When the demand of the domestic market was great, in many countries domestic consumers tried to exercise pressure on steel producers to limit exports so that quick domestic deliveries might be made. Probably the only steel exporting countries in which export prices influenced domestic prices were Belgium and Luxemburg where a major proportion of steel production was intended for the export market. In all other exporting countries export prices had little effect on domestic prices, which were not within the scope of the international cartels. When export prices were very unattractive the United States, and to a lesser extent, British producers limited exports. Continental European exporters, however, maintained exports regardless of prices, either from a necessity for acquiring foreign exchange (patriotic exports) or from a desire to maintain their positions on the export markets or in order to sustain domestic employment. The domestic steel price structure in many of these continental European countries was intended to cover losses suffered in maintaining their steel export markets.[55] A more detailed discussion of this point may be found in Chapter Eight of this volume. Tables 1 and 2 below give an approximate picture of the quantity and percentage distribution of exports of iron and steel products of major steel-exporting countries, and of the percentage of important rolled steel products exported.

---

[55] Cf. e.g., *Ausschuss zur Untersuchung der Erzeugungs- und Absatzbedingungen der deutschen Wirtschaft,* "Die deutsche eisenerzeugende Industrie," III, Unterausschuss Arbeitsgruppe 3, Volume 2, Berlin, 1930, p. 90, and *Report of the Industrial Commission* (Washington, 1901), XIII, xxv ff., 454 f., 502, 555, 512 f., 725 ff.

ICTR, January 17, 1936, p. 122, discussing exports during the depression, states: "The British industry refused to attempt to meet uneconomic competition, frequently subsidized directly or indirectly."

TABLE I

METRIC TONNAGE AND PERCENTAGE DISTRIBUTION OF EXPORTS OF IRON AND STEEL
PRODUCTS OF SIX MAJOR STEEL EXPORTING COUNTRIES*

	1913		1928		1929		1933		1934		1935	
	1000 tons	Per cent	1000 tons	Per cent	1000 tons	Per cent	1000 tons	Per cent	1000 tons	Per cent	1000 tons	Per cent
Germany...	6,562	37.3	5,098	22.3	5,883	25.1	2,139	17.7	2,566	16.8	3,217	21.2
Belgium and Luxemburg.	1,729	9.8	4,905	21.4	5,041	21.5	3,517	29.0	3,788	24.8	3,752	24.8
France.....	1,168	6.6	5,646	24.6	4,932	21.1	3,143	25.9	3,744	24.6	2,648	17.5
Gr. Britain.	5,049	28.9	4,329	18.9	4,450	19.0	1,953	16.1	2,287	15.0	2,407	15.9
U. S. A....	3,066	17.4	2,933	12.8	3,106	13.3	1,370	11,3	2,868	18.8	3,123	20.6
Total....	17,574	100.0	22,911	100.0	23,412	100.0	12,122	100.0	15,253	100.0	15,147	100.0

Source: Annual *Stahlwerks-Verband* reports.
*German figures for 1913 include Luxemburg exports. Saar exports for 1928, 1929, 1933, and 1934 are included in French exports, those for 1935 in German exports. Czechoslovakian and Polish exports (not listed here) accounted for several hundred thousand additional tons yearly. U. S. A. figures greatly deviate from official American reports. In reality U. S. A. exports were considerably smaller than those listed here.

Steel is, according to a widespread but not fully accepted opinion, especially disinclined to be permanently subject to a strongly competitive marketing situation.[56] It has been almost generally recognized that standardized commodities such as steel, whose production requires huge investments, tend to be subject to a domestic and international marketing control. In the last few decades the United States was the only country where definite attempts were made by public authorities to maintain and to enforce a competitive domestic market in steel. The governments of all other large steel-producing countries regarded it as justifiable, and even desirable, to have a collective marketing control of their domestic steel markets. Whereas in the United States the system of allegedly fixed steel prices was sharply denounced by official circles and by many economists, in other large steel-producing countries national steel cartels were often credited with and frequently praised for the maintenance of stable steel prices. This attitude towards domestic steel cartels implied a large scale publicity as to their organization and policies and good will on the part of cartel members to coöperate with their governments in actual social and economic policies pursued by those governments. A sympathetic (or at least not adverse) attitude of governments and public opinion towards steel cartels in Europe did not imply that governments would tolerate the violent suppression of outsiders in steel production or in steel trade. Previous to the turning of governments to Fascism almost

[56] "Cartels stand a better chance of holding together in this industry than in most . . ." Frederic Benham, *Great Britain Under Protection*, New York, 1941, p. 178.

TABLE 2

PERCENTAGE OF INDICATED ROLLED STEEL PRODUCTS EXPORTED, FIVE MAJOR STEEL EXPORTING COUNTRIES, 1933-1937

		Rails and track material	Structural shapes	Merchant bars	Bands	Wire rods	Sheets and plates	Tin plates	Tubular products
		Per cent	*Per cent*	*Per cent*	*Per cent*	*Per cent*	*Per cent*	*Per cent*	*Per cent*
Germany	1933	14.73	14.54	21.86	20.61	6.62	15.08	61.99	40.50
	1934	17.70	14.04	21.60	18.12	5.00	14.65	58.87	18.12
	1935	29.57	12.79	16.82	21.44	4.14	13.32	53.11	29.04
	1936	25.66	11.14	15.46	19.81	3.30	13.01	50.82	36.67
	1937	23.28	13.11	17.06	21.03	4.92	10.42	51.23	39.26
Belgium and	1933	50.73	82.16		57.96	55.62	75.83		38.74
Luxemburg	1934	56.37	86.19		54.23	51.35	77.36		40.29
	1935	61.85	82.48		65.35	35.01	56.44		63.22
	1936	44.88	62.31		65.07	36.50	50.70		68.44
	1937	–	–		–	–	–		
France	1933	28.52	41.68		39.39	30.60	15.16	–	34.99
	1934	34.75	41.88		52.99	32.71	18.95	52.61	17.94
	1935	25.66	35.16		33.48	37.69	12.56	33.00	20.33
	1936	19.92	27.94		19.47	31.05	14.55	11.37	20.12
	1937	23.77	29.63		22.35	32.70	10.91	6.33	16.40
Great Britain	1933	22.16	4.21	8.66	10.38	1.56	35.50		
	1934	29.97	5.69	10.51	8.46	0.43	31.68		
	1935	36.33	5.08	11.11	8.06	1.47	28.82		
	1936	38.29	3.97	8.18	6.98	0.57	22.79		
	1937	37.26	5.03	7.38	6.91	–	24.21		
U. S. A.	1933	6.41	2.78	1.08	1.05	0.83	1.84	5.39	6.90
	1934	4.79	3.63	1.67	1.29	1.38	4.50	11.50	7.35
	1935	4.72	3.05	1.52	1.62	1.07	3.26	7.13	4.06
	1936	3.86	2.91	1.05	1.84	1.16	3.32	0.01	2.41
	1937	7.03	5.47	2.73	3.63	1.99	7.41	13.23	4.86

Source: Annual *Stahlwerks-Verband* reports.

all of them required cartels to be moderate in exercising pressure on their own members, and not to transcend the boundaries of "fair competition" in their dealing with outsiders. Almost all European cartel laws contain provisions protecting outsiders. Naturally the success of protecting outsiders depended upon many circumstances and descended sometimes to a mere formal investigation. However, such statements as that of Franz Neumann, according to which the German Weimar Government not once utilized the powers conferred upon it according to the Cartel Decree of 1923, somewhat oversimplify the German cartel picture.[57]

---

[57] See Franz Neumann, *Behemoth, The Structure and Practice of National Socialism* (New York, 1942), p. 16.

On the international market there was no authority to enforce, and indeed, no legitimate advocate of a competitive steel market. More often than one might suppose the ISC gained the easy acquiescence of governments of importing countries to its marketing schemes. It would be worth while to ascertain just how much decadence and how much modern strife for security there is in the attitude of those who prefer to purchase on a controlled market because of its convenience rather than to seek an advantage entailing less accommodation.[58] The average entrepreneur, deviating somewhat from his classical model, prefers to abandon risky possibilities of high profits in favor of coöperation in a cartel affording lower profits but lowering risks. Many consumers, avoiding risky possibilities of buying cheaper, prefer to buy on a more stable "organized" market.

It is improbable that in a domestic or foreign market a large degree of permanent competition in a standardized commodity, such as steel, could endure under the conditions of modern communication and transportation.[59] The common experience is that Proudhon's proverbial remark, "competition destroys competition," pertains more to steel than to any other product.[60] This does not imply that among the cartel members there cannot permanently exist a certain degree of price or non-price competition. It does not imply either that out-

---

[58] *ICTR*, Jan. 26, 1934, p. 168, notes a gentle (and unsuccessful) rebellion of merchants and consumers against the establishment of a reorganized effective international marketing control in steel commodities in 1933. "The overseas markets," writes the Brussels correspondent of the *ICTR*, "were well aware of what was going on, and merchants and consumers adopted an attitude of hostility which was expressed by withholding orders until many of the continental works were starving for business."

[59] Concerning the monopolistic situation "inherent" in steel commodities, cf. Frank Albert Fetter, "The New Plea for Basing-Point Monopoly," *The Journal of Political Economy*, 1937, pp. 579 ff.; by the same author, "Rejoinder to Professor De Chazeau's Reply," *ibid.*, 1938, pp. 567 ff.; and Melvin G. De Chazeau, "Public Policy and Discriminatory Prices of Steel: A Reply to Professor Fetter," *ibid.*, 1938, pp. 537 ff. See furthermore Frederic Benham, "The Iron and Steel Industry of Germany, France, Belgium, Luxemburg and the Saar," *op. cit.*, p. 12. Benjamin F. Fairless, President of the United States Steel Corporation stated: "In this highly competitive industry, of which we are a part, competition, of course, exists at all times, but many times it is more prominent in one product than it is in another product . . ." (TNEC, *Hearings*, Part 19, p. 10490).

[60] "La concurrence tue la concurrence . . ."; Pierre Joseph Proudhon, *Système des Contradictions Economiques ou Philosophie de la Misère* (Paris, 1923), I, 225. However, Proudhon's famous proposition has often been supplemented with the sentence that unlimited freedom to contract (to combine) leads equally to the destruction of that freedom. "The struggle of particular groups of men to be stronger than one another defeats and cancels itself. Mutual agreement to restrict would benefit all collectively without individually injuring any." A. C. Pigou, *Economics in Practice* (London, 1935), p. 152.

siders cannot operate even permanently. Such competition, however, may be regarded as a small deviation from rather firmly established marketing control schemes.[61]

What the situation would have been on the steel export market in the later period had it not been even temporarily controlled is a tempting question which cannot be answered even tentatively. Some indication is found in the steel market as it was a decade ago, when concentrated control was suspended. In 1932 merchant bars were sold on the export market for as low as £2.2 (gold) f.o.b. per ton,[62] blooms £1.16.6 per ton, prices admittedly far below the average costs per unit.[63] This economically untenable situation prompted the establishment of a strong cartel in 1933, and the memory of the situation functioned as a warning ghost when critical tensions endangered the life of the cartel. The price movement in those products for which a bound market was maintained even during the critical period (1930-1933), as compared with that of products whose markets had disintegrated, served as a vivid example.[64]

---

[61] The statement of Franz Neumann (*op. cit.*, pp. 291-292), "Cartelization and monopolization are not the negation of competition, but only another form of it. . . . Entrepreneurial initiative is not dead; it is as vital as ever before and perhaps even more so" contains some truth, but an accidental accompanying feature is elevated by him into a central element.

[62] The following merchant bar prices, quoted per long ton, in £ (gold) f.o.b. Antwerp, are characteristic of the breakdown of the steel market in 1932:

Jan.	Jan.	Jan.	Jan.	Jan.	Jan.	July	Jan.	Jan.	Jan.
1927	1928	1929	1930	1931	1932	1932	1933	1934	1938
5.7.6	4.17.6	6.2.6	5.5.5	4.3.6	2.14.0	2.3.0	2.9.0	3.2.6	6.0.0

[63] "It was admitted by the French group, the *Comité des Forges,* that at the beginning of 1932, steel was being exported at 30 to 40 per cent below the cost of production." James Henderson, "The Manufacture, Sale and Use of Iron and Steel in Great Britain," *Year Book of the American Iron and Steel Institute* (New York, 1936), p. 161. According to another version, ". . . the prices then current for iron, after they had sunk to approximately one third of their original level, did not cover the actual costs of production in any of the member countries." Dr. Ernst Poensgen, "The Economic Relations, etc., *Stahl und Eisen,* Sept. 17, 1936, pp. 1063 ff.

[64] The movement of prices (in £ gold) per long ton, f.o.b. Antwerp, of billets and merchant bars on the one hand, and heavy rails and wire rods on the other from July, 1930, to June, 1933, shows the contrast between price movements on controlled and uncontrolled (or incompletely controlled) markets.

	Products in which marketing controls had disintegrated		Products in which marketing controls were maintained	
	Billets	*Merchant Bars*	*Heavy Rails*	*Wire Rods*
July, 1, 1930	4.14.0	5. 7.6	6.10.0	6. 5.0
Nov. 13, 1930	3. 6.0	3.19.0	6.10.0	6. 0.0
Dec. 25, 1930	3.14.0	4. 6.0	6.10.0	6. 0.0

The marketing policy of the ISC was determined by the economic interests of its participants in the broadest sense. Conflicting interests often had to be reconciled. Short-term interests were subordinated to long-term policies, to a point where international steel policies sometimes appeared incomprehensible.[65] Policy was not influenced only by immediate profit factors in the narrower sense; it had to be adjusted, among other things, to the domestic and foreign economic policies of many governments. Such governmental policies were one of the main reasons for the frequently discussed deviations in steel cartel prices on several foreign markets. The policy of national groups pertaining to ISC activities was increasingly influenced by the national governments after 1936, particularly that of the German national group, with whom it then naturally became difficult to continue open discussions. However, the flexibility of the ISC structure succeeded in bridging even this chasm.

Because of the generally accepted belief that the capacities of the international steel industry were more than sufficient, the ISC tended to discourage the development of new steel plants in steel-importing countries, a tendency which found expression in the marketing policy of the ISC.

VI

The Second World War put a sudden end to the ISC. At the beginning of September, 1939, the German, French, and British agreements within the ISC were automatically terminated. At the same time, and for the same reason, the general agreement with other European continental groups (Czechoslovakian and Polish) was rendered void. With the sudden end of these agreements, all agreements concerning particular commodities administered by export sales

Mar. 26, 1931	3. 5.6	3.15.6	6.10.0	6. 0.0
June 25, 1931	3. 2.0	3. 7.0	6.10.0	5. 0.0
Dec. 27, 1931	2.10.0	2.15.0	5.17.6	5. 5.0
Apr. 25, 1932	2. 2.6	2. 5.0	5.17.6	4.10.0
Aug. 22, 1932	1.18.0	2. 2.0	5.10.0	4.10.0
Dec. 24, 1932	2. 1.0	2.13.0	5.17.6	4.10.0
June 1, 1933	2. 8.0	3. 0.0	5.17.6	5.10.0

The "abnormal" margins among the single products listed above may be seen by comparing them with price margins among these same products in later years.

	Billets	*Merchant Bars*	*Heavy Rails*	*Wire Rods*
March 1, 1936	2.7.0	3.3.9	5.10.0	4.10.0
Dec. 1, 1937	5.7.6	6.0.0	5.15.0	6. 0.0

[65] See Edward Chamberlin, *The Theory of Monopolistic Competition* (Cambridge, 1938), pp. 52, 54-55, concerning long-term policies.

comptoirs, as well as the American agreement, were nullified. Understandings which established particular export marketing organizations, agreements made with shipping conferences, and a number of so-called "penetration agreements," were *ipso facto* dissolved. Innumerable legal, commercial, financial, and personal questions remained open. Thus the mighty structure of the ISC, built up with great effort, collapsed without even an orderly liquidation, and entered the realms of economic history. Under the circumstances, several entities of the ISC did not even liquidate their accounts for the business year ending June 30, 1939.[66] The ISC was not dissolved by a formal decision of its participants. On the contrary, after the outbreak of hostilities, cartel agencies attempted to operate in a limited manner, and an idea was even propagated to the effect that cartel activities might be diverted in the direction of the interests of the allied forces controlling the exports of western Europe and the Scandinavian countries.[67]

The war brought the main continental European steel producers under German domination. All of the big continental steel-producing and consuming countries, with the exception of Russia, must now coöperate with the German steel regime. Thus the continental European steel cartel was revived in the new form of an imposed combination,[68] led by the German national steel cartel (an imposed combination in itself), and controlled by German military and economic authorities. The war has thrown the world steel market, if there is any, into a *sui generis* monopolistic situation characterized by the usual features of scarcity.

After the start of the Second World War, a new form of collaboration began between American and British steel producers. However, this collaboration cannot be regarded as an extension of the old collaboration in the framework of the ISC.

---

[66] See *ICTR*, Sept. 8, 1939, p. 351; Sept. 15, 1939, p. 395; Oct. 20, 1939, p. 555; Oct. 27, 1939, p. 587.

[67] *ICTR*, Aug. 18, 1939, p. 251.

[68] Louis Domeratzky, "The German Cartel, An Instrument of Economic Control of the European Continent," *Foreign Commerce Weekly*, June 7, 1941, pp. 409-410, discusses this new function of the German iron and steel cartel and its allied selling organizations. The economic Germanization of the Luxemburg steel industry is demonstrated by Pierre Krier, Minister of Labor of the Grand Duchy of Luxemburg, in *Luxembourg Under German Occupation* (Pamphlet, London, 1941), pp. 14-15. See also *Der Deutsche Volkswirt* (Berlin), July 18, 1941, pp. 1476-77, and Anton Maier, "Die Ordnung des Eisenmarktes in der Kriegswirtschaft," *Jahrbücher für Nationalökonomie und Statistik,* Feb. 1940, pp. 224 ff.

CHAPTER TWO

The Cartel Concept

I

THE ISC REPRESENTED the most highly developed instance of an organized collectivity of marketing units, conventionally called a super or general cartel. It was a combination of combinations, or more precisely, a cartel composed of cartels. It attempted to concentrate the collective control of the world steel export market in the hands of one rather complex body which may justifiably be designated as monopolistic in tendency.

The student of industrial combinations will find an almost inexhaustible set of examples of conventional and unconventional types of marketing control mechanisms within the framework of the ISC. Members of the national steel cartels within the ISC represented almost all categories of large and small combinations of the corporate type (integrated concerns, holding companies, interlocking directorates, etc.), while the national steel cartels, the export sales comptoirs, distributor cartels, and other mechanisms included almost all representative patterns of collective marketing units referred to as cartels.[1] Scattered within the ISC framework were many auxiliary agreements accompanying intricate cartel structures that insured the smooth working of the organization.

These economic units are classified here as cartels simply to indicate that they were collective marketing controls established and maintained by legally and economically independent entrepreneurs, or entrepreneur groups. Such a classification is not intended as a judgment of the desirability of cartels from the viewpoint of one or more legal, ethical, or social value schemes. Because of the particular

---

[1] However, there were almost no cartel types represented in the ISC whose connecting link consisted of patent agreements or similar structures.

position of the term cartel in economic, social, political, and legal terminology it seems essential, even in a study specifically devoted to the ISC, briefly to review modern conceptions of cartels. In this connection is is interesting to note how changes of the last decade in the type and intensity of economic control and competition, especially in regard to steel, were evaluated.

For many years economists and political scientists throughout the world have searched for a valid meaning and satisfactory definition of the word cartel.[2] Sometimes their discussion descended to a mere play on words. Often a definition was used purposely, or half consciously, as a means of persuasion. In a majority of cases, important political and economic problems lay concealed behind what seemed to be merely terminological issues. In the eyes of many, "cartel" had an invidious connotation, and implied something socially condemnable, or legally prohibited. The literature about cartels grew to many hundred volumes without solving even elementary terminological issues.[3]

In many countries, including the United States, designating an economic structure a "cartel" is tantamount to social denunciation.[4] Referring to the domestic steel business, Mr. Eugene G. Grace, President of the Bethlehem Steel Corporation, declared explicitly that he would not favor a cartel structure in this country because it cannot

---

[2] According to Dr. Roman Piotrowski, *Cartels and Trusts,* p. 13, the term "cartel" as used in this study was used, probably for the first time, in 1879 by a member of the German Reichstag, Mr. Richter, who used the term in discussing collective industrial combinations selling abroad at a lower price than on their domestic markets.

[3] The first periodical particularly devoted to cartel problems appeared at the beginning of the century. In its first issue it attempted to justify its establishment in the founder's leading article which seems, in the light of later developments, to be characteristic. "The problem of cartels," wrote Josef Borger, the editor, in 1903, "is one of the most important among modern economic questions. It represents for the economist an inexhaustible field for research, for legal science one of the most contested issues, for the legislature a task as urgent as it is involved, for social and political groups an item subject to most violent combats, for industry and trade a frequently indispensable means of organization; thus it is one of the most eminent topics of public discussion of our time." Borger proceeded to illustrate the importance of the issue by describing the extensiveness of pertinent economic and political literature [in 1903] and the many contemporary legal and economic proposals to solve or to mitigate the cartel "problem." See *Kartell-Rundschau* (Berlin), Vol. I, No. 1.

[4] "In this country, the term 'cartelization' has always carried an alien and unfavorable connotation." Merle Fainsod and Lincoln Gordon, *Government and the American Economy* (New York, 1941), p. 527. The chairman of the TNEC found it necessary to emphasize that his committee was not prejudiced against cartels. TNEC, *Hearings,* Part 25, p. 13339. According to *Fortune,* Sept., 1942, p. 105, "Thurman Arnold has managed to invest the word [cartel] itself with a pathological aura suggesting some new, esoteric social disease."

be "constructively adapted to our domestic life and activities."[5] Even if in specific cases cartel structures are permitted, as in the Webb-Pomerene Act, they are not actually called cartels. In European countries, including Germany, where monopolistic practices and arrangements in restraint of trade were not generally prohibited, the expression "cartel" was avoided in the titles of organizations which were unquestionably cartels in the traditional sense.[6] Terms like Stahlwerks-*Verband*, Rohstahl-*Gemeinschaft*, and similar denominations were applied in Germany, though nobody denied that these organizations were proper cartels. Many authors complained that French terminology in this regard was misleading too.[7] *Comptoir, comité, entente, association,* were used for what we call cartels. Steel cartels in France preferred the expressions *comptoir*[8] and *entente* for

---

[5] TNEC, *Hearings,* Part 19, p. 10632.

[6] Sir Alfred Mond (Lord Melchett), discussing cartel definitions, made the rather strange statement that "The Germans have a term *Interessengemeinschaft*—they do not use the word cartel." *Industry and Politics* (London, 1928), p. 235.

[7] See M. Kypriotis, *Les Cartels Internationaux* (Paris, 1936), Preface.

[8] The term *comptoir* has been used in many languages for cartels and cartel-like combinations. The executive agency of the first (government-sponsored) Swedish combination of iron producers, established in 1745, was called *Järnkontoret.* (See R. Piotrowski, *op. cit.,* pp. 356-57, and *Iron and Steel,* Report of the U. S. Tariff Commission, p. 166). One of the first modern German steel cartels, the *Weissblech-Kontor* in Cologne, founded in 1862, adopted this name too. (See Dr. Arthur Klotzbach, *Der Roheisenverband,* p. 3.) French cartel literature indulged in discussions of whether or not the terms "cartel" and "comptoir" covered identical economic structures. As a matter of fact, within the international organizations of the ISC and within its French-speaking national groups, "cartel" and "comptoir" were used interchangeably. However, in international steel organizations, the expression "comptoir" was frequently used to designate single commodity cartels, as contrasted with general marketing control agencies.

"Comptoir" has been used for "cartel" for many decades in France. According to Dr. Theodore Kreps, the *Comptoir Longwy* was established in 1848, "continuing though not without a series of transformations until the present time." Several French monographs, discussing combinations in the steel industry, put the life of this comptoir from 1876 to 1922. It certainly did not operate after the reorganization of the *Comptoir Sidérurgique de France,* in 1932.

Edmond Lebée (*Trusts et Cartels Internationaux,* Recueil des Cours, 1927, IV, Académie de Droit International, pp. 154-155) attempts to distinguish between cartels flourishing in Germany, Central Europe, Scandinavia, and Holland on the one hand, and comptoirs existing in France on the other. French sales comptoirs, according to Mr. Lebée, are less oriented in the direction of the maintenance of prices and discipline than in the search for markets and in the education of clients. He remarks, however, that despite these differences comptoirs and cartels are very closely related institutions.

Karl Pribram (*Cartel Problems,* p. 275) regarded "comptoir" as a "specific cartel-form brought about by the French cartelization movement." Pribram assumed [falsely] on the basis of British official trade reports, that the *Comptoir Sidérurgique de France* was a "cartel created especially for organizing the export trade," though the *Comptoir*

their marketing controls. It is not necessary to consider here why the word "cartel" was late in entering the English and French vocabularies. Certainly not because of the absence of that type of industrial combination in English-speaking countries and in France.[9]

II

A general discussion of modern cartel concepts might well begin with the findings of the recent investigation of the concentration of economic power by the Temporary National Economic Committee of the United States Congress. Several reasons prompted this selection of a starting point. First, this investigation is the most recent among similar undertakings;[10] second, the investigation did not limit its work to the American situation; third, the TNEC devoted particular attention to American and international steel policies, especially to the combination movement in that industry. During the latter part

Sidérurgique (like nearly all similar institutions in Europe) equally organized the domestic and export markets. Paul de Rousiers (*Cartels and Trusts and their Development,* League of Nations, Economic and Financial Section, II, 21, Geneva, 1927, p. 16) writes, "The French comptoirs are related to the German cartels but have shown a certain moderation and restraint which makes them appear to be more amenable." K. Wiedenfeld states that "In France the prevalent type of combination is a loose form of price agreement, the so-called comptoirs," and that after the war impetus was given to the formation of "large concerns" which, owing in part to government pressure, eventually turned "into closely organized cartels." (Article, "Combination," *Encycl. of Social Sciences,* II, 668).

[9] It is significant that the most popular French cyclopedia, *Larousse du XXe Siècle* (II vol., Paris, 1929), did not include the cartel-meaning among the several meanings of the word "comptoir," whereas it stressed "industrial combination" as a meaning of the term "cartel." W. Tudor Davies, in a recent study, *Trade Associations and Industrial Co-ordination,* London, 1938, in a chapter devoted to "The advent of cartels," regards cartels as belonging to the European continent. Mr. Davies did not discuss the substantial reasons for his statement. *Fortune* bases its somewhat popular cartel definition also on "the strictest European sense" of the term. (Sept., 1942, p. 105.)

[10] Legislative bodies and executive agencies of continental Europe, Great Britain, and America frequently investigated general and specific problems connected with the combination movement in modern industry. As early as January 25, 1888, the House of Representatives of the United States Congress passed a resolution directing its Committee on Manufactures to investigate combinations known as associations, trusts, pools, and other like titles. On February 16, 1888, the Senate of the State of New York ordered a similar investigation. The House of Commons of Canada established a committee for the same purpose on February 29, 1888. All the pertinent documents show that the bewildering variety of patterns and the confusing nomenclature contributed considerably to the confusion in evaluating the movement toward combinations. Thus, this general confusion is not a recent one and is not limited to a single country, continent, or language. It is interesting to note that Canada, a country of little industrialization in 1888, devoted a report consisting of 750 pages to the results of the investigation of this problem.

of the 1930's, combinations of independent enterprises in Europe gradually deviated from the traditional pattern of cartels toward that of "compulsory" cartels, and this development, heavily involving units of the ISC, may well be viewed on the basis of facts and arguments brought up in the monopoly investigation.

The TNEC devoted several hearings[11] and a monograph to the nature of cartels and to the application of the term "cartel" to certain economic organizations existing in the United States. Experts were consulted about the "definition" of cartels and cartel-like arrangements. The purpose of the investigation or, as the chairman of the committee called it, of the study[12] was not only to inspect the overt features of American economic life, but also to try to determine whether severe antitrust regulations had induced entrepreneurs to adopt inconspicuous forms of coöperation[13] which would not provoke official prosecution or public condemnation. The probability of the existence of the latter situation was suggested in the message of President Roosevelt, on April 20, 1938, prompting the establishment of the TNEC: "Private enterprise is ceasing to be free enterprise and is becoming a cluster of private collectivisms; masking itself as a system of free enterprise after the American model, it is in fact becoming a concealed cartel system after the European model."[14]

At one stage of the hearings the vice-chairman, Representative Hatton W. Sumners, posed the question, ". . . why are we so much interested in what you name a thing?"[15] The assumption of Mr. Sumners that the committee, in discussing what cartels are and whether they exist in the United States, was considering "the possible failure of a complete development of what ought to have been the

---

[11] TNEC, *Hearings*, Part 25.

[12] "Let us call it study instead of an investigation. People use the word 'investigation' in a sense which this committee has never intended."—*Ibid.*, p. 13307.

[13] "Clearly illegal agreements have often been set up on a secret basis."—Fainsod and Gordon, *op. cit.*, p. 527. According to Robert Liefmann, ". . . cartels between the big American concerns are not uncommon either, but they are of a quite informal character and do not come into the open at all." (*Op. cit.*, p. 290.) Kurt Wiedenfeld judges (*Encyclopaedia of the Social Sciences*, II, 668) that because of anti-monopoly legislation and the peculiarities of business psychology, cartels in the United States "are in the majority of cases very loose associations. . . . There are no syndicates in the domestic market, nor have syndicates taken root among exporters since the passage of permissive legislation."

[14] Dr. Clair Wilcox assumes that "The parallel that may be drawn between trade associations and cartel activities lends support to the statement that was made by President Roosevelt. . . ." (*Monograph 21* of the TNEC, "Competition and Monopoly in American Industry," p. 259).

[15] TNEC, *Hearings*, Part 25, p. 13324.

governmental policy . . ." was challenged by the economic adviser of the committee, Professor Kreps. The latter considered the hearings limited "to factual exposition of what cartels are, what cartel-like arrangements are, what their economic consequences have been, and what their political consequences are abroad. These cartel-like arrangements that we have here," continued Dr. Kreps, "are similar to certain cartel developments that occurred abroad. We are interested here because they represent a type of activity quite universal throughout the modern world. . . ."[16]

The chairman of the committee, Senator Joseph C. O'Mahoney, trying to arrive at a definition, asked "What is the common acceptance of the term? . . . when we talk of the European cartel system, what do we usually mean?" Professor Kreps replied, "There isn't any common acceptance." He went on to explain that what the European cartel system means "depends in part on one's economic predilections, in part on one's political convictions."[17] The chairman, insisting on the linguistic validity of the terms under discussion, said, ". . . if there is such a thing as a cartel system, then as a practical matter it ought to be subject to easy definition, simple definition. . . ."[18]

This was not the first time that Congress had been interested in the terminological problems posed by cartels. More than a decade previous to the TNEC investigations an appropriation subcommittee of the House undertook to discover the meaning of the word "cartel." On December 5, 1927, in a discussion which heavily involved the early ISC, the chairman of the subcommittee, Milton W. Shreve, inquired of the director of the Bureau of Foreign and Domestic Commerce, Dr. Julius Klein, ". . . will you place in the record a definition of a cartel?" Dr. Klein, after stating that "The cartel [European cartel movement] is causing a great deal of concern throughout the country," submitted the following definition: "The cartel is a type of trade or industrial combination, roughly approximating our trust, but with restrictive features and governmental participation which would not be tolerated in this country. . . . They are groups of industries brought together in trade-restraining set-ups, closer than our trusts in many cases, for purposes of dividing markets, controlling prices, establishing production quotas, etc."[19]

The experts consulted by the committee not only described the

---

[16] *Ibid.*   [17] *Ibid.*, pp. 13039-40.   [18] *Ibid.*

[19] *Appropriations, Department of Commerce*, 1929, Hearing before Subcommittee of House Committee on Appropriations (Washington, 1928), p. 370.

common and specific usage of the term; they also presented their
views on the indispensable elements of the cartel concept.

The definitions of Dr. Robert Liefmann, Dr. Kurt Wiedenfeld,
Dr. Herbert von Beckerath and the one given by the League of
Nations' cartel experts in 1927 were treated in the TNEC hearings
in detail. No particular attention was paid to the relatively recent
and genuine definition of cartels by Karl Pribram.[20]

Dr. Kreps limited the application of his definition of the "cartel
system" to cartels abroad, though he admitted it had relevancy for
the United States also.[21] According to him, "the essence of the cartel

---

[20] Dr. Robert Liefmann defined cartels as ". . . voluntary agreements between . . .
independent enterprises of similar type to secure a monopoly of the market." (*Cartels,
Concerns and Trusts,* New York, 1932, p. 7). Dr. Kurt Wiedenfeld's definition is the
following: "The term designates an association based upon a contractual agreement
between enterprises in the same field of business which, while retaining their legal
independence, associate themselves with a view to exerting a monopolistic influence on
the market." (*Encyclopaedia of the Social Sciences,* Article "Cartels," II, 234). According to Dr. Herbert von Beckerath "a cartel is a voluntary agreement of capitalistic
enterprises of the same branch for a regulation of the sales market with a view of
improving the profitableness of its members' business." (*Modern Industrial Organization,* New York, 1933, p. 211.) Pribram's definition may be found on pages 18-19
of his *Cartel Problems.* Pribram, admitting that "no consensus has been achieved as
to an appropriate definition" and that the meaning of the term cartel "in popular
speech" is broader than that adopted by him, defines cartels as "combinations of independent producers or sellers of raw materials or manufactured commodities established
with a view to limiting the individual risks involved in their business activities by
controlling the markets of their products." Pribram's definition is interesting for his
emphasis on the risk-restricting tendency of cartels. He distinguishes between two
primary aspects of economic relationships, the money-exchange system, and the real-
exchange system. Cartels belong to the second concept only. "Trade associations of
the typical American varieties are thus excluded" from his cartel concept, as are so-
called price-fixing cartels. However, "cartelization might be expected to gain a firm
foothold and deeply modify the structure of the American economy." (*Op. cit.,* pp.
10, 12, 234.) Robert A. Brady recently included a cartel definition in his study "Policies of National Manufacturing *Spitzenverbände,*" *Pol. Sci. Quarterly,* LVI (1941),
216-17. Admitting that the term cartel had lost its old definitiveness, Mr. Brady states
that it now means "any sort of compact, whether recognized by law and enforceable
through the courts or not, between two or more concerns for the purpose of manipu-
lating one or more of the elements of conducting business to the advantage of the
participating parties."

[21] The relevance of the matter under discussion to the United States' industry has
apparently received recognition several times before this by legislative bodies, as the
following dialogue between Professor Jenks and Charles M. Schwab (*Report of the
Industrial Commission on Trusts and Industrial Combinations,* Washington, 1901, XIII,
474), which took place at the beginning of the century, indicates: The text referred
to is the following: Question by Mr. Jenks: "You spoke in reply to one of the earlier
questions to the effect that there were sometimes apparently agreements between the
officers of the different competing companies, so that they sold at the same rates,
Pittsburgh and Chicago to certain places. Will you speak briefly with reference to

system is an agreement among independent producers in a special line of business on some particular item, whether it be such a matter as discounts, or whether it be price, or production. It is the agreement among independent producers, voluntarily arrived at. . . . They attempt to mitigate the rigors of competition. . . . In terms of their operations, then, cartels show nearly every variation in scope from local to national and international, from relatively simple control over specified trade practices to detailed administrative control over every phase of modern business operations."[22] Professor Kreps discussed "super-cartels" or the "cartels of combines" in relation to international cartels, stating that they frequently cover a number of products. He classified international cartels, as well as national cartels, into (1) trade practices cartels, (2) price cartels, (3) territorial cartels, (4) production cartels, and (5) sales cartels or syndicates. According to Kreps, "In a strict sense only the last three are cartels, the first two types being loose associations usually depending for enforcement on mutual watchfulness of members rather than on penalty arrangements applied by an administrative officer or office."[23]

Dr. Clair Wilcox, the second TNEC expert, confined his "stricter" definition of the term cartel "to organizations which assign customers

---

previous pools as they existed before the organization of this company?" Mr. Schwab: "The steel-rail pools, as so called, were simply agreements between the managers at the various works to sell at the same price at the same point." Question: "For manufacturers before the organization of the United States Steel Corporation, were similar arrangements existing?" Mr. Schwab: "Yes, in all lines of business, not only in steel, but everything else. There were similar agreements, known as joint agreements, to maintain prices. They have existed in all lines of business as long as I can remember." Question: "Without any distribution of profits?" Mr. Schwab: "There were sometimes questions as to distribution of territory." According to *Fortune*, Sept. 1942, p. 105, "Many sophisticated arguments are put forth in this country for the cartel form of doing business—usually in the same breath with stout denials that anything like a cartel ever existed in the U. S. . . . Most of the arguments start from the plea of necessity, and retreat by stages into opportunism and outright cynicism."

[22] TNEC, *Hearings*, Part 25, pp. 13040-42.

[23] TNEC, *Hearings*, Part 25, pp. 13044-45. Dr. Kreps, classifying the British Iron and Trade Federation as a super-cartel, indicated that this type exists in the national sphere as well (*ibid.*, p. 13050). The term "loose associations" has sometimes been used to distinguish cartels from combinations of the corporate type. Dr. Kreps regarded the enforceability of agreements as one of the distinguishing points between cartels in the strict sense and loose associations. Charles H. Weston ("The Application of the Sherman Act to 'Integrated' and 'Loose' Industrial Combinations," *Law and Contemporary Problems*, VII (1940), No. 1, 42-43) distinguished "loose combinations" from "integrated combinations," defining the first as embracing "all instances where concerns not linked together by common property interests either agree to suppress competition among themselves or agree to unite in imposing restrictions upon the activities of third persons."

among sellers or divide markets among sellers or allocate production or sales quotas among sellers, or organizations in which the members market their entire output through a common sales office which assigns quotas and makes payments, or organizations which enforce quotas by pooling earnings or by the imposition of money penalties."[24] Wilcox adopted as his "broader" definition that given by the experts of the League of Nations, namely "association of independent undertakings in the same or similar branches of industry established with a view to improving conditions of production and sale."[25] Professor Wilcox defined cartels more elaborately in *Monograph No. 21* of the TNEC. "A cartel is an association of independent enterprises in the same or similar branches of industry, formed for the purpose of increasing the profits of its members by subjecting their competitive activities to some form of common control." Though membership is usually voluntary, he included organizations in which membership is required by law. "It may be limited in duration to a few months or it may persist for many years." A position of substantial monopoly is not necessary. Wilcox regards the independence of the entrepreneur in matters outside the cartel arrangement as the distinguishing characteristic of the cartel. His concept would probably exclude coöperation concerning a single business transaction, e.g. in respect to one isolated government purchase. In *Monograph No. 21*, Professor Wilcox distinguished a "strictest," "narrower," and a "widest" definition, depending on cartel types, "differentiated according to the methods which they employ. . . ." These types comprise: (1) standardization cartels, and term-fixing cartels, (2) associations to fix prices, trademark cartels, minimum-price and uniform-price cartels, (3) associations distributing particular productive activities, sales territories, and customers among their members, specialization cartels, zone cartels, customer-preservation cartels, order-allocation cartels, (4) associations that undertake to award each member a fixed share of the business, plant-restriction cartels, fixed production-share cartels, fixed marketing-share cartels, production-equalization cartels, marketing-equalization cartels, profit-sharing cartels, syndicates. Wilcox included in his "widest" definition "associations that fall within all four of these categories." The narrower definition would include those that fall

---

[24] In practice, payments and premiums paid and received by cartel participants because of the exceeding of or failure to exhaust quotas have been differentiated from fines imposed because of the violation of cartel regulations. Only these latter may be regarded as penalties in the proper sense.

[25] TNEC, *Hearings*, Part 25, pp. 13311, 13328.

within the second, third and fourth categories, and the strictest definition those within the third and fourth categories. International cartels, according to Wilcox, may include in their membership "publicly owned or operated enterprises or even governments themselves." He defined super-cartels as "composed of a number of national cartels."[26] He did not take here into account such domestic structures as represented by the *Comptoir Sidérurgique de France,* the British Iron and Steel Federation, or the German *Stahlwerks-Verband,* controlling practically all steel commodity cartels of their respective countries. Wilcox's discussion of the American cartel problem in *Monograph No. 21* of the TNEC is the most extensive and profound among recent treatments. It applies not only to American industry, but to the industry of other countries as well.

The third expert consulted in the cartel hearings was Dr. Rudolf Callman. His cartel definition covering "all essential features of the cartel" and also the underlying features of the decisions of the German Supreme Court and the German Cartel Court, reads: "A cartel is 'a *contractual* association of legally *independent* entrepreneurs in the *same* or similar field of business formed with the intent, effect or potentiality of *influencing the market* by means of *regulation* of *competition.*'"[27] Callman stressed the fact that he does not include in his cartel concept associations which only intend to influence the market without having the objective capacity to do so. According to him, "cartels have reached an advanced stage of development in the United States." His designation of basing-point systems and price-leadership systems in the United States as cartels does not seem consistent with his requirement of a "contractual association."[28] According to Callman "the distinction in substance between a very close, strong cartel, e.g. a syndicate, and a merger corporation or community of interests or fusion is sometimes negligible . . . for the problem of governmental supervision or legal enforcement it is unimportant which of the two illegal purposes of coöperation it was striving to achieve when it was created. . . ." The two purposes referred to in the statement of Dr. Callman were defense and aggression.[29] The aspect of the "illegal purposes" of the cartel which Dr. Callman introduced, indicates that he viewed industrial combinations mainly from the point of view of "legality." The TNEC did not devote par-

---

[26] *Ibid.*
[27] TNEC, *Hearings,* Part 25, pp. 13347-48 (italics in original text).
[28] *Ibid.,* pp. 13348-49.　　　　[29] *Ibid.,* p. 13350.

ticular attention to what are called legal definitions of cartels. Legal definitions, arbitrarily set up by a particular legal order, are not very important as regards this study. Besides, nearly all legal definitions, including the German, do not relate specifically to cartels.[30] Positivistic opinion in respect to the defining power of the legislator is well expressed by the proverbial sentence of Kirchmann, "One single word of the legislator transforms whole legal libraries into scrap-paper." The focusing of legal reasoning about cartels on the common-law concept of "restraint of trade" has been rather impaired by the statement of Mr. Justice Brandeis, as simple as it is brilliant: "The legality of an agreement or regulation cannot be determined by so simple a test as whether it restrains competition. Every agreement concerning trade . . . restrains. To bind, to restrain, is of their [the agreements'] very essence."[31]

The study of the TNEC accentuated the interrelation between trade associations and the cartel problem in the United States and in Great Britain. It has been claimed that in the United States several trade associations actually exercised cartel functions, operating in this manner because coöperation within an association is less conspicuous than to operate in a framework peculiar to cartels. In Great Britain cartels have been operating in the form of trade associations and in forms used by continental cartels; however, the nomenclature in that country, as in the United States, is not clear in this regard. While trade associations in the United States and Great Britain may have assumed cartel functions, on the continent cartels and trade associations functioned as separate organizations. Continental European cartels were generally organized as commercial corporations, especially the steel cartels in Germany and France, which were in both cases

---

[30] The German Emergency Decree of November 2, 1923, "Against Abuse of Economic Power (Cartel Decree)," determined in its first chapter the meaning of syndicates, cartels, conventions and similar agreements, by a common definition. The Czechoslovak statute of July 12, 1933, concerning cartels and private monopolies, defined cartel agreements as follows: "Cartel agreements according to this statute are agreements of independent entrepreneurs through which the parties in the agreement oblige themselves to limit or to eliminate among themselves freedom of competition, through regulation of production, sales, business conditions, and prices; provided that the objective of these agreements is an efficient as possible domination of the market. In case these agreements relate to transportation, credit, or insurance, the provisions of the statute relate to price-tariffs as well." Cf. Ervin Hexner, *La Loi Tchécoslovaque sur les Cartels* (Prague, 1935), *passim*.

[31] *Board of Trade of Chicago vs. United States*, 246 U. S. 231, 238 (1918).

incorporated as joint stock companies.[32] In international trade, international trade associations were not used as frameworks for cartels.

III

The purpose of the TNEC in discussing cartel definitions was obviously to determine a more exact meaning for a term which al-

---

[32] See W. Tudor Davies, *op. cit., passim.* Robert A. Brady, *op. cit.,* pp. 221-22, assumes that "In general, trade associations throughout the world are taking on cartel functions so rapidly that the distinction between different types of cartels and these associations is badly blurred, and in many respects lacking in all essential differences." Mr. Brady extends his discussion to the French and German situation after the First World War. The author assumes that Brady's information concerning the function of the main trade association of the French steel industry, the *Comité des Forges,* after 1932 is incomplete. Brady disregarded the fact that the reorganization of the *Comptoir Sidérurgique de France* was such that this agency operated as the center of all French steel cartels and not the trade association, the *Comité des Forges.* This is not to say that the *Comité des Forges* did not act in line with the general interests of the French steel industry. But it did not influence specific cartel decisions. Even less did the *Confederation Générale du Patronat Français* help in determining cartel policies. This association devoted its activities mainly to labor problems. Naturally, the new social and political order, introduced by Marshall Pétain, radically changed the whole situation. However, whereas the *Comité des Forges* was dissolved, the *Comptoir Sidérurgique de France* operates in forms adjusted to the present situation. Mr. Brady's opinion concerning the role played by the *Kartellstelle* of the manufacturers' association, the general German National Federation of German Industry, is not entirely correct. The *Kartellstelle* did not exercise any influence on business policies of German cartels. It consisted of a few economists and legal experts who advised industries and cartels on abstract questions and prepared the way for so-called lobbying. An arbitration court for cartels existed in connection with the *Kartellstelle,* but this court did not function frequently. As to the connection between cartels and compulsory trade associations during the Hitler regime, there is a certain discrepancy between the principle and its application. These associations have the right to participate in important meetings and to supervise cartel policy. In practice, cartels have been subjected directly to the Minister of National Economy. This policy was adopted after some hesitation. The men controlling steel cartel policies and compulsory trade associations were closely connected, but none of those who operated in the management of one type of organization was permitted to operate in the management of the other. (See the Decree of the German Minister of National Economy, November 12, 1936, published in *Stahl und Eisen,* November 19, 1936, p. 1395.) The compulsory trade association of the German steel industry, the *Wirtschaftsgruppe Eisen,* in coöperation with the German national steel cartel, the *Stahlwerks-Verband,* collaborated in an agency, called *Preisprüfungsstelle,* which supervised steel prices under the authority of the Minister for National Economy. See Heinz Serlo, *Das Wesen der Verkaufsverbände der deutschen Rohstahlgemeinschaft und ihre Bedeutung für die deutsche Eisenindustrie* (Diss., Düsseldorf, 1939), pp. 42, 54, 56. A discussion of the decree of Nov. 12, 1936, may be found in Henry Laufenburger, *La Nouvelle Structure Economique du Reich* (Paris, 1938), pp. 36 ff. See also Franz Neumann, *Behemoth, the Structure and Practice of National Socialism* (New York, 1942), pp. 230 f. and 270 f.

ready had a vague meaning in the minds of many. No attempt was made to reconcile differences among the various definitions presented, or to formulate one single valid proposition embodying the elements essential to the cartel concept. Even keeping in mind Aristotle's well-known admonition, "Our discussion will be adequate if it has as much clearness as the subject-matter admits of . . . for it is the mark of an educated man to look for precision in each class of things just so far as the nature of the subject admits,"[33] one cannot escape the impression that whereas the structure of industrial combinations has undergone rapid and radical change and development in the last few decades, terminology has adhered to inherited phraseology and verbal associations. Economic terminology (and political and legal as well) in the field of industrial combinations, in order to keep pace with modern developments, greatly needs the introduction of new terms indicating new developments and new distinctions. However, appropriate authorities to breach semantic lags have not yet been created in our society, and instead of bridging these lags, nebulous discussions flourish. The TNEC honestly attempted to avoid such nebulous discussions and its work is a further proof of the present difficulties in cartel terminology.

In order to make the reader realize the significance of the essential elements in cartel definitions, the most important of them should be reviewed briefly. Traditionally the following have been regarded as elements of the cartel concept:

1. A plurality of participating enterprises (economic units), as contrasted with one single economic unit composing in itself a marketing unit. There is a fairly general agreement that the participants need not necessarily be private entrepreneurs, as contrasted with public agencies. Governmental agencies may, in a collective marketing control scheme, represent economic interests either of private entrepreneurs or of government-owned enterprises.[34] If all participants in

---

[33] Nichomachean Ethics, 1094 b, *The Works of Aristotle,* translated by W. D. Rose (Oxford, 1925), Vol. IX.

[34] A publication of the International Chamber of Commerce designated the ISC as a "private entente," distinguishing it from collective marketing controls with governments as members. *International Ententes,* p. 7. Concerning government participation in international cartels, see W. Y. Elliott, *International Control in the Non-Ferrous Metals,* pp. 32 ff., and Dr. Fritz Werr, *Internationale Wirtschaftszusammenschlüsse (Kartelle und Konzerne),* Berlin, 1936, *passim.*

One of the earliest "modern" international cartels between sovereigns was established on June 11, 1470, between the owners of alum mines in the Papal State and those of the Island of Ischia, near Naples. The signers of the cartel agreement, Pope Paul II and King Ferdinand of Naples, candidly included in the covenant the statement that

the cartel are governments, however, it becomes questionable whether the economic structure thus created belongs in the realm of private economy.[35]

2. The participating enterpreneurs must be independent of each other. This independence in a certain sense implies virtually a democratic structure for cartels, and even if such a collectivism is subjected to a single will, it is presumed that such a leadership structure resembles a constitutional dictatorship, since it is temporary and is based on the volition of its followers. This virtual democracy may be naturally impaired if quota participation is very different among cartel members. The interpretations of independence in a legal sense, i.e. the implication that specific legal entities are independent of each other, as is done in several cartel definitions,[36] may cause confusion because actually legal entities may be economically dependent on each

---

their objective was to maintain prices for alum as high as it was possible. Common price policy was agreed upon, profit-sharing and sales quotas were established, exchange of statistical information arranged, and a common policy was adopted to fight outsiders. There were agents acting as a "joint sales comptoir." Credit and other conditions of sales were regulated uniformly and heavy penalties were stipulated in case of violations of the agreement. The social position of the contracting parties did not prevent a certain cartel distrust, mitigated somewhat by the provision that each party had to possess keys to the storehouses of the other in order to supervise possible circumventions. The mines were exploited by private companies, but the sovereign owners were highly interested in the prosperity of those companies. Whereas the cartel agreement conspicuously resembled a "modern" international cartel agreement, there was one provision which belonged to the arsenal of ancient times. In order to fight Turkish "outsider'" competition the Pope obligated himself to enjoin, at least once a year, all Christianity from buying and selling alum of Turkish origin. Turkish alum was outlawed and could be seized by anybody. The whole profit yielded to the Pope by the monopoly had to be used to finance wars against infidel Turks and Protestant Hussites. Cf. Jakob Strieder, *Studien zur Geschichte kapitalistischer Organisationsformen*, pp. 168 ff. and Piotrowski, *op. cit.*, pp. 152 ff.

[35] International marketing controls based on diplomatic agreements and associated with hemispheric defense have frequently been referred to as cartels. See e.g., W. L. Culbertson, "Economic defense of the Americas," *Annals of the American Academy of Pol. and Soc. Science*, Sept. 1940, pp. 186 ff. There is little doubt that these agencies have little in common with cartels in the traditional sense. However, there are many transitional patterns, where classification is based mainly on the particular view of the classifier.

[36] See e.g. the definitions of Wiedenfeld and Callman quoted above. *Fortune*, Sept. 1942, p. 105, based its cartel definition on an association of legally independent cartel members. That is why it did not distinguish combinations of the corporate type from cartels, and this is the reason why it did not separate the concept of compulsory cartels from that of free cartels. On page 106 the *I. G. Farben* is designated as "the symbol of all cartels in the American mind," thus confusing the corporate relationship with cartel relationship. The confusion grows even stronger, because the combination of the corporate type called *I. G. Farben* participated in many cartel agreements with companies which did not belong to its "concern."

other as a result of intercorporate ties, and therefore could not fulfill the requirement of independence inherent in the cartel concept. This point will be discussed more in detail below.

3. The object of the cartel is the restriction of possible competition among cartel members, which would or could exist, if the cartel were not to limit it. The commodity or service to which the possible competition relates has to be more or less exactly determined. Cartel definitions vary as to the degree of competition-restriction necessary within an economic structure for it to be called a cartel. Some are inclined to call agreements for the determination of fair practices cartels,[37] others do not call uniform price-fixing agreements cartels.[38] The restriction may relate to all possible business transactions concerning a determined commodity or service. It may relate equally to production, to the use of patents, or to other actions and forbearances affecting competition.

4. According to most cartel definitions, these collective marketing controls are established and operated on the basis of agreements[39] of the cartel members. Other opinions hold that collective marketing controls called cartels may operate without an overt or tacit act which is generally referred to as an agreement. Furthermore, some definitions view collective marketing controls as cartels, though their establishment or operation is based upon acts of public authorities. Several definitions include as an element the "intention" to restrict competition regardless of whether this intention is realized or realizable.[40] This fourth element of the cartel concept will be further elucidated below.

5. Several definitions include as cartels only those horizontal economic structures related to sales.[41] Others embrace marketing controls of buyers as well. There are definitions admitting several layers of economic activities, including activities concerning the licensing of jobbers, and those involving the establishment of contracts concerning conditions of delivery of semifinished products, etc. The ISC is one of the best illustrations for use in examining these complicated structures.

---

[37] See Robert Liefmann, *op. cit.,* pp. 10, 36. In a study published by this author in 1929, a considerable degree of restriction was regarded as an element of the cartel concept. Roman Piotrowski, *op. cit.,* p. 53, took exception to that statement, obviously misinterpreting the expression "considerable."

[38] See Karl Pribram, *op. cit.,* p. 15.

[39] See e.g. the definitions of Liefmann and Callman previously quoted.

[40] See Robert Liefmann, *op. cit.,* p. 9.

[41] See e.g. Robert Liefmann, *op. cit.,* p. 11, and Karl Pribram, *op. cit.,* p. 12.

It is generally recognized that cartels are one of the principal categories of economic structures called industrial combinations.[42] Indeed, the verb "to combine"[43] seems to apply to cartels, and marketing controls are the very essence of this type of combination. A second category of industrial combination which may, but need not necessarily, function as a marketing control, consists of combinations of the corporate type; i.e., aggregates of legal entities connected by what are broadly called intercorporate ties. A third category of so-called combinations which also may, but need not necessarily, function as marketing controls are legal entities resulting from the complete merger of two or more previously independent legal entities.

Competition on a market between legal entities connected by intercorporate attachment would be regarded as an exceptional and artificial activity,[44] whereas non-competition on a market by entities economically and legally independent of each other has been regarded rightly as an "artificial" marketing control, commonly designated as an act of a cartel. Briefly, whereas the restriction of competition in the case of combinations of the corporate type is the result of the stable structural form of the corporate interrelation (the initial act of combination), in the case of so-called cartels this restriction results not only from an initial act of combination, but also from a continued

---

[42] Various types of combinations are discussed in Milton Handler, *Cases and Other Materials on Trade Regulation* (Chicago, 1937), pp. 172 ff., 229 ff., 444 ff. The expression "trust" has been used for many decades in the United States to designate all kinds of industrial combinations. Expressions like "anti-trust" laws, and "Anti-Trust Division" are vivid proof of such terminological usage. According to E. Benjamin Andrews, "The most diverse species of joint undertakings are popularly stigmatized as 'trusts.' . . ." However, he calls one of the specific categories "trusts proper." "Trusts According to Official Investigations," *Quarterly Journal of Economics,* III (1888/9), 119, 120, 128. A revealing classification of industrial combinations may be found in E. A. G. Robinson, *Monopoly* (Cambridge, England, 1941), *passim.*

[43] A. F. Lucas uses the noun "combine" to designate what this study calls combinations of the corporate type. Lucas distinguishes "terminable associations" from "permanent combines. . . . The former involves some form of contractual relationship between the individual firms or between each firm and the central organization, while the latter is the result of complete financial unification." *Industrial Reconstruction and the Control of Competition* (London, 1937), pp. 47, 175-177, 297. Percy Ashley, in his "Memorandum on Industrial Combinations," distinguishing between "terminable" and "permanent" combinations (as Mr. Lucas does), uses the term "combine" for the second category, though admitting that there is no settled terminology. (*Report of Committee on Trusts,* p. 38.) Milton Handler distinguishes between two categories of "combines," (1) loose-knit confederations, and (2) close-knit integrations. (TNEC, *Monograph No. 38,* Washington, 1941, p. 2.) Professor Handler obviously referred to the distinction between cartels and combinations of the corporate type.

[44] See e.g. the "Goodyear Case," quoted by Wilcox, TNEC, *Monograph No. 21,* p. 49.

volition to combine. Whereas in the former case the restriction or elimination of competition is an unavoidable effect of the corporate relationship, in the second case the act organizing a cartel (if any) constitutes a temporary machine for the collective action of potential competitors. In practice, cartel members often compete keenly in branches not bound by cartel structures.[45] Using a somewhat doubtful analogy, a combination of the corporate type resembles a compound where ingredients are chemically mingled, whereas a cartel resembles a mixture of easily discernible substances. This mixture (cartels) may have a more or less frozen surface concealing movements underneath and exercising resistance only against forces outside of it. However, this surface may be split by inside or outside blows, or may melt under changed atmospheric conditions.

It is frequently difficult to apply this abstract classification to existing organizations which may often appear as a sort of hybrid mixture of both the corporate and cartel forms.[46]

Traditionally, the cartel concept is limited to marketing controls in which no compulsion to adhere to the cartel is exercised by public authorities, to controls which are not protected by public authorities through a licensing system limiting the establishment of new enterprises, and to those whose policies are not considerably influenced by general or individual regulations of the respective governments of adherents. However, some authors regard compulsory organizations, or only nominally free organizations with a government-imposed policy, as a form of cartel.[47] Those who hold the latter view make

[45] Dr. Wilcox put it thus: "The members of such an association remain under separate ownership, retaining their freedom of action with respect to matters which are not included, surrendering it only with respect to matters which are included, within the scope of their agreement." TNEC, *Monograph No. 21*, p. 215. "Common control of enterprises," writes Wilcox, describing intercorporate relations (*ibid.*, p. 189), "engaged in the same industry is not consonant with the existence of *bona fide* competition between them."

[46] Various types of interlocking directorates, personal relationships, management-engineering companies, financial affiliations, interest groupings, are examples of such hybrid forms. According to Liefmann "trusts" may be regarded "in many respects as a further stage in the development of the cartels, and frequently produce the effects of these in a still more marked degree." *Op. cit.*, p. 11. This view is neither consistent with nor warranted in practice.

[47] E.g. Dr. Heinrich Friedländer writes that cartels can be established through contracts, by-laws, or resolutions of a corporate nature ("free cartels"), and through public or private acts approved by a public authority. *Die Rechtspraxis der Kartelle und Konzerne in Europa* (Zürich, 1938), p. 11.

A very interesting example of a political stand taken toward industrial combinations is found in the still valid platform of the German Nazi Party of 1920. In its article 13 it proclaims the following high-sounding principle: "We demand the nationaliza-

no distinction between the effects of self-restraint and publicly imposed restraint on entrepreneurs. They regard it as significant (in a cartel sense) that an entrepreneur does not exercise the discretion which he legally does not possess.

"Compulsory cartels" often approach closer to the concept of public agencies, or public corporations, than to the concept of cartels. It is submitted that the legal and extra-legal influences of governments on the organization and on the determination of the policies of the economic structure discussed here have greatly differed in several countries. There were economic organizations on the borderline between compulsory and voluntary "cartels." In cartel definition, however, the compulsory element is of capital importance.[48] It is important also from the standpoint of research on economic behavior and political responsibility. Cartels are sometimes dichotomized into "compulsory" and "voluntary" types, implying that two contradictory classes are included as parts of a "more general" concept. However,

---

tion of all trusts." Gottfried Feder, the author of this platform, comments on the article in the following way. "This demand is consistent with our general war upon the capitalist idea. The first aim of syndicates and trusts in any particular branch of production is to unite with other similar businesses for the purpose of dictating prices. They are governed by no desire to distribute good wares at a cheap price. . . . Supply is regulated by pooling, by which means they are able to regulate prices in accordance with an apparently genuine 'supply and demand.' This is what interests the shareholders, who have no desire to see prices kept low by competition. New ideas and inventions are viewed with a hostile eye, and preferably suppressed if their adoption would endanger the paying capacity of older plants. Such businesses, run as huge trusts from a big central office, are clearly 'ripe for socialization,' i.e., they have ceased to fulfill any of the services to the community which individual competition performs." Gottfried Feder, *Hitler's Official Program and its Fundamental Ideas* (London, 1938), p. 91. Perhaps a statement of one of the semi-official social philosophers of Nazi Germany may convey an idea of what is meant by nationalization of trusts. According to Werner Sombart's opinion ". . . the cartel must cease to pursue a profit policy and place itself rather at the service of the community, that is that it finally becomes the bearer of political or state functions (compulsory cartels) so that it will have a sort of capitalistic guild-constitution." Cf. *A New Social Philosophy* (Princeton, 1937), p. 285.

[48] To be sure, modern legal doctrine may retort that the distinguishing mark between "free" and "compulsory" institutions is not a generic one; that the difference between them is not one of kind, but of degree. However, a certain degree of freedom may be a constituent element of a concept. For "nucleus" firms in British industry see *Concentration of Production, Explanatory Memorandum,* Presented by the Board of Trade to Parliament, Mar. 1941, Cmd. 6258. A German economist, Max Drews, expressing contempt for those who do not show sufficient understanding of the German compulsory cartel structure, states that according to the Nazi doctrine "there should not be a basic difference between peace and war economy," in which case the compulsory cartel structure would remain a permanent economic pattern. ("Die Kriegswirtschaft als Übergang zu einer neuen Wirtschaftsordnung," *Wirtschafts-Dienst* (Hamburg), July 5, 1940, p. 515.)

numerous hybrid cartel forms which defy classification in either category make doubtful the applicability of traditional categories. This is not to say that compulsory and free cartels cannot have common properties at all. However, a fruitful discussion should inquire into the degree to which "external" compulsion is consistent with the cartel concept.[49]

Is a cartel necessarily based on an agreement, or may it be established by the conscious, harmonious behavior of entrepreneurs, though this conduct is not based on and preceded by an actual getting together of parties concerning their future conduct of affairs? If economic structures, arrived at without agreements,[50] and/or lacking any external organization, are excluded from the cartel concept, an important boundary line would be fixed.[51] As a matter of fact,

---

[49] Paul de Rousiers, in *Cartels and Trusts and their Development* (League of Nations, Geneva, 1927), pp. 21-22, writes: "It cannot be too often emphasized that any agreement which possesses the smallest fraction of public authority . . . constitutes a step towards monopoly, jeopardizes freedom of competition and thus threatens to bring about a rise in prices. Under a free regime, any agreement which abuses its power by raising sale prices arouses competition from outside and thus exposes itself to the most serious danger that it can have to fear." Though this juxtaposition of free and compulsory combinations is somewhat exaggerated by Rousier, it points to a serious practical distinction between the two contrasting structures. A. F. Lucas (*op. cit.,* pp. viii and 45-46) regards the absence of close regulation by the state "an important distinguishing mark in classifying industrial combinations." According to W. Y. Elliott, "The mixture of government control and private management suggests a new form of political organization for economic life." (*Op. cit.,* p. 9.)

[50] The term "agreement" as used here does not cover contracts in the legal sense only. It includes all sorts of common understandings, whether enforceable, expressed, or tacit, about future facts and performances or forbearances. Even a so-called tacit understanding implies that one knows whose tacitness, when, where, and by whom observed, has given to it a significant meaning. A close scrutiny into the political reasons for the deliberate use of inadequate sign vehicles in formulating economic agreements would throw light on important differences in methods of government control of business.

[51] A. F. Lucas, in discussing the almost imperceptible gradation from informal understandings to highly complex organizations, dismisses informal understandings "with no more than a mention. . . . No doubt," writes Professor Lucas, "many of them exist in England, as in every country, although confirmation of their existence is, in most cases, quite impossible." The author does not share Lucas' opinion that ". . . the very informality of such arrangements makes them essentially temporary and ephemeral." Neither does he subscribe to the statement that, "While in specific cases they have substantially modified the competitive struggles, they can hardly be characterized as effective agencies of control." (*Op. cit.,* p. 201.) *The Report of Committee on Trusts* (London, H.M.S.O. 1919, Cmd. 9236, p. 17) contains the following significant remark: "What is notable among British consolidations and associations is not their rarity or weakness so much as their unobtrusiveness. There is not much display in the window, but there is a good selection inside." See concerning "Gary dinners" of

the TNEC minutely questioned entrepreneurs on several occasions about whether their collaboration to restrict competition had been based on mutual understandings or was founded solely on mutual action or forbearance, without any "agreed upon" behavior or results.[52] However, this question might be elucidated by the text of the Sherman Act prohibiting restraint of trade arrived at by agreements.[53]

It may safely be stated that even a very strong monopolistic situation, not the result of conscious relationship, but effected by mere chance or by subconscious coöperation,[54] does not fall into the cartel concept. The real question here is, "Is a conscious non-competitive attitude[55] (not based on agreement in respect to mutual restriction of competition) sufficient in itself to be an element of the cartel concept?" Dr. Wilcox seems to have answered this question in

---

the American steel industry, Lewis H. Haney, *Business Organization and Combination* (New York, 1934), pp. 183-184.

[52] E.g. Dr. Wilcox cited cases where a quota system had been attributed to "customary behavior." TNEC, *Hearings,* Part 25, pp. 13340-41. The investigation of the price-leadership system in the beryllium-copper industry questions the existence of a mutual understanding minutely. See *ibid.,* Part 5, pp. 2085 ff., 2115 ff., 2284 ff. Concerning published prices of the steel industry, cf. *ibid.,* Part 19, pp. 10486 ff., 10602 ff. Concerning extras in the steel industry, *ibid.,* Part 19, pp. 10560 ff. Wilcox discussed price-leadership in *Monograph No. 21,* pp. 121 ff. E. Benjamin Andrews, "Trusts According to Official Investigations," *Quarterly Journal of Economics,* III (1888/89), 121, referred to "Silent agreements as to prices" which "have always prevailed among contiguous dealers in a given sort of goods. . . . With wholesalers, the custom is old and not rare of fixing the minimum prices at which retailers shall vend their wares." He regarded price leadership as a particular category of "trusts": "Cases where one corporation or firm, in virtue of its peculiar power or success, is tacitly accepted by others as the standard for price-lists and methods." (P. 119.) Price leadership, as tacit coöperation, often flourished between ISC units and "friendly" outsiders. See further, Merle Fainsod and Lincoln Gordon, *op. cit.,* pp. 554 and 568.

[53] Price leadership is discussed in *U. S. v. International Harvester Co.,* 274 U. S. 693, 47 Sup. Ct. 748 (1927). ". . . the fact that competitors may see proper, in the exercise of their own judgment, to follow the prices of another manufacturer, does not establish any suppression of competition or show any sinister domination." The mere possession of potential—unexerted—economic power, unaccompanied by unlawful conduct, was not regarded as an offense in *U. S. v. United States Steel Corporation,* 251 U. S. 417, 40 Sup. Ct. 293 (1920), and *U. S. v. International Harvester Co.,* 274 U. S. at 708-9, 47 Sup. Ct. at 753-4 (1912). See, however, *Ethyl Gasoline Corp. vs. U. S.,* 309 U. S. 436, 60 Sup. Ct. 618 (1941), and *U. S. vs. Socony Vacuum,* 310 U. S. 150, 60 Sup. Ct. 811 (1941).

[54] Coöperation in this connection does not imply that competitors are aware of the harmony of their actions.

[55] Dr. Rudolf Callman, the third cartel expert of the TNEC, proposed to replace "monopoly" with "anti-competitive conduct" in legal language. It is presumed that he did not mean unconscious anti-competitive conduct. (TNEC, *Hearings,* Part 25, p. 13351.)

the affirmative by designating as cartels quota systems based on mutual "customary behavior" as well as freight equalization systems,[56] especially price leadership systems, neither of which are based on agreements. One would be inclined to put into this category so-called "honorable understandings" or "gentlemen's agreements" in which, although the parties agree on a certain conduct, there is an expressed or tacit reservation that the obligation rests exclusively in the "moral sphere."[57] A great many ISC relationships were based on tacit agreements, provable by a harmonious operation based only on expectations that if the behavior of one of the parties were changed in a competitive direction, a similar competitive act of the other party or parties would follow. It was relatively rare on the steel market for producers or merchants to be in the market only temporarily, thus they could not afford to be indifferent to the future consequences of competition.[58] Generally in the ISC sellers, distributors, and even ultimate consumers fully considered the long-run consequences of their competitive or noncompetitive acts and adjusted their behavior accordingly. Potential competitors thus coöperated ("forced by the situation itself to take into account the policy of his rival in determining his own")[59] as if a very definite agreement existed. This pattern of con-

---

[56] Professor Frank Albert Fetter assumes that the basing point system of the American steel industry was extended "for three decades or more . . . by successive agreements to all steel products and to all primary producing mills in the U. S." See "The Pricing of Steel in South Africa," *The South African Journal of Economics,* Sept. 1941, p. 238.

[57] *The Report of the Committee on Trusts* (p. 17) regards an "honorable understanding" as a kind of combination without any formal association. "The simplest (though not necessarily the most primitive) type of combination is that which occurs where a number of manufacturers or traders, who would otherwise be competitors, meet from time to time and arrive at an "honorable understanding" or "gentlemen's agreement" in regard to prices, output, division of business, etc. Such arrangements are essentially informal and temporary. There are no documents; there is no association; there is no bond except that of good faith."

[58] Sometimes a small outside competitor, assuming that the ISC would not reduce its rigid prices, particularly in the case of a small transaction, competed successfully for the business by lowering prices. As Edward Chamberlin put it, he assumed "his rival's policy constant." (*Op. cit.,* pp. 34 f.) If the cartel had met this competition by lowering its prices, an avalanche of requests to reduce official prices would have resulted.

[59] Edward Chamberlin, *op. cit.,* p. 31. According to Prof. Chamberlin "this cannot be construed as a 'tacit agreement' between the two." Though from a legal point of view the situation may be rather doubtful, from an economic point of view the difference between a tacit agreement and a lasting conscious coöperation of potential competitors is difficult to discern. From an economic point of view it makes no difference whether potential competitors "feel" their "independence" limited by tacit agreements or by expectations based on experienced harmonious conduct. In practice conscious

duct (coöperation due to fear of retribution) is not unique in economic action, and occurs on many planes of social life.[60]

IV

Most of the essential elements of the cartel concept are easily discernable within the ISC organization. A few comments should be made, however, concerning inter-corporate relationships[61] and compulsory cartel structures within the ISC. International intercorporate relationships were relatively scant within the ISC as compared with other large industries. The American steel industry had practically no intercorporate relationships with any steel industry of the world either in the active or in the passive sense. Iron and steel are mentioned among those branches of manufacturing in America in which direct foreign investments and foreign affiliations were insignificant.[62] Though the author is not in a position to quote any authorities, he has no knowledge of any notable intercorporate connections between the American iron and steel industry and other steel industries participating in the ISC. The same is true of the British iron and steel industries. No foreign steel industry had any significant corporate interests in the British steel industry and it in turn had no intercorporate relations of any consequence with countries participating in the policy-forming activities of the ISC. The French steel industry had intercorporate connections with the Belgian and Luxemburg steel industries,[63] and the French Schneider-Creuzot concern had impor-

---

harmonious conduct has often been referred to as tacit agreement. (See Chamberlin's distinction on pp. 47 and 106, *op. cit.*)

[60] Cf. Hans Kelsen, "Causality and Retribution," *Philosophy of Science*, Oct. 1941, pp. 533 ff.

[61] Gottfried von Haberler considered the ISC and its export sales comptoirs cartels, consisting of enterprises often connected by inter-corporate relationships. That is why he put them into one category with many of the combinations of the chemical and artificial silk industries. (*The Theory of International Trade*, New York, 1937, p. 330.) Louis Domeratzky placed in the category of combinations of the corporate type only combinations of the non-ferrous metal industries. "Cartels and Business Crisis," *Foreign Affairs*, X, 51.

[62] According to *Monograph No. 6* of the TNEC, Milton Gilbert and Paul D. Dickens, "Export Prices and Export Cartels" (Washington, 1940), p. 100, direct foreign investments in 1937 in the American Iron and Steel Industry amounted to $6,348,000.

[63] Because France, Belgium, and Luxemburg were not real or potential adversaries in the political sense, these financial cross-currents did not violate national loyalties. Many of the French-Belgian-Luxemburg intercorporate steel relations originated in capital transactions connected with the political changes in Lorraine and the Saar region in 1919-20, and as a consequence of the establishment of the Belgium-Luxemburg customs union, May 1, 1922. E.g., the French steel group of Schneider & Co., Paris,

tant corporate interests in the Czechoslovakian and Polish steel industries.[64] Even these relations did not exercise significant influence on ISC policies. Luxemburg-Belgian steel industries had mutual intimate intercorporate relations and this connection sometimes resulted in the coördinated policy of these two countries within the ISC, though not on basic questions. The German steel industry was almost entirely free of international corporate relations. It is true that steel plants belonging to a Luxemburg steel corporation, ARBED, existed in Germany, and that the German Mannesmann group participated to a certain extent in one of the Czechoslovakian steel companies, but these connections were insignificant in influencing steel policies within the ISC. However, the German-owned Austrian *Alpine Montangesellschaft,* the only significant steel-producing and -exporting plant of Austria, operated, even in cartel matters, according to the open and secret instructions of its German stock owner, the *Vereinigte Stahlwerke.*

It does not belong to the more immediate objective of this study to analyze intercorporate relationships within the national groups. However, it should be noted that all national groups participating in the formulation of ISC policies consisted both of small single entrepreneurs and of large concerns. Within national steel cartels one or a few large concerns played a dominant role, though frequently restricted by mutual jealousies, by the politics of their national governments, and by the potential dangers of driving smaller enterprises to outside competition. As a general fact it is safe to say that, despite the above-mentioned French, Belgian, and Luxemburg connections, no other large industry had as few significant (from the cartel aspect) intercorporate relations in the international sense as the steel industry.

bought the Luxemburg works of the *Gelsenkirchener Bergwerks A.G.,* and French, Belgian, and Luxemburg steel industries established the Hadir Company in Luxemburg in order to take over the Luxemburg, Lorrain, and Saar works of the *Deutsch Luxemburgische Bergwerks und Hütten A.G.* Those who are interested in the dark transactions through which the ownership of steel plants was transferred as a consequence of the First World War should consult the report of an investigating committee of the French lower chamber which worked under the chairmanship of Mr. Louis Cluzel. The committee concluded that the transfer of the steel works in Lorraine, into French property, which was performed with the participation and in favor of French steel industries, may be regarded as "the richest pillage ever heard of," accompanied by negligence, incompetence, and prodigality. Cf. Chambre des Députés, *Documents Parlementaires, Annexes aux Procès-Verbaux des Séances,* Annex No. 5367, Jan. 19, 1928, p. 186.

[64] The structure of the Schneider concern is discussed in Lothar Bauer, "Die Rüstungsindustrie der Welt I, Der Konzern Schneider-Creusot," *Wirtschaftskurve,* Aug. 1932, pp. 149 ff.

The pattern of several large but independent entities, national and international, is one of the characteristics of the steel industry as contrasted with many other industrial groups, especially with large chemical industries.

The new pattern of "compulsory" cartels in all of its actual gradations became significant within the ISC because of the gradually increasing influence of governments on the policies of their national steel groups. Among the national groups participating in the ISC, only the German and the Polish groups may be regarded as compulsory cartels in the proper sense. The British Iron and Steel Federation approached the compulsory cartel concept somewhat, though governmental compulsion in regard to ISC problems was exercised in an indirect and informal way. In their export trade, the American, Belgian, Luxemburg, and French national groups could be regarded as free cartels.

After 1935, important cartel policies were heavily influenced in Europe by national governments, though this influence was naturally different as to degree and form in the democratic countries. In their international cartels, national cartel groups more and more referred to the requirements of their governments in respect to the acquisition of foreign exchange, domestic employment, official barter and clearing agreements, and so forth. The TNEC hearings emphasized the intimate relationship between government and industry in Great Britain,[65] but the study did not discuss the decisive influence exercised by British public agencies on prices and production of basic commodities administered by cartels. Although regulations were promulgated by the

---

[65] TNEC, *Hearings*, Part 25, p. 13048. Dr. Kreps stated: ". . . there is an intimate relationship between members of government and ruling members of industry. That intimate relationship undoubtedly results in a give and take, in some modifications of industry policy at some times, but we have no formal evidence on that point." *The Report of the Import Duties Advisory Committee on the Present Position and Future Development of the Iron and Steel Industry*, Presented by the President of the Board of Trade to Parliament by Command of His Majesty, London, 1937, Cmd. 5507 (May Report), sufficiently proves that production and price policies of the iron and steel industry were decidedly influenced by governmental agencies. Even the agreement of the British steel industry with the International Steel Cartel was submitted to Parliament. The statement of Dr. Kreps "At present the iron and steel industry is completely controlled by a supercartel . . ." should be weighed in light of the control exercised by the government upon this super-cartel. A censuring opinion of many adherents of the British Labor Party in respect to the relationship between the British government and the steel industry is contained in Ingot (pseud.), *The Socialisation of Iron and Steel* (London, 1936), *passim*. "The heavy iron and steel products," writes Ingot, "with the aid and care of the government, have won the battle for the control of the industry." (P. 100.)

French government in 1936 and 1937 concerning the illegal augmentation of prices in general, and although the silk, sugar, and shoe industries were concentrated into compulsory code-regimes,[66] French cartels as a whole remained freer from governmental influence than the British. In all countries participating in the ISC, save the United States, Belgium,[67] and France,[68] after 1935 government influence on steel cartel policy was even stronger than that exercised by the British government. The only difference was that whereas the British system of publicity made this influence easily recognizable, in other countries it was less discernible.

Few of the countries participating directly or indirectly in the ISC influenced ISC policies through the existence of publicly owned steel enterprises which participated strongly in national steel policies. Exceptions existed in Germany, where the government was a large shareholder in the dominant steel concern, the *Vereinigte Stahlwerke, A.G.,* up to the beginning of 1936. In addition, the Polish national group was almost entirely dominated by government-owned enterprises. The same was true of the Yugoslav and Italian steel works and of those in South Africa. In Hungary, the state-owned steel works exercised considerable influence on steel policies.

V

Economic and political treatises on cartels rarely refer to opinions of business leaders in respect to the new developments in the field of marketing control schemes, and, in this connection, to their views on economic competition. It might be of interest to attach to the dis-

---

[66] The provisions relating to labor policies made these codes somewhat similar to the N.R.A. codes. These obligatory "ententes" are extensively discussed by André Piettre, *L'Evolution des Ententes industrielles en France depuis la Crise* (Paris, 1936), pp. 85 ff. The "bill" contemplating the general introduction of compulsory cartels in France was discussed in the TNEC without indicating that it had never become a statutory provision due to the non-concurrence of the French upper chamber. TNEC, *Hearings,* Part 25, pp. 13057-68. The French upper chamber resisted the Flandin-Marchandeau compulsory cartel bill because this proposal intended to obstruct the establishment of new competitive industries. Influential economic circles induced the French cabinet to answer the opposition of the upper chamber by establishing a compulsory cartel in silk (and later in shoes and sugar) through executive decrees.

[67] See a discussion of the Belgian Royal Decree of Jan. 13, 1935, concerning the government's powers to establish syndicates and to impose other restrictions in *Bulletin d'Information et de Documentation,* Feb. 10, 1936, p. 113. The application of the producers of wire products to limit the establishment of new plants based on this decree was rejected. (*Ibid.,* p. 237.)

[68] According to *ICTR,* July 14, 1939, p. 53, the establishment of the French Price Control Board retarded increases in steel prices very much.

cussion of the cartel concept a few such recent views originating in the United States and in Great Britain, which relate to steel industries and to industry in general. A conspicuous difference exists in this regard between the opinions of the British and the Americans. In Great Britain a strong and, during the last fifteen years, gradually increasing trend toward collective marketing controls in industry was generally recognized, a trend accompanied by the restriction of competition in the traditional sense. British industry regarded this development as imperative and not inconsistent with the public interest.[69] It was considered requisite to healthy economic expansion. In the United States, even in 1939, industrial and financial circles insisted that, though the forms of economic competition were changing, strong competition still existed in industry,[70] and that they preferred this competition to collective marketing controls. Professor Edward S. Mason of Harvard University characterized the American situation thus: "We are presented . . . with the spectacle of the representatives of industries in which concentration is very marked, asserting—and believing—that the prices of their products are determined by the

[69] A comprehensive analysis of this attitude may be found in A. F. Lucas, *Industrial Reconstruction and the Control of Competition* (London, 1937), *passim*. Mr. Lucas indicates as the subject of his study ". . . the progressive abandonment of free competition and the establishment of so-called industrial self-government." P. vii. Specific problems of the steel industry are discussed on pp. 103-123.

[70] The National Association of Manufacturers at the 44th Annual Congress of American Industry in New York on Dec. 8, 1939, in its *Declaration of Principles Relating to the Conduct of American Industry* (New York, 1939), pp. 8-9, included the following principle: "Pricing Under the Free Enterprise System. . . . Competition is the greatest assurance to the consumer of reasonable prices and high and improving quality of product—of getting his money's worth. Each individual enterprise, in competing for the consumer's dollar, must determine its own prices." After discussing the limitations of the range of discretionary action in this regard because of production costs, taxes, competition of like and other products, and the inequality in flexibility of demand, the *Declaration* proceeds: ". . . stimulation by price reduction will increase total consumption, the pricing policy of each individual enterprise should be one which seeks this opportunity." The National Association of Manufacturers considered the statement that "competition is no longer effective" in American industry as one of the "fallacies" of our private enterprise system. (See *Fallacies About Our Private Enterprise System*, New York, 1941, pp. 30 ff.) The National City Bank of New York, reviewing part of the work done by the TNEC, expresses the following opinion in the July, 1941, issue of its bulletin, *Economic Conditions, Government Finance, United States Securities:* "Moreover, anybody who has had industrial experience knows that monopoly in this country is much more a political bugaboo than a reality; for in every industry we see signs of vigorous competition which has steadily reduced prices . . ." (p. 82). According to Benjamin F. Fairless, "Competition is very keen in the steel industry, and it is terrifically keen in times of falling off orders." TNEC, *Hearings*, Part 19, p. 10525.

impersonal forces of supply and demand."[71] It has been a truism in
the United States that at least on the domestic market competition is
a necessary condition for the healthy development of American economy. There has been some hesitation about the kind of competition
which is desirable and appropriate for modern economic development.
The National Association of Manufacturers emphasized in this regard
that "Competition today is not just a matter of price. There is vigorous and just as important competition in the field of quality, service
facilities, allowance for old equipment, and terms of delivery and
payment."[72] The Association stated that the attitude of the man in
the street toward the new development was as follows: "At the present
time, managers of large corporations act by mutual agreement to
'regulate' prices and by this and other manipulation act to eliminate
the little fellow."[73]

A rather striking difference in views concerning the desirability
of collective marketing control schemes is noted in the opinions representative of two different industrial groups. These opinions were
presented in a discussion which took place after the birth of the ISC,
at the annual meeting of the Iron and Steel Institute in London in
1927, where Mr. Theodore Robinson, vice-president of the Illinois
Steel Corporation, and Sir William Larke, director of the National
Federation of Iron and Steel Manufacturers, London, discussed the
auspices of cartels in the United States and in Great Britain.

Mr. Robinson said that the difference in the public state of mind
was the reason for the difference between governmental encourage-
ment of the establishment and maintenance of cartels in Europe, and
the discouragement of industrial combinations in the United States.
He regarded "permissive regulation" as the desirable middle way
between unrestricted competition and uncontrolled license to combine.
Sir William Larke found it extraordinary that public opinion in the
United States "still lagged behind the view held in Europe." He
attributed this behavior to a fallacy in reasoning (often apparent in
Great Britain too), namely, that the consumer assumes that the combination must operate against him. Sir William predicted that these
combinations not only would receive the support but "the stimulus
and pressure of public opinion" in Great Britain. He stated that "it
was only by means of such organization that this country [Great

[71] "Price Policies and Full Employment," in C. J. Friedrich and Edward S. Mason
(eds.), *Public Policy* (Cambridge, 1940), p. 30.

[72] *Fallacies About Our Private Enterprise System* (New York, 1941), p. 31.

[73] *Ibid.*, p. 30.

Britain] could hope to readjust itself to the post-war economic position, without a permanent contraction in the scale of its industry and a consequent increasing burden of unemployment."[74]   Sir William Larke did not discuss the point often made in the United States in this connection, that huge economic power concentrated in private hands may in itself endanger the political structure of the state. Probably he regarded it as self-evident that combinations of independent enterprises properly held in check by the state cannot be regarded as agglomerations of uncontrolled economic power. This opinion has often been emphasized in official and unofficial circles in Europe, as has the view that combinations of independent enterprises, properly supervised by the public administration, are one of the most efficient means of moderating business fluctuations.

Several times leading representatives of the British steel industry publicly discussed economic and political problems resulting from the new developments in national and international marketing controls, and from new forms of economic competition. The leader of the British steel industry, the Earl of Dudley, felt that ". . . the days of the individualist in the industry have gone, I think for good. We have found that in modern conditions we must pool individuality without losing individual genius. I think it is quite obvious that it is only by the closest possible coöperation, both national and international, that the long-dated policy can be framed which will insure the confidence which is so essential to consumers and producers alike,

---

[74] *The Journal of the Iron and Steel Institute* (London), CXVI (1927), 30, 35. For the assumption by British steelmakers that cartels and stabilized fair prices were important measures to prevent business fluctuations, see the discussion by the Earl of Dudley, Chairman of the British Iron and Trade Federation, who said, "I see no reason why the depression in America should overcome us in this country." *Iron Age,* Mar. 10, 1938, p. 87. Gottfried von Haberler (*The Theory of International Trade,* p. 332) emphasized that the expectation that cartels lessen the severity of economic crises "is not altogether supported by experience." Though Haberler's rather skeptical diagnosis and prognosis of the possible influence of international cartels on international political and economic relations is correct, his treatment of the factual situation is somewhat simplified. His statement (*op. cit.,* p. 335) about the "proverbial individualism of the English entrepreneur" does not take into account the latest developments in Great Britain. Prof. Henry Clay discussed the influence of the new organization of British industry on technical progress and unemployment in a rather favorable light. See *ICTR,* June 11, 1937, p. 1056. A rather optimistic view concerning the moderating influence of cartels on harmful trade fluctuations was expressed by the chairman of the European continental steel cartel, Mr. Aloyse Meyer, in "Cartels and Trade Fluctuations," *World Trade,* IX, No. 6, pp. 62-63, and by *The Times* (London) Iron and Steel Number, "The Trade Cycle, Stable Prices in Good and Bad Times," June 14, 1938, p. 16.

and which will tend to iron out those trade oscillations which are so nationally fatal."[75] Similar ideas were expressed by the Earl of Dudley in his presidential address to the Iron and Steel Institute on May 4, 1938. Considering whether the production of iron and steel was moving in the right direction, he differentiated between the periods preceding the First World War and subsequently. In the first period, British-born individualists were rather slow to conform to control, even if agreed upon by industries. Individual freedom in trading had served Britain very well, but "in the post-war years we have experienced within our industry a measure of coöperation and collaboration, both national and international, such as our ancestors would never have dreamed of."

In this address the Earl of Dudley asserted that there was scope for still further expansion of this coöperation for the benefit of the nation and industries. He particularly stressed the necessity for international coöperation, pointing out that the world is an economic as well as physical unit, and expressing the hope that the ISC would ultimately include all of the steel industries of the world. Through this coöperation he expected British industry to produce the steel necessary to meet a national emergency, and secondly, through national and international coöperation, to maintain the commercial position of Great Britain in world markets.[76]

A comprehensive statement about the development of competition in the national and international steel industry (intended to apply to all industries), was made by a leading British steel industrialist, Mr. John Craig, in a presidential address before the Iron and Steel Institute in 1940. Recalling the period before the First World War when the steel industry depended for its profits on successful speculation, he observed that this was a misfortune for "industry because it attached the attention of the industry more on the buying and selling than on the costs of production." He predicted that "the old policy which clamoured for more competition, ever more competition, would not stand the strain of modern social development. These developments are symbolic of a change of attitude toward the great problems in commerce." He attacked the so-called Manchester school which believed, and possibly still believes, that competition is synonymous with price-cutting. In a separate section on "The Theory of Competition" he expounded the theory that what is called non-price competition

---

[75] See *Iron Age*, Mar. 10, 1938, p. 87.
[76] *The Journal of the Iron and Steel Institute*, Vol. CXXXVII (1938), 79-80.

should be the objective of governments, consumers, and industry,[77] and that a fair price is more advantageous for the consumer than an unreasonably low price. Extravagant prices are as dangerous as prices which are too low, and controlled stable prices are of greater service to the consumer than violent fluctuations. It is important to eliminate exaggerated profits, however, basing the prices of commodities on production costs to insure profits that make necessary investments possible. The organization of the British steel industries was imperative, he felt, for furthering international coöperation and joint control.[78]

Needless to say, the ideas of the British steel industry about the decline of competition as a historic necessity were attacked rather severely. *The Economist* in March, 1939, commented that England was experiencing a gradual cartelization and that "An entirely novel form of industrial organization is creeping upon us unawares." Discussing the tendency of industry to make public authorities and consumers assist that movement, *The Economist* wrote: "The result has naturally been to revolutionize the attitude of industry to the State: the policeman has turned Father Christmas." Assailing the steel industry, *The Economist* remarked, "The edicts of the steel cartel have been very widely criticised. . . . For all the acts of these various bodies admirable justification, usually relating to cost of production, can be pleaded. But the fact remains that, to judge by what we have seen of it to date, the self-government of industry leads to the indefinite postponement of true rationalisation and a strong bias in favour of high prices for the essential raw materials of national industry and national health."[79] Reviewing the British cartel development up to

[77] Saul Nelson and Walter G. Keim wrote in TNEC, *Monograph No. 1*, "Price Behavior and Business Policy" (Washington, 1940), p. xxi, "There is today a widespread belief in business circles that competitive efforts should be directed toward these nonprice aspects of competition almost to the exclusion of price. . . ."

[78] *The Journal of the Iron and Steel Institute*, CXLI (1940), No. 1, 58p-59p. *The May Report* (1937), *passim*, is a vivid example of how most of these views were shared by the British government. "Coming now to the main problem before us, that of the principles which should govern the future conduct and development of the iron and steel industry," writes the Import Duties Advisory Committee, "and giving full weight to the various considerations set out above . . . , we start from two broad propositions. The first is that there cannot be a return to the unorganized conduct and almost casual development and the largely unrestricted competition at home and from abroad which characterized the industry until 1932; and the second is that the State cannot divest itself of all responsibility as to the conduct of an industry so far-reaching in its scope, so vital to the national well-being, so largely dependent on State fiscal policy for its prosperity, and now being brought into a closely knit organization." (P. 29.)

[79] "The Cartelisation of England," Mar. 18, 1939, p. 551. The influence of national and international cartelization on the earnings of British steel companies may be seen

the Second World War, *The Economist* charged that ". . . for peace-time purposes the wholesale pooling, coördination and cartelisation of industry have severe and obvious disadvantages."[80] Comparing the competitive price policy of large corporations with that of cartels, *The Economist* judged that cartels "have a bias in favor of easy life, of high profits on low turnover."[81] Recently a very influential British politician expressed similar views in the House of Commons.[82]

The tendency of the British national steel group in ISC policies to live up to its principles regarding British imperial markets and international price policies in general became apparent when steel prices were fluctuating heavily in 1937-1938. As to the industry's policy toward imperial markets, the *ICTR* writes: "While prices in markets controlled by the cartel have been the subject of frequent

---

from a report of *The Economist*, Nov. 4, 1939, p. 173, "Steel Shares in War-Time." *The Economist's* annual computations of representative steel and coal company earnings (after debenture interest) give the following picture (1914 = 100):

1915	89	1923	92	1931	22
1916	119	1924	66	1932	15
1917	143	1925	27	1933	28
1918	135	1926	18	1934	52
1919	138	1927	32	1935	67
1920	64	1928	35	1936	90
1921	66	1929	51	1937	119
1922	78	1930	42	1938	125

Although *The Economist's* figures include coal companies as well, they are highly characteristic of the results of the new organization in steel, if we do not disregard the fact that after 1936 steel prices on domestic and foreign markets increased throughout the world.

[80] Mar. 8, 1941, p. 298. See also *ibid.*, June 15, 1940, p. 1933; Apr. 5, 1941, pp. 436-37. The policy of the British Iron and Steel Federation has been criticized in the House of Commons several times. See for instance *The Times* (London), Nov. 25, 1936, p. 8d. Ingot (pseud.), attacking this "self government, and all other concomitants of 'enlightened' capitalism," judged that the "aftermath will be serious" and that, "The industry's pledge to reduce prices will never be redeemed." (*Op. cit.*, p. 100.) Admitting the difficulties inherent in public ownership of so complex an industry, he included a plan for socialization in his study. (Pp. 128-159.)

[81] *The Economist*, Mar. 18, 1939, p. 551.

[82] *The Economist*, Apr. 5, 1941, pp. 436-37, in an article, "Imposed Combinations in Common Plants," quoted a speech of Capt. Lyttelton, who compared the social danger inherent in cartels with that inherent in monopolistic combinations of the corporate type. "The single large monopolistic firm—such as Unilever or ICI [Imperial Chemical Industries Limited]—has its dangers; but at least those who are in control cannot evade their social obligations, nor are they prevented from pursuing a dynamic and progressive policy. The great danger lies in the growing influence of what the common law knows (and used to condemn) as 'agreements in restraint of trade' which [operate] without securing whatever technical economies there may be in large scale production. . . ." In the opinion of Mr. Lyttelton, the cartel movement is far too strong in British industry.

adjustment in the light of changing conditions, the British participants have been able to keep prices reasonably stable for Empire countries in the past year. . . ."[83] In regard to general international prices, the same trade journal remarked: "The British representatives in the Joint Co-ordinating Committee are anxious to avoid too sensational reversal of price policy of the cartel, as they are definitively in favour of maintaining stability in world prices wherever possible. Last year [1937] they were opposed to heavy increases in cartel export prices, and they are now anxious to prevent similar trends in the opposite direction."[84]

There is every reason to assume that the views of the British Iron and Steel Federation and its representatives on modern cartel development, and on "new forms" of economic competition were shared by leading politicians supporting the government.[85] The unique fact that the British national steel cartel elected a neutral president, tacitly approved by the government, is highly characteristic of this harmony. The position of this executive officer, Sir Andrew R. Duncan, may be evaluated from the fact that after the outbreak of the war, in September 1939, he was included in the British Cabinet and now holds the office of minister of supply.

Are there now—in 1940-1942—cartels in the sense of the traditional cartel definitions? Is there potential competition in industry which might be restricted or eliminated according to cartel patterns? Is there conceivable the slightest tendency to limit output artificially? Those who regarded collective marketing controls called cartels as mechanisms belonging to the arsenal of the fight against overcapacity will deny these questions. Everywhere on the world market coöperation of entrepreneurs has been adjusted to a regime of scarcity, to the regulation of price and production conditions by governments, and private economy is frequently operating toward extra-economic objectives. The new forms of coöperation based on political emergency often move on old tracks[86] and often use outworn terms. Some of

---

[83] *ICTR*, Jan. 21, 1938, p. 100.   [84] *ICTR*, Jan. 21, 1938, p. 166.

[85] See e.g. the recognition of the work and policies of the British steel industry by Mr. Winston Churchill in *ICTR*, Feb. 19, 1937, pp. 366-67.

[86] According to *Steel*, June 30, 1941, p. 30, the Office of Price Administration and Civilian Supply "is utilizing the basing point, price leadership, and *extras systems,* presently *in effect* in the steel industry, including the *customary practice* of steel producers in gearing their own delivered prices to the base prices announced and *recognized* by price leaders." (My italics.) According to Mr. Leon Henderson, Price Administrator, "such acceptance of these systems merely as a vehicle for determining prices, should not be regarded as approval thereof, nor should this reservation be regarded as indicating disapproval."

the elements of cartels, occurring in economic structures which belong to other economic categories, are still contested from force of habit under the name of cartels.

The problem of cartel definition is relevant to an analysis of the ISC in that its structure and its operation could thereby be classified and discussed in a broader setting. Naturally the ISC and its sub-entities shared the fate of all organizations called cartels wtih the development of the war on a world-wide scale.

CHAPTER THREE

Development of the International Steel Cartel

I

A STUDY OF THE ISC should logically include the detailed history of that organization, especially since that history embraces only a span of thirteen years with one interruption. This study by no means exhaustively discusses the complete history of the organization; and only accentuates those details which are significantly associated with the most developed stage of the ISC. The earlier periods of the ISC are discussed in several papers,[1] as are early cartel devices, especially the crude steel export scheme, which were *de facto* abandoned in 1936, and therefore were relatively insignificant for the ISC's period of later development.

---

[1] An excellent report about the early history of the ISC is contained in *Trade Information Bulletin* No. 484, of the U. S. Bureau of Foreign and Domestic Commerce, by J. Joseph W. Palmer, "Origin and Development of the Continental Steel Entente," Washington, 1927. Another reliable report, containing besides the early history of the cartel authoritative information about the American steel industry's attitude toward the new cartel, was published by Walter S. Tower, "The New Steel Cartel," in *Foreign Affairs,* Jan., 1927, pp. 249 ff. See the French version of the story in C. Nattan-Larrier, *op. cit., passim.* The German version of the initial history of the cartel may be found in the article of Dr. J. W. Reichert, "Die Festländische Rohstahlgemeinschaft," *Weltwirtschaftliches Archiv,* 1927, (I), pp. 340* ff. The same author published a study about the history of the first ten years of the ISC in *Stahl und Eisen,* Nov. 26, 1936, pp. 1430 ff., "Ein Rückblick auf das zehnjährige Bestehen der internationalen Stahlverbände." An excellent critical evaluation of the cartel's operations in the first two years is contained in Otto Hoffmann, "Die Internationale Rohstahlgemeinschaft," *Die Wirtschaftskurve,* Mar. 1929, pp. 48 ff. The yearly surveys of the Belgian National Bank, "La Situation Economique de la Belgique" contain a nearly complete chain of reports concerning the development of the ISC. A comprehensive, though short, history of the ISC up to July 1938 may be found in *Bulletin d'Information et de Documentation,* Aug. 1938, pp. 95-103.

The history of the ISC is complicated by the fact that the early organization was intended to serve a double purpose; first, to reduce competition on steel markets, second, to adjust the steel industries of continental Europe to the political and economic situation created by the First World War[2] and by the peace treaties of 1919-20. Treatises on early steel cartel history are full of explanations of the second (but by no means secondary) purpose, for these two purposes were almost inextricably interwoven during the period of negotiating the establishment of the ISC and in its early operations. With later developments the two purposes for which the cartel was created became less indiscernible and the cartel structure emerged more clearly as an organization operating in the narrower sense of a marketing control.[3]

The situation of the German steel industry and that of the Saar region were of particular importance in the early development of the ISC. The peace treaties disrupted the German domestic steel market by attaching Lorraine, the home of several modern steel-producing plants and the principal source of German iron ore supplies, to France, thus detaching the steel plants politically from one of their major coke bases in the Ruhr region. The Saar territory was made a politically and economically "independent" unit. The steel-rich Silesia region was divided between Poland and Germany. After the First World War Luxemburg, until 1914 a member of the German customs union, chose to join Belgium in a customs union. As one of the consequences of these political changes the organization of the German steel industry, the *Stahlwerks-Verband,* disintegrated in 1920 because few of its former members were inclined to coöperate under the new circumstances within the old framework of the cartel. An additional disruptive influence on the German steel industry was Article 268a, Part X, Section 1, of the Versailles Treaty, which obligated Germany to admit duty-free to its domestic market a specified proportion of the raw materials and finished products originating in Alsace-Lorraine, Luxemburg, and the Saar territory until January 10, 1925. A similar provision applied to imports into the German domestic

---

[2] The Belgian steel industry accused Germans of destroying Belgian steel plants according to scientifically elaborated schemes. One of the foremost Belgian steel industrialists said, "It is therefore certain that one of the chief objects pursued was to suppress future embarrassing competition, to disable for a long period to come a rival whose energy was dreaded, and to create a market for German enterprise which the Germans imagined they would be allowed to occupy after the War." Leon Greiner, "The Belgian Iron and Steel Industry during the German occupation in the Great War," *The Journal of the Iron and Steel Institute,* XCIX (1919), 42-43.

[3] See C. Nattan-Larrier, *op. cit.,* pp. 117-126.

market from the former Silesian section. The occupation of the Ruhr region and the depreciation of German currency complicated the German steel situation considerably.

As time elapsed the tendency in Germany, shared by the Western powers, to establish "normal" economic and political relations with her neighbors, grew rapidly, particularly as the time for Germany to regain her sovereignty in determining her tariff policy approached. Several international economic agreements, closely interconnected with the first international steel pact, were intended to adjust the German steel regime to the new situation.[4] Such an adjustment required, in the opinion of many, a strong domestic organization of German steel industry and trade. This was one of the reasons for the establishment by German steel producers of the *Rohstahl-Verband,* on November 1, 1924, a domestic crude steel cartel regulating global crude steel production. The joint stock company which up to 1920 was the corporate form of the German general steel cartel, the *Stahlwerks-Verband,* was used to carry out the activities of the *Rohstahl-Verband.*[5] The establishment of the German crude steel cartel was followed by the establishment of several domestic steel commodity cartels,[6] and in

---

[4] Simultaneously with the first international steel agreement other agreements were discussed concerning import quotas of iron and steel to Germany from Lorraine, Luxemburg, and the Saar works, imports of Saar steel to France, and the relationship of Saar steel works to the German domestic steel cartel. These negotiations exercised great influence on French-German official discussions about a general trade agreement.

[5] The *Stahlwerks-Verband* was established Feb. 29, 1904, as a "general cartel." The cartel agreement, after several prolongations, expired Jan. 6, 1917. The parties to the agreement prolonged it several times, always at the express wish of the German government, until Sept. 30, 1919. From that day the German government compulsorily extended the agreement by an ordinance until June 30, 1920. On July 1, 1920, the agreement ceased to exist, though the joint stock company which carried the agreement was not dissolved. It kept its corporate form and existed as a joint stock company without really operating, existing merely as an empty framework of a corporation. An excellent account of the history and structure of the *Stahlwerks-Verband* and its predecessors may be found in Francis Walker, *op. cit.,* pp. 353 ff. According to him ". . . the individual concern has ceased to be the unit in German [steel] industry to a large extent. The modern unit is the cartel. The most important matters of commercial and economic policy are determined today by these combinations." (P. 360.)

[6] The first actual selling comptoir for semifinished steel, established Jan. 1, 1925, was ineffective from its very beginning due to heavy outside competition. On May 1, 1925, the so-called "A products" selling agency, embracing semifinished steel, structural shapes, and heavy rails, was established and joined the *Stahlwerks-Verband.* The German domestic thick plates comptoir was established and attached to the general cartel on July 26, 1925. This was followed on Aug. 1, 1925, by the establishment of the most important selling comptoir, that for merchant bars, and the comptoir for bands and strips. These later became divisions of the *Stahlwerks-Verband* as well. Separate comptoirs for wire rods and tubular products were also established but they were not

the summer of 1925 the German general domestic steel cartel, the "proper" *Stahlwerks-Verband,* was reëstablished.[7]

The negotiations of German steel producers with their own government regarding tariff protection and other problems were opposed by the steel-consuming industries which objected to the increase in steel prices which would result from the imposition of import duties. The steel-consuming industries, until January 1925, profited by both duty-free steel imports and the disorganization and competition of German steel producers.   To eliminate the obstruction of the steel-consuming industries and to gain their support in tariff and other negotiations with the government, the German steel producers in December, 1924,[8] concluded an agreement with the steel-consuming industries (generally referred to as the AVI accord), in which the steel-consuming industries were to be permitted to buy (on the domestic market) steel commodities destined to be transformed for exporting purposes, at prices prevailing on the world export market, if these "world" prices were lower than German domestic prices.[9]   This AVI agreement existed, with certain revisions, until the Second World War.   Similar accords between steel-producing and consuming industries existed in other European countries too.   Through the AVI arrangement German steel producers completed the conditions requisite to obtaining their own government's support for their negotiation of an international steel agreement.

---

controlled by the *Stahlwerks-Verband* though they shared the global crude steel quota scheme.   The *Rohstahl-Verband* became a division of the general cartel, the *Stahlwerks-Verband,* at the time of the latter's reorganization.

[7] It is significant that the reëstablishment of the domestic cartel organization coincided with the reorganization of many steel corporations.   The *Vereinigte Stahlwerke,* the largest steel firm on the European continent, an amalgamation of four large steel groups, Rhein-Elbe-Union, Phoenix, Thyssen, and Rheinstahl was established Apr. 1, 1926.

[8] This so-called "Paris AVI Agreement" which was of a provisory character was made final by an accord of Mar. 1, 1925.   Cf. Heinz Serlo, *op. cit.,* pp. 6 ff.   Former similar structures are discussed in Francis Walker, *op. cit.,* pp. 370 ff.

[9] The following figures may give a broad idea of the working of the AVI system in a period of low steel prices (summer 1932):

Commodity	German domestic price metric ton in Reichsmark	Normal AVI prices to German exporter-consumers	Export prices fob Antwerp long ton in £ gold
Merchant bars	112.00	79.00	2. 2.0
Structural steel	104.50	71.00	2. 0.0
Thick plates	127.30	103.00	2.11.0

Customary rebates have been deducted from the German prices listed here.   These prices also represent an average computed from prices at the two basing points, Oberhausen and Neunkirchen.   See also, Karl Pribram, *op. cit.,* p. 75.

It was natural for Germany to assume the leading role in negotiating international steel controls because of her position on the world steel market. Until 1870 Great Britain produced half of the world's steel output and until 1889 had the largest steel output in the world. By 1890 the leadership in steel output passed to the United States, Great Britain remaining second. In 1893, however, Germany surpassed Great Britain in steel output and German steel supremacy in Europe exists even now. After keen competition with Great Britain and other countries,[10] Germany became, before the start of the First World War, the largest steel exporter in the world. This supremacy was broken immediately after the First World War but gradually returned, not, however, with its former virility.

Her steel position before the First World War and her ambition to regain that position prompted Germany to take a leading role in the ISC negotiations. The second country which took a leading position in the early ISC was Luxemburg. More than any other country Luxemburg was interested in the pacific consolidation of the steel industry because steel is Luxemburg's dominant industry and more than 90 per cent of that country's steel production is exported. A prerequisite for international collaboration already existed in Luxemburg in the close coöperation in the domestic steel industry.

The first organization of the ISC did not resemble its structure of the late thirties, the peak period of its development. At the time of its origin, the ISC, although intended as a marketing control scheme, fell short of its purpose in that several important single commodity cartels, which rationally should have been part of such a scheme, pursued independent although not antagonistic policies. The consolidation of these separate entities into the comprehensive ISC machine only developed gradually.

Even before the First World War, as is indicated above, there were international steel cartels among several European countries and even between America and European countries. However, there is a considerable difference between the earlier cartels and the ISC in

---

[10] See Werner Bostel, *Die deutsche und die britische Eisenindustrie und ihr Konkurrenzkampf auf dem Weltmarkt,* Osnabrück, 1937, *passim.*. In a famous article Dr. Gustav Stresemann discussed the German-British competition, stating that the final issue in this regard will have "a vital importance," thus indicating the expected (first) World War. "The greater part of the actual problems, alliances of nations, and international events have their final roots in the British-German competition," wrote Stresemann. He finished his article by stating that the enlarged British fleet would not intimidate Germany in her fight for economic supremacy. "La Politique Mondiale de l'Allemagne," *Revue Économique Internationale,* July, 1913, pp. 92 and 97.

that all former cartels were focused on a single steel commodity (tubular products, or rails, or wire products), whereas the ISC attempted to establish a general, supranational marketing control in steel, embracing all semifinished and finished steel products. The comprehensiveness of its policy was the most significant difference between the ISC and former international steel cartels. The tendency of the ISC to be comprehensive in regulating the steel market led to attempts to embrace domestic as well as export markets. The attempt to control domestic markets, however, conflicted with the national policy of steel-exporting countries to such an extent that it led to the disintegration of the first ISC structure.

The historic development of the ISC is divided here into six periods,[11] each delineated by a major change which occurred in the organization. The history of the ISC throughout the first four, and one half of the fifth, of these periods practically coincides with the history of the continental European steel cartel. Until May 1935 this cartel, the *Entente Internationale de l'Acier* (EIA) was indistinguishable from the ISC as a general steel policy-determining body. After this date, the European steel cartel (ESC), developed when Britain joined the continental groups, became the policy-making body indistinguishable in structure from that of the ISC.

II

The first period in the development of the ISC dated from October 1, 1926, to October 30, 1929. The negotiations aiming at the conclusion of an international steel agreement started[12] in February 1926 at a meeting in Luxemburg. Five national units participated in the preparatory work. Germany, France, Belgium, Luxemburg, and the Saar were represented by agents of their steel industries. Two men

---

[11] The first five periods as indicated in this paper correspond generally to the periods outlined by the official statement of the EIA in *International Ententes*, p. 40. Cf. "L'Entente Internationale de l'Acier," *Bulletin d'Information et de Documentation*, Aug. 1938, pp. 95 ff.

[12] Several attempts were made before 1926, but all were unsuccessful. According to Paul Ufermann (*Der deutsche Stahltrust*, Berlin, 1927, pp. 115, 122), Louis Loucheur indicated in the *Berliner Tageblatt* (No. 463, 1926) that while Minister of Reconstruction immediately after the war, he had tried to establish coöperation on the European steel market, but his attempts broke against British and German resistance. Paul Ufermann also quotes an article by Dr. Bruhn (*Deutsche Allgemeine Zeitung*, 1926, Nos. 496, 497), one of the participants in the international steel negotiations, which stated that in the summer of 1924 the *Comité des Forges* sent a representative to Essen, Germany, to initiate negotiations concerning international coöperation in steel.

played a leading role, Dr. Fritz Thyssen of the German group, and Dr. Emil Mayrisch of Luxemburg. The governments of the five steel groups tacitly supported their attempts to organize the steel market. Whereas the German, Saar, and Luxemburg groups represented a relatively well-organized body of their respective steel industries, the Belgian and French representatives proceeded in the negotiations on the assumption that their efforts would succeed in knitting together domestic organizations of steel producers in their countries.[13] The international negotiations were considerably furthered by the conclusion of a well-instrumented international cartel by European producers of heavy rails (ERMA) on March 12, 1926, in London. Because British producers also joined the rail agreement, it presented an opportunity to inform the British of the forthcoming general steel negotiations and to attempt to induce them, though unsuccessfully, to participate.

The German group wanted to form the international organization on the pattern of the German domestic steel cartel as it existed in 1926. They intended to establish a comprehensive cartel according to the scheme of the German *Stahlwerks-Verband,* consisting of an agreement on general steel policy and sectional agreements relating to the control of particular steel commodities. In the light of later developments, it appears that such a comprehensive agreement would have been the most appropriate one on which a steel marketing control could be based at that time. The German proposals were rejected because the other national groups felt that their domestic organizations were not sufficiently consolidated to permit their entrance into such a comprehensively built international organization, and that they wanted to avoid direct influence on their pricing policies for individual steel commodities. In the opinion of several groups the actual market situation, influenced by the depreciation of franc currencies and by the relative scarcity in steel supplies due to the coal miners' strike in Great Britain, did not make advisable a marketing control embracing price policies. The dominant reason, however, for the rejection of proposals for a very intimate organization was mutual distrust, especially between the western groups and Germany.

The negotiations were put off several times because of the difficulties in organizing the Belgian national group. Finally on Septem-

---

[13] *Bulletin hebdomadaire d'Information et de Documentation,* Mar. 19, 1927, p. 280, reports efforts to induce Belgian steel producers, who had no organization whatsoever, to establish one, and efforts to encourage French producers to revive their organization. See further, C. Nattan-Larrier, *op. cit.,* pp. 289 ff.

ber 30, 1926, the five groups signed the International Steel Agreement in Brussels, establishing an international steel cartel, generally referred to as the first *Entente Internationale de l'Acier* (EIA), or the first *Internationale Rohstahlgemeinschaft* (IRG), which embraced their domestic and export markets and was effective for four and a half years, from October 1, 1926, until March 31, 1931. Part of this agreement was published in 1927, and is included here in Appendix III.[14] Official reports of the EIA designated the first international steel accord as a "gentlemen's agreement."[15] This term was generally adopted to describe the first EIA agreement.[16] Its use in connection with the first EIA agreement seems hardly appropriate. As will be demonstrated, the fulfillment of participants' obligations was secured by a system of fines, deposits, and a court of arbitration, and was by no means merely a matter of honor as is implicit in the phrase "gentlemen's agreement."[17]

In 1926 the five signatories of the EIA agreement, Germany, the Saar, Luxemburg, France, and Belgium, had a steel ingot production of about 28 million gross tons, whereas in that year United States production exceeded 48 million gross tons, and British steel production, because of the coal miners' strike in 1926, only amounted to a little more than 3½ million gross tons. Czechoslovakia, Hungary, and Austria together produced about 2½ million gross tons in 1926. Thus, in a world production of steel ingots amounting to more than 90 million gross tons, the EIA as a whole played a relatively minor role compared with the United States. In 1926 EIA countries produced about 30 per cent, in 1927 about 32.5 per cent, in 1928 about 30.5 per

---

[14] The agreement was published in *Trade Information Bulletin*, No. 484, pp. 15-16, and as an Annex to the *Memorandum on the Iron and Steel Industry*, p. 109, published for the International Economic Conference by the League of Nations, Geneva, 1927. Both publications omitted Article 15 of the agreement and printed Articles 12 and 13 incompletely.

[15] Cf. *International Ententes*, p. 40. The Chairman of the EIA, Mr. Aloyse Meyer, classified both the EIA and the IRMA accords as gentlemen's agreements. See A. S. Benni, C. Lammers, L. Marlio and Aloyse Meyer, *Internationale Industriekartelle* (Berlin, 1930), pp. 11, 17. Mr. Meyer in *World Trade*, June, 1937, pp. 62-63, discussed various forms of cartels ". . . from simple gentlemen's agreements concerning prices to common selling organizations and close market regulations."

[16] *Bulletin d'Information et de Documentation*, Aug. 1938, p. 95.

[17] H. Decugis, R. E. Olds, and S. Tschierschky, in *Review of the Legal Aspects of Industrial Combinations* (League of Nations, Geneva, 1930), pp. 5-6, state that "Cartels are sometimes simple tacit arrangements or verbal agreements of the kind which Anglo-Saxon countries call a friendly agreement or gentlemen's agreement and which have not really the legal characteristics of a contract proper." However, the same authors designate the EIA accord as being among the "essentially contractual agreements."

cent, in 1929 about 29.5 per cent, and in 1930 about 30.5 per cent of world steel production. However, the significance of the EIA agreement lies in the fact that the EIA countries occupied a relatively dominant position on the export market. In 1926 EIA countries accounted for more than 65 per cent, and in 1927-30 for more than 70 per cent of world steel exports.

The difficulties faced before the agreement was concluded and the anticipation of future difficulties are mirrored in the several provisions for the renunciation of the agreement. Article nine contained a general provision which made it possible to renounce the agreement on May 1, 1929, effective on October 31, 1929.

On February 4, 1927, the Central European group, consisting of Austrian, Hungarian,[18] and Czechoslovakian producers, entered the EIA, effective January 1, 1927.[19] These three national groups were regarded as a single unit and had to divide among themselves the quota agreed upon for the unit as a whole. The quota allotted the Central European group (ZEG), 7.272 per cent, was added to the original quota, making the total quota distributable on a basis of 107.272 per cent instead of 100 per cent. Thus, the total production allotment was considered equal to 107.272 per cent of which 7.272 per cent was the ZEG's share.[20] More than two thirds of the ZEG quota belonged to Czechoslovakia. Several attempts to make Poland enter the agreement at that time were unsuccessful.[21]

Negotiations for the entrance of Great Britain into the cartel were carried on. However, many of the continental producers did not

---

[18] In reality only one of the two great Hungarian steel works (*Rimamurány-Salgotarjáni Vasmü Részvény Társaság*) joined the cartel; the state-owned steel works remained outside of the accord. However, both companies joined the international rail agreement. The Austrian "group" also consisted of a single firm (*Alpine Montan Gesellschaft*).

[19] It happened very frequently within the ISC that agreements were concluded with a validity preceding the actual time of concluding the agreement.

[20] The Central European group functioned as a "unit" in several other ISC agreements too, especially in the rail and wire rod agreements. In July, 1928, the members of the Central European group entered the EIA individually. At the same time Czechoslovakia arranged to abolish restrictions in respect to its domestic market, receiving an export quota of about 500,000 tons, which was increased to about 560,000 tons in 1929. *Trade Information Bulletin,* No. 713, p. 16.

[21] *Bulletin hebdomadaire d'Information et de Documentation,* Mar. 26, 1927, p. 300 reports that the EIA signed a preliminary agreement with Poland and that the entrance of Poland was merely a question of days. Obviously this preliminary agreement never became effective. Reports were circulated regarding the Italian government's urging its steel industry to join the EIA. However, the industry itself did not agree with its government in this connection (*ibid.,* Mar. 19, 1927, p. 280).

consider the adherence of Great Britain vital to the success of the cartel since Britain, working under relatively high production costs, was considered an inadequate competitor. Great Britain on the other hand refused to accept the quotas offered her, deeming them too small. In addition the domestic organization of the British steel industry at that time was not strong enough to coöperate in a large international agreement.[22] The Bank of England's efforts to induce the British industry to enter the EIA were unsuccessful, due, as one source puts it, to its inability to overcome the individualism of British producers.[23]

The operation of the new cartel (EIA) was put into the hands of a chairman and a management committee. Though, according to the agreement, the chairmanship was to be rotated each year among all member groups, actually the Luxemburg group held the chairmanship throughout the duration of the agreement, because Luxemburg was regarded the most neutral country politically and because the administrative office was attached to the Luxemburg national group.[24] The management committee was composed of four members—Germany, France, Belgium, and Luxemburg—Germany and France also representing the Saar producers. The number of votes within the management committee was allotted according to the percentage of quotas. The Saar producers could never vote individually; their votes were divided between France and Germany, France holding one third and Germany two thirds of the Saar votes. The agreement did not expressly establish a business agency; however, such an agency was set up in Luxemburg. The audit service was conferred upon a Swiss firm, *Schweizerische Treuhandgesellschaft*, in Basel.

The EIA agreement centered on the production of "crude steel."[25]

---

[22] According to *ICTR*, Jan. 17, 1936, p. 121, the first decisive conference with the British, which was unsuccessful because quota requirements were regarded as exaggerated, was held in Paris, Dec. 10, 1926. Reichert's discussion of British participation shows German opposition to the adoption of British proposals. Britain was entitled, according to her production in the reference period (first quarter of 1926), to a quota of 8½ million tons, whereas she asked for 9½ million tons. *Weltwirtschaftliches Archiv*, 1927, I, 368-69*.

[23] *Bulletin d'Information et de Documentation*, Apr. 10, 1936, p. 277.

[24] Dr. Emil Mayrisch, President of ARBED, the principal steel producer in Luxemburg, held the chairmanship of the EIA until his death in 1928. His successor in the ARBED, Mr. Aloyse Meyer, succeeded him as chairman of the EIA and held that office until the disintegration of the ISC in 1939.

[25] Although fear of the effects of overproduction was the impetus which gave rise to the organization of the cartel, no attempt was made internationally to control actual plant expansion. As a matter of fact the organization of the EIA did not prevent the rapid expansion of many steel plants, particularly those in Germany. Otto Hoffmann,

Crude steel is molten steel which is poured into molds either to produce castings (steel castings) or steel ingots. The latter, after solidifying, are used either for forging or as raw material to be converted by rolling into semifinished and finished steel products. For all practical purposes, steel ingot production is very often called "crude steel production," although the expression "crude steel production" is somewhat broader, since it also refers to the production of steel castings. By influencing the production of crude steel the production of all steel products, of which crude steel is the basic material, could be regulated.

The EIA agreement required the management of the cartel to determine the quantity of crude steel which the national groups were to produce in the forthcoming quarter. These quantities were based on a quota scheme, calculated on the production of national units in the first quarter of 1926.[26] The quota scheme was flexible and was adjusted to business conditions which were expected to prevail in the future. National groups paid $1 per metric ton actual output to a common fund in Luxemburg. Groups which produced in excess of predetermined quantities paid $4 fine per ton of excess, whereas groups producing below predetermined quantities received $2 per ton as compensation. Surplus funds were first to be liquidated on April 1, 1927, and quarterly thereafter. After the deduction of general expenses, the funds were divided among the national groups (see Art. VII of the Agreement in Appendix III).

The volume of crude steel production allotted national groups by the management committee of the EIA applied not only to the production of members of the national cartels but to that of non-member producers in the respective countries as well. Thus the volume of production of non-members was included with that of national cartel adherents in applying the system of fines and compensations to the quarterly volume of national production. This assumption of responsibility on the part of national groups for the activities of outsiders was a basic principle in nearly all entities within the ISC.

In order to show the working of the agreement, a preliminary

---

in "Die Internationale Rohstahl-Gemeinschaft," *Wirtschaftskurve*, Mar. 1929, p. 51, regarded the failure of the EIA agreement to deal with this matter as a major deficiency. He argued that production could best be controlled at its source, and that its source is capacity.

[26] Because Germany regarded this reference period as less favorable to herself than to the other participants, a special sliding quota scheme was agreed upon conceding Germany higher and Belgium and France lower shares on that part of allotted quotas between 25,287,000 and 29,287,000 metric tons.

balance sheet of the cartel (October–December 1926), without deductions for administrative expenses, is here reproduced from an official American publication.[27] The first actual balance sheet as of the end of March 1927 is also included here.

TABLE 3
PRELIMINARY BALANCE SHEET OCTOBER–DECEMBER, 1926[28]

Country	Production—thousands of metric tons				Finance—thousands of U. S. dollars						
	Production quota on annual basis of 29,287,000 metric tons	Actual production	Excess production	Inferior production	Collections of $1 per ton levy	Overproduction fines, $4 per ton	Compensation for under-production, $2 per ton	Total collections, minus compensations for under-production	Repayment to national groups	Profits to members	Losses to members
Germany ...	3,161	3,736	575	...	$3,736	$2,300	$...	$6,036	$4,540	$......	$1,496
France......	2,283	2,197	...	86	2,197	......	172	2,025	3,280	1,255	......
Belgium....	846	937	91	...	937	364	....	1,301	1,215	......	86
Luxemburg .	608	598	...	10	598	......	20	578	870	292	......
Saar........	424	454	30	...	454	120	....	574	609	35	......
Total.....	7,322	7,922	696	96	7,922	2,784	192	10,514	10,514	......	......

TABLE 4
ACTUAL BALANCE SHEET OCTOBER 1926–MARCH 1927[29]

Country	Collections of $1 per ton levy	Overproduction fines $4 per ton	Compensation for under-production $2 per ton	Resulting amount for distribution after covering administrative expenses
Germany....	$7,694,000	$6,044,000	$......	$13,738,000
France......	4,202,000	....	470,000	3,732,000
Belgium.....	1,883,000	885,000	......	2,768,000
Luxemburg..	1,181,000	....	8,000	1,173,000
Saar........	932,000	428,000	......	1,360,000
Total....	....	....	......	$22,771,000

The anticipated fines for exceeding the allotted quotas were considerable and were expected to put a certain check on production.

[27] See *Trade Information Bulletin*, No. 484, p. 19. Concerning monthly figures see Dr. J. W. Reichert, *Weltwirtschaftliches Archiv*, 1927, p. 362*. Reichert's figures deviate from those contained in the U. S. publication.

[28] Source: *Trade Information Bulletin* No. 484, U. S. Dept. of Commerce, p. 19.

[29] Source: *Deutsche Bergwerks-Zeitung*, 1927, No. 103, as quoted in P. Ufermann, *op. cit.*, p. 125.

Though the $2 compensation for underproduction was not very high, the advantage in underproducing was considerably increased by the amount of the fines distributed from the common fund to the members at large.

By influencing the production of crude steel through the system of fines and compensations, it was intended to regulate the flow of the basic material from which semifinished and finished rolled steel commodities are produced. Technically this was an efficient measure, but commercially the efficiency of the agreement was hampered by the failure to fix production quantities for single semifinished and finished commodities, as well as the failure to fix prices, and to set up a price relationship between the materials supplied to the domestic and export markets. Three or four comptoirs controlling specific steel commodities did exist during the first period of the EIA, but they by no means included all of the important steel commodities. They covered only heavy rails, wire rods, wire products, and tubular products.

The honeymoon harmony of the steel pact was soon over. The German domestic demand was still very high. However, the advantages accruing to the German steel industry from this increased domestic demand were somewhat tempered by the fact that the increased production required to fill domestic needs necessitated the payment of heavy fines to the EIA for exceeding the quota. The relationship between capacity and quota in the original EIA agreement was relatively unfavorable for Germany and the Saar, although Germany had consciously adopted the agreement. Fines paid by Germany were distributed to other countries whose capacity had been given more favorable consideration in drawing up the original agreement. The German industry felt that its money was being used to some extent to support the steel industries of other countries. Another source of general dissatisfaction with the agreement among all adherents was the change which had occurred in the marketing situation since the signing of the agreement. With the end of the strike of British coal miners in November 1926, Britain not only reduced its imports from EIA countries, but actually entered into competition with them on the world export markets. Another factor affecting the market situation was the stabilization of franc currencies.

The German steel industry began a concentrated attack against the young agreement at the end of 1926 and threatened to disrupt relations with the cartel if the quota scheme were not radically revised in its favor. An American trade commissioner commented on the trembling steel pact: "A contract which the Germans were perfectly satisfied with six months ago is now declared intolerable, because the Western European inflation seems to be nearly over. . . . In any event, the present campaign is of the greatest interest to American business. It offers danger signals of the unreliability of any European combination under present economic and political conditions. It affords another good example of the soundness of the American policy of waiting an appreciable time before entertaining ideas of any participation in any European combine whatsoever. . . . It illustrates the present European state of mind, which considers any contract as open to revision unless it is furthering the particular parties' interests at the particular time."[30]

In the meetings of the management committee of the cartel in January and February 1927 Germany formally demanded an increased quota and the reduction of fines, and offered as compensation for these advantages a temporary withdrawal from export markets. After protracted negotiations, Germany's quota was broken into two parts, effective April 1, 1927. One, amounting to 72 per cent of the total quota, was to go toward domestic deliveries, while the remaining 28 per cent was to cover exports. While the $4 fine for excessive exports still remained, the fine levied against Germany's production in excess of her domestic quota was reduced to $2 and later to $1 per ton. The dissatisfaction of the German industry was only temporarily allayed; its objection to the considerable disproportion between its steel capacity and quota allotments, and its original objection to the looseness of the international agreement and its failure to serve the purpose for which it was intended, still remained.[31]

The international steel market, after a short period of improvement, faced a transitory depression in 1927. In 1928 the situation improved on the export market partly because of the placing of large credits by America in continental Europe. After a relatively short boom period in 1929, the export market at first gradually and then with increasing rapidity crumbled during the second half of 1929. In the middle of 1929 cartel members, anticipating the great depression, felt that the organization was insufficient for the maintenance of coöperation on the export market. Several proposals were made to establish export sales comptoirs for merchant bars, semifinished material, channels, and for plates, but the lack of organization within

---

[30] *Trade Information Bulletin* No. 484, pp. 25-27.
[31] See O. Hoffmann, *op. cit.*, pp. 51 f.

the Belgian group prevented their success. The dissatisfied German group renounced the EIA agreement on May 1, 1929, so that it became ineffective at the end of October 1929, coinciding with the Wall Street crash. The groups prolonged it reluctantly and only from month to month until January 31, 1930. These short prolongations of the agreement were already signs of its disintegration.[32] After the end of 1929 no payments were made to or dispensed by the cartel. Despite the many dissatisfactions among adherents of the EIA agreement, there is little doubt that the critical state in which it found itself was caused by the international economic collapse in the second half of 1929. According to J. W. F. Rowe, the sudden and drastic fall in the prices of most primary products "caused the virtual breakdown of almost all the existing control schemes, and for a short time in the spring of 1930 it looked as if the individualist *laissez-faire* system would be restored."[33]

III

On February 1, 1930, the organization of the ISC took a new shape, marking the beginning of the second period in the life of the ISC. The member groups saw that it was not sufficient to organize and to regulate the market of steel commodities by touching indirectly on the production of crude steel. They realized that to make marketing on the export market efficient prices of specific commodities had to be agreed upon. They recognized as well that interfering with the domestic supply of the member countries did not operate satisfactorily; however, they did not, during this second period, discontinue this interference entirely.

In the new arrangement the indirect control of the general production of crude steel was suspended for the period from February 1, 1930, until July 31, 1930. A set of rather weak export sales comptoirs was established by the EIA founder groups in order to control the exports of semifinished material, structural steel, merchant bars, hoops and strips, and plates by a uniform price system and by a system of quota shares. On March 13, 1930, an agreement was concluded with the Central European group (ZEG) by which they agreed to collaborate along these new lines involving specific com-

---

[32] See quotation from *Frankfurter Zeitung*, Sept. 10, 1930 (No. 675), in Carl Graeff, *Die internationalen Eisenverbände* (Diss.), Düsseldorf, 1937, p. 38.

[33] *Markets and Men* (Cambridge, England, 1936), p. 18. Professor Rowe did not include in his study a discussion of artificial control schemes in steel.

modity controls.[34]   The central administrative agency of the EIA in Luxemburg continued to operate as its coördinating agency during this second period, although on a reduced scale. The reference period for the establishment of export quotas for specific commodities was, with certain corrections, the volume of deliveries of the respective commodities between January 1, 1928, and October 31, 1929. These quotas were flexible, increasing or decreasing in proportion to the increase or decrease of the domestic sales of a member group as compared with the domestic sales of that group during the reference period. If domestic sales of a national group increased, the export quota of the group was decreased by 50 per cent of the domestic increase. Conversely, when and if domestic sales decreased, the export quota of the national group was increased by approximately 50 per cent of that decrease. However, the influence of the domestic market on the export quota could not exceed 35 per cent of the basic quota.

Even this new organization did not work satisfactorily. The reasons lay not only in the failure of the members, because of their mutual distrust, to strengthen the structure of the comptoirs, but mainly in the continuing world economic depression and in circumstances accompanying the depression. The urgency to export was so tremendous with the Belgian and Luxemburg group that they would and could not be squeezed into limitations essential to cartel agreements. The weakness of the comptoirs lay in the fact that they were nearer to being statistical bureaus than export sales syndicates in the modern sense. As the depression and the shrinkage of sales on the export market grew greater, the clamor of members for larger export quotas increased. Thus the regime of the early export sales comptoirs was not continued beyond the end of July, 1930. A rather confused quarter followed in which the old agreement was supposed to operate, but it is doubtful whether the member countries seriously followed the provisions of the original agreement.[35]

IV

The third period began November 1, 1930, when the members agreed to proceed seriously with the control of the domestic and

[34] A. S. Benni, C. Lammers, L. Marlio, A. Meyer, *Internationale Industrie-Kartelle* (Berlin, 1930), p. 14.

[35] *ICTR,* Jan. 20, 1939, p. 115, writes about the period after July, 1930: "all control of steel production ceased, although an attempt was made to revive it before it finally fell into desuetude in February 1931."

export steel markets according to the original EIA agreement, which was changed by the considerable reduction of fines for exceeding quotas. During this period, lasting until the end of January 1931, it became more and more obvious that the structure of the organization was still rapidly deteriorating. At the end of February 1931 it was generally recognized that the life of the agreement of September 30, 1926, had virtually terminated. By March 1, 1931, no pretense at a general agreement in steel policies existed, and in the middle of 1931 the cartel was definitely liquidated.

V

The fourth period in the development of the ISC dates from March 1, 1931, to May 31, 1933. During this period no formal agreement as to general steel policy existed, although several attempts were made toward collaboration in particular fields.[36]

During this period in the history of the first EIA agreement, when no general accord existed between the founder groups, the representatives of the respective steel industries often met in the meetings of the rail, tube, and wire comptoirs. They sometimes coöperated in particular business transactions; however, as a rule they fought each other desperately in noncartelized commodities. To be sure, the sharp competition to a large extent was due to the producers' desire to keep their steel plants employed and to maintain customers during the period of depression, as well as to their need for foreign exchange. However, a strong motive behind the sharp competition lay in the expectation that the next cartel, the organization of which was considered only a matter of months, would compute quotas based on the volume of past exports. A large export volume implied possible claims to larger quotas in the future. This assumption later proved correct and somewhat compensated the exporting groups for the losses they suffered in trying to maintain markets despite unfavorable price conditions.

[36] For example, even in 1932, an agreement existed among German, Luxemburg, and French steel producers regarding the mutual protection of domestic markets. Cf. H. Serlo, *op. cit.*, p. 37. Even Belgium probably participated in this domestic protection agreement at that time because Belgian steel imports to Germany were only irregular and rather scarce, which would probably not have been the case were Belgium not artificially restricted, since Belgian domestic prices were considerably lower than German. See Dr. Georg Wolff, "Neuordnung am internationalen Eisenmarkt," *Wirtschaftskurve*, July 1933, p. 169. A verbal market interpenetration agreement between Belgian and French steel producers is mentioned in *Trade Information Bulletin* No. 800, p. 34, for this same period.

In 1932 steel prices reached their lowest level, a situation which delighted consumers and terrified producers. A general feeling prevailed that cut-throat competition had attained its height. Steel producers felt that there was no particular crisis in steel, but that the export steel market was merely sharing the crisis in durable goods-producing industries. The fact that prices of cartelized steel commodities such as rails, wire rods, tubes, etc. declined only moderately indicated that the savage competition in other, unregulated commodities was as much responsible as the depression for bringing prices down to a very low level. Several steel-importing countries reacted to the decline of prices by increasing their import duties. The former cartel members were greatly affected by the introduction of an ad valorem customs duty of 10 per cent[37] in Great Britain on March 1, 1932, later increased for pig iron, semifinished steel, girders, sheets, etc., on April 26, 1932, to 33.33 per cent.[38]

VI

At the end of 1932 the old charter members of the EIA, Belgium, France, Germany, who also represented the Saar, and Luxemburg, started negotiations to establish a new comprehensive marketing control of the world steel export market. These negotiations were again hampered by the weak and unreliable internal organizations of the French and especially of the Belgian groups. The lessons of former coöperation and noncoöperation were taken into account, and the following principles, which became decisive for the next agreement, were crystallized. First, the agreement was to relate exclusively to the export market, disregarding the volume of output and domestic marketing conditions. Second, the quota system was to be extended to particular steel commodities, and prices of these commodities were to be regulated directly through export syndicates. Third, the cartel was to extend its structure to the organization of distribution, going so far as to establish or promote cartels of merchants in importing countries.

Thus France, Belgium, Luxemburg, and Germany signed a gen-

---

[37] According to Sir William Larke, in "The British Iron and Steel Industry," *Stahl und Eisen,* Sept. 17, 1936, p. 1071, the 10 per cent import duty was not intended to be protective, but was to serve revenue purposes only.

[38] For several finished steel products the general 10 per cent duty was raised to 20 per cent only, thus "perhaps the first time in British tariff history a higher duty had been put upon the raw material than on the finished product." Ingot (pseud.), *The Socialisation of Iron and Steel* (London, 1936), p. 95.

eral agreement in Luxemburg on February 25, 1933, which was to become effective as soon as sectional agreements involving six steel commodities—semifinished products, joists and channels, merchant bars, thick plates, medium plates, and universal steel—were concluded and put into operation. These sectional agreements, together with the second EIA agreement, became effective on June 1, 1933. This date marks the beginning of the fifth period in the history of the ISC, which lasted until the expiration of these agreements on June 30, 1938.

As indicated above, the new cartel arrangement of June 1, 1933, abandoned the regulation of production and thus the interference with domestic markets. Those few comptoirs, such as the ones affecting wire rods, wire products, and tubular products, which continued partly to control domestic markets, also found such activities unsuccessful.

The establishment of strong national groups was a condition upon which the new cartel structure was based. Many months elapsed, in fact years, before the Belgian and French national groups attained adequate internal cohesion. In fact they never attained the degree of unity which existed within the German, British, and Luxemburg groups.

The 1933 arrangement consisted of a general agreement and of a set of sectional or comptoir agreements of which six were organically related to the main agreement. By regulating the volume of crude steel exports, the general agreement regulated the export of all steel commodities. This general EIA agreement regulated the export of all steel commodities by evaluating them in terms of an agreed-upon amount of crude steel necessary for their production. Each commodity was assigned a crude steel value per unit.[39] The amount of

---

[39] The conversion factor for determining the crude steel value of finished products was agreed upon by the members. This factor took into account the proportion of the steel ingot which was cropped or otherwise scrapped during the rolling process. The larger the quantity of scrap, the larger the crude steel value of the rolled product. One of the national groups used in its internal relations the following scheme in computing crude steel values:

For 100 tons of rolled steel commodities:	Crude steel value in tons:
Blooms, billets and slabs	112
Sheet bars	117
Merchant bars	117
Structural steel	122
Heavy rails	119
Steel cross ties	130

crude steel involved in the production of all exported steel commodities was calculated and used as a basis for determining the quota of crude steel which each member of the EIA was to be permitted to export in the form of steel commodities. Thus all steel commodity exports, whether or not they were subject to particular controls through specific commodity comptoirs, were subject to a general control through the crude steel export quota system of the EIA.

There were, therefore, two overlapping quota systems, one in the general agreement[40] and the other in sectional agreements. If a commodity was included in a sectional agreement it was essentially included in the general agreements, but not vice versa. For instance, exports of semifinished steel, heavy rails, structural steel, and wide-

Thick and medium plates	132
Black sheets	143
Galvanized sheets	125
Hoops and strips, hot rolled	112
Wire rods	117

[40] The working quota scheme is set forth in minutes taken at the meetings of the four member groups on Apr. 25 and May 5, 1933 (see Appendix V). Fixed crude steel export quotas were established for two situations. The first quotas applied if the total crude steel value of exported steel commodities was 6,800,000 metric tons or less annually. The second quotas applied if these annual export values amounted to 11,500,000 metric tons or more. If the total crude steel value of commodity exports lay between these two amounts, the quotas were adjusted somewhere between the two already set up, according to a determined key. The two fixed quotas of the founder groups of the EIA were as follows:

Total annual crude steel value of exported commodities

	6.8 million metric tons or less Per cent	11.5 million metric tons or more Per cent
Germany-Saar	29.2	33.7
Belgium	29.0	26.0
France	20.6	23.5
Luxemburg	21.2	16.8
	100.0	100.0

When Poland entered the cartel in 1935, the total allotment was distributed on a basis of 104.197 per cent, of which Poland's fixed quota share was 4.197 per cent.

According to *International Ententes*, p. 42, the percentual quota share of each member was calculated on the basis of its actual exports during the first six months of 1932. These figures were then compared with the considerably higher average of exported crude steel tonnage for the years 1927 to 1929. "Here again, the percentual share of each group was calculated. In this way, each country received two percentage figures. The curve running between these two figures shows the actual quota claim of each country, according to the total export figures."

The annual economic survey of the Belgian National Bank, "La Situation Économique de la Belgique 1933," *Bulletin d'Information et de Documentation*, Apr. 25, 1934, p. 257, expresses great satisfaction with the advantageous position of Belgium and Luxemburg resulting from the choice of this combined reference period.

flanged beams were regulated twice; first, when the crude steel export quotas of the general cartel's members were applied to the crude steel value of these specific commodities, and second, when the quotas of the specific comptoirs controlling these commodities were applied to them. Conversely, the export of black sheets, galvanized sheets, and cold rolled strips was influenced by the crude steel export quotas of the EIA without being influenced (at that time) by specific quotas, since in 1933 no export sales comptoirs had been established for these commodities. If in 1933 there had been export sales comptoirs for all important steel commodities, probably no double quota system would have been established.[41] Because of the dual quota system, the EIA agreements were not readily comprehensible to many students, although the crude steel export quota scheme did not play the role that writers about the international steel export market attributed to it. British, American, and Czechoslovakian groups who entered the ISC after July 1, 1936, did not adhere to the general crude steel export scheme. The operation of this scheme was suspended on July 1, 1936, which meant its virtual abandonment. It was formally abolished on the occasion of the renewal of the EIA agreement on July 1, 1938.

It would be false to assume that the EIA's principal function was to divide the export of steel commodities into crude steel export quotas. The crude steel export quota scheme was intended to be an auxiliary device and nothing else. The EIA was intended principally as a central coördinating and policy-determining agency for all national groups and export sales comptoirs. These policy-determining functions of the EIA included its quarterly decisions regarding the global quantity of steel commodities to be exported by the member groups. The last such decision was made in the meeting of the management committee of the EIA, in Warsaw, October 13, 1937.[42] This activity on the part of the EIA was never of much significance.

Two conditions were requisite to the EIA agreement. First, that

---

[41] According to Dr. Reichert the German group in 1933 regarded the double quota structure as superfluous, because the system of particular commodity quotas sufficiently regulated the market. *Stahl und Eisen,* Nov. 26, 1936, p. 1435. See also Dr. Georg Wolff, "Neuordnung am internationalen Eisenmarkt," *Wirtschaftskurve,* July, 1933, pp. 168-169.

[42] The monthly global export quantity of steel (called tonnage program) was reduced from 525,000 metric tons to 425,000 metric tons. Neither the British nor the American group adhered to global crude steel export quotas, nor to tonnage program schemes. The significance of the tonnage program scheme is somewhat exaggerated in *International Ententes,* p. 42.

the four founder groups establish and maintain strong domestic steel cartels controlling domestic markets and the bulk of their national exports in steel. Second, that the four founder groups establish six international export sales comptoirs, in semifinished steel, merchant bars, structural steel, heavy plates, medium plates, and universal steel. The EIA was to coördinate the operation of its national groups in regard to export sales comptoirs, and further was to establish new export sales comptoirs for steel commodities not yet specifically cartelized. It was understood tacitly that the EIA organization would coöperate with those export sales comptoirs whose organization preceded the second EIA agreement (heavy rails, wire rods, wire products, tubular products). About the time of the EIA agreement two more comptoirs were started, one of major importance, covering hot-rolled hoops and strips, and one of minor importance, covering wide-flanged beams. Although these two cartels were not subordinate to the EIA, they were intimately connected with it. In attempting to fulfill the first requirement for a strong EIA, that calling for strong national coöperation, the Belgian national group met with particular difficulties. According to many reports, the executive officers of several Belgian steel works strongly resisted both the establishment of a strong domestic steel cartel and general coöperation within an efficient international steel export organization. Though it seems somewhat extraordinary, most of the Belgian steel works had to be compelled by their major shareholders to create a domestic organization and to become part of the international cartel. During the critical period from 1929 to 1933 Belgian steel works sold steel commodities considerably below average total costs on the export market and lost a large amount of money. The shares of steel companies on the stock market rapidly decreased in value and it has been generally assumed that Belgian banks took advantage of the unusual opportunity to buy up these shares. Besides, internecine competition between Belgian steel works on the international market had created a tension among the steel works that could not easily be bridged. Belgian banks exercised great pressure on steel works to abandon their individual disputes.[43] The principal Belgian

---

[43] The great tension and the striking difference in economic views between Belgian steel industries and their bank-shareholders did not originate in 1932-33. Mr. Hannecart, general director of foreign commerce in Belgium, discussed this unique problem in an address to the American-Belgian Chamber of Commerce, Feb. 25, 1927. He regarded it as natural that bank-shareholders should determine long-term policies as to concentration of industry whereas steel industrialists (or executives) themselves should be concerned with short-term policies "because industry itself has not sufficient time for such investigations." *Bulletin hebdomadaire d'Information et de Documenta-*

bank, the Société Générale de Belgique, held blocks of shares in most of the companies and was one of the main factors influencing the pending negotiations for coöperation. Strange as it may seem, until the end of the cartel in 1939, Belgian bank executives, in their function as members of boards of directors of steel companies, participated for the Belgian group in international steel negotiations, and several steel agreements were signed by bank executives who acted as representatives of the Belgian group.[44] The *Iron and Coal Trade Review* commented rather interestingly on the Belgian situation. According to its Brussels correspondent: "The year 1933, if we except the period of the war, has been the most eventful in the history of the Belgian steel industry; it has witnessed a revolutionary change in the principles upon which the industry has been conducted from its foundation, the relentless suppression of individualism, and the imposition of the system of international coöperation, almost socialistic in theory, upon the steel trade of the continent, of which the Belgian steel works had been the most independent section."[45] And further, "The Belgian steelmakers themselves were by no means united upon the question of establishing a selling organization for the whole trade, but forces outside the industry were at work to bring about a system of coöperation. Most of the Belgian steel works were reputed to be controlled by banks, which during the long period of depression had acquired large blocks of shares, and it was alleged, probably with

---

tion, Mar. 19, 1927, p. 272. A comprehensive article by Professor Robert J. Lemoine discusses the particular role of Belgian banks as the shareholders of industry, especially of the steel industry. Mr. Lemoine emphasizes the fact that Belgian banks, even preceding the First World War but especially after it, were exercising pressure on coal and steel industries to concentrate in domestic cartels and to join international cartels. "La Syndicalisation et la Concentration des Entreprises dans le Royaume de Belgique," *ibid.,* Jan. 10, 1936, pp. 4 ff.

Though commercial banks were large shareholders of steel industries in many continental European countries, they did not exercise their controlling role (if any) as conspicuously as they did in Belgium. It is interesting to note that in 1934 large Belgian banks were reputed to have had to put pressure on their coal industries to induce them to organize a strong cartel. See *Bulletin d'Information et de Documentation,* Sept. 1938, p. 178.

[44] See for instance the International Merchant Bar Entente agreement attached to this volume as Appendix V.

[45] Jan. 26, 1934, p. 168. See D. L. Burn, *op. cit.,* p. 453, n. 3. However, what the yearly economic survey of the Belgian National Bank for 1932 wrote about this point is not without significance. "One can expect that the reconstitution of the cartel will allow the Belgian steel industry to recuperate the forces lost by the very ardent competition during the last two years." "La Situation Économique de la Belgique en 1932," *Bulletin d'Information et de Documentation,* Apr. 25, 1933, p. 274.

truth, that these financial interests were responsible in the end for driving the Belgian industry into the cartel scheme."[46] According to a German version the German government exercised decisive pressure on Belgium by threatening to induce the German steel producers to break up the EIA negotiations. This threat implied that the German government would subsidize steel exports of the German group and make the Belgian steel situation even more difficult.[47] Belgian steel producers finally agreed to coöperate as a national unit at the end of May 1933, just before the general EIA agreement went into effect. However, the Belgian group pledged its adherence to the EIA agreement with some reservations.[48]

The organization and the operation of the central structure of the EIA as well as the specific commodity comptoirs connected with it are discussed in other parts of this study. It is sufficient to indicate here that the EIA remained the core of the international steel marketing control (the ISC) until its end in 1939.

In its fifth period the ISC developed in several new directions. It established several organizations of distributors in steel-importing countries, as is discussed in more detail elsewhere in this volume. Even in this regard it followed the organizational pattern of the *Stahlwerks-Verband* which in the first decade of the twentieth century started the establishment of merchant cartels and other distributor organizations in Switzerland, Denmark, Sweden, Norway, the Netherlands, England, and Belgium.[49]

A turning point in the cartel's history which occurred during this period was the participation of Great Britain in the general ISC organization, by an agreement signed on April 30, 1935, and effective on May 8, 1935, for a tentative period of three months.[50] On July 31,

---

[46] To the knowledge of the author Belgian banks were large stockholders of steel companies even before the depression of 1930-1933. A revealing picture of this situation may be found in an article in the *Wirtschaftskurve*, December 1929, pp. 412 ff., "Der Konzern der Société Générale de Belgique."

[47] Cf. Heinz Serlo, *Das Wesen der Verkaufsverbände der deutschen Rohstahlgemeinschaft und ihre Bedeutung für die deutsche Eisenindustrie* (Diss., Düsseldorf, 1939), p. 37.

[48] C. Graeff, *Die Internationalen Eisenverbände* (Diss.), Düsseldorf, 1930, p. 67, discusses the "Clabeque affaire," describing that the *Forges de Clabeque* reserved the right to dissolve its cartel connection until Dec. 31, 1933. According to Carl Graeff the Clabeque Works were threatened with the City of Brussels' severing its agreement concerning the purchase of electric energy if Clabeque should renounce its adherence to the cartel.   [49] See Paul Ufermann, *op. cit.*, p. 34.

[50] At the end of March, 1935, the import duties on steel commodities were increased in Great Britain from 33 1/3 per cent (of their value) to 50 per cent in order to place the British industry "in a position to negotiate satisfactory agreements with its com-

1935, Great Britain signed another general agreement effective for five years beginning with August 8, 1935, the date on which the first agreement expired. This agreement, upon the delayed fulfillment of several conditions, was made definitive in August, 1936. Poland, in a general agreement, joined the EIA on July 26, 1935. At the beginning of 1936 Czechoslovakia entered the EIA, though the negotiations regarding the terms of the Czechoslovakian agreement were not completed until early in 1937.[51]

On August 1, 1936, after infinite efforts, one of the most important sales comptoirs, that for black sheets, was established, as was the export sales comptoir for galvanized sheets. The formation of these comptoirs made the network of the export sales comptoirs practically, although not entirely, complete.

The EIA by itself and together with the British group concluded penetration agreements with producers in those countries which imported steel products because of insufficient domestic steel-producing facilities. Among these agreements the one with South Africa was the most important.

The tentative entrance of the United States steel producers into the ISC at the beginning of 1938 crowned the cartel's structure. The ISC mechanism practically embraced the entire steel-producing world and nearly all steel commodities when the fifth period of its history terminated on June 30, 1938. The rapid improvement in coöperation during this period was due not only to fortunate organizational adjustments, but also to the gradual improvement, with only minor setbacks, of the business situation on the international steel market.

---

petitors. . . ." (The *Economist*, Mar. 23, 1935, p. 653.) "A striking testimony to the efficiency of tariffs," wrote *The Times*, June 12, 1935 (quoted by D. L. Burn, *op. cit.*, p. 456). According to Sir William Larke, "The British Iron and Steel Industry," *Stahl und Eisen*, Sept. 17, 1936, p. 1072, this increase of the duty served "the interests of improving the employment position of the Industry. . . ." Frederic Benham wrote, "This is one of the clearest cases on record of the successful use of the tariff as a bargaining weapon." *Great Britain Under Protection* (New York, 1941), p. 184. The introduction of high duties was answered, according to Belgian reports, by the threat of the EIA to dissolve those comptoirs in which Britain participated, particularly those involving heavy rails (IRMA) and thick plates. See *Bulletin d'Information et de Documentation*, May 10, 1936, p. 373 and F. Benham, *op. cit.*, p. 189.

[51] An agreement for the general coöperation of the EIA and the Central European Group (ZEG) had existed from June, 1933, through May, 1934. This agreement expired without being renewed. However, even after its expiration the participants tacitly coöperated. See Carl Graeff, *op. cit.*, p. 84, and J. W. Reichert, in *ICTR*, Jan. 26, 1934, p. 167. However, in spite of this tacit "coöperation," both the cartel and the Czechoslovakian group frequently took advantage of their lack of a formal agreement and operated competitively on the markets of those commodities for which the Czechoslovakian group was not bound by comptoir agreements.

The EIA agreement and many sectional agreements were to expire on June 30, 1938. Their extension was not particularly opposed save by the Belgian group, because of internal difficulties within the latter. This obstruction was eliminated near the time for the expiration of the second EIA agreement by improving the quota of the Belgian firm, *Monceau-sur-Sambre,* belonging to the concern of the *Aciéries et Minières de la Sambre.* The agreement was then renewed and became effective on July 1, 1938. The new EIA agreement greatly resembled the old one, except for the formal exclusion of the crude steel export quota scheme, which had not been in operation for several years under the old agreement.

VII

The sixth period in the history of the ISC began on July 1, 1938, and ended when the organization disintegrated at the beginning of September 1939, with the outbreak of war. The new agreement was intended to last until the end of 1940, the date set for the termination of the EIA agreement and a majority of the other agreements, including those of the British and American groups. During this sixth period American producers put their agreement on a more secure basis. In addition, on January 23, 1939, the comptoir for cold-rolled hoops and strips was established.[52]

From the beginning of the ISC until its end, national groups concluded general and special agreements concerning mutual steel relationships among themselves and with steel producers outside of the cartel. These agreements, which received little publicity, related mainly to domestic market protection and to mutual or one-sided deliveries. Naturally, they did not conflict with the ISC structure.

Within the last period of the ISC, the organizational changes which occurred in the cartel were those resulting from the political events following the invasion of Austria, Sudetenland, and the Tesin region. The German quota shares were increased by the ISC after the invasion of Austria in proportion to the export quantities of Austria. The problem of the Tesin region[53] and the Sudetenland could not be solved so easily because the Czechoslovakian group resisted the flat abandonment of the proportion of its quotas represented by the exports of their lost plants.[54] The total invasion of Czecho-

---

[52] *ICTR*, Jan. 27, 1939, p. 210. [53] See *ICTR*, Jan. 20, 1939, p. 176.

[54] Poland received an extra quota of 17,000 tons for two months, Jan.-Feb. 1939, after the annexation of the Tesin region. Poland's supplementary quota for March of that year was reduced by 20 per cent. *ICTR*, Feb. 24, 1939, p. 392.

slovakia in March 1939 did not necessitate the immediate readjustment of quotas because the German group, either for commercial
reasons or through embarrassment, did not require the dissolution of
the Czechoslovakian group at the time. Thus Czechoslovakia remained a member of the ISC until it disintegrated.

Though it was clear that the ISC organization could not operate
after the beginning of the war, expert steel opinion would not accept
the fact that the ISC was dead. A characteristic opinion by C. S.
Richards is illustrative. In an addendum to his study dated December
28, 1939, Mr. Richards describes the functioning of the ISC after the
outbreak of the war: "All existing arrangements and agreements of
the International Steel Cartel have been rendered ineffective, and the
Cartel's activities will apparently be limited to maintaining a modified
form of control of the export trades of the Western European and
Scandinavian iron and steel industries, which are virtually divided
into those of the Allies and the neutral countries. The problem of
the Cartel will in the future apparently be not so much the maintenance of prices as the provision of adequate supplies of steel to
maintain an export trade, and in this policy, because of the membership composition of the Cartel, the interests of the Allies are necessarily bound to be paramount."[55]

Despite such expectations of activity, the ISC may be considered
as having ceased to exist early in September 1939, its projected meeting in Düsseldorf, for October 1939, never having taken place.

---

[55] *Op. cit.*, p. liv.

CHAPTER FOUR

Basic Structure and Central Agencies

I

A SUCCINCT DESCRIPTION of the structure of the ISC results in over-simplification and a sharper delineation of functions and agencies than actually existed. In this respect a systematic arrangement of such a description shares the fallacies inherent in the schematic depiction of complicated social organisms. The complete structure of the ISC developed gradually, and hardly as a result of conscious planning. The forms it assumed were the result of immediate necessities. In problems of organization the ISC followed the line of least resistance, deviating from institutional frames inherent in national legal and economic systems, though adjusting suitable features of traditional cartel patterns for its own purposes. Therefore it is vain to seek logical consistency, very distinct jurisdictional spheres, or definite hierarchies in the general structure of the ISC.

The edifice of the ISC as a whole may be visualized by four concentric circles. The innermost circle would be the symbol for the four founder groups (Belgium, France, Germany, Luxemburg) of the continental European steel cartel (EIA); the next circle would be the EIA organization, including the two associated national groups, Czechoslovakia and Poland; the third circle would represent the common organization of the EIA and the British national group, symbolizing the European Steel Cartel; the fourth, and outermost, would include United States steel producers and would represent the body of the ISC, making the picture complete. The farther a group was away from the core of the large circle, the looser its relationship to the core of the cartel.

The four concentric circles conveyed the idea that the founder groups of the continental European steel cartel maintained their leading role within the ISC until its disintegration, keeping the associated groups outside of their intimate circle. The British and American groups, deliberately placed on the periphery of the structure by their own choice, kept themselves apart from the center, a position which permitted them considerable independence of action and demanded their coöperation only on important items.[1]

Until the middle of 1935 the first circle would symbolize both the EIA and the ISC, which were practically identical until that time. In the latter part of 1935, the two associated groups began to participate with the founder groups in the determination of general steel policies, thus justifying the distinction in structure represented by the second imaginary circle. The third outer circle, symbolizing the European Steel Cartel, with Britain as well as continental Europe as adherents, would be practically synonymous with the ISC from August 1935 until January 1938. The fourth outer circle would represent the ISC as it existed after January 1938, when United States steel producers entered the main organization. It should be emphasized that the four overlapping basic units represented by four such circles coexisted from January 1938 until the end of the cartel, although, as time went on, functional spheres were naturally shifted from units designated by the smaller circles to those designated by the larger circles. Thus, until September 1939, the policies of the EIA founder groups, the whole EIA, the ESC, and of the complete ISC were distinct, though these policies were naturally interlaced and coördinated.

The three names, International Steel Cartel, European Steel Cartel, and Entente Internationale de l'Acier, were applied in a twofold manner. Each of them, on the one hand, was used to designate a complex body (a general or super-cartel) composed of a central agency and of several sub-entities, and on the other hand these names were used to designate the central agencies of the three general cartels alone, as contrasted with the component sub-entities. In the first sense, the whole structure of the ISC consisted of a basic framework, and of an extensive network of accessory mechanisms supporting the

---

[1] This isolated position of Great Britain was emphasized in *The Times* (London), by the statement: ". . . the British steel industry is not a member of the International Steel Cartel, but has signed the agreement as one industrial body to another, thus forming a dominant organization over the head of the Cartel itself." (Iron and Steel Number, June 14, 1938, p. 5.) *The Times* obviously called the EIA the "International Steel Cartel," and called what this study refers to as the International Steel Cartel, a "dominant organization." The independent position of Americans, claiming to be an entity "operating as a unit similar to Europe," is mentioned in the *Hearings* of the TNEC, Part 20, p. 10935.

operation of the basic structure. The basic structure was ultimately composed of exporter-producers of steel united in national steel cartels, called national groups. In principle these exporter-producers participated in ISC activities only indirectly, i.e. through their respective national groups. Eight national groups were the member units in both the general policy-determining bodies of the ISC, ESC, and EIA, and in the single commodity cartels (export sales comptoirs). The accessory structure of the ISC was composed principally of an extensive organization of distributors and of structures coordinating the activities of potential ISC competitors who did not participate in the policy-determining functions of the ISC.

National groups, export sales comptoirs, and distributor organizations are discussed in separate chapters of this study. The present chapter is devoted to a discussion of the basic structure of the ISC and of the central agencies heading that basic structure.

After January 1938 the basic structure of the whole ISC included two lower general policy-determining agencies (ESC and EIA), eight national groups, and seventeen export sales comptoirs. Appendix I contains a detailed survey of the basic structure, which is graphically presented in the frontispiece chart.

The ISC, and within it the ESC and the EIA, were naturally supposed to coördinate the policies of the eight national groups and of the export sales comptoirs, and to determine and to coördinate the operations of the accessory mechanisms. This coördinating policy was not limited to the settlement of real or possible conflicts among the sub-entities, but was utilized to give a general context, an objective to the workings of the sub-entities and, in view of their common economic interests, to intentionally delineate particular procedures of the sub-entities. In addition, the three general policy-determining bodies furnished the policies and mechanisms serving the interests of the organization as a whole. There was never any discussion about the all-inclusive objectives of the ISC. It was tacitly assumed that such objectives existed and that they were so obvious that to discuss them would be a waste of time. It was equally assumed as apodictical that non-coöperation on the part of one of the sub-entities not only implied damage to the whole structure in the long run, but to the interests of that reluctant sub-entity itself.

Two economic forces operated in the edifice of the ISC, both designed to make the world steel export market revolve around the parent and a group of filial centers. The first force, centripetal in nature, aimed at maintaining internal collaboration and discipline among cartel members. The second force, centrifugal, was intended to keep distributors and consumers in line and to eliminate or weaken actual and potential outside competition. Thus cartel dynamics should be viewed as a movement inside a self-centered organism and also as activities influencing the "outside" world. The maintenance of internal discipline was not easy. Self-imposed discipline among virtually coördinated national units was much more difficult to maintain than the discipline imposed on subordinate entities by a superordinate body. One should realize that violations which occurred sometimes happened many thousands of miles from the centers of cartel activities. However, more often than one might suppose, infringements of cartel regulations were reported by competing distributors within a few hours, even if they occurred in the most remote regions of the world.

An exposition of the basic structure of the ISC should focus on what might be referred to as the constitution of that organization, the guiding principles and procedures which pervaded that constitution, and the characteristics which made that structure a vigorous binding power for so many singular economic interests. These supreme rules of the ISC represented the combined will of the national groups who regarded themselves allied by a contractual relationship, somewhat resembling the political structure of a terminable confederacy. Many students of the ISC organization have tried to discover whether formulated rules determining the relationship between the central organizations (ISC, ESC, EIA) and the export sales comptoirs existed. No such written or oral understandings existed, because the national groups which constituted the central bodies in general also directed the working of the export sales comptoirs. For all practical purposes this identity of personnel efficiently guaranteed the operation of the central agencies of the ISC and the export sales comptoirs in harmony.[2]

The main actors in all policy-determining organizations of the ISC were the representatives of the national groups. Executive officers of steel exporter-producers, along with professional agents of national steel cartels, served with authority delegated by the national groups. The credentials of these deputies were never either formally or sub-

---

[2] The relationship between general policy-determining agencies and the quasi-independent comptoirs was considerably strengthened after Great Britain and the United States entered the cartel. According to *The Times* (London), Dec. 6, 1935, p. 12d, "Existing international agreements in which the British industry is participating covering rails, tinplates, etc., form an integral part of the agreement." This closer contact is emphasized in *ICTR*, Jan. 15, 1937, pp. 123-124.

stantially examined. Any action or statement of an alleged representative of a national steel group in the name of his group was attributed
to the national group as a whole without further examination. The
American group was generally represented by professional agents of
the London office of the Steel Export Association of America, who
referred all major problems to America for previous or subsequent
decision, whereas all representatives of other national groups were
bound and able to make their decisions about major problems on the
spot. This distinction between the system of representation of the
European and the American groups considerably strengthened the
feeling of the remoteness of Americans from European steel policies.

Powers and functions within the ISC were determined in rather
general terms, and the practice of delegating broad powers without
formalities among and within the ISC agencies was widespread. This
made the operation of that body strikingly flexible. Theoretically,
national groups carried an equal weight, as did the comptoirs. In
reality, however, each national group and each comptoir had a distinct power value which worked tacitly but most efficiently.

Many misunderstandings as to the ISC organization may arise from
a confusion between the three coexisting general policy-determining
units, ISC, ESC, and EIA. As a matter of fact, the cartel itself did
not particularly care to clarify the mutual status of these groupings
even in its internal relations. The enlargement of the cartel organization with the entrance of the associated groups, Great Britain and
the United States, into the general policy-determining bodies, though
tremendously important, did not produce revolutionary changes in
the structure and operations of the ISC. By ISC acquiescence the
EIA (especially the founder groups) continued to exercise far greater
powers than was warranted by logical considerations, though after
Great Britain and the United States entered the cartel the EIA itself
formally became only one of the constituting elements of the ISC.
The reader who is acquainted with modern British history will readily
compare the role of the EIA with that which Great Britain played
within the British Commonwealth of Nations after the adoption of
the Westminster Act. However, a gradual shifting of jurisdictions
resulted in an attempt to engage Great Britain, and later the United
States, in all principal policy-determining functions. This process was
interrupted by the distintegration of the cartel in September 1939.

The student of the ISC constitution must search for three constitutions, those of the EIA, the ESC, and the proper ISC.[3] All of

---

[3] The first EIA agreement and a few important items of the second have been dis-

these so-called constitutions were recorded in brief and sketchy documents, containing relatively few organizational provisions, their amplification having been intended in later, more specific agreements. The written constitutions may rightly be qualified as *pacta de contrahendo;* i.e., basic agreements, which were to be built up by sets of detailed understandings in the future. They did not contain a "bill of rights," establishing the formal relationship of members among themselves and to the main organization, and even the provisions of the documents concerning voting were not actually practiced in the manner prescribed by the constitutions. All of these written documents were only very brief fundamentals on which the network of rules, principles, and practices, which may be called the ISC constitution, was constructed.

II

The EIA organization was based on the second EIA accord, signed by the founder groups on February 25, 1933, in Luxemburg, amended on April 25, 1933 and on May 5, 1933, and put into effect on June 1, 1933. This agreement, changed several times after becoming effective, expired on June 30, 1938. Prolonged with considerable changes on July 1, 1938, it was to last until the end of 1940. The second EIA agreement regulated the relationship of the founder groups to each other, whereas their relationship to the Polish and Czechoslovakian (associated) groups was set forth in separate written understandings amplifying the basic accord. However, many of the provisions of the agreement among the founder groups were applied to the relationship with the associated groups as well. Though it was understood that the unanimous consent of all interested national groups was required in order to amend the fundamental provisions of the accords, no meticulous formalities were required or practiced in amending these documents. Changes were decided upon in ordinary business meetings and promulgated in the current minutes of the business proceedings.

The parties to the EIA constitution intended to establish an association *(Entente, Gemeinschaft)* for the pursuit of their "general" interests on the export steel market and for the coördination of the policies of export sales comptoirs, especially of those "subordinated" to or closely connected with the EIA. Most of the provisions of the second EIA agreement concerned the crude steel export quota scheme,

cussed in Chapter II, and American participation in the ISC is discussed in Chapter IX. A description of the organization of the EIA can be found in *The Economist,* Vol. 125, p. 510.

abandoned on July 1, 1936, which is discussed in Chapter II of this volume. The remaining provisions which were still operative after July 1936 could easily be placed on three typewritten pages.

The external organization of the EIA was set forth in the basic agreement of February 5, 1933, which provided for a chairman with broad powers, elected annually, and a management committee *(comité de gérance, comité directeur)*, with practically unlimited powers. Actually the chairmanship remained in the hands of the chairman of the Luxemburg group permanently. The management committee consisted of one titular member and two deputy members for each national group, but any number of representatives could participate in meetings of the committee, though the number of votes for each national group remained the same. According to the EIA agreement, the management committee was the policy-determining agency of the EIA, and it could admit new members and amend the basic accords by unanimous vote.

Actually, another EIA agency, though not mentioned in the EIA agreement, was of paramount importance in determining general steel policy and in coördinating the functions of several comptoirs. This agency was the comptoir committee, which consisted of the managing directors of all national steel cartels that were members of the EIA. Naturally, staff members of the national cartels, leading industrialists, and, depending on the type of business, members of the business agencies of export sales comptoirs, also participated in the meetings. The chairman of the comptoir committee, Mr. Hector Dieudonné, was a prominent representative of the Luxemburg group, and the embodiment of the spirit of the ISC. No sharp functional divisions existed between the comptoir and management committees, the two principal EIA agencies. The comptoir committee deliberated problems connected with price policies, the organization of distribution, outside competition, the licensing of agents, and other matters of commercial concern to the cartel. It functioned in a general supervisory and coördinating capacity in the maintenance of quota schemes. Whereas the management committee, concerned mostly with problems of principle and organization, met rarely, about once a quarter, the comptoir committee held meetings very often at no set intervals.

The EIA had an administrative agency in Luxemburg consisting of one clerk and a very small (10-15) clerical personnel which worked under the responsibility of the EIA chairman. Actually the operation of this administrative agency was directed by the chairman of the comptoir committee. The agency was charged with collecting and distributing statistics, holding deposits, keeping minutes of meetings, and all other routine matters. The routine functions of the six comptoirs (semifinished steel, merchant bars, structural steel, thick plates, medium plates, and universal steel) were partly performed by the administrative agency of the EIA, partly by their own administrative agencies.

The second EIA agreement, just as the first, provided that the vote of each national group in both the management and comptoir committees was to be proportionate to its crude steel quota percentage. In practice each national group was counted as one vote. Decisions were made by majority vote, except in a few cases requiring a three-fourths or unanimous vote. Every attempt was made to compromise differences without forcing the minority to abide by the majority's decision, and the out-voting of founder groups was, if possible, especially avoided. There were very few rules of a procedural character in the EIA accords. Procedure was adjusted to the requirements of the moment; small special committees were used frequently to deliberate and decide on special issues. Both French and German were originally intended as official languages for EIA meetings. Later, almost without exception, only French was used as the official language. However, when English-speaking members participated in meetings, French and English were generally used. Meetings of both policy-determining committees took place mostly in Brussels, Paris, London, Luxemburg, or Düsseldorf. Occasionally meetings were held in well-known resort places or in other attractive cities.[4]

The two policy-determining agencies of the EIA were supposed to be concerned with the control of the international steel market only in so far as it concerned the six national groups embraced by the EIA. In reality, even after Great Britain entered the cartel scene in 1935, and after December 1937, when United States steel producers agreed to participate in the determination of general cartel policies, the two EIA agencies constituted the general staff of the cartel as a whole. The management and comptoir committees of the EIA intercoördinated policies and all principal cartel actions even at a time when higher policy-determining agencies existed, though efforts were

---

[4] When the Italian steel producers entered the International Rail Makers' Association with a quota of less than one per cent, the government-owned Italian steel industry extended its invitation to all ISC agencies to hold meetings in Rome. In June 1938 all ISC agencies, the IRMA, the International Scrap Convention, along with other groups, were royally feted in the Fascist capital by the Italian industry which was not without some tendency to utilize the opportunity for political propaganda. See *Iron Age,* June 9, 1938, p. 77.

made to make the British and United States groups share powers and responsibilities. As a matter of fact, the chairman of the comptoir committee of the EIA, Mr. Hector Dieudonné, was regarded as the guiding spirit of the cartel organization.

Among the non-procedural provisions of the second EIA agreement, the crude steel export quota scheme, the tonnage program scheme, and the provisions for the mutual protection of home markets were the most prominent. The crude steel export quota scheme which was *de facto* abandoned on July 1, 1936, and formally eliminated from the agreement on July 1, 1938, is discussed in Chapter II of this study. In the same chapter the export tonnage program scheme is discussed. The text of the EIA management committee's decision of January 10, 1935, amending the original agreement in regard to the export tonnage program scheme, is attached to Article XII of the merchant bar agreement in Appendix V. It may be assumed that with the abandonment of the crude steel export quota scheme the penalty provisions for violations of this tonnage scheme were forsaken as well. The export tonnage program scheme, a hangover from the first EIA agreement, while never formally abandoned, was never very effective. In accordance with this scheme a total global steel export tonnage for the entire cartel was computed before each quarter, and each national group was to limit its export sales of all commodities to its proportion of the total tonnage quota. However, members paid little attention to these total tonnage quotas, taking guidance in the acceptance of orders from their quotas in the separate commodity comptoirs. If the comptoir committee of the EIA decided that for some particular quarter the total tonnage of steel exports should be reduced, such decisions received some attention from the individual EIA comptoirs, which, in determining their quota policies and in other matters, were naturally influenced by the general business policy of the EIA's comptoir committee. Thus, the tonnage program scheme, if it worked at all, worked indirectly. The scheme was originally devised because of the absence of cartelization in all significant steel commodities. The need for it, from the cartel's standpoint, decreased as individual commodity controls were established and strengthened. Another deterrent to the effectiveness of the scheme developed with the adherence of Britain, the United States, and Czechoslovakia to the general cartel, since the tonnage program scheme did not apply to them.

The non-procedural provisions for the protection of the domestic market were achieved, in the second EIA agreement, by requiring that cartel participants refrain from exporting into each others' domestic markets without the consent of the interested national groups. Several market interpenetration agreements existed among the national groups, and individual comptoir agreements contained specific provisions in this respect.[5]

The smooth working of the EIA agreement was secured by a set of mechanisms, including the compulsory supervision of the member groups and their adherent producers and distributors, a regime of fines and compensations for exceeding and for failure to exhaust quotas and tonnage programs, deposits intended to insure the orderly performance of obligations, penalties for infractions, an agency for the settlement of disputes, a system of compulsory arbitration, and compulsory payment of administrative expenses and other contributions deemed necessary for the operation of the agreement. All these mechanisms existed in addition to those provided for in specific export sales comptoir agreements, which are discussed in Chapter VI of this volume, but in many instances one such mechanism served both the general cartel and the specific commodity comptoirs. As with all other ISC organisms, the jurisdiction over the application of these mechanisms was far from clear, and it was a matter of accepted practice that possible conflicts of authority between different bodies were to be avoided by a tacit refusal to press conflicts over authority to extremes.

Provisions for compulsory supervision as a mechanism for insuring the successful operation of the agreement obligated all national groups to exercise continuous and efficacious control in their own realm over the operations of their adherents and sales organizations, and obliged national groups to keep the EIA informed about the internal organization and operation of the national groups. In addition, member groups of the EIA as well as the central agencies of the EIA were subject to an independent auditing system, exercised by a Swiss public accounting firm, the *Schweizerische Treuhandgesellschaft,* in Basel.

The regime of compensations and fines provided for rates compensating member groups who did not exhaust quotas and tonnage programs, and payments of fines by those groups who exceeded tonnage programs and quotas. In the agreement fines were set at 3 gold shillings per long ton of crude steel value for excesses of less than 5 per cent of the quota share, 5 gold shillings for excesses of from

---

[5] Appendix V A contains such a specific statement of the extent of the domestic markets of the founder groups.

5 to 10 per cent of the quota, and 10 gold shillings for excesses of more than 10 per cent of the quota share, or tonnage program share. The same amounts were to be paid, per long ton of crude steel value, as compensation to groups which failed to exhaust similar percentages of their quotas. The mechanism of fines and compensations was expected to operate along with similar provisions instituted by the export sales comptoirs. In practice this EIA mechanism was discontinued after July 1, 1936.

According to the EIA agreement, the management committee fixed rather high deposits, placed in the custody of the EIA business agency in Luxemburg, which were intended to insure the orderly fulfillment of obligations assumed with membership in the EIA and in the comptoirs closely connected with it.

The EIA agreement provided for considerable penalties for infractions of the provisions of the agreement, and for violations of the decisions of competent EIA agencies. The penalties were meted out by the management committee, and the penalized group had the right to appeal decisions to a special committee composed of the chairmen of the national groups.

Disputes arising between groups, or between groups and EIA agencies, about the execution of the EIA agreement, or about decisions of EIA agencies, were subject to a preliminary hearing by an agency consisting of the chairmen of the national groups. If one of the parties to the agreement did not accept the decision of the chairmen of the groups, the disputants were compulsorily required to obtain a ruling on the case by an EIA court of arbitration. The system of arbitration is discussed in Chapter VI of this study. As has been mentioned several times, the mechanism of penalties, conciliation, and arbitration scarcely operated in practice.

The EIA agreement permitted quota transfers among the national groups as far as such operations did not violate the interests of other groups, and if they were announced within a specified time before they occurred. The basic arrangement of the EIA contained several such transfers.[6] According to Dr. Georg Wolff, very low rates were paid in 1933 for the transfer of one long ton quota of crude steel.[7]

The second EIA agreement listed about ten circumstances under which the agreement could be prematurely denounced. Several of these circumstances related to a possible unsuccessful settlement of the

---

[6] See Appendix Vb.

[7] Dr. Georg Wolff, "Neuordnung am internationalen Eisenmarkt," *Wirtschafts-kurve*, July, 1933, p. 171.

Saar problem, which was expected to be resolved early in 1935.[8] Disruption of the operation of export sales comptoirs was also listed as a possible reason for denouncing the agreement. Three different possibilities of disharmony among the founder groups because of their mutual interpenetration agreements were listed as reason for denunciation. Two other circumstances under which the agreement could be denounced were based on the possible rise of new outsiders of some significance within the domestic markets of national groups.[9]

The EIA and its responsible chairman, as well as its executive and business agencies, were domiciled in Luxemburg. The national groups participating in the EIA may be considered partners in an adventure of restricted duration and scope. This scope did not embrace the actual sale of steel commodities, or the earning of profits for the community of members as a whole, activities common to most ordinary business firms. The EIA concluded agreements of considerable importance, and owned property in its own name. However, all EIA transactions implied that they would be covered by concrete business transactions of its sub-entities. There was a great deal of uncertainty regarding the legal status of the EIA, which neither the participants nor the Luxemburg government cared to clarify.[10] The EIA may be regarded as having the legal status of an unincorporated association subject to the legal regulations of the Grand Duchy of Luxemburg.[11]

---

[8] The change in the political control of the Saar territory made necessary several arrangements within the EIA, causing many disputes which were only eventually settled.

[9] Art. III in Appendix V contains a denunciation clause which resembles the one in the EIA agreement.

[10] The confused legal position of the EIA is apparent in the agreement with the British Iron and Steel Federation, concluded on July 3, 1935, and included in Appendix IV of this volume. In the introductory clause of the memorandum the EIA presents itself as an entity representing the collectivity of the four founder groups. However, the four founder groups, apparently unsure of the legal status of their cartel and its power to contract in its own name, deemed it necessary to enumerate, in appendices attached to the memorandum, their member-firms for which they were "responsible." The memorandum was signed "On behalf of the *Entente Internationale de l'Acier*" by the chairmen of the four founder groups.

[11] Dr. René T. Harf (now in New York), attorney appointed to the Superior Court of Luxemburg, furnished the author the following information concerning the legal status of the EIA and the laws of its domicile. According to these laws, corporation status was conditioned by actual incorporation. The EIA was not incorporated. As far as the laws of Luxemburg were applicable (because of the location of the administrative offices of the EIA in that country), the mutual legal relationship among the members of the EIA was subject to the constitution of the EIA and the other "private" agreements. "Thus, the Entente can be compared with any agreement existing between private persons basically ruled by the chapters of the Civil Code concerning 'Contracts,

III

The written basis of the constitution of the European Steel Cartel, composed of the EIA and of the British group, was an agreement signed in London on July 31, 1935.[12] It became effective on August 8, 1935 and, pending the fulfillment of certain conditions, was to be valid until August 8, 1940. In June 1938 this expiration date, as in the case of all basic ISC agreements, was postponed to December 31, 1940. The definitiveness of the agreement was made dependent on the conclusion of accords with those export sales comptoirs which maintained close relations with the EIA, and on the establishment of export sales comptoirs for black and galvanized sheets. These conditions were fulfilled in the middle of 1936, when the British accord and therefore the ESC became definitive.

Two provisions of the British accord, besides the provisions for British adherence to the system of export sales comptoirs, are indicative of the scope of the new organization. One of them states that "The aim and object of this Agreement is to establish collaboration between the Federation [British group] and EIA in respect to their general export sales and the protection of their respective interior markets." The second establishes an executive agency called the joint co-ordinating committee, "which shall be responsible for the proper carrying out of this Agreement, and for the general supervision of the various sectional Agreements."

Collaboration "in respect to their general export sales" implied what is called general policy-determining, and also implied a common marketing control on the export market. The continental-British steel export alliance never used the name "European Steel Cartel" officially. However, because after the entrance of Czechoslovakia and Poland into the cartel no significant steel exporter in Europe remained

---

Conventions, Obligations.' " Luxemburg had adopted the French Civil Code. According to Dr. Harf, neither the Civil nor the Commercial Code of Luxemburg endowed structures similar to the EIA with legal personality. "The Entente was no 'legal entity' different from the parties which constituted it. Therefore, it could not have any representative appear in court and could not own property as the Entente, but only undivided property belonging to all its parties. In order to sue the Entente, it would have been necessary to sue all its different parties separately." Dr. Harf called attention to the fact that the government of Luxemburg could not charter corporations. In order to establish corporation status, it was sufficient for an organization to have itself listed in the registry of corporations and to publish its by-laws in the official journal. Only courts might interfere with the registration of corporations. According to Dr. Harf, there were no rulings of Luxemburg courts concerning the legal status of the EIA.

[12] The British agreement is included in Appendix IV.

outside the cartel, that organization was generally referred to as the European Steel Cartel.

A considerable part of the British agreement regulated exports from EIA countries to Great Britain, and the preferential duty treatment given these exports by British government agencies. However, that part of the memorandum need not be discussed here, since it does not concern the basic structure of the ISC.

The establishment of the joint co-ordinating committee was the sole important provision of an organizational nature contained in the memorandum. No provision was made for a chairman, a business agency, and so forth. The EIA business agency in Luxemburg operated *de facto* for the ESC as well, and the chairman of the EIA, without being formally appointed, acted as chairman at meetings of the joint co-ordinating committee. The new cartel (ESC) logically should have been superior to the EIA, because in principle the EIA was deprived of the power to decide problems of general business policy and problems concerning the coördination of export sales comptoir policy by itself. In reality the superior power of the joint co-ordinating committee developed only gradually, and only became apparent from 1937 on. Beginning with 1937, the decision of principal problems was slowly but persistently shifted from EIA policy-determining agencies to the joint co-ordinating committee of the ESC. However, there was still a large abyss between the EIA and the British group. Britain, as has been mentioned several times, deliberately maintained a conspicuous aloofness from matters which were regarded with more or less justification as continental.

In negotiations of considerable importance, like those with the United States and South Africa, the British group worked along with the representatives of the EIA. Meetings of the joint co-ordinating committee generally took place quarterly, almost always preceded by a session of the management committee of the EIA.

The British agreement set up a special conciliation and arbitration mechanism for disputes arising out of either the interpretation or the application of the agreement, or out of the interpretation or application of the agreements of the British group with export sales comptoirs. Disputes had to be submitted for conciliation to a committee composed of the chairman of the EIA and the British group. If the conciliation committee could not reach an acceptable compromise, the dispute had to be submitted to a committee of two arbitrators, one of whom was nominated by the chairman of the EIA and the other by the chairman of the British group. "If the Arbitrators cannot effect a settlement, they shall, within a month, either agree upon an Umpire or request the Chairman of the International Chamber of Commerce to appoint an Umpire. The contracting parties undertake to accept without appeal the verdict passed by the Chairmen, the Arbitrators, or the Umpire as the case may be." However, the conciliation procedure was never invoked in the formal sense, and the arbitration procedure never used.[13]

The "British agreement" was recorded both in English and French, and both languages were used within the ESC.

IV

The ISC, in the sense that it was conceived after United States producers undertook to coöperate in general steel policy-determining activities, superseded both the EIA and the ESC as the highest policy-determining body. However, if the constitution of the ESC may be designated as somewhat vague, that adjective applies even more to the comprehensive ISC from the time of its inception in January 1938 until its demise. The reluctance of steel producers to remold their cartel mechanisms according to a planned scheme and the tentative nature of the American adherence to the cartel were equally responsible for the hazy character of the ISC constitution. It was an unwritten (and unformulated) constitution in the proper sense. Provisions for the organization of the super-cartel were never formally recorded, though they can be written down with some degree of precision. Because the ISC as the comprehensive cartel lasted less than two years, it developed little tradition as an organized structure.

Two agreements concluded late in 1937 between the EIA, the British Iron and Steel Federation, and the Steel Export Association of America, which are discussed in Chapter IX of this volume, constitute the written basis of the new ISC organization. These written

---

[13] For the spirit in which the British agreement was carried out and for the methods used in avoiding even potential disputes the following example may be illustrative: "Notwithstanding the efforts made by the British steelmakers . . . to maintain their deliveries of material for export, it proved impossible to keep pace with their quota of the export deliveries of the Cartel, so that when the accounting period arrived on June 30, 1937, the British makers were in deficit of their quota by approximately 20,000 tons of plates and 12,000 tons of sections. Because of the somewhat abnormal circumstances surrounding the world position, it was decided to forego all penalties and compensation in respect of such deficits and the corresponding excesses, and the fundamentally coöperative spirit behind the Cartel was typified in this agreement." (Sir Benton Jones, "The Import and Export Trade in Iron and Steel," *ICTR*, Jan. 21, 1938, p. 100.)

agreements contained short statements about the intention of the parties to coöperate henceforth in general steel export policies, implying that the American group would be kept informed of all principal problems of general steel policy, that it would participate in the determining of general steel policies, that it would furnish and receive the customary reports about business transactions, and that agreements necessary in order to carry out the basic agreements would be made later. No provisions were made for any mechanisms with which to execute the agreements. Their cohesive force lay primarily in the fact that they could not be violated without affecting the workings of the cartel organism as a whole.

The adjustment to the ISC mechanism was made by enlarging the joint co-ordinating committee by the addition of American representatives, without abolishing the original committee as a policy-forming agency for the ESC, and without abolishing the two central agencies of the EIA. However, by introducing an enlarged joint co-ordinating committee as the highest agency of the ISC, the most important problems were shifted to its jurisdiction. If Americans had remained permanent members of the ISC, a more satisfactory arrangement would probably have been found. The American representatives did not change the original joint co-ordinating committee very much. However, other national groups gave great weight to the opinions and wishes of the American representatives. Because of the power represented by the American group, no voting occurred in the enlarged joint co-ordinating committee, where, though the American group could be persuaded, it could not be overruled.

The enlarged committee held its meetings at the same time and place as the original ESC joint co-ordinating committee. Actually, the latter would meet at a specified time and a little later the American representatives would enter the meeting, thus changing it from an ESC to an ISC committee meeting. Something like the following schedule of meetings was generally arranged for the different executive bodies of the ISC: 9 A.M., meeting of the management committee of the EIA, consisting only of the representatives of the founder group; 9:30 A.M., meeting of the management committee of the EIA, consisting of all representatives of the continental European groups; 11:30 A.M., meeting of the joint co-ordinating committee of the ESC; 12:30 P.M., meeting of the enlarged joint co-ordinating committee of the ISC. On the next day meetings of the EIA comptoir committee and of comptoir executive bodies would occur.

Like the ESC, the ISC had no chairman, domicile, or business organization such as existed in the EIA. The problem of domicile was never discussed because no such necessity ever arose. The chairman of the EIA generally acted as the chairman of the ISC, and the business agency of the EIA maintained its *de facto* routine functions even after the American adherence enlarged the cartel.

The ESC through the joint co-ordinating committee, and the ISC through the enlarged joint co-ordinating committee, operated as general policy-determining agencies when they were in session. Whether the personal and written intercourse among the leading industrialists may be regarded as a substitute in the intervals between the meetings is open to question.[14]

In 1938 a special ISC agency was established in London to coordinate commercial problems between America and the ESC. It consisted of an American delegate, a British delegate, and an EIA delegate, working under the chairmanship of a neutral trustee to coordinate commercial policies between the American and European groups during the time when the enlarged joint co-ordinating committee was not in session.

The desire to maintain a coöperative propaganda for the use of steel prompted the members of the ISC to establish an agency for that purpose. This agency was to be attached to a different national group each year. The German group, after overcoming the great reluctance of the other groups, succeeded in being the first to administer the propaganda bureau. The international bureau for promoting the use of steel applied the customary means of propaganda, especially in promoting the use of structural shapes and in attempting to counteract the propaganda of producers of commodities that might substitute for steel. The bureau was financed by contributions from national groups, computed according to actual export deliveries.[15]

There was no red tape whatsoever within the cartel administration. Important understandings were rarely signed, records were kept in the most brief and informal manner, and agreements covering very important problems were frequently oral. Whereas in most commercial relationships important activities are generally formalized and

---

[14] Within the whole ISC it was the custom to deliberate and decide even important questions by letter, telegraph, or telephone.

[15] Cf. *International Cartels,* 1939, No. 1, p. 17. Before the establishment of the international bureau, the propaganda divisions of the national groups met annually to discuss collaboration. The last meeting of a special committee for the purpose of outlining the activities of the international bureau took place early in 1939, in Cologne. See *ICTR,* Feb. 10, 1939, p. 298.

recorded in anticipation of possible conflict, no conflict growing out of the lack of documentary proof of decisions and transactions was envisaged within the ISC. Cartel members felt that serious conflicts should either be compromised, or that the dissenting parties should withdraw from the cartel, or that the whole cartel should be dissolved.

Though the basic structure of the ISC may seem clumsy to the observer, and its central agencies hazy in their jurisdiction and procedure, no such impression existed among the participants of the ISC. On the contrary, they considered the structure adequate for coping with the existing situation in steel. The fact that all important ISC agreements were to expire at the end of 1940 increased the reluctance to introduce changes in the ISC organization.

CHAPTER FIVE

National Groups

I

IN PRINCIPLE the ISC and all its entities were composed of national groups. These were intermediate units between the international cartels and the coöperating steel producers. Within the general policy-determining bodies (ISC, ESC, EIA), the national groups were supposed to include all important steel producers in their respective countries. In export sales comptoirs national groups represented all important producers of the commodity which was controlled by the particular export sales comptoir. The ISC fairly consistently applied the rule that national units in the ISC and in the export sales comptoirs had to assume responsibility for the acts of all producers of their particular products in their own countries, whether or not all producers participated in the national cartel unit. Thus when the United States entered the ISC agreement it was considered natural that the Steel Export Association of America assumed responsibility for American outsiders not affiliated with that association. When French producers entered the International Merchant Bar Entente the French national group was held responsible for the exports of those French merchant bar producers who did not participate in the arrangement.

The reason for using the national group as the basic unit in building international cartels is obvious.[1] The ISC preferred to negotiate with as few entities as possible; at the same time it did not want to interfere with the domestic, economic and legal problems of particular groups. ISC agreements made it imperative to have at least the

---

[1] Cf. William Yandell Elliott and Others, *International Control in the Non-Ferrous Metals*, pp. 22 ff. Charles W. Wright, "The Iron and Steel Industries of Europe," *Economic Paper 19*, published by the U. S. Bureau of Mines, Washington, 1939, contains information about the national cartel organization of several European countries.

passive coöperation of the respective governments of member steel producers. The national group-entity concept was the easiest method of guaranteeing this coöperation. The ISC and its entities did not care to become involved in difficulties resulting from antagonisms between producers or between producers and the government of a country. Such antagonisms could arise between low-cost and high-cost producers, or between producers who preferred the domestic and those who preferred export markets; they could be caused by competition in commodities not bound by cartel agreements. These various and conflicting problems of steel production within a country were represented in the national group or cartel, which was then represented as a single entity in the international cartel.

Sometimes national groups were kept together by government intervention. Protection of domestic markets through ISC arrangements gave recalcitrant minorities an additional reason for moderating their opposition. Nationality as the primary base in grouping cartel participants in large collective marketing controls became fairly general, whereas it did not play that role in marketing controls of the corporate type. Quotas within the ISC were mostly national quotas, as were compensations, penalties, etc. However, the principle of accepting only national groups as basic entities and of making them responsible for the actions of "their" outsiders could not be realized completely and was sometimes deviated from under the pressure of actual circumstances. As is discussed elsewhere in this study, the ISC in its negotiations with the American group had to relax considerably the principle of the assumption by national groups of responsibility for outsiders. In Belgium, particular difficulties arose with a group of so-called re-rollers,[2] whose relationship to integrated steel producers was not always harmonious. In a few export sales comptoirs, especially those for wire products and for tubes, large individual producers were member entities along with national groups in the formal sense.

Broadly speaking, the eight national groups which participated in the general policy-determining activities of the ISC were member groups in almost all of the export sales comptoirs. However, there were national groups which participated in export sales comptoirs but did not participate in the general steel policy-determining activities of the ISC. Another type of national group consisted of domestic producers who directly or indirectly made agreements with the ISC,

---

[2] The Belgian national group had special quota arrangements in several international comptoirs in order to cope with re-rollers.

setting forth the conditions under which the ISC might "penetrate" their domestic market. Finally, there were national groups, or rather producer-exporters, who in their export policy tacitly coöperated with certain comptoirs or with the ISC as a whole. National groups in signing formal agreements enumerated the firms (their member units) in whose behalf they were acting. Thus the EIA agreement, all export sales comptoir agreements, and the EIA agreement with the British groups contained a clause to the effect that the national group was acting in its own name and on behalf of the enumerated member firms. Export sales comptoir agreements also indicated that in the event of a change in the ownership of a plant, the successors were equally bound by the agreement.

The eight national groups differed in many respects, although a few similarities in their structure existed. The American group was a pure export cartel.[3] The Polish group was an export cartel, intimately connected with a domestic steel cartel, which was formally a separate body. The rest of the national groups, Great Britain, Germany, France, Luxemburg, Belgium, and Czechoslovakia, controlled, at least in principle, both the domestic and export markets of their respective countries. The eight policy-determining national groups may be classified in three categories. First, the founder groups of the EIA (Germany, Belgium, France, and Luxemburg), who played a leading role in the ISC and whose coöperation was enhanced by their geographical proximity to each other. As a matter of fact they composed a single large steel region in the western part of Europe.

National groups in the second category (Poland and Czechoslovakia) were groups associated with the ISC and they were viewed within the ISC as small states are viewed by great powers in politics. Though both associated groups were rather large exporters, they did not have the same influence on ISC policies as the other national groups. However, the ISC did its best to keep them in the cartel organization, for their uncontrolled competition might be very disruptive. Great Britain and the United States fell in the third category of national groups, which might be defined as groups whose policies were coördinated with those of the EIA. Although they did not participate very intensively in ISC policies, the coördinated groups had a rather decisive influence on them.

Alliances, friendships, treaties, and conflicts existed among the national groups in the ISC, somewhat similar to patterns in inter-

---

[3] The American participation in the ISC is treated in Chapter IX.

national politics. But as soon as an alliance threatened the interests of other groups, or as soon as conflicts became sharp, the ISC organization stepped in.

The eight national groups were supposed to control the steel export markets of their countries. In reality their organization was nowhere perfect; outsiders, recalcitrant domestic cartel members, and domestic comptoirs which were only indirectly influenced by the general cartel structure existed in their midst.

The national groups were either in themselves incorporated commercial companies or they had such commercial companies as executive agencies.[4] Several of the national groups were super-cartels, having as members domestic sub-comptoirs (sub-cartels) for particular steel commodities; several others embraced all important steel commodities directly.

II

A brief discussion of the internal organization of the eight national steel groups may be useful here. There is abundant literature treating the organization of the British, German, and French groups. The British Iron and Steel Federation, established as an unincorporated association[5] in April 1934, embodied the British national group. The Federation was organized as a super-cartel having particular commodity cartels as sub-entities. The "constitution" of the Federation did not look like a cartel agreement, but resembled the by-laws of an ordinary trade association. However, its provisions established the skeleton on which the cartel structure was based. Though Article 7 of the constitution envisaged the inclusion of members from British dominions and dependencies, including the Indian Empire, in practice the Federation was concerned only with the steel production of Great Britain. The Federation, besides being concerned with pig iron and later with the purchase of scrap, controlled British production of steel, the domestic marketing of steel, the export sale of steel commodities, and steel commodity imports from ISC members. Though the Federation operated as a private association, it was under heavy governmental influence, and it exercised the jurisdiction of a quasi-

---

[4] They mostly adopted the pattern designated in cartel literature as *Doppel-Gesellschaft*.

[5] Article 37 of the by-laws of the Federation provided for the registration of the Federation or its incorporation by Royal Charter or otherwise at any time. The by-laws of the British Iron and Steel Federation are included on pp. 102-15 of the May Report (1937).

public agency in that it was the agency which issued licenses granting a reduction of import duties to certain importers. Whereas all other national groups restricted their jurisdiction to cartel functions, having at their disposal entirely separate associations exercising "typical" trade association functions, the Federation was a trade association and a cartel. This double function was openly admitted, thus it cannot be stated that the trade association structure was used to disguise cartel functions. The British Iron and Steel Federation was the result of the concerted effort of government and industry to find a solution for the very complex situation in which the British steel industry found itself after the First World War. The British steel industry was overcapitalized and had to face the difficulties inherent in an old-established but not sufficiently modernized industry.

The following salient characteristics demonstrate the peculiar situation of the British industry through 1931:

a) high production costs in comparison with continental producers;

b) no tariff protection, thus subjecting British domestic prices to fluctuations of the world steel market;

c) a conservative currency policy, which put British producers in a disadvantageous competitive position both on their domestic market and on export markets;

d) no institutionalized, strong advantages on "imperial markets";

e) no strong domestic cartel organization; and

f) no participation in the EIA.

As a consequence of Great Britain's free-trade policy, many European producers who wanted to sell their commodities at relatively good prices and for British currency could export steel duty-free to Great Britain up to March 1, 1932. British industry complained for more than a decade that foreign competition was dictating steel prices in Great Britain, and that this resulted in such low prices that the profits of the British industry were not sufficient to cover the necessary investments and the losses frequently connected with steel exports. The introduction of a general import duty of 10 per cent ad valorem on March 1, 1932, did not satisfy the steel producers, and at their request the duties on several steel products were raised, on April 26, 1932, to 33 1/3 per cent for three months. When the steel industry asked for the extension of these duties for an indefinite period, the government urged the industry to establish a national organization as a comprehensive framework in which all of its pressing problems could be solved or considerably mitigated. The extension of tariff protection was made conditional on the establishment of such a mechanism. As a result of the request of the Import Duties Advisory Committee on June 3, 1932, the steel industry formed, during the same month, a national committee which operated with the assistance of several sub-committees. The work of organization was done by the National Federation of Iron and Steel Manufacturers, the predecessor of the British Iron and Steel Federation. This association had been constituted on November 11, 1918, as a consequence of the establishment, by the President of the Board of Trade, of a committee to embrace the British steel industry in a single association. The constitution of the new Federation was adopted on April 19, 1934, with little opposition. The British Iron and Steel Federation tied together more than thirty trade associations, some of them already exercising typical cartel activities, and provided for the establishment of joint agencies to coördinate policy. The purposes of the Federation are contained in Article 4 of the Constitution. A few of them should be cited here: "to provide suitable means for adjusting matters in dispute within the Industry by arbitration; to exercise such measure of coordination in matters of general policy and matters affecting more than one Affiliated Association as is necessary or desirable to secure the orderly progress or working of the Industry; by agreement with any Affiliated Association to provide, or assist in the provision of, services of general benefit to members of that Association; to assist any Affiliated Association in any measures calculated to promote the efficient organization of the section of the Industry with which it is concerned; to organize and regulate in consultation with the Affiliated Associations concerned the control and disposal of imports of iron and steel products; to coöperate with Affiliated Associations in promoting or regulating the export trade in iron and steel products"; and "generally to take such lawful action whether alone or in conjunction with any other persons, as may be considered desirable for the protection and advancement of the interests of the Industry."

These provisions imply rather than actually call for typical cartel activities, though they provide for the necessary coördination common to collective marketing controls. Because the Federation for one reason or another wanted to maintain the appearance of a trade association, as contrasted with a trading association, it established an incorporated commercial company with limited liability, the British Iron and Steel Corporation Limited, as an executive agency which acted as a central buying and selling agency.[6] This corporation con-

---

[6] The Welsh Plate and Sheet Manufacturers Association continued to act as the central selling agency for tin plates in the export markets, and in the galvanized sheet

stituted a quasi-department of the Federation.[7] The executive officers of this corporation were practically identical with the officers of the British Iron and Steel Federation.

The form and internal organization of the Federation were quite unique in cartel history.[8] This distinctiveness was furnished by its relation to the government, to its members, to the trade, and to ultimate consumers, and by its peculiar internal organization.

The Federation covered practically all of the British steel industry.[9] The Association could not exercise self-government in the proper sense either by limiting production, by fixing prices on the domestic market, or by definitely prohibiting the establishment or enlargement of plants. The British Government exercised considerable influence on price and import policies, and it watched carefully to see that the Federation did not unduly limit the desired expansion of steel production.[10] An illustration of the views of the British Government in regard to steel price policies is contained in the *May Report:* "Unduly low prices have a crippling effect in that they prevent the maintenance of plant at a high level of efficiency or the raising of new capital for development, and may in the long run prevent the attainment of lower economic prices by improved methods. The main incentive to the formation of associations in the past has been the desire by collective action to secure that prices shall be at a sufficiently remunerative level. On the other hand, a reasonably low level of prices is of importance to the whole country, since iron and steel in some shape or form play a part in practically every industry, are largely exported, and are the materials of a very wide range of manufactured exports. In addition to its effect on consuming industries, there is a danger that the maintenance of a high level of prices in a protected industry may diminish

---

trade the Oriental Steel Company was responsible for all sales in India, and the British Sheet Marketing Company Limited controlled sales in New Zealand.

[7] Sir William Larke, "The British Iron and Steel Industry," *Stahl und Eisen,* Sept. 17, 1936, pp. 1068 ff.

[8] A comprehensive discussion of the working methods of the British cartel may be found in the paper of James Henderson, "The Manufacture, Sale, and Use of Iron and Steel in Great Britain," *Year Book of the American Iron and Steel Institute* (New York, 1936), p. 154. Mr. Henderson wrote, "There is far-reaching organization within the British iron and steel industry today for the purpose of price-fixing, regulation of selling conditions in the home and export markets, and of carrying on corporate policy."

[9] The pig iron industry, the Sheffield steel trade, the wrought iron trade, the South Wales Siemens steel trade, and the tin plate and sheet trade were controlled by independent associations (*May Report,* p. 19). However, it may be assumed that even in regard to these trades the Federation had a considerable influence.

[10] The procedure for treating proposals in regard to the expansion of plants is discussed on p. 35 of the *May Report.*

its vitality and initiative by removing the main incentive to progress. Violent and rapid fluctuations in price create serious difficulties for consuming industries as well as for producers themselves. Price discrimination, again, in the form of premiums or rebates, may be a potent factor in assisting consuming industries, e.g., in export trade. . . ."[11] British steel-consuming industries demanded lower steel prices and other benefits for steel used for products designed for export, in line with the policy practiced extensively in Germany and other central European countries. The Central Stabilization Fund of the Federation was intended to assist and expand the export of steel products and the export trade of manufacturers using steel products as their raw material.[12]

The British cartel was based on uniform delivered prices on the domestic market and on an elaborate quota scheme allotted according to the products and associations involved.[13]

---

[11] *May Report*, p. 47.   [12] *Ibid.*, p. 54.

[13] Belgian domestic steel prices were the lowest in Europe. The British domestic price situation is well illustrated by comparing indices of the two price levels of steel commodities. (Source, *Bulletin d'Information et de Documentation*, 1939, Numéro Spécial, "Situation Economique de la Belgique, 1938," p. 35.)

BASIS: AVERAGE THROUGH 1930 = 100

Date	Indices of British-Belgian disparity	Date	Indices of British-Belgian disparity
1931	Jan.-Sept. 15.1	1936	Jan. 25.6
	Sept. 22.3		Apr. 23.1
	Oct. 4.6		July 26.4
1932	Jan. 4.5		Oct. 18.6
	Apr. 25.8	1937	Jan. 14.5
	July 27.0		Apr. 6.0
	Oct. 14.5		July 10.4
1933	Jan. 14.2		Oct. 5.2
	Apr. 10.9	1938	Jan. 6.4
	July 8.2		Feb. 5.8
	Oct. 3.7		March 5.8
1934	Jan. 8.2		April 7.1
	Apr. 4.6		May 6.4
	July 2.7		June 5.3
	Oct. .... −1.8		July 5.2
1935	Jan. 1.2		Aug. 4.2
	March .... −1.9		Sept. 2.5
	Apr. 33.1		Oct. 1.1
	July 29.0		Nov. .... −0.1
	Oct. 26.0		Dec. .... −0.5

A few weeks before the British entered the international cartel (Apr. 1935), the disparity changed from −1.9 to 33.1. Dr. Burgin, Parliamentary Secretary to the Board of Trade, stated in Parliament that "the Federation had exercised a very strict control of prices. Had there been a free market prices would have sky-rocketed, and the consumer would have been very badly off, indeed. Under the Cartel arrangement the

The relationship between Great Britain and the EIA was established on a rather permanent footing by an agreement signed on July 31, 1935. The agreement was submitted to Parliament,[14] and the necessary legislative measures making possible the licensing of imports were approved in connection with the Finance Bill of 1936. The accord with the EIA envisaged the conclusion of several sectional agreements with those export sales comptoirs in which Great Britain did not directly participate as a member. It further anticipated the establishment of comptoirs for black sheets and galvanized sheets, important among steel commodities produced in Britain. All these conditions were fulfilled before the agreement was definitively approved in August 1936.[15] The British steel cartel, though under strong government influence, was still a voluntary association, no British producer or merchant being required by law to join. As Frederic Benham put it, ". . . it is a monopoly based on the consent of the member firms."[16] Several provisions in the by-laws of the Federation as to objectives and working methods were never actually realized. Those concerning the Central Stabilization Fund were applied mainly after the outbreak of the Second World War.[17] The system of licensing imports which was brought into operation Novem-

---

Iron and Steel Federation had maintained prices considerably below the prices in other countries." *ICTR*, Mar. 26, 1937, p. 581.

[14] The agreement, together with several other important papers, is included in a document presented by the President of the Board of Trade to the House of Commons in June 1936—*The British Iron and Steel Industry*, Memorandum on Clause 6 of the Finance Bill, 1936, London, 1936, Cmd. 5201. A former temporary agreement, signed in April 1935, and valid only until Aug. 8, 1935, dealt only with imports. *The Times* (London), June 17, 1935. *The Economist* (Aug. 3, 1935, p. 227) prefaced its account of the new steel agreement as follows: "Happy days are here again for the British Iron and Steel Industry."

[15] The quota relationships of 1936 between the British group and the EIA members were as follows:

	EIA	*Great Britain*
Semifinished steel	95.96	4.04
Structural shapes	90.91	9.09
Merchant bars	91.326	8.674
Thick plates	69.710	30.290
Medium plates	86.759	13.241
Universal steel	61.175	38.825
Tube strips	93.350	6.650
Hoops and strips	82.249	17.751
Wire rods	98.92	1.08

See also *The Economist*, Aug. 1, 1936, pp. 217-18; *The Times* (London), July 18, 1936; and *ICTR*, Jan. 15, 1937, p. 123.

[16] *Great Britain under Protection*, p. 199.

[17] See *The Economist*, Nov. 2, 1940, p. 559.

ber 4, 1936, as a basis of international steel relations worked effectively.[18] Under this system licenses were issued to foreign producers who might thereupon ship to Britain, at lower import duties, a certain amount of their commodities, based on the volume of their national steel exports to Britain in 1934. Since most of the British imports of 1934 were obtained from EIA groups, the licensing system, which was prerequisite to the entrance of Great Britain into the EIA, was the means used to grant almost exclusive concessions to EIA groups.

Among the national groups of large steel-producing countries, the British steel cartel ranked as one of the strongest and most cohesive organizations. Great Britain's participation in the ISC was a peculiar one because of her double relationship to the cartel as an exporting member and an importing buyer.[19] Great Britain's steel exports were to a considerable extent directed to her dominions and dependencies. She was particularly interested in reducing competition on these markets. Her moderate success at imperial conferences (in-

---

[18] This working method is discussed in detail in Burn, *op. cit.,* pp. 450 ff. See also the *Annual Report of the British Iron and Steel Federation for 1937* (London, 1938), p. 176. Sir Benton Jones, Chairman of the United Steel Companies Limited, wrote about the operation of the licensing system in *ICTR,* Jan. 21, 1938, p. 100, as follows: "The complete arrangements under which steel products, imported under quota certificates, are purchased by the Federation and then in effect handed back to the Cartel for distribution in this country in consultation with the Federation have worked well in spite of difficulties resulting from delayed deliveries. The allocation of quota certificates in itself involves considerable organization. It will be remembered that Belgium, France, Germany and Luxemburg agreed to waive as between themselves their 'most favoured' nation rights in regard to the issue of certificates in order that the Cartel might adjust their individual exports to this country as circumstances require. It was also necessary to arrange for the authorities in other countries benefitting from the quota scheme to coöperate on behalf of their exporters." W. Y. Elliott envisaged the probable amendment of the basis of the licensing system and thus the changing of the original British-EIA agreement, when he suggested in 1938: "Certain very valuable bargaining concessions such as entry of American steel into the British market at advantageous tariff rates seem to be possible at this time." "A Joint Policy for Britain and the United States," *Political Quarterly,* IX, 180.

[19] The agency in charge of exercising supervision over the operation of the British Iron and Steel Federation, the Import Duties Advisory Committee, expressed full satisfaction in June 1937, "that the quota arrangements had benefitted producers and consumers of iron and steel in this country by facilitating the equitable distribution of imports. . . . The country had," the Committee said, "been enabled to secure the main bulk of its requirements on favourable terms, thus keeping home prices at a reasonable level at a time when prices in the export markets were rising to very high levels." (Sir Benton Jones, in *ICTR,* Jan. 21, 1938, p. 100.) See also *ICTR,* Jan. 15, 1937, pp. 108, 123. The wartime role of the British Iron and Steel Federation is discussed by G. D. N. Worswick, "British Raw Material Controls," *Oxford Economic Papers,* Apr. 1942, pp. 2 ff.

cluding Ottawa) in securing decisive preferences on these markets made imperative further efforts to attain additional protection through ISC arrangements.

III

Among the national groups called founder groups the Belgian was the weakest as to its internal structure.[20] This group was embodied by the *Comptoir de Vente de la Sidérurgie Belge,* "Cosibel," established the very last day before the second EIA agreement became effective, May 31, 1933. Until that day a coöperative society, *Le Groupement des Hauts Fourneaux des Aciéries Belges, Société Coopérative,* was the bearer of rights and duties for the Belgian steel producers' collective. This group continued to exist, the Cosibel constituting the executive agency of the group.[21] The Cosibel was organized in the form of a coöperative commercial company, with a nominal capital of five million Belgian francs, and operated as a selling agency on the domestic and export markets. It did not directly control all products included in the ISC. Its jurisdiction extended to semifinished steel, structural steel, merchant bars, thick plates, medium plates, universal steel, and black sheets.[22] Other Belgian steel products were administered by specific Belgian domestic comptoirs which represented the producers of these other commodities in the international comptoirs. The internal structure of the Belgian national group was relatively the most vulnerable of all ISC national

---

[20] In a meeting at Liége on Sept. 12-13, 1930, Belgian steel producers decided to dissolve most of the comptoirs operating as agencies controlling exports.

[21] E.g. the agreement with Great Britain (July 31, 1935), lists this Belgian company as the "representative" of the Belgian group.

[22] The operation of the Cosibel may be illustrated by the following table based on data published by the Cosibel itself in the report "La Situation Economique de la Belgique en 1938," p. 39 in *Bulletin d'Information et de Documentation,* 1939. Here the comptoir lists not only the steel commodities which it controlled but the extent (in metric tons) to which it handled these commodities on both the domestic and export markets.

In metric tons:

	Domestic	1938 Export	Total
Semifinished	244,949	100,488	345,437
Structural shapes	49,797	38,606	88,403
Merchant bars	138,715	291,892	430,607
Thick plates	60,164	93,637	153,801
Medium plates	16,466	12,236	28,702
Universal steel	8,686	4,646	13,332
Black sheets	29,797	64,699	94,496
Total	548,574	606,204	1,154,778

group structures, but at the same time it was the most aggressive national group within the ISC. Its tenacious methods of bargaining and the obstructive tactics of Belgian producers in establishing and modifying international agreements became proverbial.[23] The predominant role which steel exports played in the national economy and in the economics of the particular Belgian entrepreneurs was the principal reason for this aggressiveness. Another sore point for the Belgian national group was the problem of so-called "re-rollers." Many plants which did not produce their own raw material at all or which had only inadequate steel-producing facilities had rolling facilities. These plants did not join the domestic cartel as full-fledged members. The agreement of the Belgian national group with the EIA stipulated that the Belgian group should arrange its own agreement with these re-rollers.[24] The Cosibel wanted to be the selling agency for the re-rollers as well as for the other members of the domestic cartel. Re-rollers made this concession dependent on rebates which steel-producing industries were to furnish them in their purchases of semifinished steel. According to a report originating at the end of 1933, the Cosibel proposed a rebate of 20 per cent of the official domestic price of semifinished steel. This the re-rollers rejected as insufficient.[25] Though later on an agreement was reached with the re-rollers, they remained a potential threat to the cartel during its whole existence.

On May 1, 1922, a customs union between Belgium and Luxemburg was arranged. As a result, the price policy of the Belgian group on the domestic market was to be strictly harmonized with the policy of the Luxemburg group.

The external structure of the Luxemburg national group, like that

---

[23] Alfred Plummer quotes an opinion concerning Belgian steel negotiations, stating that "The Belgian motto is: 'We are not satisfied.' It is a great motto, and it has carried them far." *International Combines in Modern Industry* (London, 1938), pp. 129-30.

[24] According to a report of the Belgian National Bank, there were in Belgium at the beginning of 1933 twenty-three "independent" re-rollers with six rolling mills for blooms and billets, twenty rolling mills for structural shapes, and fifty-six rolling mills for plates and sheets, whereas the plants with steel-producing facilities had thirteen rolling mills for blooms and billets, forty-nine rolling mills for structural shapes, five rolling mills for wire rods, and twenty-two rolling mills for plates and sheets. "La Situation Economique de la Belgique en 1933," *Bulletin d'Information et de Documentation,* Apr. 25, 1934, p. 255. Though these figures do not represent the real relationship between the two groups, because the capacity and modernity of plants is not the same, they show that the Belgian re-rollers played a considerable role on the national steel scene.

[25] *Bulletin d'Information et de Documentation,* Dec. 25, 1933, p. 414.

of its Belgian sister group, took the form of a coöperative commercial company, *Le Groupement des Industries Sidérurgiques Luxem-bourgeoises, Société Cooperative,* incorporated in Luxemburg. This cartel consisted practically of three main members.[26] The ARBED played the dominant role among these three member works, and the trading company of the ARBED, the *"Columeta" Compagnie Luxem-bourgeoise Métallurgique Société Anonyme,* was *de facto* the executive agency of the Luxemburg cartel. The Luxemburg group was regarded as the heart of the whole ISC first because it exported about 90 per cent of its production (including the part sold on the Belgian market), second because the highest EIA functionaries were furnished by the Luxemburg group, and third because Luxemburg housed the EIA administrative offices and one of the most important export sales comptoirs, the one for merchant bars.[27] This dominating position received the general support of other national groups because of the political neutrality of Luxemburg and because its government did not put any obstacles in the way of ISC policies.

The Luxemburg national group seemed extraordinarily cohesive and coöperative. Devoid of a proper domestic market, it was most interested in the existence and smooth operation of the ISC. It should be noted that among all ISC groups the Belgian and Luxem-burg groups had the lowest domestic steel prices. For all practical purposes their domestic prices moved with their export prices or were even lower.[28]

---

[26] First, the *Aciéries Réunies de Burbach-Eich-Dudelange* (ARBED), which from 1926 on was connected with its subsidiary, the *Société Métallurgique des Terres-Rouges, S.A.* whose capital it almost entirely owned. Second, the *Hauts-Fourneaux & Aciéries de Differdange-St. Ingbert-Rumelange,* generally referred to as *Hadir;* and third, the Rodange Works of a large Belgian company, the *S.A. d'Ougrée-Marihaye.*

[27] The Luxemburg steel organization was analyzed by Mr. Arthur Kippgen in an address "The Luxemburg Iron Industry," presented at the General Meeting, Sept. 13, 1934, of the Iron and Steel Institute (London). See *Journal of Iron and Steel Institute,* CXXX (1934), 11 ff. A rather early report about the structure of the Belgian and Luxemburg steel industry was published in *Trade Information Bulletin* No. 736 (1930).

[28] According to a Cosibel report the following price indices of steel products show the relationship between Belgian [and Luxemburg] domestic and export prices:

BASIS: AVERAGE 1930 = 100

Monthly average	Belgian domestic market	Export market
1928	110.37	109.50
1929	112.57	112.19
1930	100.–	100.–
1931	77.45	76.31
1932	56.39	55.96
1933	58.88	58.72
1934	59.49	57.33

The French steel industry had been organized into several cartels before the First World War. A general cartel of steel producers was established for the first time in 1920.[29] It had as its legal framework an incorporated joint stock company, the *Comptoir Sidérurgique de France, Société Anonyme à Capital Variable*. In 1921 the *Comptoir Sidérurgique* ceased to be active as a cartel, though it continued to exist as an inoperative incorporated company. The *Comptoir Sidérurgique* was revived in October 1926 as bearer of the rights and obligations of the French national group in the first EIA agreement, though the formal reconstitution of the French national group may be set as late as December 17, 1926. The national comptoir consisted of a general policy-determining division and of particular sub-comptoirs for rails, tubes, wire rods, structural shapes, and semi-finished steel. Each of the particular comptoirs was divided into a section for the domestic market and another for the export market. After 1930 the *Comptoir Sidérurgique* partially disintegrated, in that it ceased to exercise any influence on general French steel policies. On January 22, 1932, the *Comptoir Sidérurgique* was reorganized on a new basis, using as a framework the corporate structure of the old joint stock company. It was again referred to in the second EIA agreement as the French national group. After its reconstitution in 1932, the *Comptoir Sidérurgique* established or reëstablished sub-divisions for semifinished steel, structural shapes, hoops and strips, merchant bars, thick plates, sheets, rails, tubular products, galvanized sheets, wire products, wire rods, and tin plates. The French domestic agreement of 1932 expired on November 23, 1935, when the cartel was reconstituted with its former structure considerably reinforced. The French national group continued to be based on a double control, a general policy-determining agency on the one hand, and a set of comptoirs for particular products on the other. It accepted the German system of *Gruppenschutzklausel*, partly practiced by the British and other national groups, which considerably restricted the enlargement of plants by the member units even in regard to articles which were not controlled by the international or national cartels. An arbi-

---

1935	63.04	67.84
1936	72.04	80.61
1937	97.90	106.34
1938	110.50	113.57

Cf. *Bulletin d'Information et de Documentation*, 1939, "La Situation Economique de la Belgique 1938," p. 34.

[29] See C. Nattan-Larrier, *op. cit.*, pp. 158-175, and J. Tchernoff, *op. cit.*, pp. 135 ff.

tration college consisting of three persons (independent experts) who determined quotas, which were to be adjusted to particular circumstances, was a special feature of the French cartel.[30]   These arbitrators also licensed new production.   Later on, the jurisdiction of this college was decreased somewhat, but it persisted as an important agency within the French national group.   French cartel literature often saw something democratic in the fact that the French steel cartel was based on the arbitration principle as contrasted with the authoritarian structure of the German steel cartel.[31]

French re-rollers exercised considerable pressure on international and national steel cartels, and the French groups had many difficulties in dealing with them, especially in the branch of wire products and sheets, though they were less recalcitrant than in Belgium.   Their obstructions were responsible for the delay in the establishment of disciplined domestic comptoirs for wire products and sheets.   These delays notably disturbed the operation of ISC comptoirs.   Otherwise the French national group with its large number of sub-agencies[32] worked satisfactorily.   The French group was more cohesive than the Belgian; however, it was considerably weaker than the British or German groups in internal discipline.   Cartel literature has often discussed the role played in French steel policies by one of the strong trade associations of the French steel industry, the *Comité des Forges de France*.   There is no doubt that a close connection existed between the *Comité des Forges* and the *Comptoir Sidérurgique*.   However, after 1932 cartel policies were directed by the *Comptoir Sidérurgique,* which had an entirely separate staff and which did not exercise the customary activities of a "pressure" group.   The latter was the proper field of the *Comité des Forges,* which was often heavily attacked because of its reactionary policies.

The German steel cartel was the oldest and most thoroughly organized among the ISC groups.   As has been pointed out before, the German steel industry, even disregarding the invaded plants, ranked second only to the United States in the production of steel, and with few exceptions ranked first among the steel-exporting countries.   In many comptoirs Germany had the largest quotas.   This European

---

[30] This arbitration college somewhat resembled the board of arbitration provided for in the American powder pool which was established in 1886. See Lewis H. Haney, *Business Organization and Combination* (New York, 1934), p. 195.

[31] See André Piettre, *L'Evolution des Ententes industrielles en France depuis la Crise* (Paris, 1936), pp. 28-29.

[32] The fifteen French sub-comptoirs are listed in Piettre, *op. cit.,* p. 157. *ICTR,* Jan. 12, 1934, p. 67, discusses difficulties with French re-rollers.

superiority, gained in an embittered fight[33] against Great Britain, which was envisaged by Bismarck after the introduction of high customs duties on steel, was carefully guarded by the German government and cartel. The German steel industry originally comprised many large integrated enterprises, but after 1920 the process of amalgamation and integration became vigorous.

The *Stahlwerks-Verband Aktiengesellschaft,* an incorporated joint stock company, was the framework of the German cartel organization. The particular commodity cartels were separately organized groups, but operated as subdivisions of the general cartel. These subdivisions were based on a practically uniform pattern. The following introductory clause of a subdivision agreement is illustrative of this pattern: "The firms signing this agreement establish hereby a partnership *(Gesellschaft des bürgerlichen Rechtes)* under the name of Merchant Bar Association. The following agreement is concluded hereby among the partners and between the partnership as a collective on the one hand, and the *Stahlwerks-Verband Aktiengesellschaft* on the other. . . ." Save for the domestic comptoirs for tubular products,[34] that for wire rods,[35] and that for wire products, the *Stahlwerks-Verband* controlled all the separate steel commodity cartels.[36] In addition, the old structure of the *Rohstahl-Verband,* which did not exercise proper cartel activities, was included as a subdivision of the *Stahlwerks-Verband.* It performed functions somewhat similar to the discarded crude steel quota system in the old EIA agreement.

The *Stahlwerks-Verband* and most of its subdivisions were reestablished on a new basis on December 20, 1929, effective February 1, 1930. The comptoir for thin sheets joined the organization as late as 1932. The main agreement was preceded by the buying up of the last small outsiders who in 1929 accounted for about 3 per cent of all German steel production.[37] Thus the German national group controlled 100 per cent of the domestic steel production of Germany and

---

[33] Cf. Carl Graeff, *op. cit.,* p. 6.

[34] *Röhrenverband G.m.b.H.* and *Grossröhrverband G.m.b.H.*

[35] *Drahtwalzwerke A.G.*

[36] Cold-rolled hoops and strips were not subject to the *Stahlwerks-Verband* scheme. They were squeezed into that form as late as 1938 under government pressure. The organization of the *Stahlwerks-Verband* is discussed in *25 Jahre Stahlwerks-Verband* (Düsseldorf, 1929), *passim,* and *ICTR,* Mar. 10, 1939, p. 458. The new compulsory organization of the German steel industry and its recent expansion are discussed by C. W. Wright, *op. cit.,* pp. 6, 13-14.

[37] It is interesting to note that two of the outsiders were controlled by the Viag group, whose shares were mainly owned by the German government. See Carl Graeff, *op. cit.,* p. 30.

was thus placed in a particularly strong position in negotiating international agreements. The *Stahlwerks-Verband* could be regarded as the general steel policy-determining agency even in regard to those comptoirs which did not join in the narrower sense. All sectional agreements within the general cartel were concluded uniformly for a ten-year period.

All German steel producers were required to sell products regulated by cartel agreements to the *Stahlwerks-Verband,* which was virtually their exclusive selling agency. Each cartel member had a quota allotment on the domestic market, and most of them on both the domestic and export markets.

The *Stahlwerks-Verband* bought the commodities produced by cartel members and subsequently sold them on the domestic and, either directly or indirectly through subsidiaries, on the export market. The returns from these sales, after the cartel's administrative expenses had been deducted, went into a "common pot," of which there was one for each cartelized commodity. The average price of the commodity covered by a particular pot was then computed, and producer-members were paid at that average rate for the commodities they had sold to the cartel. Because prices were frequently lower on the export than on the domestic market, those producers interested only in domestic sales objected to the common pooling of returns from both markets, which naturally reduced the average return on commodities sold on the domestic market. A minimum average return was generally agreed upon by cartel members. If low export prices reduced the average return below this minimum, arrangements were made for the larger producers to export on their own account under the supervision of the cartel, thus keeping the average price from declining too sharply. The producers who exported under such disadvantageous conditions were compensated by the fact that the much-sought-after foreign exchange garnered by such transactions was deposited to their accounts in the German National Bank, to be used for the foreign purchase of their necessary raw materials. However, when export prices reached levels higher than average returns, the difference had to be put into the common pot for distribution among all members. As in other European countries, there was a strictly administered basing-point system in Germany.

The cartel operated under a provision which prohibited its members from enlarging production and from introducing the production of new articles which were protected for other members, even if these new articles were not subject to cartel control, unless the cartel gave

its approval to such an enlargement. This provision could be renounced on January 1, 1935. At that time several members had to
be put under heavy pressure in order to keep them from taking
advantage of the right to renounce this provision.

Coöperation among the several divisions of the cartel was based
on the "all or none" principle. This implied that the dissolution of
the subdivision might disrupt the whole structure. If a single commodity cartel, disregarding that potential sanction, decided to dissolve,
a three-fourths vote within the *Rohstahl-Verband* could compel it to
continue its existence within the organization.

The German government, especially after the advent of Hitler,
exercised particular influence on the export policies of the cartel.
Probably one of the main reasons for this influence was the need for
foreign exchange.

IV

The Czechoslovakian national group was the most comprehensive
structure in the ISC, due to its organization as one single unit, represented by an incorporated joint stock company which controlled both
the domestic and the export markets. This company, the Sales Corporation of United Czechoslovakian Steelworks,[38] a cartel registered
according to the Czechoslovakian cartel law, unlike other national
cartels, had no sub-comptoirs, though its quota system was divided
into a global crude steel quota scheme and into particular steel commodity quotas. Tubular products, wire products (IWECO), cold-
rolled steel, and the purchase of scrap were not within the jurisdiction
of the main cartel; but the fact that they were controlled by participants in the main agreement made for a coördinated policy. The
Czechoslovakian state-owned steel works were ordinary cartel members with a crude steel quota of 3.608 per cent. Thus, whereas one
high official of the Ministry of Commerce exercised authority as a
representative of the public interest, another high official (of the
Ministry of Public Works) participated in cartel activities as a representative of the state-owned steel works. All cartelized products were
sold through and by the cartel. The cartel paid average net returns
to its members, thus pooling the business transactions of all its members according to products. Somewhat as in Germany, if a member
wanted to participate in low-priced export transactions, which the
cartel regarded as unattractive for the sake of the common account,

---

[38] *Prodejna Sdružených Československých Železáren.*

the cartel performed those transactions for the account of that particular member, without charging them to the general pool.

Czechoslovakia took part in the first EIA agreement from January 1, 1927 on, and was not regarded as an unfriendly outsider even during the time when she was not bound to the EIA by a formal general agreement. For many years the Czechoslovakian group administered several central and eastern European agreements for the EIA and for several comptoirs, acting as their expressed or tacit trustee. Until she joined the second EIA agreement formally, on January 1, 1937, Czechoslovakia participated in the general policy-determining functions of the cartel, but in those commodities whose specific comptoirs she did not join before the end of 1936, she moderately competed with her cartelized colleagues. From that time until its end, Czechoslovakia was a member of all ISC comptoirs, except for the tin plate and the newly established cold-rolled bands comptoirs, from which she remained a not very important outsider, and the semifinished steel comptoir, where her position as an outsider was modified by hazy agreements concerning general coöperation and by permanent negotiations concerning her eventual entrance into the comptoir. Without reluctance, the EIA conceded a special position on southeastern European markets and in Italy to Czechoslovakian, Austrian, and Hungarian exporters, since the western groups were not particularly interested in delivering commodities paid for by means of clearing systems. Several cartel relationships between Czechoslovakia, Poland, Germany, Hungary, and Austria were regulated on the basis of particular accords. Because of gradually worsening political relations, the common quota systems of Czechoslovakia with Hungary and Austria disintegrated.

The quota position of Czechoslovakia, by special agreements with the particular EIA comptoirs, effective from July 1, 1934, was approximately as follows:[39] thick plates, 8.764 per cent, medium plates, 5.877 per cent, and universal steel, 2.451 per cent. By agreements effective from January 1, 1937, Czechoslovakia was given a merchant bar quota of 5 per cent, a structural steel quota of 2 per cent, and a hot-rolled hoops and strips quota of 3 per cent. The Czechoslovakian group could ask financial compensation for non-exhaustion of quotas only if it did not attain a quota of 4.373 per cent in merchant bars, 1.632 per cent in structural steel, and 2.256 per cent in hot-rolled hoops

---

[39] Czechoslovakia was the sole group in the EIA without any crude steel quota. When she formally entered the cartel in 1937, the crude steel quota scheme was no longer effective.

and strips. Other comptoir agreements gave Czechoslovakia a quota of 4.4 per cent in black sheets, with compensation if she did not attain a quota of 2.4 per cent in this commodity; and a quota of 0.5 per cent in galvanized sheets, with compensation if 0.1 per cent was not attained. Czechoslovakia had an IRMA quota of 1.788 per cent, with a guaranteed minimum export of 43,500 long tons in a pool. In wire rods Czechoslovakia's quota was 7.690 per cent, and in addition certain quota-free exports to Russia were included in the agreement, while her IWECO quota was 6.03 per cent.

The Munich agreement deprived Czechoslovakia of its steel works in the Sudeten area and in the Olsa region. The ISC made several attempts to settle the resulting quota transfer through a Czechoslovak-Polish-German Committee, but a final settlement was never reached.[40] No particular changes were made in Czechoslovakian participation as a result of the German invasion.

The Polish National Group in the ISC was an export cartel, similar in many ways to the Steel Export Association of America. The Export Association of Polish Steel Works[41] was an incorporated commercial company with limited liability. It operated, of course, in close connection with the Polish domestic steel cartel. Special flavor was given to Polish cartel policy by the fact that government-owned plants dominated the Polish steel industry, and that public authorities gradually exerted more and more influence on cartel policies. In 1938 government influence on steel policies seemed even more intensive than in Germany.

Many attempts were made to gain Poland's coöperation in international steel policies, for the relatively small Polish group was deemed a "dangerous" outsider. In July, 1935, Poland finally joined the second EIA structure as an associated group, with a crude steel global export quota share of 4.197 per cent in the EIA. At the same time Poland became a member of the renewed IRMA, with a relatively high share of 10 per cent, which was limited downwards by

---

[40] According to *Bulletin d'Information et de Documentation,* Numéro Spécial, "La Situation Economique de la Belgique en 1938," p. 29, the Czechoslovakian merchant bar quota was reduced to 3.50 per cent and the structural shapes quota to 1.337 per cent, on Oct. 1, 1938, due to territorial changes made by the Munich "agreement."

[41] The official Polish title was *Zwiazek Eksportowy Polskich Hut Zelaznych Sp. Z.O.O.* The Polish domestic cartel, *Syndikat Polskich Hut Zelaznych Sp. Z.O.O.,* was established in Katovice in 1926. The official cartel publication, *Statystyka Karteli w Polsce,* Warsaw, 1935, contains on pages 50-51 the names of Polish domestic steel cartels, on pages 82-83 international cartel connections. Poland had several specific cartel agreements, especially with Germany. See *ICTR,* Jan. 15, 1937, p. 123.

a guaranteed minimum of 45,000 tons and a maximum of 70,000 tons in an IRMA "pool." Besides, Poland received certain quota advantages in her rail exports to Germany. Poland entered the EIA comptoirs January 1, 1936.[42] The Polish position in comptoirs was approximately as follows:

Commodity	Per Cent of Quota
Merchant bars	4.233
Thick plates	1.746
Medium plates	3.375
Universal steel	7.156
Structural shapes	2.224
Hot-rolled hoops	2.420
Black sheets	3.000
Galvanized sheets	2.670
Wire rods	6.940
IWECO products	7.2478

In the semifinished steel comptoir the Polish quota was 0. This, in ISC terminology, meant that Poland was bound to coöperate at least negatively, and to pay penalties for exported quantities.

As a result of the Munich agreement, Poland occupied several large Czechoslovakian steel plants. Attempts to settle ISC quota questions between the interested groups were unsuccessful. The Polish group provisionally obtained a global quota, but it is doubtful whether a definitive solution was found before the distintegration of the ISC.

The structure of the eighth policy-determining national group of the ISC, the American group, is discussed separately in Chapter IX.

V

It seems appropriate to include in this chapter a description of those ISC connections in other countries which did not participate in the cartel's general policy-determining activities.

Among the steel-exporting countries of this type, Austria, with one dominating steel enterprise, collaborated with the ISC, whereas Hungary's two producer-exporters were divided in their attitudes toward

---

[42] *ICTR*, Jan. 15, 1937, p. 123, listed quotas which differ somewhat from those mentioned here. According to *ICTR*, a total quota of 350,000 crude steel tons was allocated to Polish exporters for conversion into exported finished products.

the ISC. Canada,[43] India,[44] and Australia maintained friendly relations with the ISC, although they occasionally "disturbed" the export market. It was, in the opinion of some experts, only a matter of one or two years' effort to make these countries parties to formal ISC agreements. Japan, a large customer of the ISC, exported very little. For a short while Japan participated to a certain extent in the comptoir for tubular products and slight but unsuccessful attempts were made to induce her to coöperate further.[45] Italy delivered only a few products to foreign countries and bound herself, though with small quotas, by five comptoir agreements. Sweden was an importing market of the ISC; however, it competed occasionally with ISC groups. The main exports of Sweden were alloy steel products, not subject to ISC agreements. Negotiations were carried on for several years to gain the formal coöperation of Swedish producers, but were obstructed by the lack of a domestic cartel organization in the Swedish steel industry.[46] Norway was an importer of steel, and one of her small works, *Christiania Spigerwerk,* Oslo, was bound to the EIA by a penetration agreement. Spain produced 500,000-1,000,000 tons of steel annually, without exporting any of its production.[46a] South

---

[43] *ICTR,* Jan. 15, 1937, mentions a "working arrangement" between the ISC and the Canadian steel industry regarding Canadian steel exports. This arrangement was probably an oral one.

[44] The ISC contemplated sending a delegation to India to induce the large Tata Steelworks to coöperate with it. See *The Economist,* Dec. 24, 1938, p. 675.

[45] According to *Rapport sur la Situation de l'Industrie et du Commerce,* Année 1936, Chambre de Commerce du Grand-Duché de Luxembourg (Luxemburg, 1937), p. 59, the first contact concerning the general coöperation of the ISC with Japan had been established in 1936. *ICTR,* July 3, 1936, p. 32 and Aug. 21, 1936, p. 306 discusses this matter. According to *ICTR,* Jan. 15, 1937, pp. 123-24 "the Japanese [steel] industry is awaiting the time when it has a more assured position in the steel export trade before committing itself to a more or less firm agreement." *ICTR,* Jan. 21, 1938, p. 100 writes, on the basis of information received, probably from cartel sources: "With an annual output of 7,750,000 tons of pig iron and 9,000,000 tons of crude steel aimed at, Japan is not likely to prove a good market for iron and steel for many years longer, and indeed, may become an important exporter of bars and rods, rails and sheets. Her sales of galvanized sheets had been advancing particularly rapidly." As a matter of fact even with her low standard of living, Japan's steel production was inadequate for the size of her population. But cartel circles were rather anxious to include low-cost outsiders, because even with a small volume of exports such outsiders could cause heavy disturbances on steel markets.

[46] The reasons for the failure of Sweden to establish sufficient steel-producing plants are discussed by Dr. Berthold Steinhoff, *Die schwedische Eisenproduktion und Eisenerzpolitik seit der Jahrhundertwende* (Berlin, 1937), pp. 37 ff. An official EIA report complains of Swedish competition [probably the *Domnarvet* works] in Scandinavia, especially in Finland. *International Cartels,* 1939, No. 1, p. 17.

[46a] A brief factual report about the present status of the Spanish steel industry may

Africa, Yugoslavia, and Finland produced insufficient quantities of steel; however, their respective steel industries had "penetration agreements" with ISC agencies, regulating coöperation on their markets. The Soviet Union was one of the best customers of continental European exporters, and did not disturb their export markets.[47] Holland was a large importer of steel. However, it developed its own steel-producing and rolling facilities rapidly, mainly with government support.[48] It therefore became necessary to conclude penetration agreements with Dutch steel producers and re-rollers. The EIA had such agreements concerning semifinished steel deliveries with the Royal Dutch Blast Furnace and Steel Works Corporation *(N. V. Koninklijke Nederlandsche Hoogovens en Staalfabrieken),* and the *De Muinck-Keizer* Steel Works, which were rather favorable to the Dutch. In addition, negotiations were started with a newly established re-roller, the *Van Lier* Works, which rolled about 150,000 tons of structural steel and sheets.[49]

The policies of the Austrian "national group," which consisted of one large steel producer, the *Alpine Montan Gesellschaft,* were largely influenced both by the Austrian government and by the firm's predominant stockholder, the German *Vereinigte Stahlwerke* in Düsseldorf.[50] The Austrian group entered the EIA, the IRMA, and the International Wire Rod Comptoir as a member of the Central European Group. It joined the thick plate, medium plate, and universal steel comptoirs in 1934. A tacit agreement existed between the EIA and the Austrian group concerning general coöperation and market protection. The Czechoslovakian group had a very extensive pen-

---

be found in Luis Barreiro, "La Industria Siderurgica en España," *Boletín Minero e Industrial,* May 1942, pp. 135-148.

[47] However, the Soviet Union was looked upon as a "potential disturbing factor" which might start sporadic competition should the home demand of the Union decrease, or should domestic circumstances require larger amounts of foreign exchange. Cf. *ICTR,* Jan. 21, 1938, p. 100. Interesting details concerning the U. S. S. R. steel industry may be found in C. W. Wright, *op. cit.,* pp. 58 ff.

According to the *Annual Report for 1938 of the Stahlwerks-Verband,* iron and steel exports of the Soviet Union in metric tons were the following:

1934	147,900	(this figure includes 115,000 tons pig iron)
1935	367,000	(includes 331,000 tons pig iron)
1936	782,000	(includes 710,000 tons pig iron)
1937	225,000	(includes 137,000 tons pig iron).

[48] Cf. *Steel,* Apr. 29, 1940, p. 23.

[49] *Bulletin d'Information et de Documentation,* 1939, Numéro Spécial, "Situation Economique de la Belgique, 1938," pp. 27-29, and *ICTR,* March 17, 1939, p. 521.

[50] After the German invasion of Austria, the German state-owned *Hermann Göring Werke* took over the shares of the Alpine.

etration accord in the Austrian market, and divided the Balkan markets and the Italian market with the Austrian group according to a quota system.[51] The EIA made several vain attempts to induce the *Alpine* to become one of its associated groups.

The two Hungarian steel works, one private and one state owned, operated as a national group only in the IRMA. In addition, the privately owned firm, *Rimamurány-Salgótarjáni Vasmü R. T.,* was a member of the wire rod comptoir and of the IWECO. The latter steel works had a tacit agreement with the EIA for the coördination of its export policies with those of all ISC comptoirs, though the firm was not a member of the ISC. This tacit agreement was a continuation of a written agreement which the *Rimamurányi* had had with the first EIA and of a later one with the second EIA as to general policies. This second agreement expired at the end of June 1934 and was not formally renewed. The *Rimamurányi* had a common penetration agreement (administered in Prague) with the Austrian and Czechoslovakian steel works concerning exports to Balkan markets. Many attempts were made to induce both the Hungarian works to join the ISC as an associated national group.[52] The privately owned works delayed negotiations, and the state-owned steel works resisted participation. The publicly owned enterprise constituted a dangerous outsider, especially in the Netherlands. When the ship plates market in the Netherlands and in the Scandinavian countries became disorganized in 1938, American outsiders and the state-owned Hungarian steel works were considered responsible. Although no national cartel for the control of exports existed, the Hungarian national group had a solid cartel agreement for the control of the home market.

Beginning on July 1, 1937, Italy participated in the IRMA with a sliding share of one half to one per cent. She was also a member of the International Scrap Convention and had limited participation, based on special agreements, in the tin plate and tubular products cartels, and in the IWECO. However, Italy was not regarded as an exporter, but as an importer of steel. The Italian "group" was organized along "corporate" lines. The four main Italian steel-producing

---

[51] A pooling of returns existed between the two groups in regard to the export of ship plates to Italy.

[52] Hungary's steel export in metric tons (according to the *Annual Report for 1938 of the Stahlwerks-Verband*), was the following:

1933	42,361	1936	139,020
1934	73,663	1937	153,038
1935	144,231		

companies were controlled by the government-owned Industrial Reconstruction Institute and by the Metal and Engineering Guild.[53] The Italian steel industry may rightly be regarded as a typical compulsory combination. In negotiations with ISC agencies, officials of the Guild,[54] along with executives of the steel companies, always participated.

Finland had inadequate steel-producing facilities. One steel-producing plant, *Vuoksenniska,* was regarded by the EIA as sufficiently important to warrant a penetration agreement. The accord, signed in Cologne on October 28, 1937, and effective until July 1, 1939, regulated several pertinent problems. It related not only to EIA comptoirs in the narrower sense, but to IRMA products as well. The EIA obligated itself not to sell semifinished steel destined to be re-rolled to any concern in Finland except *Vuoksenniska. Vuoksenniska* promised to limit its yearly steel production to 40,000 long tons until July 1939, advising the EIA that it intended, after the expiration of this time limit, to extend its steel production to 80,000 tons annually. The *Vuoksenniska* Company promised to limit its production to rolling rails, fishplates, and semifinished steel, this latter not for re-rolling purposes. Both the EIA and the IRMA promised to take into consideration the advice of the Finnish producer before determining prices of exports to Finland, and the IRMA specially promised not to offer its products to Finnish consumers without previously advising with *Vuoksenniska.* The Finnish producer obligated himself not to export more than 5,000 long tons yearly, and to limit his exports to semifinished steel which was not to be used for re-rolling.

In 1937 penetration agreements were concluded with two other

---

[53] Fascist Confederation of Industrialists, *Fascist Era Year XVII* (Rome, 1939), p. 96. See also C. W. Wright, *op. cit.,* pp. 14 ff., H. F. Geiler, "Die staatliche Beteiligung an Italiens Metallwirtschaft," *Metallwirtschaft* (Berlin), Aug. 16, 1940, pp. 724, 726, and Antonio Santarolli, "L'industria siderurgica italiana e l'attività autarchica corporativa," *Economia Italiana* (Rome), May 1940, pp. 374-380. Italy's steel export (according to the *Annual Report for 1938 of the Stahlwerks-Verband*), may be summarized as follows:

	Rails in metric tons	Merchant bars in metric tons
1933	845	11,000
1934	8810	17,000
1935	7470	14,000
1936	4669	25,000
1937	4353	20,000

[54] Vincenzo Ardissone, President of the Fascist association of the Metallurgical Industry, was regarded as speaker for the Italian group.

small Finnish plants, *Fiskars* and *Dalsbruck*.[55] Actually, the Finnish market was mainly reserved for Germany, because of various currency problems.

Yugoslavia had several steel-producing plants, among which the government-owned steel works were most important. The Yugoslav domestic cartel was guided by the policies of the state-owned works, and a government official represented the Yugoslav steel producers in negotiations with foreign colleagues. From 1927 until the disintegration of the ISC, a penetration agreement existed between central European works and Yugoslav works, for determining prices, marketing conditions, and even for the licensing of merchants. This agreement enjoyed the tacit approval of the EIA.

The Australian "national group" consisted of one large concern, the Broken Hill Proprietary Company, Ltd., at Newcastle (N.S.W.), which a few years ago amalgamated with the Australian Iron and Steel, Ltd., of Port Kembla (N.S.W.). There were many unsuccessful attempts to make Broken Hill join the cartel. Australian exports were not very large, never exceeding 60,000 tons yearly, and were limited to plates and sheets. However, the ISC was very sensitive with respect to this outsider, which gradually developed into a full-fledged outsider. Australian exports were mainly directed to New Zealand.[56] According to a decision of the comptoir committee of January 27, 1939, a delegation was to be sent to Australia to make a satisfactory arrangement with Broken Hill.[57]

The domestic organization of the steel industry of the Union of South Africa consisted of one large and four small steel producers. The large producer, the South African Iron and Steel Industrial Corporation (ISCOR), which was predominantly state owned, acted as a price leader on the domestic market, and played a leading role in international steel negotiations. The producing capacity of the whole South African steel industry did not exceed 350,000 net tons, of which ISCOR itself produced more than 90 per cent. Most of the steel consumed by the Union was imported, especially from Great Britain. The ordinary duty on steel products was very low, and most of the steel products imported from Great Britain were admitted duty-free.

---

[55] *ICTR*, Mar. 17, 1939, p. 531, mentions difficulties with Finnish producers.

[56] C. S. Richards, *op. cit.*, pp. 439-445, discusses Australian steel policies and quotes pertinent literature. He speaks with high praise of Australian price policies, which did not result in an abuse of monopolistic powers.

[57] *ICTR*, Feb. 3, 1939, page 258. Concerning Australian competition on the export market, see *ICTR*, Mar. 17, 1939, p. 521 and July 7, 1939, p. 26.

The South African market is particularly interesting from the point of view of ISC policies. It presents an excellent example of ISC penetration, and of a penetration agreement.[58] Because of the heavy competition of imported steel, the ISCOR asked the South African government either to place heavy duties on imports, or to co-operate in a suggested agreement with the ISC. The Government of South Africa chose the second alternative. At the end of November 1935, leading executives of the ISCOR together with a representative of the Government sailed for Europe to attempt to settle the problem. According to Professor Richards, the main objects of the negotiations were: "to secure for South African Steel Producers their proper share of the steel requirements of the Union, having due regard to the capacity of the local works, their range of products and the geographical area economically served them," and "to provide for a suitable control both as regards quantity and price of steel products imported into the Union." According to Mr. Richards, the government representative "carried an official letter of authority empowering him to agree to any scheme which would satisfactorily implement these and expressing the intention of the Union Government not to allow steel to be imported at prices which would menace the success of the steel industry in South Africa."[59] The ISC was represented in the negotiations by its main groups, the EIA and the British Iron and Steel Federation. An agreement was concluded on February 4, 1936, between the ISCOR on the one hand and the EIA and the British group on the other. The general purpose of the agreement was to guarantee the protection of the South African domestic market and the collaboration of the Union in the export policies of the ISC. It was concluded for five years, subject to premature rupture if the ISC should dissolve, or "if effective measures of protection to implement the Agreement were not introduced in the Union before 30th September 1936."[60] According to the agreement, which applied to all major ISC products, South African producers had the right to supply their "own" market with 350,000 net tons per year, the rest of the market being reserved for importers "in accordance with quotas based upon the percentages of actual imports from the various different countries during the year 1934."[61] In 1934 South Africa imported 377,000 long

---

[58] South African steel policies, including steel pricing, are discussed by C. S. Richards, *The Iron and Steel Industry in South Africa,* Johannesburg, 1940. Professor Richards devoted a great deal of attention to all ISC connections and to the most important implications of international steel policies. See also *ICTR,* Jan. 15, 1937, p. 123.

[59] *Op. cit.,* pp. 384-85.   [60] *Ibid.,* p. 386.   [61] *Ibid.,* p. 387.

tons of steel, and of this volume, 25,750 long tons were supplied by the United States.[62]

The supply of 350,000 net tons reserved for domestic producers was based on the actual capacity of the South African steel works. The agreement envisaged a later determination between the ISCOR and the cartel of prices for imported steel. The agreement put a ceiling on prices of imported steel products, stating that they should not transcend respective British domestic prices, plus costs of transportation to South Africa "In order to protect South African consumers against price exploitation by overseas combines."[63] This ceiling arrangement satisfied the South African delegation, though C. S. Richards, with considerable scepticism, stated that the value of this ceiling "is of course open to doubt since the cartel would *always* have the salutory and efficient competition from American products in South African markets."[64] The South African government did not adopt the ISC proposal to license imports according to the 1934 reference period.

The ISC and ISCOR were to negotiate delivered prices for each product periodically, prices which had to be "the fair average price on the world's markets plus normal insurance and freight charges to port of discharge."[65]

Both parties to the agreement, the ISC and the ISCOR, were satisfied with the operation of the accord, and American competition (probably outside of the American-ISC agreement, or preceding it) was met by South African dumping duties.

South African critics of the agreement accused the ISCOR of pursuing its own corporate profit interests, instead of trying to keep down prices, thus openly disregarding its specific duties as a government-owned corporation. The government had a double role in all negotiations, as an agency obliged to pursue the public interest, and as a shareholder of the ISCOR. The price level based on British home prices plus shipping costs was regarded as an inordinately high standard. According to Professor Richards "The price and production Agreement with the Cartel should not be necessary, nor should it ever have been sanctioned by the Government. It has worked to the detriment of the whole country, has placed the ISCOR (and the world

---

[62] According to Richards, "The subsequent attempt at agreement on these lines with the USA and Canadian exporters was only partially successful." *Ibid.*, p. 397.

[63] *Ibid.*, p. 387.   [64] *Ibid.*, p. 389.

[65] *White Paper* of December 5, 1936, issued by the South African Department of Finance, quoted by Richards, *op. cit.*, pp. 393-94.

steel industry) in the position of a privileged Government monopolist, has shielded it from virtually all competitive influences, influences which would compel it to increase efficiency."

South African steel producers participated in the last meetings of the ISC in Liége, in July 1939. A new implementation of several points of the agreement was discussed, but the disintegration of the cartel made these negotiations fruitless.

V

The system of national groups was an indispensable feature of ISC arrangements, and was the sole system by which conflicts with national governments could be avoided. Generally the principle of protecting the domestic markets of national groups was followed; however, no national group placed sufficient confidence in either the effectiveness or the permanence of its cartel arrangements to renounce its own tariff protection. This related to both cartel members and groups bound by specific agreements. Outsiders often attempted to counteract national group arrangements. These difficulties, though a permanent feature, did not disrupt a single national group.

CHAPTER SIX

International Marketing Controls of Single Steel Commodities

(Export Sales Comptoirs)

I

DURING THE 1920's many experts on international control schemes believed that any effective marketing control in steel would require a rather complete network of specific steel commodity cartels. Later developments fully justified the opinion. The establishment of the EIA on a new basis, in June 1933, marked the realization of the final ISC system, involving the exercise of general steel policies by central agencies, and of specific marketing controls by export sales comptoirs. It is true that during the first three years of the second EIA agreement (1933-1936), the crude steel export quota system was superimposed upon the marketing controls of specific comptoirs. This system, established in Article 9 of the second EIA agreement, was practically abandoned by July 1, 1936.[1] The change proved wise especially in the light of the entrance of Great Britain and the United States into the ISC framework, since these countries would never have adopted such a complementary control scheme.

All export sales comptoirs were based on separate constitutions which did not mention the fact that the comptoirs were units in a higher entity. All comptoirs had particular quota systems, uniform prices, and common sales conditions. About ten comptoirs were based on rather similar agreements, whereas the rest differed widely. Had the ISC been organized according to a prearranged scheme, its comptoir structure would probably have followed a more logical pattern

---

[1] *International Ententes*, p. 42.

as to the division of commodities and the uniformity of constitutions. Actually the comptoirs were organized at various times as a result of the interplay of various economic necessities, and once established, maintained their form through institutional inertia. The same may be said of the relationship of the comptoirs to the main organization. The degree of subordination to general steel policy-making agencies within the ISC varied widely from one comptoir to another. Again, the actual situation was at variance with any rational plan which might have been devised; it resulted from tradition, established by fortuitous circumstances in existence when and after the various organizations were formed. Whereas several comptoirs operated as subsidiaries of the EIA organization, others claimed to be independent steel commodity cartels maintaining only friendly diplomatic relations with the central agencies. To be sure, this situation was in constant flux. The close connection of the comptoirs subordinate to the EIA was somewhat dissipated after Great Britain and the United States entered the ISC, since, with the entrance of those two countries, the EIA was no longer the principal policy-making agency within the ISC. Comptoirs formerly independent of general policy-making agencies came more closely into the ISC structure after Great Britain and the United States entered the ISC.

The legal framework of the comptoirs varied between incorporated commercial companies and loose unincorporated associations. The degree of marketing control also ranged from the general supervision of quotas and prices to the directing or managing of all important individual business transactions. However, when sales were low, and as a consequence contraventions of rules frequently occurred, even comptoirs which generally allowed a considerable degree of freedom to their members (of course within the restrictions of quotas and uniform prices), attempted to intensify their control over individual business transactions. Such tendencies on the part of the comptoirs frequently met with opposition from national groups which were anxious to maintain a certain degree of independence. Frederic Benham's assumption that "to prevent price-cutting by secret rebates, all orders had to go in the first place to a comptoir which then allotted them among the various firms" did not apply to all comptoirs or to any at all times.[2] The British and American groups especially

---

[2] *Great Britain Under Protection* (New York, 1941), p. 183. Mr. Benham considered only the six comptoirs which were subordinate to the EIA. His statement is not entirely accurate even in regard to these. As a matter of fact, in the critical period of 1938, although these six comptoirs often discussed the watertight concentration of actual

insisted on a great deal of freedom in those comptoirs which were dominated by the continental groups.

The network of comptoirs embraced nearly all semifinished and finished steel commodities. A few commodities were left outside of comptoir regulation, either because they were difficult to regulate or because attempts to bring them into the comptoir structure had so far been unsuccessful (light rails, semifinished steel for seamless tubes, bright drawn material, axles, wheels, metal tires, etc.).

Whereas many comptoirs were sub-entities of the ISC in the proper sense of the word, some were on the border line of the organization, and though references to them as comptoirs of the ISC may be subject to doubt, they are usually so considered. Probably they would have become comptoirs in the proper sense of the word had the ISC endured for a few years longer. The degree of their relationship to the ISC is the best standard for a general survey of all comptoirs. Most of the comptoirs whose central agencies were located on the European continent had a particularly close relationship with the EIA, the reasons for which are more historical than rational. The connection of Great Britain and the United States with these comptoirs never became close.

All comptoirs had domiciles and business agencies. Many of these business agencies were either attached to national groups or were under the permanent leadership of some national group. As a matter of fact, a principle which with some exaggeration might be called a "spoils system" was followed in determining the location of business agencies (headquarters) of comptoirs. This principle frequently took into account which national group was most interested in a particular international comptoir. Though it would be an exaggeration to state that national groups administered their "spoils" in a biased manner, it was well understood that having an export sales comptoir attached to a national cartel organization afforded that particular national group better information and other business advantages. Thus a distinction may be made between "national group dominated" and "neutral" comptoirs. The IWECO, IRMA, and the tin plate comptoir may be regarded as examples of the second category.

---

sales, this proposal was not adopted, at least not in that general sense. In an earlier study Benham made a similar statement to the effect that ". . . all the sales of a product must be made through the sales-office of the cartel for that product." "The Iron and Steel Industry of Germany, France, Belgium, Luxembourg and the Saar," *London and Cambridge Economic Service,* Special Memorandum No. 39 (London, 1934), p. 14.

There were seventeen sales comptoirs within the ISC framework. In addition to these, the International Scrap Convention may be regarded as an entity which might be considered within the framework although it was a buying organization. One of the comptoirs, that for tubular products, had a rather loose organization after the disintegration of its formal structure in 1935, though it gradually grew more cohesive. Some of the comptoirs were of very little importance, and their independent existence was more a matter of tradition than of business requirements.

Participants in the comptoirs were mainly national groups participating in ISC policy-making activities; however, not all members of ISC national groups necessarily participated in all comptoirs, and comptoirs had participants from countries which were not ISC national groups.[3] Several comptoirs admitted individual producer-exporters as members, and called them national groups. Even the comptoirs which recognized only national groups in the proper sense as member units included in their agreements the names of the individual firms participating in the national group.

There were typical features and activities common to nearly all comptoirs. No description of them could be as revealing as an actual agreement; for this reason the most important comptoir agreement, that of the merchant bar comptoir, is included as an appendix to this study. These features and activities may be summarized under the following points:

A. The limitation of exports by a pre-determined quota system expressed either as a percentual share for a given time period, or by fixed quantities expressed in tons.

B. Uniform prices and sales conditions, and in particular cases special prices determined by the comptoir.

C. The regulation of distribution by establishing distributor cartels, by licensing merchants and agents, and by making national groups responsible for the violations of agreements by persons participating in the distribution of their products.

D. Meeting competition and the apportionment of resultant sacrifices.

---

[3] The nomenclature in this regard was often misleading. Thus an official publication of the EIA mentioned Great Britain as "non-member" in comptoirs because Britain did not participate in the crude steel export quota scheme. *International Ententes,* p. 44. In reality Great Britain participated in the EIA comptoirs, though on the basis of specific agreements.

E. The collection and dissemination of statistical information at frequent intervals, showing quota accounts, sales, and actual price data.

F. The regulation of excess and deficit quota accounts by compensations and fines.

G. The protection of home markets.

H. Obligatory supervision of the records and documents of members.

I. The punishment of infractions and the settlement of disputes.

J. The establishment of agencies for carrying out the terms of the agreement.

All export sales comptoirs were based on predetermined shares in the market, called quotas. One of the principal duties of the comptoir was to supervise its member units, to see that they fulfilled, but did not exceed, their quotas. A very severe reporting system existed, making it possible for member units to ascertain at frequent intervals the status of their own quota balance and that of other members. Several comptoirs had sub-quota systems for particular qualities of commodities and for special markets. All quotas changed frequently, because members frequently bought, sold, or exchanged their allotments, or because the admission of new members to the comptoir necessitated a reallotment of quotas. For these reasons, quota reports used in this study are only approximate.

The maintenance of uniform prices and business conditions was a basic principle of all export sales comptoirs. Several comptoirs did not regard general measures as sufficient, and set up prices and business conditions for many individual transactions. This was always the case in periods when, and in markets where, a particular commodity was subject to a competitive struggle.[4] Many European comptoirs fixed the commissions paid by their members to intermediaries. So-called official prices, as registered in literature, were only standards to be approached if possible in concrete business transactions. However, any deviation from them was always subject to approval by the comptoir. Exceptional price situations were met by exceptional measures. Thus, for instance, in 1936, when British domestic prices of semifinished products were lower than ISC export prices, the EIA gave to the members of the semifinished steel comptoir bounties of

---

[4] See *Bulletin d'Information et de Documentation,* May 10, 1936, p. 377.

1 £ gold per ton for all semifinished products delivered to Great Britain.[5]

All comptoirs attempted to influence the conditions under which their commodities were actually sold by distributors in export markets. Control of these outlets was extremely desirable, since the distributors were potential loopholes for avoiding cartel restrictions.

All comptoirs were concerned with suppressing competition among the cartel adherents, and with meeting the competition of outsiders. It is generally assumed that the suppression of competition within the cartel was mainly effected by a regime of severe penalties. In reality, these penalties remained only potential threats, exposure at cartel meetings with its attendant possibility of retribution being the device utilized. Even in periods when violations were known to occur, it was very difficult to secure proof of them; however, the presentation of a strong case against a member reflected strongly against him, and if proved, made his position in the comptoir very precarious. Early in 1938, the circumvention of cartel prices became fairly general, and the ISC in an official communique admonished its members and distributors to adhere to their agreements.[6] Outside competition was met either by general action, of which a general price reduction was the most radical measure, or by individual competition where the cartel required one or several of its members to enter the business transaction as a competitor, cutting their prices to the level of the outsider. The cartel's regular buyers did not purchase from outsiders; however, they took advantage of outsiders' offers to force down cartel prices. Outsider competition very often required sacrifices on the part of the comptoirs. "This has led in practice to the actual pooling of all the prices obtained, which in its turn has made it possible to secure absolute equality of prices obtained among the groups."[7] Such

---

[5] *International Ententes,* p. 47.

[6] The following excerpt from this official communique, printed in *Iron Age* (Mar. 17, 1938, p. 93B) indicates the concern with which members viewed the discipline situation within the cartel. "The various groups decided unanimously to apply very severe penalties to any party who through breaking the general rules compromises that discipline which is essential. These penalties will be inflicted without discrimination either upon member firms or upon accredited merchants who fail to observe in the strictest sense the obligations they have undertaken towards the cartel."
Following this strong resolve, a special penalties committee was actually set up late in 1938. However, a notice in *ICTR* (Jan. 13, 1939, p. 64) indicates that the first general meeting of this committee had been indefinitely postponed.

[7] *International Ententes,* p. 44.

a pooling existed in certain comptoirs only among the founder groups, and was discontinued in 1938.[8]

Protection of the home markets was an indispensable device in all comptoir agreements. However, the groups among each other concluded specific protection and interpenetration agreements. The home market was defined in each particular comptoir agreement; these definitions were rather uniform. One definition of home markets may be found in the merchant bar agreement in Appendix V A.

Those comptoirs which were subordinate to the EIA conferred upon a Swiss firm of auditors, *Schweizerische Treuhandgesellschaft* in Basel, the jurisdiction to supervise and audit their records, documents, plants, and stocks in order to ascertain compliance with cartel regulations. Other comptoirs made such provisions for supervision only occasionally.

Almost all export sales comptoirs had a uniform system of sanctions intended to guarantee the smooth operation of their quota and price mechanisms. These sanctions may be divided into two categories. The first carried no punitive implications but related to the exceeding of quotas, implying that those who did not exhaust their quotas should receive compensation. Broadly speaking, the fines for exceeding quotas and compensations for not exhausting quotas were corresponding. The rates, although uniformly applied, were not uniform for all groups within the cartel and for all products. In addition there were quotas whose non-exhaustion was not compensated. The British and American groups especially had special arrangements concerning fines and compensations.

The following rates may give an approximate picture of the fines and compensations per long ton, in gold shillings: semifinished steel 15, merchant bars 20, structural shapes 20, thick plates, medium plates, and universal steel 25, hot-rolled bands 20, black sheet from 30 up, galvanized sheet 50, heavy rails 10-20, and wire rods 20. The system of fines and compensations did not mean that the comptoir had no other means (e.g. the compulsory transfer of business transactions) of compelling a national group to operate within the quota framework. The accounts of quotas were balanced yearly, and fines and compensations were determined yearly. The settling of accounts often

---

[8] There was great dissatisfaction among members who did not receive appropriate compensation for fighting outsiders. In July 1939, at what was to be the last meeting of the ISC in Liége, an attempt was made to console those who were required to meet outside competition with the promise that a new system of compensation for their losses was being considered for the current year. *ICTR*, Aug. 11, 1939, p. 214.

led to controversies. In June 1934, the EIA comptoirs reduced their fines by half, because Germany resisted payment of substantial fines for plates, France for bars, and Belgium for semifinished steel.[9] After July 1, 1936, the EIA groups in the EIA comptoirs practically abandoned the payment of fines and compensation. In June 1939, when accounts had to be settled, several groups insisted that the system of fines and compensations be applied according to agreements. The matter was under deliberation when the cartel disintegrated.[10] The exceeding of quotas or the failure to exhaust quotas was not generally regarded as a circumvention of rules. It was considered a problem of business strategy whether a group preferred to pay fines and enjoy a volume of business in excess of its quota share or to receive compensation by failing to fulfill its quota allotments. Generally, national groups preferred to acquire as much business as possible and the fines were not, under ordinary circumstances, high enough to deter exporters from exceeding quotas.

The second category of sanctions was intended to prevent and to punish violations of agreements and other comptoir regulations. Penalties, determined in the agreements, were either charges of a certain quantity of commodities, though actually not delivered, against the quota account of the offending member, thus in effect reducing his quota, or monetary penalties. Price-cutting was a typical form these violations of agreements took, involving the offer or actual sale of commodities at lower prices or under more favorable conditions than stipulated in comptoir regulations.

Comptoir agreements provided for settling disputes between members or between the comptoir and members in the first instance by conciliation, in the second instance by compulsory arbitration. The arbitration clauses of the comptoir agreements were rather brief and incomplete and it is possible that most national courts would declare them ineffective because of their incompleteness or because they might be construed as purporting to oust the courts of jurisdiction entirely. The contending parties were expected to choose arbitrators who elected a chairman of the arbitrating committee. If the arbitrators could not agree on the selection of a chairman, the latter was to be appointed by the President of the International Chamber of Commerce in Paris. To the author's knowledge no arbitration committee was ever invoked in the history of the ISC. When a rather serious

[9] See *Iron and Steel*, Report of U. S. Tariff Commission, p. 403, n. 11.

[10] See *Bulletin d'Information et de Documentation*, June 10, 1936, p. 630 and May 10, 1937, p. 391, and *ICTR*, Aug. 18, 1939, p. 251.

dispute between one of the comptoirs and the British group arose concerning the date upon which the computation of the gold value of a paper sum should be based, the presidents of the EIA and the British group settled the disagreement, in March 1939, by flipping a coin. Such a procedure, showing a slight contempt for the regular pattern of deciding disputes, was founded on the recognition that the issue arose because of the rather incomplete formulation of agreements, which could not be supplemented by the reasoning of arbitrators. Thus the arbitration procedure within the ISC comptoirs may be looked upon as a mere safety valve, which if ever put into actual operation might have indicated the faulty operation of the whole structure.

Comptoirs may be classified, according to their relationship to central agencies, into five categories.[11] First, those directly subordinated to the EIA; second, those closely connected with the EIA; third, those connected with the ESC; fourth, those having a coördinated policy with the ISC; and fifth, those whose policy was only loosely coördinated with that of the ISC. As mentioned above, the relationship of a comptoir to a central agency is the result of historical development rather than of economic factors. Thus, although the administration of merchant bar policies was specifically subordinated to the EIA, this did not mean that Great Britain or the United States (which were not EIA groups) did not participate in the comptoir.

II

A complete outline of the comptoir structure within the ISC is included in Appendix I. The following description of individual comptoirs within the ISC is necessarily of a fragmentary nature in order to confine this study to reasonable limits.

The first category, that comprising comptoirs directly subordinated to the EIA, included the comptoirs administering the markets of six products: semifinished steel,[12] structural shapes, merchant bars,[13]

---

[11] In an official publication the EIA discussed comptoirs as falling into three categories, first, "directly subordinated to," second, "more or less affiliated with," and third "independent of" the central agencies. *International Ententes*, p. 44.

[12] According to figures, published in metric tons in the *Annual Report for 1938 of the Stahlwerks-Verband,* exports of semifinished steel of major steel-exporting countries were the following:

	1933	1934	1935	1936	1937
Germany	123,163	185,255	155,916	191,000	111,000
Belgium and Luxemburg	305,580	387,283	329,255	361,107	427,036
France	289,451	352,482	240,812	289,359	278,553

thick plates, medium plates, and universal steel. They had rather
uniform constitutions, which did not indicate their particularly intimate relationship with the EIA. According to the texts of their basic
agreements, they appeared to be independent cartels endowed with
their own executive bodies. Their relationship to the EIA could be
inferred only from provisions envisaging their dissolution if the EIA
or important comptoirs of the EIA should disintegrate, and from
provisions for EIA participation in the settlement of disputes. These
comptoirs followed the ISC scheme in having founder groups, associated groups, and groups with a coördinated policy. All six comptoirs were established or reëstablished June 1, 1933, when the second
EIA agreement was put into effect.

Article VII of each comptoir constitution provided for a management committee, a separate chairman, and a vice-chairman. Further,
it set up a business agency called the central bureau for which the
chairman was responsible. In reality, the management committees
of these comptoirs did not exist, their functions being exercised in
organizational problems by the management committee of the EIA,
and in commercial questions by the comptoir committee of the EIA.
Because of this tacit delegation of functions, these six comptoirs were
classified as "subordinated" to the EIA. No chairman and vice-
chairman existed in the proper sense; the functions of these officers
were exercised by the national group to which each comptoir was
attached. The largest of the comptoirs, that for merchant bars, was
attached to the Luxemburg group; that for semifinished steel to the
Belgian group; that for structural shapes to the French group, while
the ententes for thick plates, medium plates, and universal steel were
administered together by the German national group. These last
three comptoirs were referred to in cartel jargon as the "Centitol"
group. Only the thick plate comptoir was important among the

Great Britain	27,230	28,306	20,922	15,017	44,017
U. S. A.	3,209	19,900	40,420	21,742	341,353

There is little doubt that the rapid increase in semifinished steel exports of the United
States was caused by the conspicuous increase of prices for semifinished steel in 1937.

[18] Major steel exporting countries exported the following quantities of merchant
bars, in metric tons, according to the *Annual Report for 1938 of the Stahlwerks-Verband:*

	1933	1934	1935	1936	1937
Germany	319,766	538,390	568,260	628,807	773,247
Belgium and Luxemburg	929,969	1,026,581	1,015,178	809,857	1,068,706
France	1,049,314	1,268,810	696,760	581,557	702,955
Great Britain	117,859	188,488	223,003	208,886	215,987
U. S. A.	25,017	47,627	57,203	53,921	143,627

three, because of the volume of its exports, particularly that of ship plates. The latter was a particularly difficult commodity to handle due to the fact that buyers were themselves large entrepreneurs versatile in exploring all trading possibilities. The thick plate entente collaborated closely with the merchant bar comptoir on prices and deliveries of the steel sections controlled by the latter which were necessary for shipbuilding purposes.

There were several quota systems within the six comptoirs. The main quota system arranged the sharing of the market among the founder groups, while special quotas were arranged for associated and coördinated groups. The following table gives an approximate picture of the percentage distribution of the quotas of the founder groups by the six comptoirs as of January 1938:

	Semifinished steel	Structural shapes	Merchant bars	Thick plates	Medium plates	Universal steel
Germany	21.541	30.426	29.655	46.184	32.655	51.497
Belgium	24.298	13.110	28.719	42.779	32.935	38.484
France	39.396	38.689	12.560	8.473	13.651	10.019
Luxemburg	14.765	17.775	29.066	2.564	20.759	—
	100.000	100.000	100.000	100.000	100.000	100.000

These quotas underwent a change during 1938, largely as a result of the German invasion of Austria and the consequent increase of German quotas. According to a Belgian report[14] these quotas were, at the end of 1938, the following:

	Semifinished steel	Structural shapes	Merchant bars	Thick plates	Medium plates	Universal steel
Germany	26.276	30.703	31.097	47.659	33.019	52.134
Belgium	22.832	13.058	28.173	46.606	32.756	37.979
France	37.018	38.535	12.300	8.241	13.578	9.887
Luxemburg	13.874	17.704	28.430	2.494	20.647	—
	100.000	100.000	100.000	100.000	100.000	100.000

At the same time, the Belgian report indicates, the following special quotas were allotted to Czechoslovakia, Poland, and Great Britain:

	Semifinished steel	Structural shapes	Merchant bars	Thick plates	Medium plates	Universal steel
Czechoslovakia .	—	1.992	4.926	8.764	5.847	2.419
Poland	—	2.213	4.315	3.293	3.356	7.056
Great Britain ...	3.450	9.478	8.606	30.340	14.285	37.915

[14] *Bulletin d'Information et de Documentation,* "La Situation Economique de la Belgique en 1938," p. 29. The reported quota participation in thick plates seems to be erroneous.

These quotas were derived from those of the founder groups, each of the latter surrendering an amount proportionate with his share of the original quota. The Belgian report also indicates that with the detachment of the Olsa region from Czechoslovakia after the Munich agreement, the Czechoslovakian quota in merchant bars was reduced to 3.500 per cent, and its structural shapes quota to 1.337 per cent.

The marketing system of the International Thick Plate Entente was the most complex among these six comptoirs. The first thick plate entente had disintegrated in December 1932 due to Belgian and French competition.[15] The reëstablished comptoir concluded an agreement with the British group regarding shipbuilding material, effective January 1, 1934, giving it a quota participation of 25 per cent and reserving imperial markets for it. This agreement was twice prolonged until the British entrance into the ISC.[16] The comptoir also had a special agreement with Austria. The entente did not succeed in disarming the Hungarian State Steel Works which remained a dangerous outsider. It also had difficulties with American outsiders even after concluding an agreement with the Steel Export Association of America, effective January 1, 1938. The agreements binding all six comptoirs in this category expired June 30, 1938. Renewed agreements, to expire at the end of 1940, were of course interrupted by the outbreak of war.

III

The comptoirs in the second category were closely connected with the EIA. Their policies were often heavily influenced by the comptoir committee of the EIA but they maintained their separate business administrations. Only those for wire rods and for hot-rolled bands and strips were important among them.

The International Wire Rod Entente was established as an unincorporated association on October 1, 1927. Its business office was attached to the administrative organization of the steel works in Ougrée-Marihaye, Belgium. The accord concluded among the founder groups in 1927 operated with several suspensions and monthly prolongations until the end of 1931. Beginning with January 1, 1932, a new agreement was concluded, effective until December 31, 1936. This agreement among the founder groups regulated not only exports

---

[15] *Bulletin de l'Institute des Sciences Economiques,* Feb. 1933, p. 236.
[16] *ICTR,* Jan. 12, 1934, p. 60. *The Economist,* Jan. 13, 1934, p. 63.

but also part of the domestic output, according to a preëstablished tonnage program system. The founder groups experienced great difficulties in attempting to renew the comptoir agreement after its expiration at the end of 1936, mainly because of difficulties between French wire rod producers (members of the entente) and wire products producers. These difficulties still existed in June 1938 when the EIA agreement was prolonged, but were removed with the establishment of a domestic comptoir among the French wire products producers in May 1939, after which the formal agreement maintaining the international entente was renewed.[17]

The Central European Group, consisting of Czechoslovakia, Austria, and Hungary, joined the International Wire Rod Entente on January 1, 1933, with a joint quota. They had coöperated even earlier in respect to uniform prices. Great Britain joined the entente in 1935, and the United States in 1938.

The wire rod comptoir worked in close connection with the international wire products cartel (IWECO). The wire rod comptoir deliberately limited the number of its direct customers (Sweden 4, Norway 5, Denmark 1, Finland 4, Holland 5, Switzerland 2, Italy 6, Brazil 1, Mexico 1, etc.) because most of the members were also producers of wire products and in this way tried to lessen competition in the field of wire products. It had special marketing organizations in a few countries, particularly in Bulgaria.

The wire rod entente was merely an export cartel in respect to those national groups which were not founder groups of the EIA. The founder groups of the EIA had a quota system embracing not only exports of wire rods, but also deliveries to domestic producers which were destined to be exported in the form of wire products. These mixed quotas comprised, in June 1939: Germany 47.6637 per cent, Belgium 22.9729 per cent, France 19.6094 per cent, and Luxemburg 9.7540 per cent, whereas the pure export quotas of the continental groups at that time were 29.0589 per cent for Germany,

---

[17] *Bulletin d'Information et de Documentation,* Numéro Spécial, "Situation Economique de la Belgique, 1938," p. 29.

Wire rod exports of major steel exporting countries are listed in metric tons as follows in the *Annual Report for 1938 of the Stahlwerks-Verband:*

	1933	1934	1935	1936	1937
Germany	44,608	39,287	42,526	37,674	59,431
Belgium and Luxemburg	209,328	220,707	141,965	161,169	246,598
France	136,446	153,888	128,807	110,017	132,046
Great Britain	5,292	1,840	6,369	3,051	—
U. S. A.	17,147	24,112	26,510	35,430	60,971

17.5251 per cent for Belgium, 33.1872 per cent for France, 7.2561 per cent for Luxemburg, 7.2478 per cent for Poland, 3.9814 per cent for Czechoslovakia, and 1.7435 per cent for Hungary.[18]

The only other comptoir of any magnitude among the five in the second category of comptoirs was the International Hot-Rolled Bands and Strips Entente which was reëstablished along with the six EIA comptoirs on June 1, 1933, with an agreement similar in pattern to that of the EIA comptoirs. Because of the peculiarities of the commodities involved in this entente, marketing control was rather difficult. The EIA founder groups constituted the core of its organization. The rest of the ISC groups were attached to the main accord by specific agreements. The quotas were as follows in 1938:

	Per cent
Germany	28.34
Belgium	44.29
France	15.60
Luxemburg	11.77
	100.00

Czechoslovakia had a special quota share of 2.97 per cent and Poland 2.40 per cent.

The comptoir for cold-rolled bands and strips was administered together with the comptoir for hot-rolled bands. It was established January 23, 1939. Because of difficulties among the group of German producers of cold-rolled bands, the establishment of this organization was postponed several times. Finally the intervention of the German government made the new arrangement possible. Before its formal establishment, the cold-rolled bands entente operated informally, without Germany, for eight months. It took as its base for the establishment of quotas the exports of the first half of 1937. These quotas were: for Germany, 58.08 per cent; Belgium, 23.98 per cent; France, 12.00 per cent; and Luxemburg, 5.94 per cent. According to a report of the Belgian National Bank, the International Black Sheet Comptoir only agreed to the establishment of the cold-rolled bands comptoir in October 1938.[19] If this report is true, the permission of the black sheet comptoir was probably conditioned on the limitation of competition between the two interrelated products.

---

[18] *Bulletin d'Information et de Documentation, 1939,* "Situation Economique de la Belgique, 1938," p. 29.

[19] *Bulletin d'Information et de Documentation,* Jan. 25, 1939, p. 40.

The International Wide-Flange Beams Entente was established February 26, 1934, by producers in Luxemburg, Germany, and France. It was an unincorporated association with very little formal organization, and was relatively unimportant among the ISC comptoirs. Due to the fact that wide-flange beams were rolled by only a few mills, control of the export market was not difficult.[20]

The International Sheet Piling Association was an inconspicuous comptoir, with a small turnover. It fixed quotas and prices for sheet piling. There are very few facts available concerning its operation and organization; however, the official report of the EIA lists it with the group of "independent" comptoirs.[21]

IV

The third group of comptoirs collaborated with the European Steel Cartel (ESC) in general steel policies though it carefully maintained its independence. Of the two comptoirs in this category, the International Black Sheets Comptoir was of most consequence. Established, after considerable effort, on August 1, 1936, as an unincorporated association with headquarters in London, its organization was a condition of British adherence to the ISC. The permanent chairman of the comptoir was the largest British producer of sheets. This comptoir had been preceded by many temporary arrangements concerning black sheets, but the complexities inherent in the thin sheet market had made the establishment of a definitive arrangement very difficult. Even at the time of the establishment of the comptoir, there was no organized French national sheet group in the proper sense. The domestic French comptoir was not established until November 17, 1937.[22]

The black sheets comptoir faced considerable difficulties from outside competition. American exporters, particularly, took advantage of the higher prices which resulted from its activities. The cartel succeeded in making arrangements regarding the sharing of markets with the largest American exporters only in the second part of 1938.

The quota distribution in the comptoir, in June 1938, was as follows: Great Britain, 31.98 per cent; Germany, 22.86 per cent; Belgium, 22.42 per cent; Luxemburg, 9.70 per cent; France, 7.64 per

---

[20] Cf. *ICTR*, Mar. 2, 1934, p. 380, André Piettre, *op. cit.*, p. 150, n. 1, and *International Ententes*, p. 44.

[21] *International Ententes*, p. 44.

[22] *ICTR*, July 16, 1937, p. 118, and Nov. 26, 1937, p. 907.

cent; Poland, 3.00 per cent; and Czechoslovakia, 2.40 per cent. These quotas were adjusted after July 1, 1938, in favor of Belgium and Poland.[23]

The introduction of the continuous strip rolling process revolutionized the sheet rolling industry and constituted another difficulty which the comptoir faced in attempting to control prices and markets.

The International Galvanized Sheets Comptoir was a small comptoir organized precisely on the same lines as the International Black Sheets Comptoir. Both comptoirs were administered by the same people, according to similar plans. Meetings of the two comptoirs regularly followed each other. The quota participation of this group, in June 1938, was as follows: Great Britain, 52.55 per cent; Germany, 5.99 per cent; Belgium, 36.52 per cent; Luxemburg, 1.16 per cent; France, 1.01 per cent; Czechoslovakia, 0.10 per cent; and Poland, 2.67 per cent.[24]

V

Comptoirs in the fourth category were those which were entirely independent as organizations but whose policies were coördinated with those of the ISC. The International Railmakers' Association (IRMA), a comptoir in this category, may be said to have been the "aristocrat" among the comptoirs in the ISC. It was the oldest, the best disciplined, and the best administered comptoir in the organization. The IRMA preceded the organization of the ISC by many decades. It was an unincorporated association, whose affairs were handled by a public accounting firm in London, according to well-established principles of business administration. The modern IRMA organization was established by a comprehensive agreement concluded on March 12, 1926. Special agreements were also concluded with the American, Central European, Polish, and Italian groups. Besides provisions for a business agency, the accord set up an all-powerful management committee and a permanent "London Committee." The maintenance of quotas, prices, and other regulations was much more rigidly supervised within the IRMA than in other comptoirs. Not only was the system of fines and compensations actually operative, but an additional device against the violation of quota and price regulations existed in the comptoir's practice of allot-

---

[23] *Bulletin d'Information et de Documentation,* Numéro Spécial, "Situation Economique de la Belgique, 1938," p. 32. Czechoslovakia had in reality a quota share of 4.4 per cent, with compensation if she did not attain 2.4 per cent in this commodity.

[24] *Ibid.,* p. 32.

ting individual orders to the different member groups. Thus, all inquiries regarding the purchase of heavy rails and track material exceeding 250 tons were reported to the London Committee, which then designated the national groups which were to fulfill orders as well as the prices and conditions under which orders were to be accepted.[25]

The fact that representatives of all members were present in the London Committee, meeting at least once a week, made it possible not only to handle negotiations in this manner, but also to secure a degree of coöperation and continuity unique among large international cartel organizations. All relevant decisions were voted upon by the London Committee, the number of votes determined by the size of quotas.

The management committee of the IRMA held meetings quarterly, generally in conjunction with ISC meetings. It decided major organizational problems, including amendments to the constitution of the comptoir, and fixed minimum prices which served as standards for the London Committee. Each member of the comptoir was represented in the management committee.

Besides the national groups which constituted the membership of the IRMA, two individual Belgian producers had special quotas. One was the steel works in Ougrée-Marihaye owning rail-rolling plants in Belgium, France, and Luxemburg, which had a common quota for its whole concern, independent of the quota of the national groups. The second Belgian firm was Beame and Nimy, which had a fixed quantity quota for track material only.

The IRMA administered the export of all heavy rails (thirty-six pounds or more per yard), except grooved rails for tramways and cranes. Exports of fish plates and certain other track material were also subject to the control of the IRMA.

After the First World War, in 1925, Great Britain, Germany, France, and Luxemburg began to coöperate informally on the rail export market. In the spring of 1926 they established a business agency in London, attached to the public accounting firm of Peat,

---

[25] Exports of heavy rails and track material of major steel exporting countries in metric tons, according to the *Annual Report for 1938 of the Stahlwerks-Verband.*

	1933	1934	1935	1936	1937
Germany	93,965	138,900	270,000	252,832	215,205
Belgium and Luxemburg	83,341	117,895	129,060	99,120	186,180
France	152,915	199,000	117,270	73,980	116,412
Great Britain	93,716	167,108	163,337	212,708	211,700
U. S. A.	55,897	87,467	62,952	87,740	172,315

Warwick, Mitchell, and Co. The United States joined the agreement by a special accord on April 1, 1929; the Central European group entered this cartel on January 1, 1927; Poland, October 1, 1935; and Italy on July 1, 1937. In March 1935 the agreement was renewed for three months only. This provisory prolongation was due to the difficulties connected with the entrance of Great Britain into the ISC organization. The conditional prolongation implied the possibility that the EIA members might overthrow the IRMA agreement if they failed to reach a general agreement regarding the participation of Great Britain in the ISC. After Great Britain's entrance, the IRMA agreement was prolonged for five years. British claims for a major quota increase were satisfied mainly by a quota cession from the United States.

With the entrance of Great Britain into the ISC, the IRMA became more closely related to that organization. This intimacy increased further after the United States' entry into the ISC.

After February 1937, but before the entrance of Italy, quota participation in the IRMA was as follows: Great Britain 28, the United States 12.471, France 14.421, Germany 15.603, Belgium 6.940, the Ougrée group 4.303, Luxemburg 3.282, Czechoslovakia 1.788, Austria 0.734, Hungary 1.740, Beame and Nimy 1.306, and Poland 9.412 per cent.[26]

The other comptoir categorized as "coördinated in policy with the ISC," was that for drawn wire and wire products called the International Wire Export Company *(Compagnie Internationale pour l'Exportation des Produits Tréfilés, Société Coopérative, IWECO)*, established in the form of an incorporated commercial company on January 1, 1932, in Brussels. As early as 1927, German, Belgian, Dutch, and Czechoslovakian producers agreed to coöperate to protect their domestic wire products markets. Later, other national groups and firms joined this alliance, which was extended to insure uniform prices. However, no strong cartel with centralized selling of products was established until January 1, 1932. The IWECO was the most cohesive comptoir in the ISC.

While the activity of most of the comptoirs was limited to directing the general conditions under which members were to transact business, or at most, as was true of the IRMA, to requiring permission of the comptoir before an order could be accepted and filled

---

[26] According to *Kartell Rundschau,* 1929, No. 5, the quota shares before the First World War were: Great Britain 37.36, U. S. A. 25.70, France 4.47, Belgium 12.34, and Germany 20.13 per cent.

by a member, the IWECO transacted all business deals itself, obtaining the supply from its members and delivering it to consumers. Returns were pooled in the IWECO and then allotted to members.

Another factor influencing the effectiveness of the comptoir was its close connection with the comptoir controlling the supply of raw material necessary for the manufacture of IWECO products. The International Wire Rod Entente which controlled these raw materials adjusted its price and delivery policies to the needs of the IWECO.

Despite the existence of an extremely well-instrumented organization, the IWECO had many difficulties in controlling the export market. These difficulties arose principally from the activities of producers outside the comptoir both in exporting and in importing countries. Since the drawing of wire and the production of wire products require a relatively small investment, and, in comparison with other steel products, production methods are relatively simple, competition arose easily.

The IWECO was established by the German and Belgian wire products cartels[27] and by two Czechoslovakian firms, four Dutch firms, one Hungarian, and one Danish firm. The agreement extended from January 1, 1932, until December 31, 1936, at which time it became impossible to negotiate another permanent agreement, mainly because of the opposition of Belgian and French members. Agreements for short periods continued to exist. The differences with the Belgian group were settled early but those with the French group were not resolved until May 1939, when the French rejoined the IWECO and a permanent agreement was concluded.[28]

The original quotas established in 1932 were: Germany 53.37 per cent, Belgium 35.17 per cent, Holland 3.96 per cent, Denmark 0.61 per cent, Czechoslovakia 6.03 per cent, and Hungary 0.86 per cent. Later on, agreements were made with France, affording it a quota of over 5 per cent; and there were agreements with English and United States' producers as well as with producers of other countries.

Although the IWECO was a commercial company, it was governed by a management committee under the direct management of a hired executive. It was dominated mainly by the German group, though its headquarters were in Brussels.

---

[27] The German cartel was known as the *Drahtverband Gesellschaft m.b.H.* located in Düsseldorf, and the Belgian one as the *Société Coopérative Union des Tréfileries et Clouteries Belges,* in Brussels.

[28] *ICTR,* May 26, 1939, p. 940; *Ibid.,* June 30, 1939, p. 1134.

VI

The three comptoirs listed in the fifth category of comptoirs, those whose policies were only loosely coördinated with those of the ISC, were those involving tubular products, tin plates, and scrap.

The International Tube Convention was temporarily established on April 13, 1929, by British, American, and Canadian producers in conjunction with the Continental Tube Cartel. It included several accords. First, a general export agreement which covered merchant tubular products, especially gas pipes and similar tubes; second, an oil agreement covering oil pipes; and third, a South African market agreement covering pipe exports to the South African Union. Along with these agreements a special accord was concluded between the Continental Tube Cartel and the British group concerning the protection of domestic markets and exports of locomotive tubes. In April 1933, the International Tube Convention was extended to include boiler tubes. On April 15, 1933, Swedish tube producers entered the international agreement. Effective September 3, 1933, the French group as a trustee of the international cartel concluded a penetration accord with the Japan Steel Tube Company. This agreement was intended to last until July 1937. Later the Continental Tube Cartel entered into a separate agreement with the Japan Steel Tube Company.[29] Because of the distintegration of the Continental Tube Cartel, the International Tube Convention dissolved itself on March 12, 1935, at a meeting in Brussels.

After its disintegration many attempts were made to reconstitute the International Tube Convention, which were only partially successful. A network of informal oral understandings concerning the maintenance of prices grew out of negotiations with the United States. The European groups even attained quota agreements without succeeding in reëstablishing the former strong cartel. From the very beginning, the International Tube Convention revolved in its structure and operation around a core, the Continental Tube Cartel. The failure of the latter to reorganize on strong lines was responsible for the lack of success in reorganizing an international tube comptoir, in spite of the fact that many groups actively promoted such a reorganization.

The International Tube Convention covered only gas pipes and similar tubes, oil pipes, and so-called boiler pipes, whereas the Con-

---

[29] Cf. *Iron and Steel*, Report of the U. S. Tariff Commission, p. 285 and *International Ententes*, pp. 51 f. Also see TNEC, *Hearings*, Part 20, pp. 10926 f.

tinental Tube Cartel embraced nearly all kinds of tubes. The International Tube Convention was concerned only with tube exports, whereas the Continental Cartel embraced, until the time of its disintegration, both the domestic and export markets. The International Cartel was based only on quotas and uniform prices, whereas the Continental Tube Cartel pooled export returns.[30]

The origin of the Continental Tube Cartel may be traced to a cartel agreement between Germany and Czechoslovakia concluded in the summer of 1925. One large Polish producer joined this agreement in October 1925. The actual Continental Tube Cartel was established on June 11, 1926. At that time the original groups were joined by the French group and the sole existing Hungarian tube producer. In November 1927, the remaining Polish producers joined the agreement. Even before the establishment of the International Tube Cartel, the Continental Tube Cartel coöperated to a certain extent with Stewarts and Lloyds Tube Works in Glasgow. On April 1, 1930, the Continental agreement was extended and adjusted to new conditions. This new agreement embraced the following six groups, designated within the organization by the first six letters of the alphabet: A—*Röhrenverband G. m. b. H.,* Düsseldorf; B—Central Office of Czechoslovakian Tuberollers, in Prague; C—*Huta Batory,* in Hajduky-Wielkie (Poland); D—*Comptoir Franco-Belgo-Sarrois pour la vente des tube d'acier à l'exportation, S. A.,* in Paris; E—Manfred Weiss, in Budapest; and finally F—those Polish producers who did not belong to group C, united in the Selling Office of Polish Tube Rollers, *z.o.o.,* in Katovice.

According to a cartel publication, the objective of the Continental Tube Cartel as set forth in paragraph 1 of its agreement was:

a. The determination of sales quotas. b. The reservation of the domestic markets for the competent members. c. The determination of export prices and the assurance to producers of average profits from export sales. d. The determination of the markets with reference to geographical position of the plants. e. The rational specialization of management. f. The standardization of tube types and the simplification of technical conditions of delivery.[31]

---

[30] Cf. *International Ententes,* p. 54. The first Continental Tube Cartel agreement is published almost in its entirety in *Bulletin Hebdomadaire d'Information et de Documentation,* May 21, 1927, pp. 510-512.

[31] *International Ententes,* p. 52.

Both the Continental Tube Cartel and the International Tube Convention were administered by a business agency attached to the German domestic tube cartel.

The formal reason for the disintegration of the Continental Tube Cartel was the difficulty which arose in adjusting quotas after the incorporation of the Saar region into Germany. In reality the cartel was doomed to failure because of the difficulties inherent in international marketing schemes embracing domestic markets also. Though attempts were made early in 1935 to confine the activities of the cartel only to exports, no agreement could be reached concerning German export quotas.[32]

At the time of the dissolution of the tube cartels the parties to the agreement expressed their intention to protect each other's domestic markets. Later on, European continental producers and British and American tube makers agreed upon prices and subsequently on quotas, without establishing a formal comptoir comparable in business organization with the earlier one. In 1939, just prior to the disintegration of the whole structure as a result of the war, it appeared likely that a new organization would be established, with as great a degree of organization as the old comptoir.[33]

The International Tin Plate Association was an unincorporated association administered by the same public accounting firm as the IRMA, in London. A control committee consisting of representatives of all member firms was in charge of managing the cartel. The tin comptoir was more independent of ISC policies than any other comptoir; as a matter of fact, its relationship to the ISC was established more by literature than by facts.[34] The predecessor of the association was a rather simple organization composed of the tin plate exporters of Great Britain and the United States, who divided the total exports in a ratio of 70 per cent for Great Britain and 30 per cent for the United States. This accord was concluded in 1928 and disintegrated in 1931.[35]

---

[32] *Ibid.*, p. 54.

[33] Cf. *International Ententes*, p. 55. Laurence Ballande, *Essai d'étude monographique et statistique sur les ententes économiques internationales*, Paris, 1936, pp. 34 f. *Iron and Steel*, Report of U. S. Tariff Commission, pp. 384 ff. *The Times* (London), May 6, 1938, p. 23. *The Iron Age*, Mar. 23, 1939, p. 59. *ICTR*, Jan. 27, 1939, p. 218 and July 28, 1939, p. 144. *Bulletin d'Information et de Documentation*, Mar. 1939, p. 194, and *ibid.*, Numéro Spécial, "Situation Economique de la Belgique, 1938," p. 32. Ervin Hexner, "American Participation in the International Steel Cartel," *Southern Economic Journal*, July, 1941, p. 61.

[34] See *Iron and Steel*, Report of the U. S. Tariff Commission, p. 391, n. 65.

[35] *Ibid.*, p. 391.

The International Tin Plate Association was established on July 1, 1934, to be effective for three years. It was then extended until June 10, 1938, when a new agreement, to extend to June 30, 1941, was made.[36]

The United States, Great Britain, Germany, and France were regular members of the cartel. Italy and Norway joined the association on the basis of special accords and Belgium joined in 1938 with a yearly participation of about 24,000 long tons.[37]

Though the tin plate cartel was a relatively strong organization, its price policy had to take into account outsiders, particularly Czechoslovakia.

The third organization whose policy was loosely coördinated with that of the ISC was, in contrast with other comptoirs, a buying comptoir concerned with the purchase of scrap for steel production, thus restricting the buying activities of individual steel makers and of national groups. (It is understood that the main source of scrap was the United States.) The International Scrap Convention was established on March 11, 1937, for the purpose of preventing scrap buyers (steel works and their organizations) from bidding against each other in purchasing imported scrap. There was even a provision for rationing imports for countries based on a reference period (1934-1936 average), if scrap should become scarce. The convention was administered by its permanent president who was the managing director of the British Iron and Steel Corporation in London.[38] Though ISC agencies did not influence scrap policies directly, according to the president of the scrap convention, "The policy involved is fundamentally integral with that of the International Steel Cartel."[39] The members of the convention were Great Britain, Germany, Italy, Sweden, Poland, Czechoslovakia, Austria, Hungary, Rumania and Yugoslavia.[40]

The rapid displacement of iron ore by scrap as the most important steel ingredient has occurred in the last two decades and prices of scrap have reacted violently on demand.[41] The convention did not

---

[36] Cf. TNEC, *Hearings*, Part 20, p. 10928. This last agreement had not been signed, though it was operative. Mr. Bash designated it as a "proposed" agreement. *Ibid.* See *Iron Age*, Aug. 4, 1938, p. 58.

[37] *Bulletin d'Information et de Documentation*, Numéro Spécial, "Situation Economique de la Belgique, 1938," p. 32.

[38] *The Economist*, Mar. 9, 1940, pp. 424-25, severely censured the past scrap purchasing policy of the British Iron and Steel Corporation.

[39] *ICTR*, Mar. 24, 1939, p. 551.

[40] The U. S. Tariff Commission mentions a report of an informal scrap agreement with Japan. *Iron and Steel*, Report of the Tariff Commission, p. 381.

[41] A very instructive chart comparing widely fluctuating scrap prices with frozen

attempt to stabilize purchasing prices, it aimed to eliminate disadvantages due to buyers' competition at times when there occurred a real or imagined scarcity.[42]

The United States Tariff Commission described the convention as follows: "The cartel members agree to buy all foreign scrap exclusively through the cartel's representative, the British Iron and Steel Federation in London; transgressing members are fined 1 pound for each long ton purchased independently. Administrative expenses are defrayed by a levy on transactions."[43] In the words of its president, I. F. L. Elliott, ". . . the Convention fulfills the important function of pooling knowledge as to all surplus supplies, of focusing the import requirements of members, and of thus matching supply and demand by the shortest and most economical route." The interest of the ISC in the scrap convention was indicated by Mr. Elliott in stating, "It might become exceedingly difficult for the Cartel [ISC] to maintain prices for steel in the export markets at a level calculated to promote consumption and to guard against a mushroom growth of indigenous plants if the cost of the principal raw materials became excessive."[44]

A month after the convention began to operate, principal shipbreaking firms held a meeting in Venice to make preparations for establishing an opposing organization to protect shipbreakers from the activities of the Scrap Convention. Shipbreakers of principal European countries and of Japan continued with these negotiations at a meeting in London in June 1937.[45] The establishment of the

---

iron ore prices is contained in *Institute of Scrap Iron and Steel Yearbook*, New York, 1940, p. 4.

[42] Changes in scrap prices are summarized in the heavy melting steel scrap composite prices of *Iron Age*. These prices were per gross ton:

Jan. 1933	$ 6.77	Nov. 1937	$13.50
Jan. 1935	12.29	June 1938	11.18
Jan. 1937	18.33	Jan. 1939	15.68
Mar. 1937	21.25	Aug. 1939	16.10
Sept. 1937	20.30		

According to *ICTR*, Mar. 24, 1939, p. 550, "In the United States the Pittsburgh price [of scrap] was reduced from over $23.— in the spring of 1937 to $10.— within the space of a year, although since then the rate was again advanced to $15.— 16.—. . . . These reductions are evidence that the convention has not only studied the pockets of its members but has also been of use to steel-makers of countries having a scrap surplus." This opinion, addressed principally to United States steel producers, disregarded somewhat the rapidly decreased demand for steel all over the world as the principal factor influencing scrap prices.

[43] U. S. Tariff Commission, *Iron and Steel*, p. 381.

[44] *ICTR*, Mar. 24, 1939, p. 551.   [45] *ICTR*, June 18, 1937, p. 1100.

shipbreakers convention did not meet with success,[46] because of the difficulty in organizing the widely separated units and because of the small amount of tonnage.

In the United States, which was the principal source of scrap, large scrap dealers reacted similarly to the buyers' international comptoir. They organized the Scrap Export Associates of America on May 27, 1937, for the purpose of opposing a power structure of sellers against that of the buyers. However, their organization was not sufficiently comprehensive and was dissolved in November 1937.[47]

The International Scrap Convention did not exercise the same strict control over its members as the ISC sales comptoirs did. Contraventions were practically disregarded. The convention disintegrated at the outbreak of the Second World War.

---

[46] The U. S. Tariff Commission notes an Italian report to the contrary. *Iron and Steel*, p. 382.   [47] *Ibid*.

CHAPTER SEVEN

Control of Distribution

I

THE CONTROL of the distribution process seemed, to ISC members, an essential corollary of the ISC marketing system. The problem of distribution played a very important role in cartel operations, and this part of ISC activities was deemed essential to the maintenance of cartel disciplines, particularly those connected with the maintenance of comptoir prices. The distribution control schemes of the cartel embraced the limitation of national groups to sell either directly to ultimate consumers or through distributors approved by the cartel; the determination of price and collateral terms under which distributors could operate; and the restriction of cartel-approved intermediaries to the sale of commodities produced by cartel members.

The cartel's interest in limiting the number of distributors and restricting its members to approved distributors arose from the need to sustain established prices and sales conditions, which might otherwise be undermined in the sphere of distribution. Unorganized or uncontrolled distributors might compete among themselves by cutting prices with or without the connivance of cartel adherents anxious to acquire more business. The same purpose was served by the regulation of commissions or price-margins for distributors.

Besides official selling agencies of national groups who sold directly to consumers, participants in the distribution of steel may broadly be classified into two categories: first, those who operated from the producing or exporting countries, although they may have had branch offices, agents, or subsidiaries in importing countries; and second, local agents and jobbers in steel-importing countries. Distributors in the first category, those in exporting countries, might further be classified as either independent distributors, or subsidiary companies of the steel manufacturers.

Independent steel distributors were few in number because of the need for large capital and for an extensive and expensive international organization. Steel producers and their cartels were disinclined to recognize new independent distributing organizations. Most of the distributors (except local jobbers) were connected through corporate ties to one or more steel producers. Through their distributing subsidiaries the producers not only absorbed the additional profits arising from the distribution process, but also were able to maintain their connection with consumers, a valuable consideration should the cartel disintegrate.

The organization of distribution was not unified among the comptoirs and even in commodities where distribution was supposed to be highly controlled, practices were far from uniform. Thus the control of the distribution of British steel exports by the cartels was rather weak, while the cartels exercised practically no control over the distribution of American products. A few of the comptoirs attempted to exclude distributors in the proper sense from business transactions, admitting only, if unavoidable, agents of the producer-members. This was generally the case with IRMA products, wire rods, and semi-finished steel. In other cases the chairman of the EIA comptoir committee negotiated direct contracts with particular customers.

II

The system of licencing distributors at home (in exporting countries) and abroad (in importing countries) was included in the marketing scheme of the EIA at the time of its reëstablishment on June 1, 1933. This system met with severe opposition. Early in 1934 several independent German and Belgian distributors who failed to receive a licence from the cartels protested their exclusion; the Belgian merchants even tried to engage their government in the controversy. The EIA thereupon compromised by recognizing a lower category of distributors who were to receive only half of the standard commission, i.e., two shillings (gold) per ton. Merchants in this new category were to place their orders with the licenced distributors.[1] Early in 1935 independent German distributors complained that the licencing system was an obstacle to business development and that Belgian producers were establishing their own distribution organizations under the auspices of the EIA, avoiding Hamburg exporters.[2] Although

---

[1] *ICTR*, Jan. 5, 1934, p. 27, and Jan. 19, 1934, p. 105.
[2] *ICTR*, Jan. 25, 1935, p. 193.

these complaints did not subside, those distributors who finally were licenced later resisted further licencings.

Large steel concerns had their own subsidiary distributing firms; smaller producers united to establish common agencies.[3] The licencing of such subsidiaries was naturally supported by the national groups controlling them, usually with success. The steel producers did not limit the distribution of their products to their own subsidiaries entirely, but used them in most transactions. Distributors were licenced by the six EIA comptoirs at the meetings of the comptoir committee, and by other comptoirs at their normal business meetings. The two sheet comptoirs had their own list of approved distributors, who were assigned quotas based on a predetermined reference period.[4] Large United States' producer-exporters generally distributed through their own subsidiaries. After entering the cartel, they too considered the introduction of a licencing system.[5] The national groups were responsible for those licenced distributors whose licencing they had sponsored.

Non-licenced distributors could not, under ordinary circumstances, obtain steel commodities from cartel adherents for export purposes. Even if it were possible for these merchants to obtain steel on the domestic market without indicating its destination, it was unfeasible to export commodities purchased in this manner because most domestic steel prices were higher than export prices. Domestic and export prices were practically equal in Belgium, which led to "abuses" in regard to exports. When, early in 1936, foreign currencies had a high exchange rate in Belgium, and export prices were therefore attractive, several non-licenced merchants attempted to operate in exports and then to compete with cartel distributors. A report of the Belgian

---

[3] Some of the licenced distributors were well known in world steel markets. The ARBED group used as its distributor "Columeta," *Compagnie Luxemburgeoise Métallurgique,* Luxemburg. The Hadir works mainly employed the *Société Davum-Exportation.* The Ougrée-Marihaye concern organized *Société Commerciale de Belgique,* called "Socobelge," whereas for distribution purposes the Belgian producers John Cockerill, La Providence, Angleur-Athus, and Laminoir de Monceau established the *Union Commerciale Belge de Métallurgie* (Ucometal). The Belgian Clabecq, Hainaut, and Boel works all had their particular sales companies. The largest German steel concern, the *Vereinigte Stahlwerke,* established as its subsidiary for export sales the *Stahlunion-Export G.m.b.H.,* the *Gutehoffnungshütte* sponsored the *Ferrostahl A.G.;* and the Mannesmann-works also had its own export company.

[4] *ICTR,* Mar. 19, 1937, p. 540.

[5] According to TNEC, *Hearings,* Part 20, p. 11019, the American group envisaged the European system of licencing exclusive brokers, jobbers, or export merchants, who were responsible for applying the regulations of the cartel.

National Bank termed this activity a "special fraud." The same report described how licenced merchants and the Belgian national steel cartel asked the government to stop these "clandestine" business practices. The Belgian government, complying with this request, introduced the compulsory licencing of exports in coöperation with the Belgian national cartel.[6]

III

In principle, that category of local merchants who were recognized as intermediaries in importing countries was required to organize distributor cartels with a quota system. These organizations agreed either with the EIA or with particular comptoirs to sell cartel commodities exclusively and to operate according to other cartel provisions.[7] The countries in which the ISC established such organizations were called "organized markets." Business conditions were more stable in organized markets. Competition of outsiders was decreased, thus making organized markets more attractive to cartel members. Subquota systems were in effect in the comptoirs by which the extent of all adherents' exports to each organized market was determined. If a national group could not exhaust its entire comptoir quota in organized markets, it could sell to "unorganized" markets. In addition, the local merchants of a particular organized market determined their quota participation in the distribution of these imports. The local distributors' agreements were made under the auspices of the EIA. Merchants who did not participate in the local pools could not function as intermediaries for cartelized commodities. An official explanation of the EIA may throw more light on this point. "This pool has to deal with a local commercial organization embracing all resident trading firms interested in the product in question. This commercial organization determines the purchasing quota of its members. It also fixes the sales price for the different articles and determines the measures of control designed to ensure the observance of its regulations. The relations between the EIA and the commercial groups are accordingly based on mutual exclusivity. The trade abstains from buying from outsiders without previous agreement to this effect with

---

[6] *Bulletin d'Information et de Documentation,* May 10, 1936, p. 375.

[7] In 1938 the merchant bar comptoir had to face the competition of so-called "merchant bars No. 3," produced from scrap by very cheap and primitive methods. Merchant organizations asked the EIA whether they might be permitted to handle these merchant bars, promising to call buyers' attention to the lower quality of this commodity. After protracted deliberations, the EIA set up conditions under which "its" merchants could sell these goods. See *ICTR,* Feb. 3, 1939, p. 258.

the 'comptoirs.' In exchange, the EIA guarantees to them a margin of profit by the creation of a system of tonnage rebates and bonifications. In so far as a local steel industry exists in the commercial areas concerned, an attempt is made to include this industry in the market organization and thus stabilize its production."[8]

The United States did not participate in the organized market scheme, and Great Britain participated only to a limited extent. The organization of an export market did not exclude direct business transactions with large consumers, according to the decisions of the comptoir committee of the EIA. Tables 5, 6, and 7 give an approximate picture, as of December 1937, of the participation of EIA countries in the organized markets for merchant bars, structural shapes, and thick plates.

TABLE 5

ORGANIZED MARKETS FOR MERCHANT BARS, DECEMBER 1937. QUOTA DISTRIBUTION OF ORGANIZED MARKETS AMONG INDICATED EIA MEMBERS (PERCENTAGES)

Organized markets in importing countries	Germany	Belgium	France	Luxem-burg	Poland	Czecho-slovakia	Total
Great Britain.....	14.095	50.280	13.424	22.201	0	0	100
Holland*.........	–	–	–	–	–	–	
Switzerland......	28.205	0	52.301	13.494	0	6.000	100
China...........	30.000	29.400	6.240	34.360	0	0	100
Norway..........	15.523	19.172	14.493	34.285	11.199	5.328	100
Sweden..........	22.802	21.556	13.615	35.881	3.243	2.903	100
Denmark........	35.428	22.509	11.120	28.943	0	2.000	100
Syria...........	0	22.312	24.575	46.145	6.968	0	100
Palestine........	26.471	19.182	9.854	22.988	12.784	8.721	100
Egypt..........	6.384	19.520	13.696	45.388	7.622	7.390	100

*The apportionment of Dutch merchant bar quotas among the national groups of the EIA is not known to the author.

The British import market was under the control of the British Iron and Steel Corporation. This agency conducted negotiations between ISC exporters and British buyers, even though the sellers had their own representatives in Great Britain. Yugoslavia, though an organized market, was under the direct control of the Central European Group in which Czechoslovakia functioned as the guardian of ISC interests. The organization of markets in several Balkan countries and northern Italy was equally conferred by the EIA upon the Central European Group in conjunction with Germany. The market

[8] *International Ententes*, p. 44. See also *Iron and Steel*, Report of the U. S. Tariff Commission, p. 401, and *Bulletin d'Information et de Documentation*, Aug. 1938, p. 101. Regarding dissident Dutch merchants see *ICTR*, Jan. 6, 1939, p. 28.

TABLE 6

ORGANIZED MARKETS FOR STRUCTURAL SHAPES, DECEMBER 1937. QUOTA DISTRIBUTION OF ORGANIZED MARKETS AMONG INDICATED EIA MEMBERS (PERCENTAGES)

Organized markets in importing countries	Germany	Belgium	France	Luxem-burg	Poland	Czecho-slovakia	Total
Great Britain.....	8.037	21.678	50.448	19.837	0	0	100
Holland..........	49.907	18.567	20.203	4.159	5.269	1.895	100
Switzerland......	48.562	0	46.786	4.152	0	0.500	100
Norway..........	24.417	10.572	44.267	7.692	11.277	1.775	100
Sweden..........	28.788	11.930	45.758	11.645	0.385	1.494	100
Denmark........	31.583	11.916	42.896	11.605	0	2.000	100
Syria............	0	12.406	74.129	8.095	5.370	0	100
Palestine.........	27.110	9.236	42.458	7.885	3.679	9.632	100
Egypt...........	10.288	11.179	62.783	7.689	5.218	2.843	100

TABLE 7

ORGANIZED MARKETS FOR THICK PLATES, DECEMBER 1937. QUOTA DISTRIBUTION OF ORGANIZED MARKETS AMONG INDICATED EIA MEMBERS (PERCENTAGES)

Organized markets in importing countries	Germany	Belgium	France	Luxem-burg	Poland	Czecho-slovakia	Austria	Total
Gr. Britain.	36.433	45.181	16.281	2.105	0	0	0	100
Holland....	47.433	46.046	4.029	0.462	2.030	0	0	100
Switzerland.	28.972	0	56.358	2.840	0	8.830	3.000	100
Norway....	40.330	43.753	10.437	2.320	3.160	*	0	100
Sweden.....	49.327	45.032	3.967	1.344	0.330	*	0	100
Denmark...	49.030	45.181	4.194	1.595	0	*	0	100
Syria......	0	41.911	42.910	13.149	2.030	*	0	100
Palestine...	41.000	42.779	5.630	10.591	0	*	0	100
Egypt......	5.687	44.264	35.795	12.224	2.030	*	0	100

*Czechoslovakia never reached an agreement within the EIA concerning a share in the quota distribution of these organized markets.

of the Soviet Union was naturally controlled by the Soviet government, to which the ISC fostered exports. Because of specific sales conditions required by the Soviet government, and because of the magnitude of single orders, special prices were determined for each transaction. Several comptoirs offered special allowances in quota computations for exports to the Soviet Union.

Table 8 indicates, approximately, in which countries organized markets existed for the specified steel commodities. The EIA dissolved the association of importers in Egypt in December 1938, and replaced its general contract by individual accords with merchants undertaking to observe ISC rules. The Chinese merchant organiza-

TABLE 8
PRODUCTS IN WHICH ORGANIZED MARKETS EXISTED

Importing countries	Wire rods	Semi-finished products	Merchant bars	Structural shapes	Bands and strips	Thick plates
1. Great Britain.....		*	*	*		*
2. Holland.........			*	*		*
3. Denmark........			*	*		*
4. Sweden.........	*		*	*	*	*
5. Norway.........	*		*	*		*
6. Switzerland......	*	*	*	*	*	*
7. Portugal........					*	
8. Bulgaria........	*					
9. Greece..........	*					
10. Japan..........	*				*	
11. China..........			*			
12. Egypt..........			*	*		*
13. Syria..........			*	*		*
14. Palestine........			*	*		*
15. India..........					*	

tion also ceased to exist at this time. Difficulties arose regarding the renewal of the EIA's agreement with the organization of Dutch importers.[9] In Switzerland the EIA had particular agreements with the Swiss State Railways, and with two other large importing plants.

The ISC made great efforts to extend its distribution organization to as many countries and as many products as possible. In importing countries merchants and sometimes consumers resisted resale price controls, as the ISC intended to exercise them. However, as mentioned before, experience had proved that such measures were necessary to the ISC marketing scheme.

---

[9] *International Cartels,* 1939, Nr. I, p. 17.

CHAPTER EIGHT

Price and Pricing Policies

I

A DISCUSSION of prices and pricing policies on the steel export market deserves more comprehensive research than falls within the objective and the framework of this study. Recent research in the United States and abroad has revealed many interesting facts and conclusions concerning the peculiarities of domestic steel markets.[1] However, no adequate treatment exists of steel price patterns, pricing techniques, price trends, and general price relationships on the international market, nor on these aspects of the subject as they have developed under the impact of artificial marketing control schemes.

Prices and pricing policies were the crux of ISC activities, and it is in the behavior of steel prices, and in their relationship to other important economic factors that the kind and the degree of effectiveness of ISC marketing control schemes and measures are best revealed. It is necessary, of course, to view export steel prices in their broadest economic setting, always judging their trends, their flexibility or rigidity in regard to many other relevant economic and political circumstances besides marketing control schemes.[2] There is little doubt,

---

[1] C. R. Daugherty, M. G. De Chazeau, and S. S. Stratton, *The Economics of the Iron and Steel Industry.* Vols. I and II are limited to the domestic marketing problems of the United States steel industry. The TNEC hearings (see *Hearings,* Parts 19, 26, 27) and monographs are also related to domestic marketing problems, though *Hearings,* Part 20, contains items indirectly related to international price policies of steel.

"Proposals for Research on Prices and Pricing Policies in the Iron and Steel Industry," *Price Research in the Steel and Petroleum Industries,* New York, 1939, contains significant aspects and elements which every investigation on steel prices should take into account. However, these proposals completely omitted export problems, export prices of domestic industries, and price patterns and price relationships on international and foreign markets.

[2] E.g. *ICTR,* Jan. 21, 1938, attributes the rise in steel exports and the boom in steel prices in the first seven months of 1937 to various factors. The agricultural and raw-

for example, that the sinking of many steel commodity prices below the average total costs per unit, and in several cases even below the average prime costs per unit, in 1932, was partly due to the deterioration of concerted marketing controls. However, the mere comparison of these fluctuations with those of steel commodities in which marketing controls persisted even during the crisis years, is not sufficient as a commentary on the effectiveness of control. Other factors, such as contemporary price fluctuations of other basic materials, the nature of the controlled commodities, and general economic conditions accompanying such changes must be taken into account.

This chapter merely attempts to outline the methods used by the cartel in administering world steel prices, and to describe how prices responded to those policies. No attempt is made here to discuss price and quantity variations in terms of modern theoretical analysis.

Price decisions of the ISC assumed the existence of a permanently uniform interest among all cartel members in regard to prices, and these decisions were intended to satisfy all individual cartel adherents. In practice, however, price decisions did not take into account the real or potential desires of marginal, i.e., high-cost producers. Price decisions were not based on differences in production costs among cartel members, although these differences probably influenced the policies of the groups which did not regard maximum steel exports as imperative under all circumstances. Cartel adherents did not object to prices discussed or set up by the cartel on the grounds that their average total costs per unit were not covered and that they did not want to sell below these costs. Such an argument would probably have been greeted with malicious joy by other adherents, who would then willingly divide among themselves the share of the market which the "unfortunate" member felt he could not supply. Thus it was assumed that a group which did not or could not afford to take orders at prices deemed best by the cartel should withdraw from the market. The necessity to export large quantities of steel was of such elementary

material-producing countries were prosperous in 1937, and their foreign exchange position was considerably improved, thus making possible the purchase of durable goods such as steel. The high domestic demand for steel in 1937 in Great Britain, Germany, and U. S. A. reinforced by the rearmament demand, caused fears of a shortage on the export market. The Spanish war caused anxiety about iron ore deliveries, and disturbances in ore supplies and the reduction of steel output were expected to result, according to the report, from the general industrial unrest and from the introduction of the forty-hour week in France. The report also comments on the existence of industrial unrest in the United States at that time, resulting in a strike in the leading steelworks which reduced steel output considerably.

force with several continental European steel groups, that no cartel tactics aimed at maintaining high prices would have succeeded, if these exporting groups seriously felt that price concessions would notably increase the demand for their products.[2a] Experience on domestic and foreign markets had revealed to cartel members that the price level had less influence on the quantity of steel sold than other factors connected with the general business situation.[3] One of the most contested points in steel price discussions has been how far the reports of steel industries about their experiences in this regard are warranted by facts. Sometimes an increase in the export price of steel was not only a consequence of, but also a stimulus for, higher demand. This seeming paradox may be explained by expectations of distributors and consumers of further increase in steel prices. Thus the fear that the trend of steel export prices might take an upward turn stimulated the demand. However, such expectations operated in the opposite direction as well. The hesitation of cartel agencies to lower official prices was often influenced by fear that price reductions would induce steel consumers to withhold orders expecting further decreases.

Though the cost-price mechanism is weakened on all markets which lack a strong marketing control scheme, its relative ineffectiveness on the controlled steel export market is highly significant. Whereas in the long run steel prices on domestic markets did not fall below the average total unit cost line, this was considerably less true on export markets, where many groups tacitly assumed that overhead costs would be covered by transactions on domestic markets. The steel price level on the export market did not decidedly influence the decisions of many national groups as to whether they should produce and export. The compulsion to maintain national export balances in order to obtain foreign exchange, to maintain employment levels at home, and the desire to safeguard their position on the export market, were greater influences on the quantities produced and exported by these groups than were export prices. Several forms of export promotion schemes were introduced by European governments in attempts to reduce possible losses of their producers in export markets.

A study of the price spreads between several ISC-controlled steel commodities, including commodities with quality variations, confirms

---

[2a] "The special regulations relating to the third and to the following year," included in Appendix V A to this volume, show that several national groups intended to loosen their cartel connections in case that the demand for steel should considerably decrease.

[3] See TNEC, *Hearings*, Vol. 26, pp. 13655 ff.

the relatively smaller extent to which the cost-price mechanism operated on the export market in contrast with its operation on domestic markets. A comparison of price margins, on both the domestic and export markets, between merchant bars, standard rails, wire rods, structural shapes, and thick plates, products whose spread in average total unit costs was relatively small and did not change considerably in the period on which this discussion focuses, illustrates how on the export market prices varied with no consistent relationship to each other, indicating that although these costs were relatively equal, factors other than cost were evidently in operation. On the domestic market, however, margins between prices for these same products were much more stable, regardless of actual price fluctuations.

Since cost factors have relatively little relevance to the development of steel export prices, it is of little consequence that the secrecy of each producer concerning cost elements, and the problem of comparing cost factors of producers in different national groups, make it difficult to determine what the average cost per unit of production for steel commodities on the world steel export market actually was. If these difficulties were surmountable, conclusions of interest, though not germane to the scope of this study, could be drawn regarding the general pathology of international trade, the pressure under which national groups had to operate in order to export, and the extent to which domestic prices covered losses on the export market.

The ISC did not attempt to influence price policies by artificially creating an absolute scarcity of steel commodities. Thus it did not resemble in this regard large international cartels of raw materials, determining in advance global supplies, to be produced and "released." The restriction of sellers not to make long-term contracts without special permission of cartel agencies, and the prohibition of accepting orders below prices and conditions determined by the cartel were in themselves curbs on unlimited supply. The several quota schemes implied a further restraint of producer-exporters from supplying unlimited orders. This restraint, however, was merely a medium by which the supply of steel commodities was to be channelized or assigned to certain national groups satisfying as large a demand as actually existed with reference to a certain price level, and was not used to create an artificial general scarcity of steel. Steel distributors and consumers knew that if one national group was out of the market for a while because of quota excesses, commodities could still be purchased from other national groups. Large distributors were duly informed about the quota positions of the national groups. Even during the regime of the first EIA agreement, which attempted to restrict output by a system of fines and compensations, the policy of restraint was ineffective, producers readily risking fines for exceeding their quotas in order to accept additional export orders. As a matter of fact, after 1936 neither the so-called EIA comptoirs, nor the EIA itself practiced the regime of fines and compensations in connection with quota excesses and deficits. The so-called EIA tonnage program, discussed elsewhere in this volume, also failed to exercise any restricting influence on the general volume of supplies. Except for a very short period in 1937, when demand for steel boomed greatly on both domestic and export markets,[4] no major complaint was made against the ISC for limiting supplies. Thus with reference to a certain price level only certain producers and national producer groups were quantitatively limited to take orders, whereas the collective of the producers (the marketing unit as contrasted to its sub-entities), did not put self-restrictions on supply. And the price level just mentioned almost never resulted in returns exceeding those from deliveries on the domestic market.

It is generally assumed that steel prices on domestic markets are a particle in the cellular system of a well-framed national economy, interrelated with a corresponding system of wages, taxes and currency, and part of an interrelated general national price system. In addition, it is taken for granted that in all steel-producing countries the industry and its pricing policies are actually or potentially controlled by one national government to which producer and consumer are equally subject. Whatever the relationship between government and business might be, no national government could for long tolerate the considerable disharmony in its economy caused by steel prices which fall far below the total cost line. Any national government could at least potentially find suitable means of breaking down exaggerated steel prices which were seriously interfering with the operation of steel-consuming industries and with the general living standards of the small consumer. To view steel prices in the mosaic of an assumed international economic cellular system and to relate them to "general"

---

[4] Complaints that supplies were being limited were made on both domestic and export markets in 1937, though the steel industry was expanding production as fast as possible, in order to take advantage of the booming prices. Heavy attacks of domestic producers in Belgium against the cartel for favoring foreign customers to the detriment of home economy are mentioned in *ICTR*, Feb. 19, 1937, p. 380, and *ibid.*, Feb. 26, 1937, p. 419; also in *Bulletin d'Information et de Documentation*, Sept. 1938, p. 179. Concerning Great Britain see *The Times* (London), Nov. 3, 1937, p. 8a, and Sept. 29, 1938, p. 18d.

wages and taxes, and to a general price index is immeasurably more complex.

The international steel market might rightly have been called an orphan in regard to the controlling force of government. No authority existed to say whether export steel prices should be competitive, administered, flexible, high or low.[5] No supranational agency cared what the relationship of production costs and steel prices was or should be, whether prices were adequate, and whether international steel-pricing policies furthered or obstructed employment and consumption in steel-producing and importing countries. Studies in economic policy or international trade made no criticisms in this respect, nor did they reveal any principles according to which international steel price policies could be evaluated.[6] That their steel industries should export as much as possible at the highest prices attainable, was of great concern to the governments of exporting countries. Governments of importing countries, on the other hand, were interested in low steel prices and in a sufficiency of imports as far as such policies did not interfere with the development of their own steel industries if they had any. Tariffs and other trade barriers were vivid expressions of such national policies. Thus the hotly contested concept of a just steel price on the domestic market is a rather nebulous conception if applied to export, and utility, as contrasted with costs, was a stronger criterion on the export market than on the domestic one. The difference indicated here between domestic and international prices applies, of course, to many other monopolistically controlled commodities, as well as to steel.[7]

The expression "marketing control" is often associated with the concept of an extensive discretion in price-fixing, which was not warranted by the actual situation on the international steel market. Steel commodity prices, collateral terms, and selling conditions were "administered" according to the ISC scheme; i.e., they were subject to decisions by organized sellers, and were influenced relatively little by buyers and by transitory impersonal forces on the market. Though

---

[5] Ceilings on export prices, as introduced in the United States, and export certificates, as introduced in Great Britain and elsewhere, do not belong among the instruments of international trade applied under ordinary circumstances.

[6] J. B. Condliff (*The Reconstruction of World Trade,* New York, 1940, pp. 340-41), remarked briefly that an economic organization "which works towards a freer market and acceptance of competitive forces is not only economically beneficial, but politically wise."

[7] See Donald B. Marsh, "The Scope of the Theory of International Trade under Monopolistic Competition," *Quarterly Journal of Economics,* May 1942, pp. 474 ff.

it sounds somewhat paradoxical, the administration of steel prices by the cartel did not permit a large volume of discretion in the determination of a general steel price level. There was of course considerable latitude in the cartel's power to determine business and price strategy, particularly for individual business transactions. However, prices in general could not be arbitrarily determined without regard for the total economic situation on world markets and for particular circumstances on single markets. An examination of steel prices after 1933, when the modern phase of the cartel's operation began, indidicates that steel prices were much more highly associated with fluctuations in the world's economy than with the desires of the steel cartel for increased returns. Steel export prices from 1933 to 1936 were low in the opinion of producers and consumers. The controlling agency was obviously not strong enough to make them higher. One may safely assume that export prices of several steel commodities did not cover in that period the average total unit costs of many exporter-producers. However, it would be impossible to determine the influence exercised on cartel price policies at that time by the anxiety that an increased price would considerably lessen demand, on the one hand, and by outsider competition, by the incompleteness of the cartel organization, and by the dynamics of opposing forces within the cartel, on the other. The cartel was much more effective in preventing prices from sliding below the price level attained in 1933, than in increasing prices beyond this level.[8] The ISC marketing control did not prevent independent buyers who were familiar with the intricacies of the steel market and who were not pressed by the need for quick deliveries from attaining competitive advantages, either by playing off one ISC distributor against another, or by drawing an outsider into the market. However, the possibilities for such activity were few, and the methods intricate.

The world steel export market cannot be located in a single geographic locality. As it was affected by ISC agencies, the world steel export market implies an aggregate of marketing operations in many places throughout the world. In the United States the steel export market may be considered identical with those centers which were most significant for the domestic steel market, with the addition

---

[8] The Economic Intelligence Service of the League of Nations, analyzing price levels in the period after the reëstablishment of the EIA, says that many of the substantial increases in commodity prices were caused by marketing controls. *World Economic Survey,* 1934-35 (Geneva, 1935), p. 65. But steel is not listed among those commodities whose export price notably increased between 1933 and 1935.

of New York, the domicile of important steel-exporting firms. British steel exports and European exports of those commodities in which Great Britain played a decisive role were focused on the London steel market. Brussels may be regarded as the most significant center for continental European exports, and in a sense for the world steel export market. Trade journal reports originating in Brussels were the most exhaustive and reliable. The weekly reports of the Belgian correspondent of the *Iron & Coal Trade Review* constituted a barometer of the world export market in steel. Hamburg, the seat of steel-exporting firms of old tradition, to a certain extent lost its significance in favor of Belgium. Steel export prices were listed on the commodity exchanges of several commercial centers, the most renowned of which were those in Brussels and London. However, with the establishment of export sales comptoirs the effectiveness of these quotations practically vanished, since they now reflected only the efficacy of the workings of cartel agencies.

II

An important distinction between the methods and purposes of different marketing control schemes lies in the extent to which they impart market information about actual offers, prices, and their price policies to potential distributors, buyers, and the general public. Knowledge of these facts may considerably lessen the economic and psychological strain under which distributors and consumers are put by the very existence of sellers' concerted business strategies. An enlightened policy of furnishing information implies great advantages for the buyer, making easier the range of choices in purchasing. Such information makes price discrimination, both general and individual, more difficult. Conversely, the restriction of full market information to cartel adherents only, enables the latter to negotiate business with unorganized and uninformed buyers who are weakened by all the disadvantages of an unknown market.

Within the ISC fairly full market information was released among the cartel member groups, and in addition a rather liberal policy of informing distributors and consumers of the market situation was generally followed.

ISC members were informed both about prices actually obtained in business transactions and price policies (including terms of payment, etc.) to be followed. This information was either general in nature or it was related to individual business transactions, depending on the organization of the particular comptoir, and on particular circumstances. It was understood that the prices which comptoir members were instructed to apply to transactions were minimum prices, and that members were under no obligation not to ask higher prices than those determined by cartel agencies. Under exceptional circumstances, however, comptoirs could require national groups to transact business under the exact conditions determined by cartel agencies. In 1937, when customers, in order to obtain quick deliveries, freely offered premiums in addition to cartel-determined prices, ISC agencies admonished cartel members not to require such premiums.[9]

There was no uniform system of informing ISC members about price decisions. Information was conveyed in business meetings of the ISC agencies, in minutes of those meetings, in periodic reports, and in special messages transmitted by writing or by wire. As has already been mentioned several times in this study, the connection of the American group with this price-regulating and reporting service was rather loose, except in those comptoirs in which the American group participated directly (e.g., IRMA).

Distributors, consumers, and the general public were informed about ISC price policies through the usual channels of trade journals and daily newspapers. Distributors intimately connected with national steel groups obtained further information from those national groups or from exporter-producers to whom they were subsidiary.

No statistics or other comprehensive information were or are available for distributors, consumers, or for the general public regarding the actual prices paid in business transactions of ISC members. What is generally referred to in literature as international steel commodity prices are nominal prices (official prices) which served as guides in computing actual prices. Trade journals often discussed the degree to which actual prices deviated from official prices. In periods when for any reason a commodity was not regulated by cartel agreements, trade journals published prices of significant exporting groups as the "official" prices for these commodities. Whereas actual prices were rather sensitive to the conditions of the individual business transaction, and often reflected what might be called an intimate relationship between seller and buyer, nominal prices showed a certain resistance to adjusting to business fluctuations in steel. That is why

---

[9] See the report about the meeting of the joint coördinating committee, Paris, Jan. 17, 1938, *The Times* (London), Jan. 18, 1939, p. 17. *ICTR*, Jan. 21, 1938, p. 137, reports that the cartel increased prices by the practice of quoting British (higher) extras for some markets.

nominal prices (like so-called published steel prices on domestic markets) appeared to have much greater price inflexibility than actually existed. Any change in general business conditions was rather quickly reflected in actual steel prices, though there was great reluctance in ISC circles to admit the existence of such changes by adjusting nominal prices.[10] Discussions of world steel prices were often based on the boring uniformity of nominal steel commodity prices over long periods of time, since data about actual prices were not available.

Nominal prices were generally the result of abstract price decisions by ISC agencies. The relationship of nominal (official) prices to actual price quotations varied greatly at different times and in various comptoirs. In many comptoirs, especially most of those subordinated to the EIA, actual prices followed the fluctuations of official prices with fair regularity; in others, such as those for wire rods, wire products, and black and galvanized sheets, they often deviated greatly from official prices. In the semifinished steel comptoir, where immediate profit motives frequently had to yield to other considerations, official prices were of relatively little significance. The student of steel prices who does not want to penetrate the whole network of commodity prices may best obtain an approximate picture of them by studying nominal merchant bar or structural steel prices, which deviated relatively little from actual prices and which were rather significant for the whole steel market. In addition, it is useful to read trade journal marketing reports, interpreting the nominal price quotations of merchant bars and structural steel in the light of actual current markets.

Nominal prices within each comptoir related to a specified standard or base product with a determined chemical composition, gauge, length, thickness, tolerance, minimum quantity ordered, etc. The base commodity for which the nominal price was determined by the comptoir generally corresponded to the standard or base commodities for which national groups on their domestic markets also quoted so-called base prices. Besides determining nominal prices, the cartel also set up lists of so-called extras and deductions which could be applied to the nominal prices of specific base commodities in order to transform them into prices for commodities differing in some detail from the base commodities. With the aid of these lists and with

---

[10] Similar conditions existed in many domestic steel markets. See e.g., TNEC, *Hearings*, Part 19, pp. 10506 f.

consideration of other pertinent decisions of the comptoir, the prices of numerous commodities of different specifications which were subject to the control of the respective comptoirs could be determined. The nominal price was usually related to a set of ports, either to Channel or North Sea ports, or to British ports generally.

Decisions concerning nominal prices were not published with precision and exactness, which is why trade journals and other publications often furnished somewhat contradictory data. These journals published, besides the official set of nominal prices, so-called British export prices, which were computed for commodities of British origin, most times including extras for steel of open-hearth quality, and which took into account certain advantages which the British group enjoyed in their imperial markets.[11] No nominal prices were published for American exports, but it may safely be assumed that American export prices after January 1938 did not deviate considerably from European export prices.

Within the ISC system actual price quotations followed a double geographic price pattern. Customers received price quotations in the form of delivered prices computed according to cartel-determined standards, implying that the seller had to arrange and pay for transportation to the port of delivery, and also that he was to bear the responsibility of shipping the commodity from the place of production to the port of delivery. The geographic price structure was undoubtedly one of the most efficient accessory means of restricting competition between cartel members, otherwise exporter-producers situated more favorably in regard to shipping expenses would enjoy competitive advantages, and opportunities to conceal price concessions would occur.[12] Official freight rates on which delivered prices were computed were fixed by the cartel for European cartel members. These rates were mostly based on agreements of the EIA with the cartels of shipping companies, so-called shipping conferences.[13] Be-

---

[11] Spreads between British and continental European prices were listed in trade journals as considerable. This was not always true, especially in regard to rails and sheets.

[12] See e.g., Art. XIV in Appendix V.

[13] See *ICTR*, July 23, 1937, p. 158, and *ibid.*, Dec. 30, 1938, p. 1126. The agreements between the cartel and the shipping conferences included clauses making shipping rates dependent on higher or lower steel price levels. See *ICTR*, Jan. 1, 1937, p. 23. In particular, shipping rates were to be increased during boom periods. On the other hand, if the cartel attested the fact that an adherent was selling at a low price for some reason, especially if the price was reduced in order to fight outside competition, the shipping conference agreed to lower rates for that business transaction.

sides the delivered-price pattern, by which cartel discipline could more easily be maintained, in several comptoirs an additional geographic price structure of nominal prices existed, prompted by mere business strategy. The specific nominal prices of this second type related to certain geographic zones, e.g., Straits Settlements, China, South Africa, Argentina. These particular nominal prices for geographic zones took into consideration domestic conditions in the importing country, outside competition, the particular wishes of the British or American groups in regions which they preferred to serve, and so on. Whereas the general geographic price system was mainly directed toward restricting competition among cartel members, the system of specific geographic base prices was aimed at the elimination of outside competition and at the adjustment of prices to specific local business situations. Thus, many comptoirs had a general nominal price for markets for which no geographic zone prices existed, and special nominal prices for particular markets. Fixed freight rates were applied to specific geographic base prices by ISC agencies just as they were applied to the general base prices, in order to establish uniform delivered prices for the specified areas or zones.

A few examples will illustrate the application of the specific geographic base price system. The official general base price for merchant bars in November 1935 was, per long ton, fob Channel or North Sea ports, £3.3.9 (gold.) However, the official geographic zone price fob Channel and North Sea ports for Argentina was 3.8.6, for Egypt 3.7.6, for Denmark and Norway 3.7.0, for Brazil and the East Indies 3.5.0, and for South Africa 3.0.0. The South African price was so low because immediately before the conclusion of the South African penetration agreement, competition in that region was particularly severe.[14] At the end of 1937, geographic zone prices were raised on Far Eastern markets only, while the general nominal price for mer-

---

[14] See C. S. Richards, *op. cit.*, p. 378. According to *Bulletin d'Information et de Documentation*, Sept. 25, 1934, p. 163, regional prices in gold livre sterlings, per long ton, fob Antwerp, were:

	Billets	Sheet bars	Thick plates	Structural steel	Merchant bars
China—Shanghai and Hong Kong	—	—	4.1.6	3.5.7	3.6.7
China—other places	—	—	4.2.9	3.6.10	3.7.10
Japan and Manchuria	2.9.10	2.10.10	3.18.6	2.15.0	3.0.0
Argentina	2.7.11	2.8.10	4.1.3	3.5.2	3.6.2
Denmark	—	—	4.0.0	3.4.0	3.5.0
Rumania	2.5.5	2.6.7	4.0.0	2.19.0	3.0.0
British India	2.7.0	2.8.0	4.0.0	2.15.0	3.0.0

chant bars remained unchanged.[15] In 1937, when demand was particularly heavy and the cartel did not want to change official prices, a semiofficial system of premium payments in addition to official prices was introduced for many commodities, including merchant bars. The zone price pattern was followed for the premium system also. Thus the premium paid on merchant bars was twenty shillings gold in Japan, China, Manchukuo, and India, and ten shillings gold in Canada and the United States, whereas the general nominal premium amounted to fifteen shillings gold.[16] During the first half of 1939, when the official general base price for merchant bars was £5.5.0 (gold), the nominal zone price for Sweden was £4.17.0, for Finland £4.17.0, for Yugoslavia £5.15.0, and for Norway £4.17.6 (gold). In order to meet American outsider competition, the cartel lowered its official zone price in Central America to £4.15.0 (gold) in 1939, and because of Australian competition, the zone prices in the Straits Settlements and China were decreased to £4.11.6, and those in the Dutch Indies to £4.12.6 (gold).[17]

Nominal prices were uniform for large and small buyers. However, small buyers were at a competitive disadvantage in that concessions were frequently made to consumers of large quantities. The latter, well acquainted with ISC pricing techniques, often demanded concessions in the form of fidelity rebates, i.e., rebates for promises to buy only from cartel members. In this respect the situation did not greatly differ from that of domestic markets. The rebate system was most common in the field of ship building materials, particularly in times of heavy competition with outsiders.

Actual steel commodity prices of European groups were quoted either in British currency, called "paper sterlings" after its depreciation, or in the domestic currency of the buyers. The confused currency relationships which existed in the late thirties and the so-called clearing and barter agreements between nations complicated the cartel's price control system. Many attempts were made to find a suitable device for restricting the indirect price-cutting and the monopolizing of markets which developed because of the existence of barter and clearing agreements. These attempts were unsuccessful since several

---

[15] *ICTR*, Feb. 12, 1938, p. 333.   [16] *ICTR*, May 21, 1937, p. 950.
[17] See *ICTR*, May 5, 1939, p. 818, and *ICTR*, July 14, 1939, p. 67. *Bulletin d'Information et de Documentation*, May 10, 1936, p. 377, mentions a case where distributors ordered steel, naming Siam as the destination of the order, though it was destined for the Straits Settlements, in order to take advantage of the cheaper regional prices for Siam.

national groups, particularly the German, found a ready excuse to perpetuate their bartering system in the compulsory regulations of their national governments.

Nominal steel prices were determined for cartel purposes in gold livre sterlings by most of the ISC comptoirs.[18]   The conversion rate by which gold livre sterlings were to be transformed into British currency was determined by ISC agencies, mostly by the comptoir committee of the EIA. This conversion factor first changed monthly, but from June 1935 until the end remained 1.675 of the gold value.[19] The artificial conversion rate did not vary exactly with the gold value of the British pound sterling; changes in, or maintenance of, the conversion rate were based on business considerations as well. By maintaining the established conversion ratio when the gold value of the British currency changed, or by changing the conversion rates when no corresponding change in the gold value of British currency warranted such revision, the cartel was able somewhat to influence nominal and actual prices indirectly, without making its business strategy conspicuous. For instance, raising the conversion ratio from 1.55 to 1.65 and maintaining the same nominal gold price had the effect of raising nominal and actual prices without alarming those who did not consider this conversion factor.[20] Though this technique was by no

---

[18] As a matter of fact, after the depreciation of British currency, when prices could no longer be quoted in that medium, trade journals listed nominal prices in gold livre sterlings, maintaining the custom of quoting prices with a British base, although at that time most of the comptoirs which might ordinarily decide to quote their prices with such a base were nonexistent.

[19] The first conversion rate, effective July 1, 1933, was 1.463 paper per one gold livre sterling. This conversion factor was changed as follows:

Date	Conversion rate	Date	Conversion rate
August 1933	1.489	October 1934	1.675
September 1933	1.552	November 1934	1.650
October 1933	1.553	January 1935	1.675
November 1933	1.519	February 1935	1.700
December 1933	1.486	March 1935	1.750
January 1934	1.550	April 1935	1.725
March 1934	1.625	May 1935	1.700
September 1934	1.650	June 1935	1.675

According to *ICTR*, Jan. 20, 1939, p. 153, the ISC raised the conversion ratio from 1.675 to 1.80. This report seems to be erroneous because according to *ICTR*, Jan. 27, 1939, p. 218, the ISC decided to retain the old conversion ratio, which "is equivalent to a reduction in export prices of between 5s and 6s per ton." In 1938 the ISC modified its conversion rate for the Balkans and northern Italy (called secondary markets) from 1.675 to 1.75. *Bulletin d'Information et de Documentation, 1939,* "Situation Economique de la Belgique, 1938," p. 34.

[20] Following is an illustration of how the artificial conversion ratio system operated:

means secret, it frequently made nominal prices seem more inflexible than they were in reality. The maintenance of the old conversion rate despite the decrease in the gold value of the British currency with more than 5 per cent in the second half of 1938 is an example of that.[21] Prices expressed in currencies other than paper livre sterlings were computed from the current exchange value of these currencies into paper livre sterlings. For certain countries whose currency had not depreciated, the cartel determined prices directly in the currencies of those countries.[22]

Official prices of steel related, as mentioned above, to standard or base commodities, implying a minimum quantity ordered. It was not the most frequently ordered commodity which was considered standard in each comptoir, but the one which was deemed most appropriate to use as the basis for computing the price of many varying specifications in the commodities ordered. Tariffs for extras and deductions were determined by the same ISC agencies that dealt with other pricing problems. However, the ISC did not succeed in unifying American, British, and continental European extra lists in regard to several commodities. Attempts to eliminate this gap from the cartel scheme were in progress when the ISC disintegrated.[23]

Printed or mimeographed lists of extras and deductions existed, the application of which required considerable familiarity with steel-pricing in general and with steel-export marketing in particular. Extra charges were an excellent field for open and concealed price concessions. Price-cutting by waiving extras, charging lower extras, or delivering better material than invoiced, were frequent accusations leveled at cartel members in periods when orders were scarce. It

---

The base price for merchant bars fob Antwerp in November 1933 was £3.2.6 (gold) per long ton; at the conversion rate of 1.519, the paper livre price was actually £4.10.10. In Sept. 1934, still at the same gold livre price (£3.2.6), but at a conversion rate of 1.650, the paper livre price of merchant bars per long ton was actually £5.3.1.

Following are the gold parity values of British currency at the indicated dates:

	1931	1932	1933	1934	1935	1936	1937	1938	1939
Mar.		74.8	70.5	62.3	58.1	60.3	59.3	60.5	56.9
June	100	74.9	69.3	61.6	60.1	61.3	59.9	60.2	56.8
Sept.	93.1	71.3	64.6	60.3	60.2	61.1	60.1	58.3	48.5
Dec.	69.3	67.4	67.3	60.4	60.1	59.6	60.6	56.7	47.7

[21] A comptoir committee meeting in Dec. 1938 was reported in *The Economist* (Dec. 24, 1938, p. 675), as justifying the maintenance of the conversion ratio by referring to the recovery of the British currency.

[22] See *ICTR*, Mar. 19, 1937, p. 540, concerning prices for Holland and Switzerland.

[23] However, the British group insisted that continental producers use British extra lists for many commodities on British and Empire markets. *ICTR*, Sept. 17, 1937, p. 477.

would be difficult to learn to what extent these indictments were based on fact.

Deductions from standard prices were rare. They were applied mostly to material which was below that of the standard commodity in quality, or to large orders for commodities of one size, one chemical composition, and so forth. Extra lists were made up mainly of additions to be added to the prices of standard commodities, expressed in nominal prices, either because of orders of less than one ton of a single item, or because, as has been mentioned previously, the specifications for the commodities ordered deviated from the specifications of the standard or base commodity in gauge, size, length, shortness, chemical composition, etc. Extras were charged for special services, such as heat-treating, annealing, oiling, painting, cement washing, pickling; for separate laboratory or other tests, and for several other special processes. The most frequent extra charge in non-British deliveries was the separate or additional charge for steel manufactured by the open-hearth process. Whereas official British prices implied steel of open-hearth quality, American export prices were related mostly to Bessemer, and continental European prices mostly to Thomas qualities. Though sellers of Bessemer and Thomas qualities were free to substitute the more expensive open-hearth steel at the prices set up for the cheaper qualities by stating that they could not supply commodities produced according to the Bessemer or Thomas processes, if the buyer originally specified open-hearth quality steel in ordering, he had to pay extras, which for merchant bars amounted to 7.6 gold shillings. The problem of deliveries in open-hearth (Siemens-Martin) quality was a frequent subject of confusion inside and outside of the cartel.

III

In studying published accounts of steel export prices and their fluctuations, allowances must be made, as several times mentioned in this study, for the fact that the prices discussed were not actual but were only nominal prices, subject to the unexposed effects of price concessions, conversion rates, extra charges, premiums, etc. Although, during the cartel regime, publications listed prices as "official" prices, they were not published by the cartel. Therefore, the verification of contradictory reports is not possible without the existence at hand of cartel reports.

There were a few steel commodities, especially heavy rails, prices of which were subject to a strong marketing control during the whole period between 1926 and 1939. The prices of these commodities did not fluctuate heavily, and at first glance one might assume that the sole or dominant reason for the relative stability of their prices was the fact that they were subject to control. As has been suggested several times in this study, an investigation in this regard should inquire into the reasons for the uninterrupted operation of those international marketing controls, while strong marketing controls were impossible to achieve for most steel commodities between 1930 and 1933. Such an inquiry would disclose that even within the range of standardized steel commodities, technical and economic circumstances made some steel commodities much more readily subject to international marketing controls than they did other commodities. However, the number of commodities which survived the great crisis after 1929 without interruption, and thus did not participate in heavy price fluctuations, was very limited.

Most semifinished and finished steel commodities were subject to heavy price fluctuations between 1929 and 1933. After June 1932, especially after the reëstablishment of the cartel structure in 1933, steel prices recovered slightly and with some improvements remained stable until the fall of the year 1936. At the end of 1936 a rapid price increase occurred, reaching a peak in the second quarter of 1937. A decrease in steel prices followed in the second half of 1937, lasting until the disintegration of the cartel. However, this decrease did not reach considerable proportions, and did not bring steel prices down to the 1936 level. Actually, steel export prices in 1937-1939 did not differ greatly from those of 1929.

Figures published by the Economic Intelligence Service of the League of Nations indicate that steel commodities were among those articles whose prices, in the order of the magnitude of price drops during the period 1929-1938, did not decrease considerably.[24] Though the League publication took into account only Belgian export prices of steel girders,[25] its example is most appropriate, since Belgian export prices were most characteristic of the steel export market, and since the commodity chosen was relatively one of the most significant commodities illustrating the development of the steel export market as a whole. A few items from the League's survey are quoted here for

---

[24] See *Review of World Trade,* 1934 (Geneva, 1935), pp. 14-15, and *ibid.,* 1938, pp. 12-13.
[25] See *Review of World Trade,* 1934, pp. 14-15, and *Review of World Trade,* 1938, p. 13. Steel girders are practically synonymous with the article listed as structural steel in steel price statistics.

possible comparison. The percentage change in average gold export prices from 1929 to 1938 is given as follows:

	1929 to 1930	1930 to 1931	1931 to 1932	1932 to 1933	1933 to 1934	1934 to 1935	1935 to 1936	1936 to 1937	1937 to 1938	1929 to 1938
Raw silk (Japan)	−30	−28	−37	−17	−38	+19	+12	+ 9	−12	−79
Cotton (U. S. A.)	−27	−38	−19	− 1	+ 0.2	+ 2	+ 0.4	− 5	−17	−71
Copper (U. S. A.)	−26	−31	−34	−11	−17	+ 1	+19	+40	−23	−67
Petrol (U. S. A.)	−11	−37	− 6	−24	−21	− 0.7	+ 8	+10	− 9	−66
Rubber (British Malaya)	−42	−51	−45	+ 5	+77	+ 3	+35	+21	−28	−59
Newsprint paper (Canada)	− 3	−10	−20	−33	−25	− 2	+ 2	+ 6	+17	−57
Tin (British Malaya)	−29	−27	−10	+ 5	+ 7	− 6	− 9	+20	−24	−47
Mechanical wood pulp (Finland)	+ 5	−11	−46	−11	− 0.2	−10	+ 4	+18	+15	−43
Steel girders (Belgium)	− 1	− 7	−11	−16	− 8	−25	+ 1	+19	+ 9	−37
Coal (United Kingdom)	+ 3	− 9	−23	− 7	− 9	− 2	+ 5	+ 9	+11	−23
Mowing machines (Germany)	+ 1	− 7	+ 2	− 6	− 3	− 2	−10	− 1	+ 4	−21
Pig iron (United Kingdom)	+ 3	−16	−29	− 5	−10	− 2	+14	+41	+18	− 2

In order to illustrate the degree of caution necessary in drawing conclusions from statistics relating to steel export prices, it might be interesting to compare the fluctuation figures published by the League of Nations (a source rightly regarded as very reliable) with the figures published by other sources. According to reports of the Belgian National Bank, published in the *Bulletin d'Information et de Documentation,*[26] the average Belgian export prices for structural steel, per long ton, fob Antwerp, in gold £, were:

1929	1930	1931	1932	1933	1934	1935	1936	1937	1938
5.1.5	4.12.11	3.6.0	2.5.2	2.10.8	3.0.3	3.1.6	3.2.10	4.12.8	5.0.7

Thus prices between 1929 and 1938 do not show a fall of 37 per cent, as in the report of the League, but a decrease of less than one per cent. Between 1929 and 1932 the League's report notes a price fall of 17 per cent, whereas a decrease of more than 54 per cent is apparent in the prices published by the Belgian National Bank. For an even more interesting comparison, according to the figures of the League of Nations, gold export prices of steel girders continued to fall after 1932; after dropping fully 25 per cent between 1934 and 1935, they slightly recovered between 1935 and 1936 with an increase of one per cent. However, according to the statistics of the Belgian National Bank, gold prices of structural steel reached their lowest point in 1932

[26]See e.g., Jan. 10, 1938, p. 26 and Dec. 1939, p. 575.

and steadily, though slowly, increased until 1936. Whereas the League publication indicates a price increase of 19 per cent between 1936 and 1937, the prices in the report of the Belgian National Bank show a rapid increase of almost 50 per cent for the same period. It should be noted that the figures reported by the Belgian National Bank correspond roughly to those published in trade journals, those included in the report *Iron and Steel,* published by the United States Tariff Commission, and to those quoted in official German reports.[27]

Official German statistical reports published composite index values of the fluctuation of iron and steel prices and of other basic materials on the world market. Table 9 is an abstract of such a report.

TABLE 9

INDEX VALUE OF PRICES ON THE WORLD MARKET 1925-1938 (1925/1929 = 100)

Date	Composite index of raw mat. and partly mfd. commodities	Iron and steel	Non-ferrous metals	Coal	Petrol products	Raw material for industry	Products of industry
1925.....	113.3	105.4	109.2	96.2	117.0	115.9	106.9
1926.....	103.6	101.3	104.9	131.0	115.1	104.6	113.9
1927.....	97.1	95.0	95.8	91.5	89.5	95.1	92.9
1928.....	95.1	97.9	93.1	84.7	87.1	93.7	90.2
1929.....	90.9	100.4	97.0	96.6	91.3	90.7	96.1
1930.....	70.6	89.5	70.3	87.7	79.4	70.4	81.0
1931.....	51.2	68.4	49.6	77.7	49.4	51.2	60.8
1932.....	40.3	50.4	39.7	60.1	48.2	39.4	49.4
1933.....	37.7	53.9	40.7	55.0	40.2	38.9	47.0
1934.....	35.8	55.1	38.7	50.6	33.8	37.6	43.8
1935.....	36.4	55.0	42.7	50.4	32.9	37.4	44.6
1936.....	39.5	56.2	40.8	55.4	34.2	40.1	46.0
1937..... Jan.-June	47.6	89.2	49.9	73.4	41.7	49.6	61.7
1938.....	40.7	85.1	38.6	68.2	35.6	40.7	54.7

Source: *Statistisches Jahrbuch für das Deutsche Reich,* 1938, Internationale Übersichten, p. 179.

These index values clearly indicate the significant fluctuation of world steel prices between 1930-1933, when the cartel structure practically disintegrated. They show the influence of the reëstablishment of the cartel structure in 1933. In 1937 steel prices reacted to the general prosperity with a stronger swing upwards than did other listed commodities. Significantly, the considerable decrease in the demand for steel in 1938, reducing the quantity of steel exports that

---

[27] The *Statistisches Jahrbuch für das Deutsche Reich,* 1938, Internationale Übersichten, p. 194, lists an average gold price of £5.3.7 for 1937.

year to 25 per cent less than those of 1937, did not influence published steel prices by bringing them down to the level of 1936, though a majority of the other prices listed slid down considerably. This is partly due to the fact that published steel prices in 1937 had not revealed the addition of official and unofficial premiums to prices, nor did they reveal the disappearance of these premiums in 1938. On the other hand, many concessions from official prices were made in 1938 and 1939, because of competition outside of the cartel, and because of the somewhat loosened cartel discipline, which was the usual consequence of small demand. However, the controlling influence of the cartel and the psychological situation caused by expected orders for armaments saved steel prices from a more rapid disintegration. It should be noted that in 1937 steel export prices for the first time since 1929 reached (and somewhat surpassed) the domestic price level of steel-exporting countries.

Tables 10, 11, and 12 reproduce listings in trade journals, particularly in *Steel,* of the export prices of several steel commodities, per long ton, fob Antwerp, quoted in British currency, and after the depreciation of British currency in 1931, in gold livre sterlings. Table 10 embraces the period of the first EIA marketing scheme, extending from the third quarter of 1926 to the first half of 1930.

Table 10 shows a notable increase of prices accompanying the conclusion of the first general steel agreement, though it would be diffi-

TABLE 10

EXPORT PRICES PUBLISHED FOR SEVEN STEEL COMMODITIES, PER LONG TON, FOB ANTWERP, IN BRITISH POUNDS, JUNE 1936-JUNE 1930*

Steel commodities	June 1926	Dec. 1926	June 1927	Dec. 1927	June 1928	Dec. 1928	June 1929	Dec. 1929	June 1930
Merchant bars......	4.14.6	5.12.0	4.14.9	4.16.0	5.15.0	6. 2.6	5.18.9	5. 5.0	5. 4.6
Structural shapes....	4.12.0	5.11.6	4.13.9	4. 8.0	4.18.0	5. 1.0	5. 4.9	4.17.9	5. 1.6
Thick plates......	5. 0.0	6. 7.6	6. 1.0	5.19.0	6. 7.9	6. 6.6	6. 7.6	6. 4.0	6.10.6
Hot-rolled bands and strips.....	6. 2.6	6.17.6	6. 0.3	5.10.0	6.15.3	6. 5.0	6. 7.6	5.12.6	5.17.6
Black sheets....	9. 5.0	11.10.0	9.18.0	9.14.0	10.14.0	10. 3.9	10.12.6	10.15.0	9.15.6
Standard rails......	6. 0.0	6. 0.0	6. 5.0	6. 7.6	6. 7.6	6.10.0	6.10.0	6.10.0	6.10.0
Wire rods......	5. 8.0	6. 2.6	5.10.0	5.10.0	5.16.9	6. 2.6	6. 7.6	6. 7.6	6. 5.0

*All prices quoted are as of the end of the month indicated.
Source: *Steel.*

cult to ascertain whether the establishment of a rather loose continental European marketing control, or the British strike, which made large imports to Great Britain necessary and temporarily eliminated Great Britain from the export market, is more responsible for the increase in prices. Probably the second reason influenced prices more than the first. The transitory boom period at the beginning of 1929 is mirrored in the prices listed at the end of December 1928. It is rather interesting to note that the disintegration of the first general steel cartel and the beginning of the great depression were not accompanied by a sudden breakdown in steel prices. Though steel exports dropped 20 per cent from 1929 to 1930, prices did not decrease considerably below the average level of the last six years.

In the period between June 1930 and June 1933 no proper general marketing control scheme existed for steel exports. Special cartels were operating for a few products, such as rails, wire rods, wire products, and tubular products. Nominal prices for noncontrolled commodities gradually declined far below the total unit costs of even the lowest-cost producers. Table 11 indicates the extent to which several noncontrolled and two controlled commodities fluctuated. The relative stability of the controlled commodities during the critical period is obvious.

TABLE 11

NOMINAL EXPORT PRICES OF 8 STEEL COMMODITIES PER LONG TON, FOB ANTWERP, IN GOLD LIVRE STERLINGS, JUNE 1930-JUNE 1933*

Steel Commodities	June 1930	Dec. 1930	June 1931	Dec. 1931	June 1932	Dec. 1932	June 1933
Thomas billets..........	4.14.0	3.14.0	3. 2.0	2. 9.0	1.19.0	2. 1.0	2. 7.0
Merchant bars..........	5. 4.6	4. 6.0	3. 7.0	2.14.0	2. 2.0	2.13.0	3. 0.0
Structural shapes.......	5. 1.6	3.15.0	3. 5.6	2.13.0	2. 0.0	2. 2.6	2.15.0
Thick plates............	6.10.6	4.17.0	4. 0.0	3. 7.0	2.13.0	3. 1.0	3.18.6
Hot-rolled bands and strips...............	5.17.6	4.12.6	4. 2.6	3.10.0	3. 5.0	3.10.0	3.12.6
Black sheets............	9.15.6	8. 6.9	8. 0.0	6.17.6	5. 6.0	5.17.6	5.17.6
Standard rails..........	6.10.0	6.10.0	6.10.0	5.17.6	5.10.0	5.10.0	5.10.0
Wire rods..............	6. 5.0	6. 0.0	5. 0.0	5. 0.0	4.10.0	4.10.0	4.10.0

*All prices quoted are as of the end of the month indicated.
Source: *Steel* and *Bulletin d'Information et de Documentation.*

During the critical period prices of semifinished steel, listed in Table 11 as Thomas billets, decreased from £3.14.0 to 1.19.0, and the margin between the prices of semifinished steel on the one hand, and merchant bars and structural shapes on the other, practically disappeared. Merchant bars were obtainable in June 1932 for £2.2.0, and many trade journals reported that merchant bars could also be purchased for £2.0.0. Standard rails and wire rods, examples of controlled commodities, resisted the general disintegration of prices rather well. The reëstablishment of the general marketing control on June 1, 1933, was accompanied by a general increase in steel export prices, though the demand remained on the level of 1932. As in 1932, steel exports in 1933 amounted to about 50 per cent of the export quantities attained in 1927, 1928, and 1929.[28]

Table 12 indicates the trend of ISC prices after the reëstablishment of the cartel in 1933 until its disintegration in 1939.

During the period which marks the proper existence of the modern ISC, 1933-1939, prices of those commodities which even before were comptoir-controlled fluctuated within narrow latitudes. The short period of boom in steel in 1937 is clearly mirrored in the official prices, though, as has been mentioned above, they did not indicate the premiums paid in various guises at that time. In boom periods the regime of extras worked in a relatively severe manner, and this fact is not indicated in the table either.

Thus, from June 1933, the date which marks the establishment of a comprehensive marketing control in steel, to the end of 1936, steel export prices, though somewhat improved, remained fairly stable. December 1936 marks the rapid rise of steel prices, a trend which continued until the second half of 1937, when prices decreased about 15 per cent, remaining at this level through the first half of 1939. The

---

[28] As is elsewhere indicated, exporter-producers of different countries did not reduce their exports under the impact of price-disintegration in equal proportions. The iron and steel exports of major exporting countries were the following in million long tons:

Year	Belgium and Luxemburg	France*	Germany*	Great Britain	U. S.
1927	4.6	5.6	4.3	4.2	1.9
1928	4.5	5.0	4.6	4.3	2.4
1929	4.5	4.2	5.5	4.4	2.5
1930	3.9	4.0	4.5	3.2	1.6
1931	3.3	3.5	4.0	2.0	0.8
1932	3.3	2.4	2.2	1.9	0.4
1933	3.1	2.7	1.9	1.9	0.6
1934	3.3	3.0	2.4	2.3	1.0
1935	3.3	1.8	3.1	2.4	0.9
1936	3.2	1.6	3.6	2.2	1.2
1937	3.9	2.1	3.6	2.6	3.4
1938	2.5	2.0	2.8	2.0	2.1
1939 Jan.-June	1.4	1.1	1.5	0.9	0.9

* Steel exports of the Saar territory are to Feb. 1935 included in the export figures of France, later in the export figures of Germany.

TABLE 12

NOMINAL EXPORT STEEL PRICES PER LONG TON, FOB ANTWERP, IN GOLD LIVRE STERLINGS, JUNE 1933-JUNE 1939*

Dates	STEEL COMMODITIES							
	Thomas billets	Merchant bars	Structural shapes	Thick plates	Hot-rolled bands and strips	Black sheets	Standard rails	Wire rods
June 1933......	2. 7.0	3.0.0	2.15.0	3.18.6	3.12.6	5.17.6	5.10.0	4.10.0
Dec. 1933......	2. 7.0	3.2.6	2.17.6	4. 1.0	3.17.6	5.15.0	5.10.0	4.10.0
June 1934......	2. 7.0	3.3.6	3. 1.6	4. 2.6	4. 0.0	5.10.0	5.10.0	4.10.0
Dec. 1934......	2. 7.0	3.3.6	3. 1.6	4. 2.6	4. 0.0	5.16.0	5.10.0	4.10.0
June 1935......	2. 7.0	3.3.9	3. 1.6	4. 2.6	4. 0.0	5.16.0	5.10.0	4.10.0
Dec. 1935......	2. 7.0	3.3.9	3. 1.6	4. 5.0	4. 0.0	5.16.0	5.10.0	4.10.0
June 1936......	2. 7.0	3.3.9	3. 1.6	4. 5.0	4. 0.0	5.16.0	5.10.0	4.10.0
Dec. 1936......	2. 7.0	4.2.6	3.10.0	4. 7.6	4. 0.0	6.15.0	6. 0.0	4.10.0
June 1937......	4. 6.0	6.0.0	4.17.6	6. 2.6	6.10.0	8.10.0	5.15.0	7. 0.0
Dec. 1937......	5. 6.0	6.0.0	5. 7.6	7. 2.6	6. 0.0	8.15.0	5.15.0	6. 0.0
June.1938......	5. 6.0	5.5.0	4.17.6	6. 2.6	5.10.0	7. 2.6	5.15.0	5. 2.6
Dec. 1938......	5. 0.0	5.2.6	4.17.6	5.12.6	5. 5.0	7.10.0	5.15.0	5. 2.6
June 1939......	4.10.0	5.2.6	4.12.6	5.12.6	5. 5.0	7.15.0	5.15.0	5. 0.0

*All prices quoted are as of the end of the month indicated.
Source: *Steel*, and *Bulletin d'Information et de Documentation*.

following index of nominal merchant bar prices is a simplified indication of the nature of the export price trend from 1933 to 1939:

End of June 1933	100	End of Dec. 1936	138
End of Dec. 1933	104	End of June 1937	200
End of June 1934	106	End of Dec. 1937	200
End of Dec. 1934	107	End of June 1938	175
End of June 1935	107	End of Dec. 1938	171
End of Dec. 1935	107	End of June 1939	171
End of June 1936	107		

Before the outbreak of hostilities, in July-August 1939, prices had a somewhat decreasing trend. After the outbreak of the Second World War the fiction of "official" steel prices was maintained for a while. According to a report of the Belgian National Bank in October 1939 "official" steel export prices rose about 25 per cent above the prewar level. These prices, quoted in Belgian francs, per long ton, fob Antwerp, were 1,500 francs for merchant bars, 1,475 for structural shapes, 1,750 for thick plates, and 1,900 for black sheets.[29]

[29] *Bulletin d'Information et de Documentation*, Oct. 1939, p. 348, and Nov. 1939, p. 455.

IV

If the study of export steel prices, their mutual relationships, and the magnitude of cyclical fluctuations is obstructed by the lack of source material about actual prices and by insufficient general research in the field of export steel prices, even greater difficulties obstruct any attempt to compare the domestic steel prices of exporting countries and to contrast them with nominal export prices.[30] Though trade journals, for instance *Steel,* in their weekly surveys attempted to reduce domestic steel prices of large steel exporters and world steel prices to a common gold denominator, and other authors endeavored to approach this problem in several ways, the net result of these efforts may be regarded as very insufficient, and great caution should be applied in drawing conclusions from these figures. Currency relationships, changes in currency values, and the fact that published domestic prices often deviated from actual prices are, among others, circumstances which make for unreliability.

Whereas the process of controlling steel export prices is little affected by the influence of governmental pressure, by regard for the interest of steel-consuming industries, and by what is called "patriotic spirit," the situation on domestic markets is considerably different. In the 1930's, especially during the second half of the decade, all governments of European steel-exporting countries exercised a decisive influence in the fixing of domestic steel prices. Most of the domestic steel cartels of European countries, either voluntarily or under government pressure, had to take into account the economic situation of "their" steel-consuming industries, especially if the latter exported their products. And it is most significant that Mr. Thurman Arnold regarded "patriotic spirit" as one of the elements which influenced American domestic steel price policies in 1939.[31]

Steel prices fluctuated less on the domestic markets of steel-exporting countries than on export markets, with the sole exception of the Belgian and Luxemburg markets, where no considerable difference existed between domestic and export prices. The relatively low level of Belgian and Luxemburg steel prices, and the parallel fluctuation of domestic with export prices, were due to the fact that in both countries the greater part of all steel commodities was destined for exports. Several factors account for the ability of Belgium and

---

[30] See TNEC, *Monograph No. 6,* "Export Prices and Export Cartels," *passim,* particularly pp. 7-8.

[31] See TNEC, *Hearings,* Part 18, p. 10216.

Luxemburg to maintain large exports in times of low export prices, without having to resort to the system of higher prices on the domestic market. Among these factors were the favorable location of these two countries in regard to the supply of raw material and the shipping of export commodities, the relatively low wage and tax scales which prevailed in both countries, their favorable credit conditions, the type and quality of steel produced, and the particularly alert business methods by which their products were sold. C. S. Richards called attention to "the relative similarity of domestic values and the price levels in Great Britain, Germany, France, and the United States, all of which countries have large domestic markets," and compared them with the conspicuously low domestic prices of Belgium and Luxemburg, where the domestic market is relatively small.[32] German official statistics contain comparisons between domestic steel prices and export prices, of which the figures relating to merchant bars are reproduced in Table 13.

TABLE 13

AVERAGE PRICES* OF MERCHANT BARS ON MAJOR DOMESTIC MARKETS AND ON THE EXPORT MARKET

Date	DOMESTIC PRICES					Export prices fob Antwerp
	Germany	Belgium	France	Great Britain	U.S.A. Pittsburgh	
1913.........	108.50	117.11	150.61	163.46	143.52	103.04
1925.........	132.35	113.47	112.59	178.39	187.04	......
1926.........	133.62	102.51	111.35	165.42	185.19	......
1927.........	134.−	98.60	98.79	165.82	170.37	96.75
1928.........	139.46	117.17	112.67	156.13	173.15	114.54
1929.........	141.−	......	122.27	160.63	177.78	115.81
1930.........	139.−	......	105.20	158.86	158.34	97.20
1931.........	126.50	......	81.43	132.06	150.93	69.37
1932.........	110.−	......	85.70	96.30	145.37	49.26
1933.........	110.−	60.35	90.14	92.38	121.74	56.72
1934.........	110.−	64.18	92.12	97.04	101.85	63.98
1935.........	110.−	53.70	92.12	98.88	99.46	64.09
1936.........	110.−	56.14	91.57	111.74	105.94	64.40
1937.........	110.−	84.58	92.61	131.07	132.04	106.60
Jan.–July 1938.........	110.−	92.46	80.−	144.50	133.50	102.−

*Computed in Reichsmarks, per metric ton. German prices do not take into account special prices offered steel consumers who export their products. German, French, and Belgian prices, and export prices fob Antwerp relate to Thomas quality, British prices to Siemens-Martin quality, and U. S. A. prices to Bessemer quality.
Source: *Statistisches Jahrbuch für das Deutsche Reich*, International Surveys.

---

[32] C. S. Richards, *op. cit.*, p. 379.

Table 14 lists another version of merchant bar prices on the export market (fob Antwerp and British ports) and domestic prices in large steel-exporting countries, computed in United States currency.

TABLE 14

AVERAGE PRICES* OF MERCHANT BARS ON MAJOR DOMESTIC AND ON EXPORT MARKETS

Date	Great Britain	France	Belgium and Luxemburg	Germany	U.S.A. Pittsburgh	European cont. export price fob Antwerp	British export price fob British port
1930 End June...	1.74	1.22	1.25	1.52	1.65	1.18	1.74
End Dec....	1.68	0.97	1.01	1.48	1.60	0.95	1.68
1931 End June...	1.63	0.81	0.82	1.38	1.65	0.74	1.63
End Dec....	1.07	0.90	0.69	1.38	1.58	0.60	1.07
1932 End June...	1.06	0.95	0.53	1.19	1.60	0.49	.99
End Dec....	1.01	0.95	0.70	1.19	1.60	0.58	.93
1933 End June...	1.28	1.23	0.84	1.49	1.60	0.66	1.22
End Dec....	1.73	1.57	1.07	1.85	1.75	0.69	1.56
1934 End June...	1.94	1.68	1.16	1.90	1.90	0.71	1.69
End Dec....	1.90	1.68	1.16	2.01	1.80	1.17	1.66
1935 End June...	1.90	1.68	0.90	2.01	1.80	1.16	1.66
End Dec....	1.90	1.68	0.90	2.01	1.85	1.17	1.64
1936 End June...	2.03	1.67	0.99	2.00	1.85	1.14	1.74
End Dec....	2.05	1.46	1.05	1.98	2.05	1.38	1.86
1937 End June...	2.53	1.77	1.46	1.98	2.45	1.82	2.43
End Dec....	2.55	1.62	1.65	1.98	2.45	2.22	2.73
1638 End June...	2.71	1.40	1.65	1.98	2.41	1.93	2.44
End Dec....	2.56	1.30	1.65	1.98	2.25	2.03	2.30
1939 End June...	2.42	1.44	1.65	1.98	2.15	1.97	2.30
End Dec....	2.25	1.43	1.88	1.98	2.15	2.90	2.16

*Computed in United States dollars per hundred pounds.
Source: Weekly quotations of *Steel* and *Annual Statistical Reports of American Iron and Steel Institute.*

Several tables comparing domestic and export prices of steel are published in *Iron and Steel,* Report of the United States Tariff Commission,[33] and by D. L. Burn.[34] Burn's work, which analyzes British domestic price policies in detail, including their relationship to costs and to other circumstances, is most revealing.

---

[33] *Op. cit.,* pp. 489 ff.   [34] *Op. cit.,* pp. 427 ff.

The history of the ISC indicates that domestic price policies did not influence the price decisions and price policies of the ISC to any great extent. However, many price patterns, including geographic price systems developed on domestic markets, were applied in international steel marketing controls as well.

V

The listing of steel prices of former decades and of the nineteenth century, without discussing circumstances accompanying price changes, especially the changes in steel technology, is of little significance in this study. However, a few figures, rather fragmentarily listed, may be of interest to the reader.

German statistical reports contain a composite index of domestic iron and steel prices between 1792 and 1937 which shows fluctuation between the index number, 295 for 1809 and 62 for 1886, taking 1913 = 100 as a base.[35] British prices of wrought-iron marked bars are listed in the annual reports of the British Iron and Steel Federation for the period between 1810 and 1938. These prices, indicated for long tons, vary between £5.15.0 in 1843 and £33.10.0 in 1920.[36]

---

[35] See *Statistisches Jahrbuch für das Deutsche Reich,* Berlin, 1938, p. 320. Large fluctuations are indicated by the following figures:

Year	Index	Year	Index	Year	Index
1792	155	1843	82	1900	132
1800	203	1847	143	1903	83
1802	170	1851	92	1907	109
1805	228	1854	151	1909	77
1809	295	1860	94	1913	100
1810	218	1873	181	1924	125
1814	180	1874	130	1926	112
1815	136	1875	105	1930	115
1818	180	1879	76	1932	93
1830	107	1886	62	1933	86
1832	96	1890	103	1937	86
1836	143	1894	70		

[36] Major fluctuations are indicated by the following prices:

Year	Prices in £	Year	Prices in £	Year	Prices in £
1810	14.10.0	1837	8.0.0	1919	25.10.0
1813	12.10.0	1843	5.15.0	1920	33.10.0
1816	8.10.0	1845	12.10.0	1921	16.0.0
1817	12.0.0	1861	7.10.0	1922	13.10.0
1820	7.10.0	1872	14.10.0	1932	12.0.0
1825	14.5.0	1876	9.10.0	1936	13.0.0
1827	9.0.0	1914	8.10.0	1937	15.15.0
1828	6.10.0	1918	17.0.0	1938	15.15.0
1836	13.0.0				

Table 15 lists average prices of steel products, compiled from quotations in *Iron Age* and also from other authoritative sources

TABLE 15
AVERAGE PRICES OF STEEL PRODUCTS, PER 100 POUNDS, IN PITTSBURGH, IN UNITED STATES DOLLARS

Year	Soft steel bars	Tank plate	Beams	Year	Soft steel bars	Tank plate	Beams
1898....	0.95	1.08	1.17	1914....	1.15	1.14	1.15
1899....	1.84	2.21	1.81	1915....	1.31	1.31	1.30
1900....	1.59	1.54	1.91	1916....	2.67	3.53	2.55
1901....	1.42	1.55	1.58	1917....	3.64	5.88	3.67
1902....	1.58	1.70	1.81	1918....	2.89	3.24	2.99
1904....	1.33	1.54	1.54	1919....	2.49	2.72	2.53
1907....	1.60	1.70	1.70	1920....	3.22	3.28	2.95
1911....	1.26	1.31	1.32	1921....	1.87	1.93	1.93
1913....	1.55	1.50	1.50				

Source: *Annual Statistical Report for 1934*, p. 72.

published by the American Iron and Steel Institute. James M. Swank listed some American iron and steel prices dating from the end of the eighteenth to the end of the nineteenth century, which show immense fluctuations.[37]

It is highly probable that early export steel prices, of which there are no particular records, did not fluctuate less than the domestic steel prices of exporting countries.

---

[37] See James M. Swank, *History of the Manufacture of Iron in All Ages* (Philadelphia, 1892), p. 514. Hammered bar iron is listed per long ton in dollars 77.50 (1794), 106.50 (1796), 144.50 (1815), 82.50 (1824), 111.- (1837), 75.- (1844). Best refined rolled bar iron was sold per long ton in dollars, 85.62 (1844), 54.66 (1853), 91.33 (1854), 91.04 (1863), 146.46 (1864), 87.08 (1867), 44.24 (1878), 61.41 (1882), 40.32 (1885). Iron rails were marketed for 45.63 (1851), 80.13 (1854), 41.75 (1862), 126.- (1864), 33.75 (1878). Steel rails, sold in 1867 for $166.-, went down in 1885 to 28.50. The change in iron prices before and after the American Revolution is discussed by Alexander Hamilton in his "Report on the Subject of Manufacturers," *Industrial and Commercial Correspondence of Alexander Hamilton* (Chicago, 1928), p. 301. See also Arthur Harrison Cole, *Wholesale Commodity Prices in the United States 1700-1861* (and Statistical Supplement), Cambridge, 1938, *passim*.

CHAPTER NINE

American Participation

I

THE WEBB-POMERENE ACT in 1918 to a considerable extent lifted the restrictions imposed on American exporters by the range of general antitrust regulations against uniting in collective national marketing schemes for the control of exports, and against joining international marketing controls. The legal obstacles in the path of American steel export-producers' collaboration in international cartels were thus removed. However, both the national organization which United States' steel exporters formed, and the form of the exporters' adherence to international cartels deviated considerably from customary European patterns. In their national organization American steel exporters did not follow the European model of national groups with strong cohesion and strictly unified business strategy, and the ties of American steel exporters to international steel cartels bore unmistakable signs of the unwillingness to participate too intimately in compacts dominated by Europe. Besides such traditional differences, the fact that collective marketing controls of the European type were prohibited on the American domestic steel market and that a relatively high percentage of exporter-producers did not join the Steel Export Association of America accounted for the looseness of the American export steel organization. Another difference between the form of United States' and European adherences to the international cartels arose from differences in their marketing methods. In addition, the peculiar relationship between government and business in the United States, the remoteness of the American steel industry from the central agencies of international steel cartels, and its comparatively small interest in steel exports except under relatively attractive circumstances, were further reasons for the differences between the American and

European national groups in their relationship to international steel cartels.

United States' steel exporter-producers participated in negotiations and made agreements with the ISC and its sub-entities according to the provisions of an act of Congress, passed April 10, 1918, entitled An Act to Promote Export Trade and for Other Purposes, generally referred to as the Webb-Pomerene Act. Associations of exporters engaged solely in export trade were exempted from the provisions of the Sherman Anti-Trust Act by the Webb-Pomerene Act, provided that any such association was not acting in restraint of trade within the United States, that it did not exercise restraint in export trade upon any domestic competitor of such an association, and that the association did not act to enhance or depress prices within the United States, intentionally or artificially, or to substantially lessen competition within the United States.[1]

The association formed for the purpose here discussed was the Steel Export Association of America, incorporated in 1928 under New York State law. The United States Steel Products Company and Bethlehem Steel Export Corporation, both of New York City,[2] founded the association in June 1928. The association was intended to function as an entity in international steel agreements, representing United States' exporting-producers,[3] to direct its members' export business, without preventing them from taking export orders through their established subsidiary distributors and through their agents abroad.[4] The board of directors of the association was composed of the delegates

---

[1] In Europe, even among experts, a somewhat mistaken interpretation of the American antitrust acts existed to the effect that these regulations prevented American exporters from making international agreements entailing the possibility of exporting at prices lower than those existing on the American domestic market. See *ICTR*, Dec. 3, 1937, p. 940.

[2] The members of the association are listed in *Monograph No. 6*, of the TNEC, pp. 218-19. The association reported as its chief advantages under the Webb-Pomerene Act "ability to meet foreign competition through establishing uniform terms and contracts for export sales, standardizing weights and qualities and the collection and exchange of information regarding foreign markets." (*Ibid.*, p. 218.) According to the testimony of one of the executives of the association, its purpose was to "allow us to get together and establish prices, to divide the world's business amongst ourselves and if possible, if we could arrange it, with Europe." TNEC, *Hearings,* Part 20, p. 10922.

[3] United States' exporting-producers, united in the Steel Export Association of America, were generally referred to as the "American group." Cf. TNEC, *Hearings,* Part 20, p. 10933.

[4] The association, unlike comparable export cartel organizations in Europe, did not serve either as an exclusive selling agency, or as an exclusive intermediary in business transactions.

of the participating steel exporters, who were also stockholders of the company.[5] United States' negotiators, whether stockholders or directors of the company or not, had to act on behalf of the association, or be subject to the previous or subsequent approval of the association, to satisfy the provisions of the Webb-Pomerene Act. The members of the association made arrangements among themselves for such items as the domestic allotment of export quotas, for premiums, if any, for particular cartelized steel commodities, for the apportionment of expenses arising from the administration of these agreements, and for the apportionment of any fines resulting from the exceeding of international quotas and fines resulting from deliveries of exporters who were not members of the association.[6] These arrangements were necessary in order that the American group might function as a national group within the ISC and/or its sub-entities. The Steel Export Association of America maintained a bureau and a representative in London.

It is interesting to note that the French politician, Edouard Herriot, regarded the establishment of the Steel Export Association of America as an indication that on the world steel market a "fight for world supremacy" between America and Europe was not far distant.[7]

In making international agreements American steel producer-exporters were in many respects freer from government interference than their European colleagues. Apart from the provisions of the Webb-Pomerene Act[8] the United States government, unlike European governments, did not exercise any direct influence upon negotiations. However, two previously mentioned characteristic provisions of the Webb-Pomerene Act that are peculiar to the American legislative regulations had to be complied with by the American group.

---

[5] Cf. TNEC, *Hearings,* Part 20, p. 10955.

[6] Cf. Exhibit 1447, TNEC, *Hearings,* Part 20, pp. 11018-19. According to TNEC, *Hearings,* Part 20, p. 10926, ". . . the Steel Export Association of America consisted of various members who were in various groups. If they manufactured one product, they would be in that group but not necessarily in another group."

[7] *The United States of Europe,* p. 108.

[8] According to Section 5 of the Webb-Pomerene Act, annual reports have to be filed with the Federal Trade Commission, on blanks for this purpose, describing the methods according to which a Webb-Association is doing business, the plan under which it is operating, and stating its relations with other associations, corporations, and individuals. The question of whether or not American laws require exporters to inform governmental agencies about international agreements and to furnish details to any public agency has been answered in the negative. TNEC, *Hearings,* Part 20, pp. 10982-83. However, the Webb-Pomerene Act empowers the Federal Trade Commission to make inquiries according to Section 5 of the act.

The American group concluding an international marketing control agreement could not (1) restrain trade of American exporters not joining the agreement, (2) ask for or agree to the protection of its internal market, because such protection could artificially or intentionally enhance or depress prices within the United States (Section 2 of the Webb-Pomerene Act).

When the American producers were minutely questioned about their mutual understandings and their understandings with European producers at the hearings before the Temporary National Economic Committee, they testified that they had always observed those two points.[9] This is not the place to discuss whether or not the said legislative provisions are consistent with the purpose of the act. It seems that there were some doubts in this regard among governmental officials participating in the hearings.[10] However, the representative of the Steel Export Association of America did not recommend a clarification or a modification of the Webb-Pomerene Act by legislative action.[11]

Thus international steel cartels negotiating with Americans about

---

[9] Mr. Bash testified before the TNEC (see *Hearings,* Part 20, p. 10933) that the Steel Export Association of America incorporated expressly in all of its international agreements what, in effect, is a paraphrase of Section 2 of the Webb-Pomerene Act. Clause 1-D of the Agreement of the International Rail Makers' Association of Aug. 1, 1937, containing such a paraphrase, may be regarded as a means of incorporating this provision. This clause reads as follows: "It is understood that the Steel Export Association of America (hereinafter referred to as the American Group) is an association constituted under an Act of Congress of the United States of America approved Apr. 10, 1918, and entitled, 'An Act to Promote Export Trade and For Other Purposes,' commonly known as the Export Trade Act. As used in this paragraph the term 'United States' shall have the meaning given in the Export Trade Act. Materials sold in the United States other than for export and sold for export to the United States shall not be covered by this agreement, and this agreement shall not be construed as in any way referring to trade in materials so sold and shall not be allowed directly or indirectly to restrain trade within the United States or the export trade of any domestic competitor of the American group or to enhance or depress prices of such material or to lessen competition therein within the United States."

[10] TNEC, *Hearings,* Part 20, p. 10965. The representative of the Treasury Department, Mr. Joseph J. O'Connell, remarked in this connection (p. 10960): "It isn't a question of what would be reasonable for you to do, but what you are permitted to do under the law." And Mr. A. H. Feller, special assistant to the Attorney-General said (p. 10963): ". . . therefore the question really rises—and I think the fundamental question here is if the provisions of the Webb-Pomerene Act, to the effect that the export business of the outsiders should not be restricted, is to be adhered to, whether it is possible to have an export association at all in this situation." Outright repeal of the Webb-Pomerene Act is proposed by *Fortune,* Sept. 1942, p. 152.

[11] TNEC, *Hearings,* Part 20, p. 10965.

common marketing controls had to take into account the somewhat peculiar position of United States steel exporters, especially in respect to American outsiders, who were protected by the Webb-Pomerene Act. This point—not sufficiently realized by Europeans—caused considerable difficulties within the ISC.

II

American marketing collaboration with the organization of steel exporters of other countries may be separated into two periods: the first before January 1938, and the second after that date. In the first period American producers were members of the international sales comptoirs of tin plate, rails and tubes.[12] This membership did not imply coöperation on general marketing conditions with the International Steel Cartel as a whole, although the comptoirs mentioned were parts or annexes in the framework of the international organization. Neither did it imply coöperation with other export sales comptoirs that were part of the International Steel Cartel.

American membership in the International Rail Makers' Association goes back to 1904. This most famous international cartel was dissolved in 1914 with the outbreak of the First World War. In 1925-26 a new European Rail Makers' Association (ERMA) was established. America entered this cartel through the Steel Export Association of America on April 1, 1929,[13] and remained a member up to the suspension of cartel operations in September 1939. America participated in the weekly business meetings of the IRMA ("London Committee") through the London representative of the Steel Export Association. According to general agreement, the Steel Export Association of America was a member of the International Tinplate Association from July 1, 1934, up to the beginning of the Second

---

[12] According to S. Tschierschky, "Chronik der Internationalen Kartelle und Trusts," *Weltwirtschaftliches Archiv*, XXXVII, Part I, 290, American steel producers had an agreement concerning the maintenance of prices of wire products on the export market with the International Wire Export Company (IWECO), the selling organization of European wire-products producers. *ICTR*, Oct. 22, 1937, p. 672, refers to a price convention between the IWECO and the American wire industry concerning the Brazilian market. Dr. Ernst Poensgen, chairman of the German national steel cartel, lists an understanding between American and European wire producers, which already existed in 1910. ("The Economic Relations Between The English and Continental Iron and Steel Industries," *Stahl und Eisen*, Düsseldorf, Sept. 17, 1936, pp. 1063 ff.)

[13] TNEC, *Hearings*, Part 20, p. 10928. After Americans joined the cartel, the European Rail Makers' Association (ERMA) changed its name to International Rail Makers' Association (IRMA).

World War.[14]   The American association had various agreements
with foreign producers concerning tubular products.   The most important of these was the so-called general export agreement, which
existed with several changes from December 1928, to March 31, 1935,[15]
when the cartel based on that general agreement disintegrated.   After
the dissolution of that strong organization, United States producers
coöperated with European producers on the world export market for
tubular products from 1935 to September 1939, under an "informal"
agreement to maintain prices and to meet to discuss business strategy.

In the second period, beginning in January 1938, the American
group remained direct members in the rail and tin plate comptoirs
and collaborated with Europe on tube exports.   In addition, according
to two agreements concluded late in 1937, the American group began
coöperating with the ISC organization as a whole in general and in
some special marketing questions, and with other important comptoirs,
of which it did not become a member until 1938.

This striking change was largely due to two factors.   First, both
American and European producers increasingly felt the pressure of
competition in several important markets.[16]   Second, and more significant, the European organization grew more complete and vigorous in 1935-36, by extending its structure to include all important
European steel-producing countries, especially Great Britain, Poland,
and Czechoslovakia, and by establishing more comptoirs, the most
important of which was that for black sheets.   In previous years, not
only had American competition been too insignificant to make it imperative that American exporters participate in a general control, but
European groups had not been sufficiently organized to be partners
to such a general control.

When the EIA was first formed in 1926 many wondered what its
attitude would be toward the American producers, and vice versa.
At that time a competent authority, Walter S. Tower, wrote: "With
British and United States producers outside the agreement, steel consumers in neutral markets have little ground to fear price gauging by
the syndicate."[17]   British experts did not then regard the question of

---

[14] TNEC, *Hearings,* Part 20, p. 10926.

[15] *Ibid.,* p. 10927.

[16] American competition was growing, especially in European markets, thus increasing the eagerness of Euorpean national groups for greater American participation in the
cartel. See *ICTR,* Nov. 12, 1937, p. 821 and *ibid.,* Nov. 19, 1937, p. 866.

[17] *Foreign Affairs,* V (1926-27), 266.

American participation so important as their own. "With America practically out of the foreign trade running—save on the Canadian market," wrote *The Economist* in September 1928, "the steel importing world must depend almost entirely on those producing countries controlled by the steel cartel and Great Britain. In other words, competition is between our country and cartellized Europe. In no other part of the world but this—or these two parts—can steel be produced at a truly competitive or economic cost."[18] According to one report, Americans felt some anxiety over the establishment of the cartel, although they had frequently been assured that the cartel "is not a war machine directed against them."[19] A notable German economist, in discussing the necessity for German adherence to the continental steel entente, declared bitterly that the German iron and steel industry, before establishing the new form of coöperation, was doomed to operate without profits at a time when the "American Steel Trust" (probably the United States Steel Corporation) was earning a 40 per cent dividend.[20] Walter S. Tower felt that, as matters stood in 1927, there was nothing much for the American industry to gain by joining, and nothing to lose by staying out.[21]

In the first half of the 1930's steel exports from the United States were on a low level. However, after 1933 they gradually increased,[22] and European producers began to worry about what United States' exporters would do if the depreciation of the dollar and rising steel export prices should make foreign markets, especially those which Europeans regarded as their domain, more attractive to Americans.[23]

---

[18] *The Economist*, Sept. 1, 1928, p. 382. Other British views are quoted by J. Joseph W. Palmer, "Origin and Development of the Continental Steel Entente," *Trade Information Bulletin* No. 484.

[19] *Revue Economique Internationale*, III (1926), 391.

[20] Dr. J. W. Reichert, "Die Festländische Rohstahlgemeinschaft," *Weltwirtschaftliches Archiv*, XXV, Part I (1927), 348*.

[21] *Foreign Affairs*, V (1926-27), 264.

[22] Yearly exports of finished steel products from the United States in thousand net tons:

1926	2,401	1933	641
1927	2,134	1934	1,101
1928	2,549	1935	1,023
1929	2,750	1936	1,295
1930	1,818	1937	2,905
1931	934	1938	1,830
1932	416	1939	2,593

[23] Professor C. B. Richards had the opportunity to compare delivered costs actually paid by a South African importing firm for structural steel imported from continental

III

European steel producers, including the British, approached American producers in the second quarter of 1936 with a proposal to start negotiations aiming at a general understanding about the export steel market.[24] A delegation of the ESC, led by the Earl of Dudley and Sir Andrew Duncan, visited the United States to pave the way for that agreement.[25] A tentative draft of an agreement was prepared by both sides in February 1937, at a meeting in London. The draft consisted of two parts. The "heavy steel" agreement concerned semifinished steel, merchant bars, plates, structural shapes, and wire rods. The "sheet agreement" covered hot-rolled hoops and strips, cold-rolled strips, black sheets, and galvanized sheets.[26] The second group of products was put into a separate draft because of a fear that the chances of coöperation among exporters of these products was slimmer;[27] later experience proved that the fear was well founded. Indeed, the unworkability of this second draft threatened the whole scheme of American coöperation.[28]

Europe and from the United States. The following table is an excerpt from Richards' figures:

Competition of Continental European with United States Structural Steel on the
South African Market
(Prices in British £ per net ton)

Date	Structural Steel Exported from Continental Europe			Structural Steel Exported from the United States		
	Price fob Antwerp	All charges via Durban to Johannesburg	Delivered cost actually paid in Johannesburg	Price cif South African port	Landing charges duty and railroad (via Lourenço Marques to Johannesburg)	Delivered cost actually paid in Johannesburg
July 1935	5. 4. 6	7.15.11	13. 0.5	7.13.7	5.11.11	13. 5.6
Feb. 1936	6. 2. 7	7.14.11	13.17.6	7.13.7	5.11.11	13. 5.6
Sept. 1936	6.16. 2	7.14.11	14.11.1	8. 2.6	5.12. 2	13.14.8
June 1937	10. 0.11	7.16. 5	17.17.4	12. 3.4	5.13. 5	17.16.9

Source: C. S. Richards, *op. cit.*, Appendix 6B.

[24] *Bulletin d'Information et de Documentation,* "La Situation Economique de la Belgique en 1937," May 10, 1938, p. 391, states that the principal American steel producers already had a gentlemen's agreement concerning general steel policy in 1936 with Europeans.

[25] See *The Times* (London), Apr. 8, 1939, p. 17, and TNEC, *Hearings,* Part 20, p. 10928.

[26] TNEC, *Hearings,* Part 20, pp. 10928, 10929.

[27] See *Iron Age,* Dec. 16, 1937, p. 76, and *ICTR,* Dec. 3, 1937, p. 940.

[28] See TNEC, *Hearings,* Part 20, p. 10948. In a letter written by a well-informed and competent agency, the sheet agreement is spoken of as to be formed later than the heavy steel agreement. *(Ibid.)*

There was a special discrepancy in production conditions and costs between the American and European producers of commodities included in the sheet agreement. This discrepancy was mainly due to the rapid development of continuous hot-strip mills in the United States.[29] In the last few years before 1939, $850,000,000 had been spent on such mills in America, with a resulting capacity of 13 million net tons a year.[30] In the United States 26 mills of this type were operating; while in the whole of Europe only a very few such mills could be found.[31] The revolutionary effect upon competition resulting from this technical evolution may be seen in the reduction of the price of automobile fender sheets on the American domestic market from $135 a ton in 1923 to $59 in 1939.[32] It is interesting to note that the ISC did not adapt the cartel organization to these technical achievements. It maintained separate comptoirs for strips and for sheets with separate quota and pricing systems, and separate commercial organizations. During 1938 and 1939 attempts were still being made to straighten out the difficulties arising from the slow coördination of marketing policies in commodities belonging to the "sheet agreement."[33]

Late in 1937 the tentative draft of the agreement between the American and European producers was adopted.[34] However, only the section concerning "heavy steel" was put into effect immediately, that is, in January 1938,[35] whereas the "sheet agreement" went into

---

[29] See Daugherty, De Chazeau, Stratton, *op. cit.,* I, 19. With reference to the identity of the expressions "continuous sheet" and "continuous strip," see TNEC, *Hearings,* Part 19, p. 10689.

[30] See TNEC, *Hearings,* Part 19, p. 10689.

[31] *Ibid.,* pp. 10411, 10694. The first continuous strip mill in Germany was put in operation in the fall of 1937 by the *Bandeisenwerke A. G.* at Dinslaken, a subsidiary of the *Vereinigte Stahlwerke A. G.* The mill was licensed to use American Rolling Mill Company patents, and is a 55-in. hot unit capable of rolling 500,000 tons of sheets a year. The strip output was mainly to be converted into automobile sheets at the Wissen works of the *Vereinigte Stahlwerke* where a new cold-rolling mill was erected for this purpose. A second mill of this same kind was contemplated by the Neunkirchen Steel Works, and by the Röchling and Hoetsch companies. See *ICTR,* May 7, 1937, p. 865, Nov. 19, 1937, p. 841, and Jan. 6, 1939, p. 28. Only two British firms, Richard Thomas & Co., Ltd., and John Summers & Sons Co., own mills of this type. They are located in Ebbw Vale, South Wales, and at Shotton, near Chester, England. D. L. Burn (*op. cit., passim*) discusses in detail the introducing of this new production method in Great Britain and the background of these activities.

[32] TNEC, *Hearings,* Part 19, pp. 10527, 10701, and Part 20, p. 11001.

[33] See "Observations on the Working of the International Steel Agreement," in *International Cartels,* I, No. 2, 14.   [34] See *ICTR,* Dec. 3, 1937, p. 940.

[35] The agreement went into effect with reference to some products in December, 1937. TNEC, *Hearings,* Part 20, p. 10938.

effect six months later. The parties declared subsequently that they regarded the period between January and June, 1938, as a testing period,[36] although the whole accord, intended to run till 1940, had been regarded in a certain sense as a test. The accord was often referred to as an "understanding," a "tentative agreement," and a "modus vivendi" as distinguished from an "agreement."[37] This terminology customarily has been used to indicate the unwillingness of the parties to be subject to any obligation save a "moral" one. In another sense the term "understanding" may suggest that, although there is already an enforceable obligation, many important details have still to be agreed upon. It is in this sense that the term was used by the American group itself,[38] this in spite of the fact that the pact was never signed. Such a procedure was not unusual; in the operation of the International Steel Cartel important agreements often remained unsigned. As a matter of fact, the accord was regarded by the three parties (EIA, the British, and the American associations) as obligatory though concluded for a "trial period."[39]

The Steel Export Association of America acted as party to the agreement for the American group and representatives of the ESC, that is both the EIA and the British group, for the European group. The ESC representatives also acted for the interested comptoirs. The American group considered that the Webb-Pomerene Act determined who could represent it.

The British group played an outstanding role as party to the agreement and as mediator in the American negotiations. This was partly

---

[36] According to Mr. Bash's testimony (*ibid.*, p. 10982), the obligations of the agreement had become incumbent in June, 1938. "The principles of the draft agreements with the American industry were confirmed on June 14, 1938, with certain amendments the necessity of which had come to light during the test period since December, 1937," reads an official communication of the EIA. "Prolongation of the International Steel Agreement," in *International Cartels*, I, No. 1, 14.

[37] The accords were designated as "tentative agreements" which should be made more effective, according to a draft of a report published as annex to Part 20, TNEC, *Hearings*, p. 11018. The report had been sent to the presidents of the member companies of the board of managers of the Steel Export Association of America. *The Economist* (Dec., 1937) spoke of coöperation with America secured by an "informal understanding on prices, covering most products apart from sheets." . . . "While the United States," continues *The Economist*, "cannot be expected to join the Cartel, an informal understanding, if observed, would achieve the same object." *The Economist*, CXXIX, 468. Mr. Walter S. Tower regarded "an informal, friendly understanding" as an act which could accomplish "everything that a full membership in the syndicate has to offer." *Foreign Affairs*, V (1926-27), 266. The pact was called a "modus vivendi" as contrasted with a permanent agreement, in *Steel*, Jan. 2, 1939, p. 260.

[38] TNEC, *Hearings*, Part 20, p. 10982. [39] TNEC, *Hearings*, Part 20, p. 10982.

due to the independent position which the British held in the framework of the European steel organization and partly because of the natural ease with which they could negotiate with another English-speaking country. During the time the steel pact with America was in operation, the British representatives very efficiently bridged gaps, sometimes very deep, between European and American interests.

The written text of the continental-British-American steel understanding was very brief and sketchy, covering not more than two typewritten pages. The most important provision of the accord was the agreement to collaborate on the world steel market. However, many details of coöperation were expected to be agreed upon later. It was implied that Americans would participate in the most important management and policy-making activities of the European cartel[40] without interfering with small internal problems.

Differences of opinion, especially as to price policy and business strategy, were not to be settled by vote or in graver cases by arbitration tribunals. Such a system would not have worked. Though the agreement was effective only until 1940,[41] the three parties to the pact knew that if the agreement did not operate, it would be dissolved even earlier, that is, before its contemplated expiration date. The understanding intended to establish a close collaboration of the American group with individual comptoirs, even with those comptoirs which America did not join before 1938. Such close coöperation required a set of "sectional agreements."[42] However, when the cartel disintegrated in September 1939, these sectional agreements were still incomplete. America was not placed "on the same strict statistical basis" as Europe and the agreements did not function in a "watertight manner," according to Spencer Summers.[43] There was a striking difference between the position of American producers in comptoirs entered before 1938 and their position in those comptoirs entered as a consequence of the general pact. Whereas in the former (e.g. rails, tin plate) Americans were ordinary members, although subject to fewer limitations than their fellow cartel members, in the latter comptoirs (e.g. semifinished steel, thick plates) American coöperation was rather

---

[40] ". . . as partners, we consider that we are entitled to know what they are actually doing." (Quoted from a letter published in the TNEC, *Hearings,* Part 20, p. 11020.) In order to facilitate collaboration with the ISC and with export sales comptoirs, the Steel Export Association of America maintained a representative and a bureau in London (Brettenham House, Strand, W.C. 2.).

[41] See TNEC, *Hearings,* Part 20, Exhibit 1448, p. 11020.

[42] *Iron Age,* Mar. 10, 1938, p. 86, states that quota agreements were reached in about twelve comptoirs.   [43] *ICTR,* Jan. 20, 1939, p. 104.

loose, and the comptoirs did not direct American business strategy. However, the collaboration extended to quota regulations and uniform prices and extras.

The American group obligated itself not to sell in the interior markets of the European national groups,[44] although it avoided, in compliance with the Webb-Pomerene Act, a demand for the artificial protection of its own domestic market from European intrusion.[45] "Spheres of influence" were recognized for the American group.[46]

Quotas of the American group in particular commodities were determined with exports of the year 1936 as a reference period. The American group insisted on taking 1936 as a base period because that year was more favorable than 1934, which was the reference period in most of the EIA comptoirs for the British group.[47]

Originally the exports of all American exporters were included in the American quotas. This meant that it made no difference whether members or non-members of the Steel Export Association of America were responsible for exhausting or exceeding the quota. In quota arrangements, the American group was responsible for its outsiders too. This system of responsibility for outside producers was generally adopted in the ISC framework. For American exporters to exceed quotas meant that the American group would be charged with penalties.[48] Thus it might happen that the members of the association

---

[44] See TNEC, *Hearings*, Part 20, p. 10931.

[45] Imports intended to be weapons of foreign producers against domestic production could be met by several provisions of the existing tariff legislation. The present tariff laws and their influence on imports has been officially analyzed in Report No. 128, *Iron and Steel*, of the U. S. Tariff Commission, *passim*, and in *Monograph No. 10* of the TNEC, Clifford L. James, "Industrial Concentration and Tariffs." Mr. James judges that duties on the main rolled steel products probably restrict imports appreciably. He believes that (the author does not follow his opinion in this regard) even for these products ". . . removal or substantial reduction of duties would assist in offsetting monopolistic elements in the domestic industries . . ." (pp. 23, 220-228). The TNEC analyzed the "danger" of European imports in connection with international cartel negotiations. See *Hearings*, Part 20, pp. 10951 and 11018 and W. A. Irvin, "Competition from Imports of Foreign Steel Products," *Yearbook of American Iron and Steel Institute,* 1936, pp. 46 ff.; also Abraham Berglund and Philip G. Wright, *The Tariff on Iron and Steel* (Washington, 1929), *passim*. Concerning the proposition "Either reduce your prices or in will come competitive material," see TNEC, *Hearings,* Part 20, p. 10808. See also Haberler, *op. cit.*, pp. 324-25, 331.

[46] TNEC, *Hearings,* Part 20, p. 10930.

[47] According to TNEC, *Hearings,* Part 20, p. 10935, the year 1934 was used as a reference period "among the Europeans." The reference periods used for quota allotments are discussed in Chapters III and VI.

[48] *ICTR*, Feb. 17, 1939, p. 351, said that the arrangement with the Americans was subject to severe criticism within the cartel because exports of United States' steelmakers

would be obliged to pay penalties even though they themselves did not exceed the quotas, that is, even when non-adherents to the agreement were responsible.

The American group felt that its situation in regard to the outsider problem was more difficult than the position of the European national groups. The first reason for the allegedly greater difficulties was that there were several strong outsider-exporters[49] in America, though the association united more than 80 per cent of the regular exports. The second reason was that the Webb-Pomerene Act prevented American members of the association and the association itself from taking aggressive measures to eliminate the outsiders from the market or force them to join the association. The difficulties were even stronger because the outsiders allegedly entered the export market only when conditions on the home market were unfavorable in regard to employment or when prices on the export market were more favorable.[50] It was stated in the TNEC investigations that European cartel members were advised that American members of the association did not mind the reduction of prices on the world market by European cartel members if the prices were "sufficiently low actually to eliminate the American outsiders."[51] The representative of the Steel Export Association claimed that the policy of the association was not detrimental to the outsider and thus not in violation of the Webb-Pomerene Act. He contended further that the association's policy did not act as a compulsion on outsiders to join the cartel.[52]

---

signatory to the agreements were much in advance of the tonnage agreed upon. Excluding the exports of American outsiders, the quota excess of American adherents during the last months of 1938 amounted to 40,000 tons. According to *ICTR*, Apr. 7, 1939, p. 642, an exchange of views took place in the ISC because America exceeded its 20 per cent quota in thin sheets.

[49] They were called "have nots," in TNEC, *Hearings*, Part 20, p. 11018.

[50] *Ibid.*, and *ICTR*, Jan. 20, 1939, p. 115.

[51] TNEC, *Hearings*, Part 20, pp. 10949 ff., 10958, 11020, and Poor's *Industry and Investment Survey in the Iron and Steel Industry*, Apr. 12, 1939, quoted *ibid*. According to a report in *ICTR*, Jan. 20, 1939, p. 115, the cartel reduced the prices of a majority of steel products 10 to 15 per cent in order to combat a wave of competition from American outsiders. The reduction consisted partially in abolishing premiums for early delivery. *ICTR*, Jan. 28, 1938, p. 203. According to *The Times* (London), Apr. 8, 1939, p. 17a, and the *ICTR*, Jan. 21, 1938, p. 166, some of the American members of the cartel cut prices as well. At the same time some of the European cartel members were also suspected of cutting prices. *ICTR*, Jan. 17, 1938, p. 23, and Jan. 14, 1938 (Report on Belgium).

[52] TNEC, *Hearings*, Part 20, pp. 10959, 10966. Concerning the extent of American outside competition in South Africa and in the Far East, see the report about the London meetings of the cartel, *Iron Age*, Sept. 22, 1938, pp. 78-79. However, *The*

During the test period, that is, in the first months of 1938, the American group felt that to pay penalties because of excessive exports of American outsiders would be too onerous. Principally for this reason, it approached the European members of the cartel about amending the original agreement by differentiating between quota excesses of members and of non-members of the association. An agreement was reached relatively soon; however, even with this amendment, the American group was still held slightly responsible for its outsiders. A report, obviously derived from well-informed circles, says that the provisional agreement in force was replaced in June 1938 "by a definitive agreement covering both export tonnages and prices."[53] Thus, by changing the original agreement in June 1938, the first test period was regarded as terminated.[54] The confirmation of the amended agreements may be seen in the official communique of the cartel issued after the meeting in Rome.[55] Smaller readjustments of the American understandings were agreed upon early in 1939.[56]

The American agreement provided for uniform prices according to periodic or incidental accords between the groups. The application of this provision met with some difficulty, for one reason, because the American group was not yet familiar with the intricacies of the pricing system of the European groups, and vice versa. Difficulties also arose because the extra lists pertaining to size, quality, quantity, and lengths of the American and the European groups were not coördinated.[57] The greatest difficulty resulted from the fact that during the first part of 1938 circumstances often required the use of special prices, agreed upon for individual transactions between exporters and the particular export sales comptoir.[58]

Economist saw American competition diminishing at that time, whereas Belgian rerollers were sharply raiding the market. Vol. CXXXIII, 675.

[53] *ICTR*, Jan. 20, 1939, p. 115.

[54] *International Cartels*, I, No. 1, 16, 17 (1939), and *Iron Age*, July 7, 1938, pp. 84 ff. *The Times* (London) described the situation as it was on June 14, 1938, after the Paris meeting of the enlarged joint co-ordinating committee, as giving "fair promise that an effective agreement will be reached at an early date" with the Americans. June 15, 1938, p. 21.

[55] *Iron Age*, June 9, 1938, p. 77.   [56] *Iron Age*, Jan. 12, 1939, p. 84.

[57] According to the extra lists of the comptoirs, as mentioned above, such items as the desire of the customer to have the commodity necessarily delivered in open-hearth steel played an important role.

[58] See e.g., *Iron Age*, Mar. 30, 1939, p. 57, about the authorization of comptoirs to deviate from general price policies. C. S. Richards, *op. cit.*, Annexure B, n. 4, remarks that large South African consumers, especially the Railway Administration, have occasionally secured considerable reductions from official cartel prices to meet in particular American competition. Richards mentions one case (Tender No. 1718)

One striking incident characteristic of American-European competition in steel should be mentioned here. In January 1938 the government-owned South African Iron and Steel Corporation, Limited (ISCOR), charged United States steel exporters with selling thick plates, merchant bars, and sheets in South Africa far below fair average world prices, below South African domestic prices, and below domestic prices of cartel countries. These commodities were, according to ISCOR, "dumped," at prices materially lower than American domestic prices. Besides these "ordinary" dumping charges, American exporters were accused of "freight dumping" because the freight calculated in the prices of the products mentioned was from 4 to 20 British shillings lower than what ISCOR regarded as "normal freight."[59] ISCOR objected bitterly to American exporters' disturbing the harmonious steel relations of South Africa with the ISC.[60] One should note that the complaints were made at a time when United States' exporter-producers began their general coöperation with the ISC. It is not known whether American outsiders or members of the American group were involved in the business transactions complained of by the ISCOR. As a consequence of the ISCOR charges, the government of South Africa on August 5, 1938, introduced "freight dumping duties," and in addition, on October 11, 1938, "ordinary dumping

---

where the cartel, in May 1938, quoted a price of £2/15/0 per ton below the official price to meet American competition.

[59] Freight rates for plates per net ton in British currency from British and European continental ports, and from United States Atlantic ports to Capetown were the following, according to C. S. Richards, *op. cit.*, Appendix 6 F:

From British and continental ports:

1929	1930	1931	1932	1933	1934	1935	1936	1937	1938
1.15.8	1.15.8	1.15.8	1.5.10	1.15.8	1.15.8	1.12.4	1.5.8	1.15.8	1.15.8

From U. S. A. Atlantic ports:

1929	1930	1931	1932	1933	1934	1935	1936	1937	1938
2.7.8	2.7.8	2.7.8	2.7.8	1.9.8	1.4.9	1.5.6	1.5.2	1.2.7	0.19.10

Thus whereas the freight rates from Europe remained rather stable, those from United States ports decreased considerably. Concerning fluctuations of British ocean freight rates see *World Economic Survey*, 1937-38 (League of Nations, Geneva, 1938), p. 83.

[60] Early relations between ISCOR and ISC were not very harmonious. ISCOR, before concluding an agreement with the cartel, attempted to prompt the South African government to introduce dumping duties against steel commodities originating in Belgium and Luxemburg. But according to C. S. Richards, *op. cit.*, p. 383, "It was officially admitted impossible to prove dumping, and the plea of the ISCOR for dumping duties against imports from these two countries became a demand not for duties against dumping, but for protection against the products of two countries with which . . . it could not compete." Comprehensive information about South African dumping duties on steel may be found in C. S. Richards, *op. cit.*, Statistical Appendix No. 5. and 366 ff.

duties" for steel plates, merchant bars, and sheets originating from the United States. Both dumping duties were withdrawn on May 5, 1939. Richards, sharply attacking the South African government for introducing these dumping duties, censures the role of the ISC in encouraging the South African Steel Corporation during this incident.[61]

Soon after the beginning of the testing period, early in 1938, it became necessary to discuss several important problems of coöperation between European and American groups.[62] One set of problems arose from the sharp competition by European groups and American outsiders at the end of 1937 and at the beginning of 1938. To be sure, 1938 was a bad year for sales on the export market. The second set of obstacles arose because of the nonrealization of the so-called "sheet agreement." The hearings of the TNEC disclosed the American group's difficulties in trying to get all pertinent sheet producers to join the association. In order to eliminate these two sets of difficulties, four leading personalities of the European Steel Cartel sailed to America at the end of January 1938. The delegation consisted of the Earl of Dudley, at that time president of the British Iron and Steel Corporation, Mr. I. F. L. Elliott, director of the same corporation, Mr. Spencer Summers, member of the Board of Directors of the British Iron and Steel Corporation and chairman of both the International Black and Galvanized Sheet Comptoirs, and the versatile Mr. Hector Dieudonné, chairman of the comptoir committee of the EIA. The negotiations between the Europeans and the representatives of American exporters were quite frank.[63] The European delegation expressed itself as satisfied with the results of its American trip.[64] The leader of the European delegation, the Earl of Dudley, two days after his return from New York, at the annual dinner of the Staffordshire Iron and Steel Institute said that he had discussed with the leaders of the American steel industry, "the machinery already established within our cartel arrangements for insuring that stupid and senseless cutthroat compe-

[61] See C. S. Richards, *op. cit.,* pp. 412 ff.

[62] See *Iron Age,* Feb. 3, 1938, p. 114 D (Report about the cartel meeting of Paris, Jan. 17, 1938).

[63] TNEC, *Hearings,* Part 20, pp. 10948, 11018.

[64] According to a report (*The Times* [London], Feb. 11, 1938, p. 21), with a New York dateline, the British delegation sailed from New York on the Queen Mary on Feb. 10, 1938, without revealing the outcome. "The impression in interested quarters here is," reported Reuter, "that the results are entirely negative." *The Financial Times* (London) remarked in its issue of Mar. 7, 1938, that "The Cartel has now entered upon a new phase. . . ." An extract of the article in *The Financial Times* which gives a good survey of the situation at that time may be found in Alfred Plummer, *International Combines in Modern Industry* (London, 1938), p. 258.

tition would not be added to the other difficulties in the way of export business. . . ." He had the impression that the leaders of the American steel industry wholeheartedly agreed with these objectives.[65]

In order to support a close coöperation with separate comptoirs, an agency had been set up in London to enhance coöperation with America.[66] It consisted of the London representatives of the Steel Export Association of America, a representative of the comptoir committee of the EIA, a representative of the British Iron and Steel Federation, and a neutral chairman, probably a partner of a public accounting firm in London.[67] It is difficult to say whether this agency operated during 1938. An official EIA report of June 1939 says that the members of the special agency met frequently and worked satisfactorily.[68]

IV

The general participation of America in the international steel agreements lasted, including the testing period, eighteen months altogether. It may safely be stated that the collaboration did not approach perfection but improved steadily. The period of its duration was too short and political and economic circumstances during the time that coöperation took place were too extraordinary[69] to secure perfect collaboration. An official communication of the EIA in Luxemburg, published a few months before the outbreak of the Second World War, regarded the collaboration between American and European exporters as perfected, although some details were still to be settled and disturbances by American outsiders were still felt.[70] However,

---

[65] Quoted from *Iron Age,* Mar. 10, 1938, p. 87.

[66] ". . . a direct result of recent negotiations in New York will be the establishment of a central office in the United Kingdom. Its special duty will be to take stock of the activities of outsiders. . . ." *Iron Age,* Mar. 10, 1938, p. 86.

[67] Plummer, *op. cit.,* p. 258, *Iron Age,* Mar. 10, 1938, p. 86, and Mar. 17, 1938, p. 93 B.

[68] *International Cartels,* I (1939) No. 2, 14. Up to Mar. 1939 the London Bureau was regarded as more or less dormant. *ICTR,* Mar. 31, 1939, p. 604. At the beginning of Apr. 1939 it was decided that this committee would meet regularly in the future. (*The Times,* London, Apr. 8, 1939, p. 17a.) *ICTR,* June 9, 1939, p. 1016, stressed a better liaison with the London Bureau.

[69] An official document of the League of Nations registering international agreements between producers and others—No. E. 1067—dated in Geneva, March 15, 1939, says on p. 8 regarding the American Steel coöperation, "In spite of the agreement concluded between the Cartel and the Steel Export Association of America, American competition is still noticeable. The agreement between Europe and the United States does not yet seem to be firmly established."

[70] *International Cartels,* 1939, No. 2, p. 14. According to *ICTR,* Mar. 31, 1939, p. 604, American outsiders were securing a substantial portion of merchant bar exports,

reports existed to the effect that even American "insiders" were competing with European cartel members.[71]

After the start of the Second World War, a new form of collaboration began between American steel producers and the British Iron and Steel Corporation as the representative of both British and Canadian steel producers.[72] However, this coöperation cannot be regarded as an extension of the old collaboration within the framework of the ISC.

---

30 per cent of sheets and 16 per cent of shapes. Another report of the *ICTR*, July 7, 1939, p. 26, states that American outsider competition compelled rebates of 12s 6d (gold) per ton.

[71] See *The Times* (London), Apr. 8, 1939, p. 17a, *ICTR*, Feb. 24, 1939, p. 392, *ibid.*, July 21, 1939, p. 107.

[72] *Iron Age*, Jan. 30, 1941, p. 84.

CHAPTER TEN

Political Implications

I

THE STRUCTURE, ramifications, and operations of the ISC have often been regarded as highly characteristic of that economic period which ended with the beginning of the Second World War. Indeed, many people considered large international industrial combinations, such as the ISC and its sub-units, important pillars in the political development of that period as well.[1] Although neither the leaders of nor the participants in national and international steel cartels were anxious to have their organizations under discussion on a national or international scale, the structure and activities of these steel cartels were often the focus of political discussion and argument. Criticism centered on the concentration of huge economic power in private hands, on possible abuses of such power in limiting output and supplies, on the dangers of monopolistic power in determining prices and discriminatory policies, and in influencing employment and labor problems. On the other hand, such organizations as the ISC were credited with the promotion of international peace through harmonious economic collaboration, and the moderation of great trade fluctuations.

Steel is not the sole but is one of the most significant elements in determining the war potential of a nation.[2] Admittedly, the war potential of a nation is a political problem even in times of peace. The lack of appropriate coal, iron ore, scrap, and auxiliary materials on

---

[1] "Of the importance of these efforts to the relations between nations there could be no doubt. Unless the economic struggles which underlay political rivalries could be reached, a great part of the machinery of peace would simply be going round out of gear with the forces which it must effectively control if the whole mechanism were not to break down." (W. Y. Elliott, *International Control in the Non-Ferrous Metals*, p. 3.) See also Herman Kranold, *The International Distribution of Raw Materials*, London, 1938, pp. 2 ff. and 165 ff.

[2] See Sir Arthur Salter, *Security* (New York, 1939), p. 72.

the one hand, and the lack of capital with which to finance investments on the other, are reasons for the inability of some nations to develop adequate steel industries of their own.[3] For instance, among the totalitarian warring powers, Japan and Italy may be regarded as so-called "have-nots" in steel, whereas Germany has a sufficiently large steel production, although that country has been dependent on other nations for its iron ore and scrap supply. That an international artificial steel control scheme might work against the interests of political entities in their desire for self-sufficiency in regard to steel, lends political significance to the operation of that control scheme.

There are many political questions involved in the international marketing of steel, only part of which relate specifically to international marketing control schemes, the subject under discussion. In the latter connection, the question arises whether it might be considered politically dangerous for a single agency, such as the ISC, to be responsible for the exclusive supply of a material vital to the security of steel-importing nations. A further question arises as to whether this restriction of the source of supply might imply a limitation in quantity and discrimination in prices which might either cause or result from political pressure on national governments.

Apparently neither national governments nor such international agencies as the League of Nations ever felt apprehensive about the effects of the monopolistic control of markets by the ISC on the political security of steel-importing nations. Though it was suggested that the ISC and its sub-entities be placed under the supervision of some international political agency and that the interests of steel consumers and of labor should be safeguarded by this supervision, neither the League of Nations, nor such politically sponsored economic conferences as that of Geneva in 1927, and of London in 1933, expressed the desirability of establishing a competitive international steel market.

Tendencies of the ISC to discourage the establishment of new steel-producing facilities in countries which, in the opinion of the ISC, did not possess "natural" conditions for the establishment of steel industries, did not originate in political considerations. The fear of losing markets and the persuasion that abundant steel-producing facilities existed within the ISC were the exclusive motivating forces behind this attitude.

In regard to the possibility of a limitation of supply and its con-

---

[3] See Erich Walter Zimmermann, *World Resources and Industries* (New York, 1933), pp. 612 ff.

sequent political effects on the security of steel-importing nations, there is no reason to believe that any nation had to face a real or potential scarcity of steel deliveries in times of peace. As a matter of fact, in peacetime any political pressure which the ISC or its national groups could exert was directed toward the enlargement of markets rather than toward exercising pressure by limiting supplies. The abundance of raw materials and steel-producing facilities, and their dispersion throughout the world, have given steel a peculiar position among the politically important commodities. Save the American embargo on scrap and steel to Japan, which incidentally did not occur during the ISC period, no official or unofficial restraints were put on steel deliveries for political reasons. Japan's war potential despite her relatively small steel capacity is a striking example of this fact. This does not mean that governments failed to exercise pressure on their domestic steel industries to satisfy their domestic demand first, particularly when export prices were attractive.[4] However, such pressure caused some delay but no serious hampering of deliveries to steel-importing countries.

Although ISC prices in many importing countries frequently differed, this discrimination had no political origin. An attempt to introduce "political prices" in steel would have been blocked by the fact that ISC leaders did not belong to one single political group. Soviet Russia for instance bought and received steel under favorable conditions and the ISC made great efforts to enhance its exports in that direction.[5] This whole subject is developed more fully in the chapter devoted to the price policy of the ISC.

Though national groups of private entrepreneurs actually controlled ISC actions, there is no doubt that the problem of entering the

---

[4] *Bulletin d'Information et de Documentation,* Sept. 1938, p. 179, discusses the complaint of Belgian domestic jobbers that Cosibel, the Belgian national steel cartel, was disregarding the domestic market in favor of exports. The motion presented to British Parliament by Mr. Ernest A. Lake to restrict English steel exports since the domestic steel shortage was hindering rearmament and causing unemployment was not carried because steel export trade was considered of "fundamental" importance. *The Times* (London), Oct. 9, 1937, pp. 7 f.

[5] Just before Germany turned Nazi, it exported heavily to Soviet Russia, setting rather favorable prices with government support. The following figures show the significance of German steel exports to the Soviet Union in 1932, in 1,000 metric tons, according to Carl Graeff, *op. cit.,* p. 54.

	Thin and med. sheets	Thick plates	Semifinished steel	Structural shapes	Merchant bars
All exports	156.5	158.7	74.8	81.6	484.5
Those to U.S.S.R. ...	113.0	138.0	22.0	50.0	290.0

ISC, and of policies within the ISC, were heavily influenced at least in Europe by the respective governments of the member groups. No case is known of any government's opposition to the participation of its steel industry in the ISC. Conversely, many cases are known where home and foreign governments exercised pressure on steel industries to enter or reënter the ISC.

There is a certain parallelism between several political highlights of the period 1920-1939, and important events in the development of the ISC. The great political tension ensuing after the First World War was first considerably moderated by Germany's entering the League of Nations in September 1926. It is not without significance that the birth of the ISC occurred in the same month. After the disintegration of the first EIA agreement, it was reëstablished on a permanent basis in 1933, the same year in which the Economic Conference in London, which was expected to reëstablish world economy, took place. The completion of the European Steel Cartel by the entrance of Great Britain coincided with the signing of the politically significant British-German Naval Treaty.

II

At its birth the ISC was hailed throughout the world as an event of dominant significance in international politics. As time went on its political significance was less and less emphasized. The establishment of the ISC was openly supported by the governments of the participating countries. For example, in steel-exporting Belgium, where socialists played a dominant role in the national government, the socialist Foreign Minister, Mr. Vandervelde, made every effort in the name of his government to force the Belgian steel industry to enter the EIA. According to contemporary reports, he even approached British iron and steel manufacturers, asking them to join the cartel.[6] Belgian Senator Louis de Brouckère, chairman of the Labour and Socialist International, regarded the steel pact as a favorable result of the new Locarno policy. However, he took exception to the accumulation of economic power in private hands. Public supervision of large combinations would be more desirable, according to de Brouckère, because of the role of heavy industries in the preparation for war.[7] In Luxemburg the government regarded the EIA as a secure foundation for international economic and political coöperation.

---

[6] "Continental Steel Trust Negotiations," *ICTR*, Oct. 1, 1926, p. 493.
[7] *Berliner Tageblatt*, Oct. 1, 1926, No. 463.

Though in France critical voices were raised against possible repercussions on the domestic market, the ISC was received with a feeling
of great relief. The former minister for reconstruction, Louis Loucheur, emphasized the great political significance of the steel pact
which he had advocated for many years, although he seemed to doubt
whether the governments sponsoring the pact had sufficient regard for
the interests of ultimate steel consumers.[8]

Germany's reaction to the new steel accord may be regarded as
most significant because it was generally evaluated as a turning point
in her attitude toward international collaboration. The official opinion
of the coalition government was proclaimed the day following the
signature of the EIA accord by the German Foreign Minister, Dr.
Gustav Stresemann, in emphatic words: "I regard the conclusion of
the international steel cartel as a landmark of international economic
policy the importance of which cannot be overestimated. I welcome
this agreement though clearly realizing the dangers which it implies
in the fact of the concentration of such great economic power in a
few private hands. It has been the objective of my life to realize in
the political field what has been accomplished in economics by this
pact. Groups of industries which a short time ago regarded their
interests as irreconcilably opposed, met to bridge their differences and
to regulate their production in conformity with their mutual requirements and with the demands of the world market. Although the
International Steel Cartel was preceded by other international economic agreements, none of them approached it in importance, both
because of the extent of the capital involved, and because of the significance of steel as the key commodity in public economy. I expect
that the creation of this new accord will be accompanied by a marked
change in the basic attitude of large industries on the international
market. Before the [First] World War and especially in the emergency following, the general attitude of large industries was expressed
by the desire to expand their production to the limit, and to use this
production to appropriate the world market by eliminating competitors. We realize now that such an eternal struggle necessarily implies
a permanent fluctuation of market conditions accompanied by a pathological fluctuation of prices which cannot bring a lasting advantage
to either party. An atmosphere full of tensions caused by opposing
economic interests not only conceals dangers for the development of
industries themselves but also implies threats to the political peace of

---

[8] *Ibid.*

the nations. I hail this attempt to dispel these heavy strains. The most valuable point in the steel pact in my opinion is its tendency to become sincerely international. This seems to me expressed by the clause of the agreement which invites other nations to join it. It is to be hoped that before too long it will be generally recognized that friendly coöperation is sounder than unlimited competition in the economic field also. I hope that this great idea of collaboration will be fruitful and that other industries without regard to state boundaries will follow the example of the steel industries."[9] Dr. Stresemann saw international political coöperation vitally affected by the establishment of international control schemes and by the elimination of *laissez faire* and unlimited competition in economic life.

At the end of November 1926 the international steel pact was discussed at length in the German lower chamber. Significantly, the matter was reviewed in detail in a joint meeting of the committees for foreign affairs and economic policy. The German minister of national economy, Dr. Curtius, emphasized the fact that though the discussions preceding the accord were carried on by private groups, the German government had been kept informed about all phases of the negotiations. He stressed the fact that the government expressly permitted these negotiations, with certain conditions. "If the large German industries obligate themselves to buy steel products from France, an agreement to regulate competition on the world market should accompany this obligation." According to Dr. Curtius, it was not an accident that during the two years preceding 1926 German governments of various political colors found such an agreement an important means of enhancing the political peace of Europe. He regarded it imperative that the huge economic power put in private hands should not be abused. Dr. Curtius felt that an increase in the world price of steel should be one of the objectives of the new cartel.[10] The reaction of the rather strong Socialist party to the speech of Dr. Curtius may be summarized by the opinion of a famous Socialist, Dr. Hilferding, member of the Reichstag and former minister of finance. He also regarded the steel pact as an important landmark in the development of an international economy. According to Hilferding, the definitely anti-Socialistic creators of the cartel acted as Marxist propagandists in a most effective manner by establishing this organization. To him, international cartels seemed stronger than

[9] Quoted from the *Frankfurter Zeitung*, Oct. 2, 1926, No. 735, p. 1.
[10] *Frankfurter Zeitung*, Nov. 24, 1926, No. 874, p. 2.

modern states endowed with sovereignty. He attacked the Communists' opposition to the cartel, calling Communists anti-Marxist. Mr. Hilferding proposed to confer upon the League of Nations the supervision of the activities of international cartels. The joint meeting of the two Reichstag committees was closed with the emphatic statement of its chairman that the world had obviously arrived at the beginning of a new economic period.[11] However, an editorial in the *Frankfurter Zeitung* looked upon the political significance of the steel pact rather skeptically, stating that real peace could result only from political measures, though admitting that political harmony might be complicated by economic struggles. The editorial emphasized the fact that the relation of the state to cartels should be reconsidered, from the aspect of the necessary democratizing of the highly capitalistic economic structure. The editorial writer was obviously disturbed by the non-participation of Great Britain and the United States in the agreement. The editorial predicted that unless England joined the agreement as soon as the internal disorganization of the British industry was remedied, a fight might develop between the EIA on the one hand and the British-American groups on the other, which would complicate political problems.[12] German Nazi circles at that time called the steel accord "a felony against the German economy."[13] The Communist party in the German Reichstag proposed the cancellation of customs duties on steel, stating that the German domestic market was sufficiently protected by the cartel agreement. This proposal was heavily opposed by the industry and by several political parties, and finally rejected.

The reëstablishment of the EIA in June 1933 did not arouse loud political repercussions. Though the chairman of the German group, Ernst Poensgen, hailed the new cartel as an accomplishment leading to an "economic Pan-Europe,"[14] a leading German economic magazine, recalling earlier expectations of a moderation of political tension because of the existence of the cartel, wrote: "Hopes attached to the conclusion of the steel pact in the field of international politics had to be buried soon. Nobody speaks today [July 1933] of its political effects any more."[15]

---

[11] *Ibid.*

[12] *Frankfurter Zeitung*, Oct. 1, 1926, No. 732, pp. 1-2.

[13] Dr. J. W. Reichert, "Die Festländische Rohstahlgemeinschaft," *Weltwirtschaftliches Archiv*, 1927, I, p. 340*.   [14] *Wirtschaftskurve*, July 1933, pp. 168-169.

[15] Dr. Georg Wolff, "Neuordnung am internationalen Eisenmarkt," *Wirtschaftskurve*, July 1933, p. 172. However, according to R. D. Charques and A. H. Ewen

III

During the decade following the First World War, and even later until the demise of the appeasement policy, a limited number of politicians and economists on both sides of the Atlantic assumed that Europe as an entity on the one hand, and America on the other, were or might become rivals in international politics, including international economics. They advocated aggressive and defensive measures on their own continents in order to gain world markets for themselves. Especially at the time of the establishment of the ISC (1926), both the advocates of the concept Pan-Europa and the proponents of the idea of dividing the world into large spheres of influence detected indications of pungent economic competition between the power groups of both continents. National and international cartelization was often considered as the institutional blueprint on which either economic collaboration throughout the world, or European internal coöperation in case of economic conflict with America, could be based.

In an often-quoted speech at the World Economic Conference in 1927, the French politician Louis Loucheur pointed to the European-American rivalry as one of the reasons for the necessity of establishing European international cartels.[16] Another famous French politician, Mr. Edouard Herriot, regarded international cartels as an important means of establishing a new political and economic order in Europe. Anticipating (in 1930) a rivalry (especially in steel) between Europe and the United States on the export market, retarded only by the extraordinary capacity of the American market for absorption, he stated that: "in such a competition a disunited Europe would be defeated in advance."[17] Opinions of Americans may be also cited.

(*Profits and Politics in the Post-War World,* London, 1934, p. 278), the new *rapprochement* of the German and French heavy industries was sponsored by Herr von Papen, in collaboration with Mr. François-Poncet, the French ambassador in Berlin.

[16] *Report and Proceedings of the World Economic Conference* (Geneva, 1927), I, 132-133.

[17] *The United States of Europe* (London, 1930), pp. 108-109, 121, 146. Similar statements in connection with the international steel pact may be found in Lucien Romier, *Qui sera le maître? Europe ou Amérique?* (Paris, Hachette, 1927), *passim.* Sir Arthur Salter notes that the problem of "how to increase world prosperity" had gradually taken the form in the public mind of "how can Europe compete against America." Although this conception was rather confused it "usually assumes an anti-American form." Sir Arthur, designating these views as regrettable, and admitting that American progress might injure certain special European industries, emphasized that "it does not diminish European prosperity *absolutely:* it increases it." His statement that ". . . the United States of Europe must be a political reality or it cannot be an economic one," preceded the statement regarding the need for a fundamental general

Commercial Attaché Cooper found that "the conclusion of the European steel agreement has been hailed by some of its sponsors as the greatest recent economic development and a first step toward the formation of an "Economic United States of Europe.""[18] The Director of the Bureau of Foreign and Domestic Commerce, Dr. Julius Klein, referred to the steel pact in a Congressional committee as "a most aggressive drive" against American export markets.[19] After the EIA agreement had operated for fourteen months, the same official, on December 5, 1927, in a statement before a subcommittee of the House Committee on Appropriations, called attention to the "formidable" stiffening of European competition in the export markets "notably in the development of cartels and combinations." As an example he pointed to "the greatest alarm regarding the steel situation" on the Pacific coast, remarking that "a number of new steel industries have cropped up all along the coast." According to Dr. Klein, "Recently there has been a very marked increase in European exports of steel to the Pacific coast. . . ." Referring to the fact that the first international steel cartel was established more than a year before, he concluded that European industries were "striving rather blindly toward comparable advantages" with those enjoyed by the American industry because of its large domestic market. Considering the EIA "a formidable new competitive weapon" he inferred that an attempt was being made to set up a "European steel industry which would counterbalance the American steel industry. . . . Steel, of course," according to Dr. Klein, "is one of the biggest items in our export trade." He

---

subordination of the economic to the political problem included in Briand's *Memorandum on European Federal Union*. ". . . the main competition of every country in Europe is not with America but with other European countries; it was this competition and not American which was the origin of the tariffs; and if American competition and tariffs are an additional obstacle to their removal, as they are, they are not the only one." Sir Arthur made it clear that "the object is to encourage not cartels and monopolies, but security of equal opportunity." *The United States of Europe* (New York, 1933), pp. 89-90, 92, 99. As a matter of fact, all European governments which answered the Briand *Memorandum* were in agreement with the basic idea of a closer European coöperation, but most of them disagreed about the methods of attaining coöperation. A great many governments, including the British, expressed their opposition to the idea of inter-continental rivalries. A summary of the Briand *Memorandum* and the answers of the European governments to it are included in the *Bulletin of International News*, Royal Institute of International Affairs, Sept. 11, 1930, and in *International Conciliation*, Special Bulletin (June 1930), and No. 265 (December 1930).

[18] *Trade Information Bulletin* No. 484, p. 41.

[19] Subcommittee of House Committee on Appropriations, *Appropriations, Department of Commerce, 1927*, pp. 219 ff. See also the corresponding document for 1928, p. 305.

proceeded, expounding the theory that "the development of the European cartel situation has, of course, roused universal concern in all of the affected industries in this country."[20]   However, a competent representative of the American steel industry, Walter S. Tower, spoke about the European cartel situation with considerable calm, stating that "that policy would be more to the advantage than disadvantage of British and American steel makers. . . . The suggestion that the syndicate may try to drive United States and British steel from neutral markets, and then invade both the United States and Great Britain with added volume of imports, is highly fanciful." Mr. Tower did not attribute much importance to European steel exports to Gulf and Pacific coast points, though "it is always likely to persist, to some extent. . . ."[21]   The general interest in the international cartel movement prompted another high official of the Department of Commerce, Mr. Louis Domeratzky, to indicate the attitude of the average American businessman toward international cartels.   The businessman believes, according to Mr. Domeratzky, that "such organizations are aimed primarily at the American producers and consumers, and represent the alleged combination of Europe against the economic hegemony of the United States."[22]

Walter S. Tower regarded the young EIA as "An industrial syndicate on a scale never before approached. . . . In its reach beyond national boundaries this agreement marks a new phase of economic relations. It opens great possibilities." Dr. Tower, registering skeptical opinions concerning the life prognosis of the international steel pact, wrote that many people looked on the steel cartel as marking "a new political and economic alignment in Europe and consider it the greatest guarantee for peace Europe ever had."[23]   Both the desire for self-protection and the "preparations for a war for supremacy in world steel markets" may have motivated the establishment of the EIA, according to Dr. Tower. "As a force in the steel industry in particular, the syndicate is of special and continuing concern to producer and consumer alike."[24]

---

[20] *Appropriations, Department of Commerce, 1929,* Hearing before Subcommittee of House Committee on Appropriations (Washington, 1928), pp. 363 f.

[21] Walter S. Tower, "The New Steel Cartel," *Foreign Affairs,* Jan. 1927, pp. 263-266.

[22] "The International Steel Cartel Movement," *Trade Information Bulletin* No. 556 (Washington, 1928), p. 2. Similar ideas may be found in an article by A. Cressy Morrison, "The League of Nations, cartels and the tariff," reprinted in the *Congressional Record,* May 8, 1928, pp. 8483 ff.

[23] "The New Steel Cartel," *Foreign Affairs,* Jan. 1927, p. 249.

[24] *Ibid.,* p. 258.

The desire to fight American competition was considered by the British magazine, *The Economist,* as one of the motives on the part of Germany for the signing of the rather recent (March 16, 1939) Düsseldorf agreement, discussed in the preface to this volume, between the British Federation of Industries and the *Reichsgruppe Industrie,* contemplating the establishment of international cartels and, according to *The Economist,* an expected securing of complete coöperation not merely in export trade by joint British-German export subsidies, but by "complete domestic cartelization." The agreement contained the following provision: "The two organizations realize that in certain cases the advantages of agreements between the industries of countries or of a group of countries may be nullified by competition from the industries in some other country that refuses to become a party to the agreement. In such cases it may be necessary for the organizations to obtain the help of their governments, and the two organizations agree to collaborate in seeking that help." According to *The Economist,* "The United States is one country that would be most unlikely to 'become a party to the agreement.' The clause consequently means that in given circumstances the Federation of British Industries contemplates seeking British Government subsidies to help German trade against American. Is there something in the atmosphere of Düsseldorf that causes sensible men to lose their wits?"[25] The sharp words of *The Economist* indicate and a calm consideration of the Düsseldorf accord supports the opinion, that it is more than probable that no British industry and no British government would have participated in fighting American competition in this way.

IV

One may ask whether or not the personal contacts of outstanding business leaders, like those participating in ISC operations, may be regarded as a factor, positively or negatively, influencing the international policies of their governments. Though it is true that the domestic influence of important steel executives might be used to influence international political relations negatively by transforming the private international economic problems of the industrialists into inter-governmental issues, thus disturbing government relations, conversely there is little reason to believe that smooth international steel relations could exert any positive influence on inter-governmental

---

[25] *The Economist,* Mar. 25, 1939, p. 607. See also Preface to this volume.

political relations. Generally speaking, this author shares the opinion of Jacob Viner in not believing "that the international contacts which the conduct of international trade promotes, as between individuals and groups, themselves lead to international good will and understanding," though Professor Viner went too far perhaps in his skepticism when stating "I have a suspicion that the contrary may be nearer the truth."[26] The collaboration on the world steel market within the ISC has been regarded as a pattern for political coöperation. Edouard Herriot, an experienced politician, extolled the attitude of businessmen in concluding the continental steel pact by stating that this attitude "ought to be an example to the politicians."[27] He pointed to the opinion of economic and political experts of the League of Nations who stated that the establishment of international cartels is a "contribution to a general organization of production and of peace."[28]

Although not so popular as before, the conception of international steel coöperation as a pattern for political collaboration persisted in the minds of many literally up to the outbreak of the Second World War. In the minds of many the easing of the greatest political tension which ever existed in history was regarded as attainable, if only "practical" men could do the work of politicians. A few months before the outbreak of the Second World War on May 4, 1939, many outstanding representatives of the major steel industries of the world attended the annual dinner of the Iron and Steel Institute in London. The British government was significantly represented by the Minister for the Coördination of Defense, Lord Chatfield. The main address was delivered by a renowned British politician and steel industrialist, the Viscount Greenwood of Holbourne, who emphatically declared, to his approving audience: "The representatives of the steel industries and, indeed, of all other industries from all parts of the world can sit around the common table, and without raising their voices come to quick decisions of national and international importance, affecting the lives of millions of men throughout the world, but it is an odd thing and a sad fact that the representatives of government cannot sit

---

[26] "International Economic Relations and the World Order," in *The Foundations of a More Stable World Order* (Walter H. C. Laves, edit.), Chicago, 1941, p. 36. Mr. Viner's statement to the effect "that some enthusiasts, and particularly the Cobden-Bright School and their followers, have exaggerated the importance of economic factors in determining the state of international relations, and especially that they have exaggerated the efficacy of a free-trade policy in promoting international peace," *ibid.*, p. 37, is surely pertinent especially in regard to international steel policies up to the Second World War.

[27] *Op. cit.*, p. 146.   [28] *Ibid.*

around a common table but live in atmosphere of shouting and suspicion that interferes with the normal, healthful economic development of the world for which we stand above all else."[29] There is no doubt that Nazi propaganda did its best to shelter and foster such illusions, especially in Western democracies. Oversimplification of responsibilities for huge economic and political difficulties was not limited to the steel industry.[30]

Those who controlled the production and marketing of steel commodities were often suspected of using—or abusing—economic power concentrated in their hands to influence "politics." In most of the ISC countries politically reactionary tendencies have generally been attributed to steel industrialists, leading executives of steel concerns, and even to associations connected with national steel marketing controls.[31] Such indictments were not limited to steel industries[32] but they often were focused on them. Thus, it has often been alleged that the interest of steel industrialists in domestic politics lay not only in their desire to increase their profits (e.g., by influencing tariff and conservative social policies) but that they were also interested in undermining political democracy, inciting war, in appeasement, and even in conspiring with the enemy against their home countries. The discussion of these accusations is made particularly difficult because, according to a well-established universal habit, none of the accused nor

---

[29] *Journal of the Iron and Steel Institute,* CXXXIX (1939), 29 P. The same idea was expressed by the then British Secretary for War, A. Duff Cooper, *ibid.,* CXXXIII (1936), 488. Mr. Duff Cooper, in a fiery speech before the Iron and Steel Institute, promising the fast rearmament of Great Britain, exclaimed: "I sometimes think the day will come when the politicians of this country will have to get together with the Untouchables of our Great Indian Empire, as being the only two sections of large communities which are universally despised." Concerning the belief that our major political and economic troubles and confusions may be solved by intellectual processes of economists, practical businessmen, and other experts, see E. H. Carr, *Peace Conditions* (New York, 1942), p. 114.

[30] Alfred P. Sloan, Jr., discussing the economic blindness of some politicians remarked: ". . . they preach the gospel that accomplishment is a crime—the greater the accomplishment, the greater the crime. They teach the concept of something for nothing. This, in one form or another, has influenced our national economic thinking for many years." *Adventures of a White-Collar Man* (New York, 1941), p. 130.

[31] See e.g., Robert A. Brady, "Policies of National Manufacturing Spitzenverbände," *Political Science Quarterly,* June, 1941, p. 217 ff.

[32] "Fascism, all over Europe and in its nascent state in Mosley's English blackshirts, is subsidized by imperialistic and capitalistic reaction, which has been thoroughly frightened by democratic Socialism. . . . It is effectively controlled by the banking interests and the big industrialists to whom it grants special favors and control over the state's finances." William Yandell Elliott, *The Need for Constitutional Reform* (New York, 1935), pp. 76-77. See Walter Sulzbach, "Capitalistic Warmongers, A Modern Superstition," *Public Policy Pamphlet,* No. 35 (Chicago, 1942), *passim.*

their governments substantially answers such indictments. Left un-answered, these accusations do not reach the stage of fair discussion and therefore become simultaneously reinforced and weakened.

Among the politically flavored accusations against national steel groups participating in ISC general policies, those made against the American steel industry are, from the viewpoint of this study, the least significant. The American industry has been reproached with supporting conservative political tendencies in America, concentrating huge economic power in private hands and occasionally abusing that power, keeping artificially high and inflexible uniform steel prices, and pursuing in many other regards its selfish interest, for instance, in failing immediately to adjust its production capacity to the require-ments of the emergency and its dilatory, allegedly half-hearted man-ner of industrial mobilization. Though these charges have been made against the American steel industry in the aggregate, they do not relate to organized efforts to undermine the Constitution, to over-throw the legally established government or to introduce fascism.[33] Heavy accusations were often extended to business and industries in general.[34] For instance, Donald C. Blaisdell, in an official publication, writes: "Speaking bluntly, the Government and the public are 'over a barrel' when it comes to dealing with business in time of war or other crises. Business refuses to work, except on terms which it dic-tates. . . . The experience of the World War, now apparently being repeated, indicates that business will use this control only if it is 'paid properly.' In effect, this is blackmail, not too fully disguised."[35]

[33] Kemper Simpson, *op. cit.,* p. 6, quotes a statement of Judge Elbert H. Gary, former president of the United States Steel Corporation, made during the early twenties, to the effect that what the United States needed was a Mussolini. The present author was not able to verify this statement.

[34] "American business houses, in conspiracy among themselves and in alliance with foreign commercial interests, had suppressed the production of critical materials, de-prived the Allies of weapons of war, and unwittingly divulged military secrets and vital production data to foreign governments.". . . "Agreements between American and foreign concerns are startling, their implications obvious and their damage to our war effort is serious." Thurman Arnold and J. Sterling Livingston, "Antitrust War Policy and Full Production," *Harvard Business Review,* Spring, 1942, pp. 265 and 269.

[35] See "Economic Power and Political Pressures," TNEC, *Monograph No. 26,* pp. 172-73. A well-known conservative British scholar, who is now a high-ranking official in government services, writes: "In the United States, 'big business' aquired almost undisputed control of the machinery of government" (Edward Hallett Carr, *Conditions of Peace,* p. 84). A recent decision of the Supreme Court (*U. S. vs. Bethle-hem Steel Corporation* [1941]) contains a discussion of business regimentation in times of emergency. Mr. Justice Black for the majority of the Court reaffirmed that the power of Congress to draft business organizations is not less than its power to draft men for military service. He states that "this [the case of Bethlehem Steel Company],

ISC operations were particularly subject to prompt adjustments to changing political situations in the years 1938 and 1939. It became more and more obvious that Germany was going to use its steel industry as a springboard for large-scale political activity.[45] Germany began to establish large new steel plants, to have them ready for action when the "battle of steel capacity" started. The timing of the international steel agreements to last only until the end of 1940, and no longer, was due to the unpredictability of political events in the next years.

---

[45] See Volkmar Muthesius, *op. cit.,* pp. 129-130. Literature regarding Germany's preparation for the First World War through international economic penetration reads like an account of contemporary occurrences. See e.g., Henri Hauser, *Germany's Commercial Grip on the World* (New York, 1918), *passim.*

CHAPTER ELEVEN

Conclusions

I

IN DESCRIBING the structure and operation of the ISC, including a few considerations of a more general nature in the foregoing chapters, an attempt was made to discuss this small but significant section of international economic and political relations in the 1930's. Adjectival coloring has been carefully avoided and comments have mostly been limited to explaining the significance of facts. Dispassionateness in depicting the working scheme of the largest international cartel may be unwelcome to those who placed a taboo on the calm discussion of the economic pattern of international cartels. These cartels were merely an economic mechanism, gradually developed, resulting from a complexity of underlying social and economic forces, rather than themselves the cause of social and political developments.[1] People who looked upon large international collective marketing controls as both the requisite element for, and the symptom of a peaceful co-operation among nations, now confronted with the cataclysm of the Second World War, in disillusionment turn their view to more substantial influences on the political and economic relationship of states. Those who condemned large collective international marketing schemes as an evil *in se,* though realizing that on a known market, endowed with modern communication and transportation facilities, a

---

[1] Mr. Justice Holmes put it thus many decades ago: ". . . it is plain from the slightest consideration of practical affairs, or the most superficial reading of industrial history, that free competition means combination, and that the organization of the world, now going on so fast, means an ever increasing might and scope of combination. It seems to me futile to set our faces against this tendency. Whether beneficial on the whole, as I think it, or detrimental, it is inevitable, unless fundamental axioms of society, and even the fundamental conditions of life, are to be changed."—*Vegelahn vs. Guntner,* 167 Mass. 92, 108 [1896]. "The trouble is that the individual obstinately refuses to remain an individual," writes E. H. Carr (*Conditions of Peace,* p. 73).

regime of free competition in certain standardized commodities cannot operate permanently, face an impasse. Though they realized from
experience and simple reasoning that in certain markets free competition is untenable as a permanent situation, they still advocated it because they could offer no substitute for free competition which would
not in their minds endanger a cherished image of the desired status of
political society. For them, "There is the old, well-known story about
the man who, during the Lisbon earthquake of 1775, went about
hawking anti-earthquake pills; but one incident is forgotten—when
someone pointed out that the pills could not possibly be of use, the
hawker replied: 'But what will you put in their place?' "[2] Finally,
those who in the past proposed that large international marketing controls be put under the direction of supranational agencies, should today
recognize that their recommendation, though it may sound attractive,
failed to indicate the substance of international economic and social
policies which such supranational agencies were to pursue. For nowhere were economic and political principles of a substantial nature
indicated by which those supranational agencies should be guided in
determining international price and pricing policies in the case of a
clash of national economic interests, nor was much consideration
given to the fact that such supranational economic controls imply
intimate political coöperation within the international community.

In the author's opinion, the relevance of the pattern of international
cartels to the political and economic problems of the last two decades
has been heavily exaggerated by representing international cartels as
demiurges of good and evil.[3] To attack the cartel pattern, for ex-

---

[2] Quoted from L. B. Namier, "Diplomacy, Secret and Open," *The Nineteenth Century and After*, Jan. 1938, p. 45. "To acknowledge that industrial competition is
dead, and will stay dead," wrote Upton Sinclair in 1906, "would be to acknowledge
that the evils of the time were without a remedy; and the people would not stand
that." "Markets and Misery," *North American Review*, Apr. 1906, p. 592

[3] The *New York Times*, June 6, 1942, p. 21, reproduced, for instance, the following
excerpt from a speech of a high government official: "To the international cartels, . . .
we owe the peace of Munich, we owe the failure to expand American industry prior
to Pearl Harbor, and to the interests of these cartels in stabilizing prices and restricting
production we owe our present scarcity in all basic materials." One of the foremost
Nazi leaders, Baldur von Schirach, recently stated that the United States and Great
Britain use "big cartels" to obstruct the establishment of a "United Europe, real,
sovereign, and master of its destiny." Cf. *The Nation*, Oct. 3, 1942, p. 298. *Fortune*,
Sept. 1942, p. 105, put it thus: "The cartel has been variously represented by its foes
as an International Octopus, a Financial Fifth Column, and the Four Horsemen of
the Apocalypse. Its defenders have tried to describe it as a striving for international
order, an enlightened internationalism, and a conduit for the interflow of civiliza-
tion. . . . Needless to say, the cartel is neither the one nor the other. . . ."

ample, because of the cartel's alleged role of putting profits before
patriotism, is to put the cart before the horse. It should be the role
of an efficient government to cope appropriately with split loyalties,
if any, of entrepreneurs, and to require its citizens, with proper sanctions, to disclose those of their economic relations which the government deems necessary in the interests of the national community.[4]
Thus, because a joint stock company may have served as an appropriate implement in corrupt practices, it does not necessarily follow that
the joint stock company pattern should be specifically castigated. The
substance of the issue is not the joint stock company pattern, which
might be used for neutral and even socially useful purposes as well.
Naturally, this is not intended as an argument against an investigation into any possible contribution which the joint stock company
pattern itself may have made toward the corrupt practices. If an
economic pattern, such as the joint stock company of our example, is
not merely the instrument, but by its very form contributes socially
undesirable effects, then the opposition to the pattern itself is fully
justified. An international cartel might be an excellent vehicle through
which to commit criminal or social offenses; it might be neutral from
those two viewpoints, or it might serve socially useful purposes. An
international cartel might be composed of national units which use
the cartel organization for the darkest political purposes of a fascist

---

[4] Mr. Donald M. Nelson formulated the duties of the individual with reference to
wartime rather bluntly. "Anybody"—said Mr. Nelson—"I don't care who it is, that
holds their private interest above the interests of the United States is guilty, in my
opinion, of treason and ought to be tried for treason." He extended his concept of
treason to the behavior of people who make accusations "without knowing all the
facts." Senator Gillette, chairman of the Senate Subcommittee in which Mr. Nelson
made the above quoted statement, commended Mr. Nelson's opinion as "very refresh-
ing and very encouraging" and endorsed it heartily not only in the name of his
committee, but in the name of every true American. (*Utilization of Farm Crops,
Industrial Alcohol and Synthetic Rubber,* Hearings before a Subcommittee of the Committee on Agriculture and Forestry, United States Senate on S. Res. 224, Part 3, July 6,
1942, p. 856.) Reports about the undermining of the war effort by businessmen,
especially in connection with industrial combinations, have been very frequent. The
man in the street has been somewhat confused by these reports because these indictments
were not followed by court actions appropriately sentencing offenders and acquitting
those who were accused innocently. It is true that the mere public exposure of certain
offenses may cause the offender to discontinue permanently certain practices, and this
public exposure contains an element of retribution by the community for the violation
of legal rules. However, in the minds of many, serious offenses "ought to be tried," as
was indicated by Messrs. Nelson and Gillette. It should be noted that in recent accusations against combinations based on patents and on business experiences the expression
"international cartels" has been used rather loosely. No agreement belonging to the
framework of the ISC was subject to adverse public criticism in connection with the
war effort of the United Nations.

government; it might consist of national groups striving for business profits, trying to act according to the intentions of their democratic national governments, and if occasion arises resisting abuses of concentrated economic power. Extreme generalization in this respect diverts the light from economic racketeers and other elements undermining vital interests of the political community. This is done by not discriminating socially dangerous combinations from socially neutral and socially desirable combinations. The responsibility of people participating in undesirable cartels becomes diluted by putting them in a too large common bag and by concentrating the attack against the cartel pattern instead of prosecuting individuals using that pattern for criminal purposes. This is not to say that a legislature may not prohibit the coalition of entrepreneurs in certain forms. Even in that case it is essential to distinguish between violations of the law by restricting competition without undermining vital interests of the nation, and violations which approach what is generally called treason.

This chapter attempts to draw a few fragmentary conclusions from the facts which have been presented regarding the international steel market. These conclusions will show that the ISC did not contribute actively to the maintenance of international peace, nor did it serve as a link in an international conspiracy of capitalists directed against world peace.[5] It contributed substantially to the establishment of col-

---

[5] The Vice-President of the Belgian Senate, a recipient of the Nobel prize for distinguished achievements in the field of promoting international peace, prefaced a book which discussed international steel relations, with the following words: "A puissant bellicose triumvirate consisting of industry, finance, and the press, dominates, in effect, the world." He proceeded to explain that these three groups compose an international family closely connected by blood and business relationships similar to the interrelationships of traditional dynasties. According to the Belgian Senator, these interests constitute a gigantic entente, appearing in most diversified forms, destined to provoke plethoric orders of armaments for the massacre of human beings, their main purpose being to make their governments order armaments and instruments of death and destruction at usurious prices. In order to win public opinion in all countries the triumvirate administers the opinion of citizens by persuading them that their defense is conditioned by large-scale armaments. (Henri La Fontaine, in Louis Launay and Jean Sennac, *Les Relations Internationales des Industries de Guerre,* Paris, 1932, Preface.) In the light of the experiences of the Second World War, one has better insight into the reality of the alleged armament races of the democracies during the 1930's. To ascribe the lack of international and national supervision of private industrial policies (especially in relation to armaments) primarily to the dominating influence of a triumvirate of international industry, finance, and the press is, moderately speaking, unrealistic, and merely aids, to say nothing of echoes, those who regard the case of democracy as a hopeless adventure in political development. The reasons why the international control of armaments and armament industries proved unsuccessful are fairly clear. Primarily, the reasons for those failures are broadly identical with the

laboration in one specific, important section of international business relations. It did not abuse economic power, concentrated in private hands, by creating general artificial scarcity in steel supplies, nor did it use concerted business strategy to increase its returns substantially over returns from domestic sales in steel-exporting countries. Those who are inclined to search for the ideological background of the achievements of the ISC, should realize that these achievements were not the result of the ethical considerations of ISC adherents, but that they resulted from an enlightened economic egoism, which was neither better nor worse than that contemporarily existing among many international businessmen at large. In addition, as has been pointed out in a foregoing chapter, the discretion in using economic power was much more limited in the determination of steel policy by economic circumstances and national policies accompanying ISC policies, than is usually realized.

II

An examination of the following questions may help in evaluating effectively the role of the ISC in the economic development of the period of its operation:

1) Did the ISC organization satisfy its participants, i.e., did they consider the marketing scheme that actually developed the one most feasible under given economic and political circumstances?

2) Did the operation of the ISC cause an increase or decrease in the steel consumption of steel-importing countries?

3) Did the ISC scheme cause an enlargement, a restriction, or a shifting in steel-producing facilities; did it support the preservation or even the expansion of high-cost capacity?

4) Did the ISC contribute to a technical rationalization in steel production, did it contribute to rationalization in distribution by restricting the wastage of competition?

5) Did actual tariff policies of governments condition the very existence of the ISC; and were trade barriers affected by the existence of the ISC?

---

failure to create a close international coöperation among Great Britain, France, the United States, and the Soviet Union. It is interesting to note that General von Seeckt, *The Future of the German Empire,* transl. by Oakley Williams (New York, 1930), p. 150, expressed somewhat similar ideas as those discussed here. "It is impossible to shut one's eyes to the fact," said the famous soldier, "that the intertangled, international monetary powers and monetary interests are beginning to acquire a super-State influence . . . [which] is aspiring to world power to-day. Wars may be prevented in the interests of international finance just as they may be launched by them."

6) Did the existence and the operation of the ISC exercise any influence on labor problems?

7) Did it, by its business policy, exercise any influence on business fluctuations, and did its operation influence general employment or unemployment, or the extent of employment or unemployment in particular countries?

8) What was the degree of pressure exercised by the ISC on its own members, on outside producers, on distributors, and on the ultimate consumer, as compared with the pressure which would have been exercised on these groups, if the ISC had not controlled the steel export market?

9) Finally, did the ISC fit into the general ideological background of the two decades following the First World War? What ideological basis made possible an intimate economic coöperation among national groups in the late thirties, when the world was rapidly and visibly running into a stage of political disintegration?

These questions may be fragmentarily answered as follows:

1) It may safely be assumed that ISC participants, almost without exception, regarded the ISC structure as an appropriate framework for the realization of their aims for a concerted control of the world steel market. The very nature of the cartel structure, the fact that it was built on independent entities, connected temporarily only in respect to determined business relationships, conveyed the idea of a genuinely coöperative venture, not unduly dominated by leaders imposed upon the adherents. Though cartel agreements were concluded for several years, a common tacit assumption existed that every national group might quit at any time, without having to face legal consequences attached to the breaking of contracts. The elastic cartel framework, which was a masterpiece from the point of view of business administration, permitted units to coöperate who were at the same time allies and rivals. This situation takes us back to the early meaning of the word competition, when this term signified both rivalry and a striving toward a common end.[6] The fact that large-scale integration and corporate concentration occurred more on the

---

[6] Present usage of the words "compete" and "competition" in English, and *"concurrencer"* and *"concurrence"* in French is a direct opposite of their original meaning. Both sets of words are used today to designate "to contend in rivalry," whereas their etymological sense was "to strive together for a common end." The word "concurrence" still has its original meaning in English as opposed to its present meaning in French and German. The verb *"concourir"* and the noun *"concours"* are used in French to designate both to coöperate and to compete.

national than on the international plane in steel, and that technical secrets did not constitute a specific tie among steel-producing entrepreneurs, accounts for the adoption of the international cartel pattern, rather than international intercorporate relationships.   Basing the structure of the cartel on general policy-determining agencies, national groups, and export sales comptoirs seems, in retrospect, the only sound foundation for coördinating the various interests of the participants, though they probably recognized that the system of assigning commodities to specific export sales comptoirs required a more logical arrangement.

2) The operation of the ISC probably did not cause steel consumers to consume considerably less than they would have consumed in a competitive marketing situation, nor did the ISC succeed in enlarging steel consumption as a whole.   However, this statement is more an impression than a substantiated judgment because of the great difficulties in visualizing a permanently unrestricted competitive situation on the international steel market.   The nature of the demand for steel on domestic markets has been subject to many sharp controversies. There is no reason to assume that this issue is less controversial in respect to the export markets; on the contrary, an investigation of the elasticity of demand for steel on the international market is considerably more complex.   Even the question whether the demand for steel is more or less inelastic on the export market than on the domestic one would require an extensive examination.   Without such investigations the answer to the question posed here is necessarily vague.   There is no doubt that ISC policies were aimed at enlarging steel consumption on importing markets.[7]   A few comptoirs experi-

---

[7] According to Mr. A. H. Feller, "To choose the cartel as an instrument for securing an expanding economy is as logical as placing an atheist on the papal throne." ("Public Policy of Industrial Control," *op. cit.,* pp. 138-139.)   This statement may apply to entrepreneurs who prefer a marketing situation characterized by absolute scarcity, and who base their business policy on high profits resulting from the artificial limitation of supply.   It assumes an impotent government which supports such cartel policies by trade barriers and by other measures which obstruct the establishment of outside plants. However, many examples could be quoted of the expansion of the steel industry in Europe in the last two decades, where governments used the pattern of national steel cartels to secure an expanding economy in steel.   No one single European government expected the expansion of its steel economy from the enforcment of a competitive steel market.   In the United States the steel industry has often been accused of short-sighted policies, preferring high prices and small production to lower prices and large production.   A magazine which is not unfriendly to industry, wrote in 1936, ". . . steel men have geared their industry to the philosophy of high prices and restricted production." "U. S. Steel, II: Prices," *Fortune,* Apr. 1936, pp. 130-132, quoted in E. G. Nourse and H. B. Drury, *Industrial Price Policies and Economic Progress* (Washington, 1938),

mented with various devices to increase the use of their products. Thus the IRMA, late in 1938, considered a large project to allocate great quantities of heavy rails in a complicated transaction involving a credit pool among its members. However, there is no reliable evidence that ISC measures to increase consumption were very effective, or that the regularity of the market, resulting from the existence of the cartel, induced consumers to enlarge their volume of buying.

3) The ISC exercised no influence on the enlargement or restriction of steel-producing or rolling facilities in steel-exporting countries. This is not to deny the existence of strong national cartels, mostly concerned with the regulation of production among all ISC policy-determining national groups, with the exception of the United States. But the ISC and its sub-entities, taught by experience that an international steel cartel had better refrain from all output problems, rather definitively accepted the principle of limiting its influence to exports in the strictest sense. It is true, for example, that the disintegration of a strong international cartel for tubular products in 1935 was accompanied by a doubling of German exports in tubular products, but it is very doubtful whether such changes in exports affected the expansion of production capacities in Germany and the restriction of capacities elsewhere. The entrance of Great Britain into the ISC framework, and the simultaneous organization of a domestic marketing scheme in steel were admittedly intended as a basis for an enlargement of British steel capacity. The British prime minister was prompted by these plans to state: ". . . I make bold to say that in four or five years the [British] steel industry will be second to no steel industry in the whole world—and that is the natural position of a British industry."[8] It is doubtful whether any British steel industrialists agreed with Mr. Stanley Baldwin's elated prediction, though he himself had expert knowledge of steel. In itself the adherence of the United Kingdom to the ISC was not an immediate incentive to increase its steel capacity, though the resulting regulation of imports and exports might

---

p. 301. This problem was sufficiently aired in the TNEC investigations. However, American steel industries never attempted to induce ISC agencies to limit supply on the international market in order to secure higher prices.

[8] Cf. *The Times* (London), July 1, 1935, p. 10, column b. Speaking of labor employed in the steel industry, the Prime Minister said: "Those are men who must have been wondering through the early part of the year what chance they had of keeping their work. And now, under the shelter of that terror, that great trade is rearming itself under the skillful chairmanship of Sir Andrew Duncan. . . . That is practical reconstruction and practical progress. We have not so happy a story to tell of all industries." *(Ibid.)*

have influenced the enlargement and modernization of British steel plants indirectly.

Whether the success of the ISC in contributing to the development of an attractive price on the steel export market may be regarded as an incentive to enlarge steel production in steel-exporting countries is more than doubtful. Even if the self-limitations in regard to expansion which were imposed on their members by most of the domestic steel cartels are disregarded, it should be realized that the increase in steel prices came during a period of political and economic uncertainty, when the problem of expansion of steel industries was dominated by considerations other than the success or failure of the ISC. It should also be realized that a notable expansion of steel industries requires considerable time. As a consequence, steel industrialists are rather cautious about investing large amounts of capital in expansion because of the constant uncertainty of the duration of increased demand for exports. The question of preserving or expanding high-cost capacity in steel remained a problem of the national groups. As is discussed elsewhere in this study, the ISC did not support the preservation of high-cost capacity, and experience showed that high-cost capacity plants generally did not participate in supplying the export market, neither did they profit from it.

The ISC influence on enlarging steel industries or establishing new steel industries has to be considered from an entirely different angle in regard to steel-importing nations. It has never been denied that ISC agencies attempted through their pricing policies, through delivering cheap semifinished steel, and through other appropriate measures, to slow up the establishment or the enlargement of steel-producing and rolling facilities in importing countries. It may be assumed that these measures were moderately effective until about 1937. Beginning with 1938 almost all national governments, even in countries which believed themselves secure against future offensive and defensive wars, induced their nationals to establish and to enlarge steel plants often under heavy government support. They took this course because they were anxious to have sufficient steel if the countries from which their usual steel supplies came should be involved in a war, or if transportation should become difficult because of war.

4) The ISC did not attempt to introduce a rationalized correlation among its members according to the principles of technical efficiency. It was not guided by the principle of concentrating export orders of commodities to producers who would produce these articles in the cheapest and best way, although the actual quota systems had devel-

oped somewhat along these lines. It did not focus on single producers or single national groups to export one article or quality of steel. For instance it did not agree upon concentrating semifinished steel exports in one or two national groups, rails in another group, or ship plates in still another. If some of the international sales comptoirs were dominated by a few national groups with large quotas this dominance was less attributable to a desire for efficiency than to the "vested rights" of these groups derived from previous large exports. Speaking of technical rationalization within the ISC one should realize that except for the Luxemburg, and partly the Belgian group, all national groups were influenced in their production programs and systems by considerations of their domestic markets. In addition, no group regarded the cartel ties as sufficiently strong and permanent to induce them to give up the export of commodities, sizes, or qualities, which would be of potential disadvantage if the cartel structure disintegrated. Certain markets remained, however, the domain of groups which specialized in steel products customary to that region. Thus the American group, which produced certain types of heavy rails, was sure of receiving certain orders by the very fact that no other group produced that gauge and quality.

The ISC did not provide for an exchange of patents and technical experience, as emphasized elsewhere in this study. The erection or enlargement of a modern steel plant, with almost no exception, could not be prevented by refusing to grant patent licenses, or by the non-conference upon entrepreneurs of secret technical knowledge. The establishment and enlargement of steel-producing facilities remained a problem of raw materials and of the availability of capital.

Though there was no particular mechanism within the ISC for standardization of steel commodities, the uniform price and rather uniform extras system contributed to the efforts of specific associations of the steel industry to standardize their products, and to make customers coöperate in this direction.

The ISC exercised great influence on the rationalization of the distribution process on the steel export market. Even though national groups and big steel concerns maintained their own distribution mechanisms, the open price system, the uniformity of sales terms, the system of licencing intermediaries and limiting their number, and last but not least, very restricted competition made the distribution process considerably simpler and cheaper than it would have been in a truly competitive export market.

5) It is a provocative question whether or not the existence and

the operation of the ISC were conditioned by the tariff policies of governments during the time of the ISC. According to many authors large international marketing control schemes were conditioned by tariff policies of governments, and without appropriate tariff policies these international organizations would have disintegrated. To quote Gottfried von Haberler, "Many of the present international cartels owe their existence to tariffs. . . . Beyond doubt the majority of cartels hold together only because of protective tariff. . . . If all tariffs were removed tomorrow, very many entrepreneurs would lose the monopolistic position which each today possesses in his own line and country, while most of the existing cartels would vanish or would cease to exercise any power."[9] To analyze this statement is of increasing importance because of the growing tendencies to restrict future tariffs to a minimum.

Although it was true in the past that national and international collective marketing controls were adjusted to actual tariff policies of governments, and that frequently their form and substance were conditioned by their tariff policies, the question as to whether they would have existed at all if there had been no tariffs seems to be too narrow. Let us broaden the question in this way. Would the elimination or considerable restriction of tariffs, all other things being equal, have resulted in the breaking down of international cartels, or would it have resulted in even more cohesive monopolistic combinations? According to the opinion of this author the elimination of all tariffs may result, according to the character of commodities and to other circumstances, either in a breaking down of particular international marketing controls, or in a readjustment of those structures which can be even more cohesive than they were under tariff protection. Whereas for example, in pig iron, the lack of adequate tariff protection in many countries was one of the circumstances which made the establishment of a comprehensive international marketing control less attractive, this author assumes it rather probable that the general breaking down of tariffs on steel would not result in an elimination of comprehensive international steel cartels. No doubt it would modify their structures and policies considerably. It seems that the United States Tariff Commission, viewing the relationship between ISC and tariffs from the other side of the picture, was not far from the same conclusion when it stated in its excellent discussion of the ISC, "Such complete power renders governmental trade barriers for steel

---

[9] *The Theory of International Trade* (New York, 1937), pp. 324-25, 331.

practically superfluous in most European and some non-European countries."[10]

Several economists and politicians regarded national and international marketing controls as a means to eliminate or restrain tariff protection. Louis Loucheur considered international cartels the "only course" to be followed to solve the problem of custom barriers.[11] E. Benjamin Andrews, as early as 1888, predicted that "We may . . . expect that the dependence of trusts upon tariffs will steadily decrease. Perhaps it is to disappear altogether. The interest hitherto centered in the tariff question will then go over to that of trusts."[12] The above two quotations are a simplified presentation of the problem. Tariff policy is only one part of economic relationship among nations, and only one circumstance, though a very important one, which makes commodity controls rise.

For the relationship between tariffs and international commodity controls the whole international trade situation is significant. Because a deeper analysis of the international trade situation in general would go far beyond the scope of this study, the author will limit his characterization to the international trade situation in the thirties. With special reference to tariffs, two rather arbitrarily selected quotations are presented. However, these quotations will indicate very well the confusion of the international trade situation, of which the international steel trade was a part. They indicate that governments, in their international trade policies, and also national economic organizations were obsessed with a short-sighted economic egoism which did not create a situation favorable to restrictions of trade barriers. It would be trite to state that this situation was created or supported by international political considerations on the part of the great democratic powers which did not regard it essential to coöperate sufficiently in the establishing of what is called a comprehensive world order even by risking military actions against fascist powers. It was also created and supported by political fear and uncertainty on the part of smaller nations, whose economic egoism was often not genuine but rather derived from the egoism of the so-called great powers.

Mr. Sumner Welles, at the World Trade Dinner of the twenty-eighth National Foreign Trade Convention, New York, October 7, 1941, said that nations ". . . have considered foreign trade a cut-throat game in which each participant could only profit by taking

---

[10] *Iron and Steel,* Report of the U. S. Tariff Commission, p. 410.

[11] *Report and Proceedings of the World Economic Conference,* I, 132-33.

[12] *Quarterly Journal of Economics,* III, 152.

advantage of his neighbor. Our own policy at times in the past has, as we all know, constituted no exception. . . . We might have realized much earlier that our tariff policy was striking at the very roots of our entire export trade. We might have avoided the colossal blunder of 1930 and the less serious, but equally misguided action of further tariff increases under the guise of the so-called excise taxes in 1932. Many foreign countries, which had not recovered from the shock of our tariff increases in 1921 and 1922 and were tottering on the brink of economic and financial collapse, were literally pushed into the abyss by our tariff action of 1930. Throughout the world this withering blast of trade destruction brought disaster and despair to countless people. The resultant misery, bewilderment and resentment, together with other equally pernicious contributing causes, paved the way for the rise of those very dictatorships which have plunged almost the entire world into war."[13]

The second characteristic opinion is requoted from a study by a left-wing socialist, John Strachey, *The Coming Struggle for Power*. "Lord Beaverbrook . . . recently issued the slogan 'Thou Shalt Not Steal.' He told the readers of his newspaper that the livelihoods of British workers and farmers were being stolen from them by wicked foreigners who sold goods on the British market. The remedy lay to hand. Exclude foreigners from the British market and take from them all those markets over which Britain has political control. The same idea," writes Mr. Strachey, "has, curiously enough, occurred to the French, German, Italian, Dutch, American, Japanese, Polish, Spanish, Argentine, and Czechoslovakian Beaverbrooks."[14]

That this sharp self-criticism, which is one of the best signs of political maturity, emanated mainly from American and British sources, deceives nobody about the fact that the responsibility for the sad status of the international trade situation between the two world wars was not confined to English-speaking countries.

With little exception steel tariffs all over the world had one single dominating motive: short-sighted economic egoism and artificial support of domestic steel markets to protect existent and support developing domestic industries.

---

[13] *Press Release of the Department of State*, No. 483, Oct. 6, 1941. According to Dr. P. E. Corbett, "in 1930 the United States . . . had emphasized by the Smoot-Hawley tariff its unwillingness to accept foreign goods in payment. Partly in retaliation, the British Commonwealth transformed itself into a close trading corporation by the introduction of the United Kingdom tariff of 1931 and the system of preferences established in the Ottawa agreements in 1932." *Post-War Worlds* (New York, 1942), p. 39.   [14] New York, 1935, p. 260.

Within the range of steel-exporting countries Luxemburg and Belgium belong to a particular category. Under existing circumstances these two countries did not have to fear imports of steel, except as measures of retaliation. After 1932 Great Britain introduced a rather high tariff on steel products, in order to strengthen her domestic steel industries. The development of British tariff policies after the middle of 1935 showed a flexible compromise between the protection of domestic steel industries and efforts to obtain sufficient steel supplies at prices approved by the government. These British tariff policies attempted as far as possible to satisfy the ISC. France, Germany,[15] Czechoslovakia and Poland maintained rather high tariffs and also various other trade barriers to protect their domestic steel markets. They did not regard the severe provisions of cartel agreements, which were designed to protect their home markets, as sufficient.

As discussed many times in this study, no ISC adherent looked upon the cartel structure as essentially permanent. Without tariff protection they would have regarded themselves as considerably weakened in ISC negotiations. Speaking objectively, the "danger" of large quantities of steel commodities being imported by outsiders or by cartel members to steel-exporting countries was negligible. But even the import of small steel quantities, outside of the control of domestic steel cartels, could and did impair the rigid domestic price structures and the relationship between domestic cartels and consumers. The United States maintained rather high custom duties on steel commodities, especially after 1930, though they were somewhat reduced in 1935-36 by the Belgian, French, and Swedish trade agreements. As in European steel-exporting countries, there was little danger that large quantities of foreign steel could invade the American domestic market. But American steel producers, like their European colleagues, did not like their domestic price structure disturbed by even small imports which were not subjected to considerable custom duties.[16]

---

[15] The German government derived its jurisdiction to exercise pressure on cartels through tariff policies from Art. 4 of the Statute concerning Changes in Custom Duties, of August 17, 1925. Such powers were expressly conferred by the Decree of the Reichspresident concerning Relief from Financial, Economic and Social Emergency, of July 26, 1930. See Max Schlenker, *Die Eisenindustrie in der Welt, etc.* (Jena, 1927), p. 33.

[16] See the Report of the U. S. Tariff Commission, *Iron and Steel, passim,* TNEC, *Monograph No. 10,* pp. 23 and 219 ff., and Abraham Berglund and Philip G. Wright, *The Tariff on Iron and Steel* (Washington, 1929), *passim.*

In steel-importing countries the tariff policy mirrored governmental policies in regard to protection of steel producers and steel consumers. However, there were governments which did not impose high custom duties on imported steel, in order to maintain low steel prices. These governments heavily supported the building up of a domestic steel industry by other measures. Holland, in which the government participated as a shareholder in steel industries, is the best example for this category.

Except in Great Britain and South Africa, the ISC did not influence tariff policies of governments directly.[17] The indirect influence of ISC policies on tariff policies of individual governments would require an extended investigation transcending the objective of this study.

6) The ISC plan did not provide for coördinated labor policies of steel industries, nor did any informal or tacit understanding in this respect exist. The very fact that the ISC exercised no influence on domestic markets of steel exporters—and these markets were the main concern of the prevailing majority of ISC members—would in itself explain this negative attitude. A further fact to consider is that labor problems would have burdened the frail ISC structure considerably. Also social conditions were entirely different even within continental European countries. The differences in these social conditions would have doomed any attempt to coördinate labor policies in steel industries. Several of the governments which watched the policies of their own ISC national groups had socialist members and members belonging to liberal parties. These governments could probably have prevented their national group from participating in the ISC if there had been the slightest suspicion that the ISC interfered either directly or indirectly with labor policies.

7) Several publications from ISC official sources show that it had very definite intentions of influencing international business fluctuations by maintaining a relatively stable price policy. It was often assumed that the ISC partly succeeded in this respect.[18] In spite of the fallacies shielded in the rigidity of published official steel prices,

---

[17] According to *International Ententes*, p. 7, "The activity of the Association [ISC] has in many cases formed the direct basis of the decisions of several governments in respect of commercial policy."

[18] See Aloyse Meyer, "Cartels and Trade Fluctuations," *World Trade*, IX, No. 6, 62-63; The Earl of Dudley, quoted in *The Iron Age*, Mar. 10, 1938, p. 87; Henry Clay, quoted in *ICTR*, June 11, 1937, p. 1056; "The Trade Cycle, Stable Prices in Good and Bad Times," *The Times* (London), June 14, 1938, Iron and Steel Supplement, p. 16.

no doubt steel prices would have fluctuated more than they did had there been no efficient marketing control. The kind of stabilizing influence on prices exerted by the ISC was shown first by the fact that it was always somewhat late in increasing or decreasing the official price level with reference to the demand of the existing business situation. Second, the ISC attempted to limit the frequency and extent of such adjustments.

Even if we assume that, in steel, price inflexibility has a moderating influence on business fluctuations we must keep in mind that the ISC controlled only the export steel markets. The steel marketed for export represented only a fraction, probably not exceeding 10 per cent, of world steel consumption, thus the influence of the ISC was very restricted. Though a detailed investigation would disclose a sharper picture of this situation, the known facts do not warrant the statement that the ISC was able to influence world business fluctuations to any visible extent.

There is little evidence that ISC policies had any influence on general employment or unemployment. This problem, however, in particular steel-exporting countries was somewhat affected by the ISC quota scheme. Probably without the operation of the ISC, high-cost producing countries would have participated less in the export market than they actually did.

8) The ISC marketing schemes, requiring a rather strict and comprehensive internal discipline, exercised considerable pressure on the business behavior of all adherents. But because of the self-imposed character of that restraint, and also because the adherents felt there was no other choice, this discipline was regarded as a necessary corollary of collective business action. Even within the ISC scheme there was plenty of opportunity for exercising the creative forces inherent in the classical idea of entrepreneurs.

Outside producers, including those who were not considered by the ISC as so-called friendly outsiders, had to accept several ISC marketing patterns because these patterns were generally adopted by almost all customers. The pressure exercised against unfriendly outsiders was not directed to the elimination of those outsiders, but rather toward turning them into adherents of the ISC. However, the ISC had often to wage sharp price-wars against truculent outsiders. According to the experience of the ISC even the selling of small quantities of steel below ISC price schemes could cause considerable "disturbances" on the market.

Distributors and consumers were naturally less free in purchasing than they would have been on a free market. Nonconformists came to recognize the futility of fighting the ISC, but the ISC was always prone to make compromises without regard to its prestige, if it could gain the coöperation of former foes. After 1937 there were relatively few objections against ISC marketing schemes from customers. Distributors who did not find their place within the ISC scheme remained naturally antagonistic to ISC marketing methods. Their opposition was divided between the ISC and their fellow distributors.

9) The ISC organization and its working methods were not too conspicuous in the political and economic setting of the fateful period between the two world wars, but were a representative pattern of one of those entities on which the international, economic and political setting was based. Ostensibly, the fact that an agency controlling the world steel export market was established the same month after the First World War in which Germany entered the League of Nations— while before the First World War attempts to establish general international marketing controls for steel had never been successful— indicated, for many, a landmark in the development of social philosophy, a development which, indeed, can be more realistically viewed in the light of international events surrounding this second world struggle. Such a reinterpretation of international political and economic coöperation, from the point of view of this study, necessarily has to inquire whether the establishment and operation of such large international collective marketing controls as the ISC were a symbol or a sign of an alleged profound transformation in the conception of political and economic relationship among nations, and thus in social philosophy. One has to question whether it is true or not, as often stated with vitriolic skepticism, that international collaboration between 1919 and 1939 composed only a huge involuntary political pantomime in which many internationally minded participants did not notice, or were not courageous enough to confess, that while they were stating high-sounding principles, for other politicians this dramatic performance merely represented a continuation of pre-First World War national power politics in a new shape.[19] The frequently posed question, how could national steel groups of democratic countries, bound by loyalties to their nations and governments, collaborate

---

[19] "What matters is," writes Professor E. H. Carr, "that these supposedly absolute and universal principles were not principles at all, but the unconscious reflections of national policy based on a particular interpretation of national interest at a particular time." Cf. *The Twenty Years' Crisis 1919-1939* (London, 1941), p. 111.

intimately inside a large marketing control scheme with Germany, Italy, and in a certain sense with Japan, can be answered only by courageously facing conclusions resulting from a reëxamination of the broader framework, i.e., the political coöperation between democratic and fascist nations in the period between the world wars.

The fact that in the operation of the ISC the discussion of items which were not directly connected with steel export policies was avoided with the utmost vigor, does not contribute to a satisfactory explanation. More enlightening are utterances about international politics and economics by men who had leading roles in ISC controls, though these views were made outside of the ISC. They emphatically stated the possibility of peaceful intimate collaboration among nations, democratic and fascist, if only sufficient good-will among politicians would exist.[20] They regarded the possibility of harmonizing economic interests between and within nations as a problem which could be easily solved by human reasoning and a right procedure.[21] There is no reason not to attribute to these opinions a large degree of sincerity, even if they contain inconsistencies and contradictions. They give what may be called an ideological background to the ISC collaboration. This ideological background of ISC collaboration reflected the background of international political coöperation during that era. That is why examples chosen from political life are highly significant for the explanation of ISC concerted action, which may best be characterized by a brief indication of the polarity between extremely idealistic[22] conception of the objectives and methods of international coöperation, and a realistic pragmatism which was supposed to serve the attainment of international harmony.[23]

---

[20] See e.g., the speech of Viscount Greenwood of Holbourn, quoted in Chapter X.

[21] Several of these utterances are reproduced in Chapter II of this volume.

[22] The expression idealistic means here "pertaining to ideals" as contrasted to the meaning "pertaining to ideas."

[23] A discussion of this chasm may be found in E. H. Carr, *The Twenty Years' Crisis, passim*. See also Leonard Woolf, "Utopia and Reality," *The Political Quarterly*, 1940, pp. 167 ff. A severe criticism of E. H. Carr's conception of world politics and economics may be found in Sir Norman Angell, *Why Freedom Matters*, Harmondsworth (England), 1940, pp. 37 ff. Angell discusses Carr's opinion under the heading "Hitler's Intellectual Allies in Britain," stating that "the disparagement of those things for which we fight is to be found in very high places in Britain. These arguments of profound defeatism—often an apology for the Hitlerian philosophy—should be faced and answered. . . ." J. B. Condliff, *The Reconstruction of World Trade* (New York, 1940), p. 116, comments on "The Victory of Political Realism," as discussed by E. H. Carr, from the point of view of political economy. Professor Condliff quotes the following significant sentence of Gottfried von Haberler (*The Theory of International Trade*, p.

The idealistic conception of international political and economic relations between 1919 and 1939 was based on the more or less sincere belief that there may exist, without a basic revision of the doctrine and practice of national sovereignty, a status of international political and even social equilibrium which entails the political and economic interest of the human community as a whole. This status may be reached and maintained by a continuous judicious balancing of economic and political operations of national units according to a predetermined democratic procedure. Such common interest of the family of nations equally represents the interest of all nations, all social classes, and all members of the human race. This international harmony was never described in a substantial sense since it was presumed evident to people of "good will." It was tacitly assumed that those interested in an economic and political *status quo* and those craving a radical change of political, economic and social *status quo's* might be brought to a common platform by a peaceful procedure. This warranted an equalization of those interests in what may be called an impartial way. Such a sound political platform may find a compromise among national interests, between free entrepreneurs who developed their creative individualism and the suppression of competition by the combination of these entrepreneurs. It may find a compromise between systems of fair profits and fair wages, between economic freedom and state or international interventionalism. This conception of international politics and economics was implied in the underlying principles of the League of Nations. A critical analysis of its Covenant shows that this famous document contained very few, and only general, substantial statements about the desired status of political society. It limited itself to an elaborate procedure of how to attain and maintain that presumably "self-evident" status.[24]

---

221), "It can be proved that, at any rate under the usual assumptions of general economic theory (free competition, absence of friction, and so on), the unrestricted international exchange of goods increases the real incomes of *all* the participating countries." Winston Churchill, discussing traditional views of politicians, indicated the gulf between extreme idealism and pragmatism, in stating: "But what have they to offer but a vague internationalism, a squalid materialism, and the promise of impossible Utopias." (Speech delivered to the Royal Society of St. George, in 1933, quoted by T. P. Conwell-Evans, "The Statesmanship of Mr. Churchill," *The Nineteenth Century and After,* Jan. 1941, p. 58.) An indirect but brilliant exposition of realistic pragmatism may be found in Robert Bendiner, *The Riddle of the State Department* (New York, 1942), *passim.* See also the review of this book by Frederick L. Schuman, in *The Nation,* Sept. 5, 1942, pp. 195 f.

[24] It is encouraging to study the brilliant results attained by the League in non-

It would be rather unjust not to recognize that the League contributed in large scale to a moderation of human suffering. Its work greatly facilitated the possibility of establishing a more perfect political machine in the future, one which might serve international collaboration on a more secure basis. However, there exists today in democracies an almost unanimous opinion that the political actions of the great powers which touched on the substance of great political and social issues did not follow principles which would have led to the realization of their (in general terms) expressed ideals. Instead, in their actions, they adopted the principles of short-sighted realistic pragmatism. This pragmatism helped conceal substantial political and economic issues. It made it possible for the great powers to pretend an international collaboration, although this concerted action was frequently nothing more than a diplomatic farce.

Realistic pragmatism made it possible for democratic governments to sit at a table with government leaders whose main aim was to destroy them and their ideals about international collaboration as soon as possible. It is not in the scope of this study to discuss causes and responsibilities for the state of things as they actually occurred,[25] nor does this study entail a discussion of what degree of realistic pragmatism is required in all political and economic negotiations. However, the characterization of the economic atmosphere in which leaders of national steel groups within the ISC coöperated requires some examples from the broader political atmosphere which influenced their social behavior.

An excellent illustration of realistic pragmatism is furnished by the proceedings and results of the two official World Economic Conferences, in 1927 and 1933. These sharply indicated the dangerous abysses in collaboration among nations, without even attempting to bridge them. As soon as concrete economic issues were discussed in those conferences it turned out that "in practice" the members of

---

political problems, where there was no compelling reason to evade touching on substantial political items.

[25] "It is a moot point"—writes E. H. Carr—"whether the politicians and publicists of the satisfied Powers, who have attempted to identify international morality with security, law and order and other time-honored slogans of privileged groups, do not bear as large a share of responsibility for the disaster as the politicians and publicists of the dissatisfied powers, who brutally denied the validity of an international morality so constituted." *The Twenty Years' Crisis,* p. 289. Such exaggerated statements originating from a well-known professor of international relations and a man who for many years was a member of the British Foreign Service are rather remarkable. They show the great variations in value-systems according to which political responsibilities can be judged.

the international community did not intend to deviate from their national interests even if their reluctance endangered the pillars of their widely heralded idealistic structure of international coöperation. A few more examples from different stages of international politics may be quoted to illustrate realistic pragmatism. Naturally, the quotations are deliberately chosen from the actions of great democratic powers, as it would make little sense to quote from the practice of those governments whose political conception of international harmony was bare of all idealism accepted by modern democracies, and based only on their desire to dominate the international community through a large-scale gangsterism. Great and small powers, led by "practical considerations," refused to incorporate into the Covenant of the League of Nations the restriction of offering membership only to those nations whose constitutions were based on giving the basic freedoms to their own nationals. Count Sforza bitterly emphasized that, "Such a clause in the Covenant would have prevented fascism in Italy." He regards it as a major error on the part of President Wilson to yield to the pressure of so-called "realists" in dropping this proposal.[26]

In the first great crisis in 1931, when Japan started its series of aggressive moves, the League of Nations was expected to create an example to deter similar actions in the future. According to Professor Lindsay Rogers, though America was desirous of coöperating in such an action of the League, "Great Britain refused to support Secretary of State Stimson in his desire to restrain Japan. . . . Indeed," says Mr. Rogers, "at Geneva the Japanese representative could thank Sir John Simon for having said in twenty minutes what he had been trying to say for several days." And discussing the policies of realistic pragmatism Professor Rogers states, "Americans, therefore, think of Sir John Simon and Monsieur Laval as the principal architects of the Japanese and the Italian empires, and indirectly of the German Empire."[27]

---

[26] See *The Nation*, July 4, 1942, p. 14, and Florence Wilson, *The Origins of the League Covenant* (London, 1928), pp. 19, 106-107.

[27] Lindsay Rogers, "Munich: American Opinion and Policy," *The Political Quarterly*, 1939, pp. 12-13. For another version see E. H. Carr, *Conditions of Peace* (New York, 1942), p. 174. Henry L. Stimson, *The Far Eastern Crisis*, New York, 1936, p. 224, quotes a report of the *Manchester Guardian*, December 8, 1932, according to which the Japanese representative, Mr. Matsuoka, remarked, after listening to Sir John Simon's speech in the Assembly of the League of Nations: "Sir John Simon had said in half an hour, in a few well-chosen phrases, what he—Mr. Matsuoka—had been trying to say in bad English for the last ten days." See also Arnold J. Toynbee, *Survey of International Affairs, 1933* (London, 1934), p. 493.

A third example originates in a period when the great drama in which we are living became apparent with the Munich agreement. The Prime Minister of Great Britain, Neville Chamberlain, gave expression to his realistic pragmatism in a national broadcast, September 27, 1938, in the following words, "How horrible, fantastic, incredible it is that we should be digging trenches and trying on gas-masks here because of a quarrel in a far away country between people of whom we know nothing."[28]

This rather fragmentary description of the great chasm between ideals and realistic pragmatism in the conception of what has been called international collaboration was reflected by the collaboration

---

[28] See Neville Chamberlain, *In Search of Peace* (New York, 1939), p. 174. See also the editorial "Price of Peace," in the *New York Times*, Sept. 30, 1938, quoted by Lindsay Rogers, *op. cit.*, pp. 10-11. As late as August 1, 1941, evidences of such exaggerated realistic pragmatism were found in the leading article of *The Times* (London), "Peace and Power." This article, which has been much commented upon, reads: "The direct community of interest created by Hitler's invasion can be projected into the future and becomes applicable to the future settlement of Europe. Leadership in Eastern Europe is essential if the disorganization of the past twenty years is to be avoided, and if the weaker countries are not to be exposed once more to economic disaster or to violent assault. This leadership can fall only to Germany or to Russia. Neither Great Britain nor the United States can exercise, or will aspire to exercise, any predominant role in these regions; and it would be fatal to revive the Allied policy of 1919, which created a bond of union between Germany and Russia against Western Europe." The assumption that the lack of German or Russian leadership in Eastern Europe was the decisive cause of the disintegration of that region between the two world wars is in itself somewhat bold. Furthermore, one may consider from various aspects the problem of whether or not the Soviet Union is politically, economically, and psychologically equipped, or willing to exercise, what *The Times* calls leadership in Eastern Europe. One may even modestly suggest the possibility that East European countries will refuse in future to be subject to the leadership of great powers. To advocate such a leadership for Germany, in August 1941, is, gently speaking, a political blunder. According to Z. Grabovski ("A Dangerous Theory," *The Fortnightly* (London), Sept. 1941, pp. 257 ff.), "The press of the Third *Reich* and the German radio devoted long articles and commentaries to the statement of *The Times*. The German propaganda machine stressed the fact that the nations in the East of Europe are now confronted with a clear choice and that Great Britain proclaimed frankly and openly her disinterestedness in the affairs of Eastern Europe." Though it is safe to assume that many people in the United States and in Great Britain disagree (and did disagree in August 1941) with the leadership principle in international relations in the form advocated by *The Times* (see e.g. the opinion of Professor Ernest Barker on p. 218 of the issue of *The Fortnightly* quoted here), the statement of the leading conservative daily of Great Britain is highly significant as a revelation of the chasm which existed between opinions regarding future political adjustments necessary for the establishment of harmony in the community of nations. See also, Paul Einzig, *Appeasement: Before, During and After the War* (London, 1942), *passim*. Dr. Einzig discusses extensively the economic aspects and economic implications of several appeasement waves following Munich. See also Josef Hanč, "Eastern Europe and the United States," *America Looks Ahead*, Pamphlet No. 7, Boston, 1942, *passim*.

within the ISC. It indicates that the First World War only super-
ficially transformed political nationalism, though it did give a powerful impetus to the forming of ideals and to those politically beneficial
international actions which did not touch on the conceptions of what
were shortsightedly considered national interests.

III

In the rebuilding of the shattered world, and in the rebuilt world
that follows, international steel policies, whether regimented or voluntary, will have a significant role. This role may be indicated, although only most tentatively and very fragmentarily, in the light of
past experiences with international steel marketing control schemes.
These past experiences with international steel marketing controls
can be utilized in the reopening of trade channels for other basic
materials also. Naturally, considerations about the formidable recon-
version of our present life into peaceful coöperation require constructive ideas about the general necessity for, and the future forms
of entrepreneur collaboration on international markets.

Considerations in regard to these reconstruction periods are overshadowed by the tremendous importance of the present effort to win
the war. Also, any such projection is of necessity tarred with the
brush of prediction. But in order to avoid the great risks of a complete "muddling through" policy, every effort should be made to
examine and to develop considerations on future possibilities.[29] There
is bound to be a certain amount of "muddling through" in any case,
but the risk of such policies may be considerably alleviated by previous
extended research.

The world steel industry, compared with its pre-Second World War
situation, will be greatly changed after the present war is over. In an
organizational sense, the silencing of arms will find all over the world
national steel industries coöperating strongly. There will also be several international steel organizations among allied nations, all of them
under strong governmental control. Production on high gears causes

---

[29] Mr. Walter S. Tower, President, American Iron and Steel Institute, emphasized
that it is not too early to begin speculating about problems of peacetime economy in
steel. In the opinion of Mr. Tower, "Whatever the date of the war's ending, the
steel industry will find itself equipped with capacities and facilities for which there
will be little, if any, need. . . ." According to Dr. Tower, ". . . one may conclude
that one vital question of the future is the kind and condition of market which the
steel industry will face." ("A Speculative Look at the Future," *Steel in a Year of
War.* Address at the fifty-first general meeting of American Iron and Steel Institute,
New York, May 21, 1942. Pamphlet.)

many steel-producing facilities to become outworn. These will urgently require reconditioning. Almost all steel plants will have to be more or less reconverted to peacetime purposes. Both of these tasks can be effected gradually without completely interrupting production. Some plants have been, or still will be, destroyed, many have been enlarged, others newly established under the impact of war. Depletion and destruction of industries, ships, railroads, and of other transportation facilities, of buildings, ports, and so forth, will probably create in the first postwar years a violent public and private demand for steel. Great quantities of scrap iron and steel, originating from scrapped war material, available almost everywhere in the world, will transitorily influence the situation regarding raw material supplies in the steel industries. The overabundance of appropriate steel scrap may induce in various areas the establishment of primitive furnaces and rolling plants. Out of this scrap certain steel commodities may be produced, for instance, reinforcement bars, or third-class sheets, in simple and cheap processes.

In and outside of steel industries the armistice will find tremendous quantities of ready and half-ready war materials of steel. Part of these surely may be converted for peacetime purposes, but just how much use these materials may be given will require a detailed investigation. The same problem arises in regard to finished and semifinished steel commodities which have been prepared for military purposes. Substitute products for steel, especially aluminum, may compete with steel even in the first period of transition, more strongly than they did before. New technical developments, especially in the field of alloy steels, may create a shifting demand in steel commodities. However, all these fragmentarily indicated technical problems are strongly overshadowed by possible and probable changes in the steel market resulting from developments in the political and social sphere.

Even tentative statements regarding political and social developments as they effect steel policies require a hypothetical background concerning the outcome of the war. These statements have to take into consideration the social and psychological adjustments which will be the results of collective and individual experiences of the last two decades. Such assumptions by this author embrace not only an expected victory of the Allied nations, without a previous stalemate of several years. The author also assumes that English-speaking democracies within and among themselves will develop and adopt fundamental principles concerning formal and substantial items of international collaboration.[30] This study further embraces the assumption that a basic agreement concerning these fundamentals will be reached with the Soviet Union. Those who regard this latter assumption as little substantiated by political realities may take into consideration that the Soviets in a state of political security will probably be inclined to put into practice the constitution of 1936. And this may be an appropriate first step towards the willingness of the Soviet Union to participate in international collaboration on a democratic basis.[31]

The postwar world as a whole will be strongly affected by the political and economic ideas which are being developed in English-speaking countries. The democratic process has never stopped in these countries, while people in other areas, including China and India, are living in a psychological atmosphere which makes it difficult for them to prepare for the future. After the war, the democratic process will immediately be given free play in English-speaking countries, while in other countries this may take a considerable time. Apart from power factors, the fundamental political and economic patterns which develop immediately after the war in English-speaking countries will serve as a model for political thinking in those countries which are starting or re-starting their political life.[32] These patterns may be particularly pertinent in regard to industrial organization.

---

[30] There is little difference in opinion among conservatives, liberals, and socialists in English-speaking countries regarding the most vigorous prosecution of the war. However, in respect to postwar objectives and as to methods of how international collaboration can be achieved in the future, vast intellectual abysses are apparent in contemporary literature. These seemingly unbridgeable gulfs are more noticeable in British than in American writings. The English situation is well illustrated by an editorial of the conservative *The Nineteenth Century and After* ("The Obscurantists," Mar. 1941, pp. 209 ff.). The article contrasts the political left, which is said to be very vocal on the subject of the war and of the peace which will follow, with "patriotism" which is almost silent about these subjects. The political left is identified with "socialism and internationalism." Among the adjectival colorings used in this article in criticizing those writings of Sir Norman Angell, Harold Laski, H. G. Wells and Sir Richard Acland which discuss postwar problems, "unsurpassed unpersuasiveness, confusion, superficiality, pettiness" are the less offensive ones. There is no doubt that the bitterness of the discussion would be considerably lessened by descending from generalities to less attractive but more concrete items in postwar politics and economics. Such concrete studies could be of great assistance in formulating the necessary understanding about generalities.

[31] See Arnold Wolfers, "Anglo-American Post-War Coöperation and the Interests of Europe," *American Political Science Review*, Aug. 1942, pp. 656 ff.

[32] One may safely assume that after the Second World War the great majority of nations will amend their constitutions or they will adopt new constitutions. These constitutional changes will be decidedly influenced by the effects of the working of

As these patterns develop, they will bear the imprint of an accepted reluctance on the part of English-speaking countries to change basic political and economic concepts and institutions in a revolutionary way. In contrast, the patterns themselves cannot escape a considerable remodeling when we compare them to former economic and

---

democracy in English-speaking countries in the period immediately following the war. This relates particularly to the operation of political parties in the United States and in Great Britain, i.e., how the regime of representative democracy will show itself adapted to what is somewhat vaguely called, "winning the peace." There is no doubt that in English-speaking countries under the present constitutional mechanism an unexpected outcome of elections may counteract many hopes in respect to an intimately collaborating family of nations. And even if all major political parties will, after this war is over, sincerely desire to establish and support an intimate collaboration among nations, each political party, or political grouping, will pursue its own plans. The British economist, Professor D. H. Macgregor ("Actual War Influences On Reconstruction," *Agenda,* Jan. 1942, pp. 11-12), indicating the difference among reconstruction plans, asks, "Will all this just be thrown into public debate, so that the path chosen will really depend on whichever party first obtains power? Or what is the alternative?" Mr. Macgregor proposes for determining reconstruction policy a revolutionary change in British government by establishing a technical and comparatively uncontroversial council. This agency would be truly national, as contrasted with agencies which are subject to temporary and accidental political party regimes. He finishes his study with the statement: "Either no promise is reliable, or 'we' must have some organ for shaping a [national] policy." Doubts similar to those expressed by Mr. Macgregor were raised regarding the United States Congress by Jacob Viner, "The International Economic Organization of the Future," in Howard Robinson and Others, *Toward International Organization* (New York, 1942), p. 121. Professor Gilbert Murray put it thus: "Our objection to 'commitments' is no doubt chiefly due to intellectual laziness encouraged, or made possible, by our long insular security; but the argument is sometimes used that 'commitments' are somehow inconsistent with democracy. The House of Commons, it is argued, is supreme; and no one can bind a future House of Commons or tell how it will act when the *casus foederis* arises. A different party with different views may be in power. If this contention were true it would prove too much. It would prove that Great Britain was not a continuous unity, but only a series of governments without any consistency or sense of honour; . . . I agree . . . about the necessity of this country accepting a large permanent responsibility for the guidance and reorganization of Europe. . . ." *The Fortnightly,* October 1941, pp. 331-32. Edward Hallett Carr (*Conditions of Peace,* New York, 1942, pp. 34-35), discussing postwar constitutional problems of democracies, indicates that the rebuilding of the political system and the reconstruction of the economic system are the same problem viewed from different aspects. Comparing the holders of economic power to the holders of military power in former centuries, he regards it as a prerequisite for the revival of political democracy that economic power should be brought under the control of the community "in exactly the same way as military power was brought under control in democratic countries before the nineteenth century." See also R. H. Tawney, *The Acquisitive Society* (New York, 1920), pp. 44 ff. There will be no constitutional difficulty in bringing economic power under the control of the community. As a matter of fact economic power has been under the potential control of the community for many decades. But whereas the will of the community as to the organization and operation of military power proved to be rather unequivocal in modern democracies, it may be questionable whether, and how, the community will take

political patterns. The first great influence for change will be a new emphasis on international economic and political policy rather than national and isolationist. The second great influence will be the idea of full-time employment.[33] Neither of these is revolutionary in the proper sense, but both have already become essential to any speculations regarding future international and political developments.

After the laying down of arms in countries which have been victorious, and even in those which have been defeated, every effort will be made to reintroduce or maintain steel production, first for reasons of reconstruction, and second for social reasons to employ returning labor. No doubt military authorities, which will more or less transiently occupy important steel areas, will be obliged to arrange these operations according to a preëstablished program. Europe, including Great Britain, will probably not export steel commodities outside of Europe in the first postwar years, though mutual trade in steel may develop. If the British, Belgian, Luxemburg, French, German, Czechoslovakian, Polish and Italian steel industries are not considerably impaired in a technical sense, European countries will probably not need to be supplemented by American steel, even in the first months. They may even be able in a short time to supply steel to the Soviet Union. That country will probably import huge quantities in the first years after the war is over. The Far East and the Western Hemisphere will certainly remain, at least for the first years, an uncontested market for the United States,

---

advantage of its control over the holders of economic power. Thus the jurisdiction of the community over economic power need not be established in English-speaking countries on a stronger basis; what is needed is a reëxamination of short- and long-run principles as to the exercising of the existing power of the community. And in this regard the degree of success of the peoples in the United States and in Great Britain will influence the constitutional life of the majority of civilized nations.

[33] John Maynard Keynes' famous sentences about the obligation of sound statesmen to cope with unemployment through employing people, will probably become accepted as a basic principle of constitutional doctrine. "If the Treasury were to fill old bottles with banknotes, bury them at suitable depths in disused coal mines which are then filled up to the surface with town rubbish, and leave it to private enterprise on well-tried principles of laissez faire to dig the notes up again . . . there need be no more unemployment and, with the help of the repercussions, the real income of the community, and its capital wealth also, would probably become a good deal greater than it actually is. It would, indeed, be more sensible to build houses and the like, but if there are political and practical difficulties in the way of this, the above would be better than nothing." (*The General Theory of Employment, Interest and Money,* London, 1936, pp. 128-29.) Permanent large-scale investments in the realm of national and international economies may change profoundly the former structure of the international steel market. The struggle for import markets may give way to other—yet unknown—problems. See also Peter F. Drucker, *The Future of Industrial Man,* New York, 1942, *passim.*

especially if currency and credit problems do not interfere. This also applies to South Africa. If the European steel industries, including those of Britain, are destroyed to a considerable extent, the demand from these areas will have to be met by the United States steel industries. In consideration of the fact that the reconstruction of large steel plants requires a great deal of time, this factor may become a major bottleneck in European reconstruction. It is difficult to tell, at the present time, how far transportation difficulties will disturb the raw material supply of European steel industries.

The European steel situation will be significantly influenced by the fact that the postwar period will bring about major changes in the ownership of steel industries as compared with the prewar period and also the period of German domination. In almost all German-dominated countries, steel industries were transferred under pressure to German ownership.[33a] To retransfer ownership and to solve the ownership problem of the steel industries will pose difficult questions.

No doubt, ownership problems of steel industries, like those of other industries, will be influenced by considerable changes in shareholders who acquired their stocks as beneficiaries of the Hitler-Mussolini-Petain-quisling regimes. Personnel problems in steel industries will be influenced by the holding to account of those executives of steel corporations and steel organizations who were co-responsible for the rise and maintenance of all brands of totalitarian regimes.

Many continental European steel industries will be run by public authorities before the problem of ownership has been finally solved. Efforts will be made on the European continent to engage American capital as a complete or partial stockholder in any rearrangement. One of the most important problems of rearrangement of ownership of European steel industries will be the violent demand of many people to socialize steel industries by making them subject to public ownership. In this regard even Great Britain cannot be exempted.[34]

[33a] The methods by which the Nazi regime acquired the property of steel industries in invaded countries excellently fit into the picture of Nazi morals. One of the best known cases was the attempted acquisition of a major part of the shares of the largest Czechoslovakian steel corporation, *Vitkovice,* by keeping Baron Louis Rothschild, the man who had these shares under control, under arrest until he consented to transfer his property "legally." The transfer of French, Belgian and Luxemburg steel industries to German control after the invasion of these countries is discussed by Louis R. Franck, *French Iron and Steel from Prewar Time to German Rule,* Washington, 1942 (Brookings), *passim.*

[34] A proposal calling for state control of key industries in wartime, introduced at the end of 1941 in the House of Commons, was rejected with a large majority of

It is a matter of conjecture whether demands for public ownership will become apparent in the United States. Socialist parties all over the world will be eager to emphasize this point of government ownership. This is not the place to discuss advantages and probable disadvantages accompanying the transfer of such complex industries as the steel industry represents to public agencies. A detailed investigation was made after the First World War by a German official committee on socialization. Besides this, experiences in Germany, Italy, Poland, Yugoslavia, Rumania, Czechoslovakia, Hungary, the Netherlands, South Africa, and other countries show that a certain caution is necessary in this respect.[35] With some trepidation, one may suggest that the outcome of these issues will be determined not so much by experience and sober reasoning as by political volition. Those who favor a private entrepreneurial system will probably have

---

votes. The fact that only a small fraction of Labor voted in favor of the proposal prompted Mr. Louis Fischer to remark: "Verily, the revolution is not just around the corner in England." (*Dawn of Victory*, New York, 1942, p. 131.)

[35] The combination of the profit motive and the social motive is heavily attacked by Dwight Macdonald, "Jesse Jones, Reluctant Dragon," in *The Nation*, Feb. 14, 1942, which designates "state capitalism" as a theoretical impossibility, as "a monster uniting mutually irreconcilable principles." He concluded that "Either the profit motive or the social motive may be a spur to economic effort, but a compromise between the two seems to take the dynamism out of both." According to Mr. Macdonald the falsity of the proposition "that there is any particular virtue, from a democratic, progressive point of view, in state enterprise . . . should have been pretty well discarded by now anyway. . . ." Though this author disagrees with Mr. Macdonald in several generalizing points, he regards his article as a brilliant presentation of the "combination of the vices of private capitalism and state bureaucracy." C. W. Wright (*op. cit.*, pp. 5, 21, 94-95), says that in Great Britain "The tendency to nationalize industry, as in Germany, is regarded as a downward step toward inefficiency and higher production costs." According to Mr. Wright, "Political control over the iron and steel industries, particularly in Germany and to a smaller extent in Italy, Poland and Rumania, is thus waxing greater, and private interests are becoming less powerful. Such control, however, usually has resulted in decreased efficiency, higher production costs, and inferior quality of products, as competition is largely eliminated. These conditions may continue for a number of years, as has been the case in Russia, but if and when the trade barriers of these nations are broken down and consumers are permitted to buy their requirements at world market prices, these protected, high-cost producing mines and plants will have to be scrapped." Furthermore, "As the number of State-financed mining and metallurgical companies in Germany and Italy expands, the desire to nationalize the entire industry becomes greater and the actual control by private interests is replaced by Government control. Such control, however, often results in decreased efficiency, higher production costs, and inferior quality of products, as competition is eliminated. This tendency toward nationalization of the industries is causing a gradual break-down in the heretofore balanced economic set-up." Naturally this problem, once touched upon by Mr. Wright in an official publication, deserves a more penetrating investigation and evaluation.

to answer the demand for socialization with certain guarantees of full employment. They will also state that industries subject to heavy criticism may be subject to even more stringent attack under government ownership. They will point out that, especially in politically unsettled periods, it is preferable that the role "of a battered buffer between consumers, labor, investors, and government"[36] be played by private entrepreneurs rather than by public agencies. In passing it may be stated that this exposed role of entrepreneurs in steel industries, especially certain guarantees of full employment, would in itself be a radical incentive for collective marketing controls on the national and international scene. It would require even more complicated and extensive collective marketing mechanisms than before.

It may be interesting to note that people concerned with the efficient guarantee of future peaceful coöperation of nations have been considering a supranational control of world steel industries as a measure of world peace. The extent of this proposed measure varies from outright supranational public ownership to supranational management control. The plans vary, one embracing the steel industries of Germany, Italy, and Japan only, another enclosing European steel industries, and still another including the steel industries of the world.[37] Whereas supranational control of the heavy industries of the defeated countries, probably embracing some regulations concerning their ownership, may be a step envisaged for a period until those nations can be regarded as definitely pacified, the problem of subjecting to supranational control the steel industries of other nations would imply a degree of international collaboration which may be referred to as world government. However, if the intimacy in collaboration among nations attains the degree of world government, the guarantee of peace by concerted control of steel industries may be regarded as superfluous. This is not to say that national governments may not in the framework of international conventions regulating armaments subject their steel industries to supranational supervision. Such measures would probably meet little opposition in governments and industries.

While the American steel industry will dispose of problems of technical readjustment rather smoothly, the main problem will be

---

[36] J. M. Clark, "Economic Adjustments After Wars, The Theoretical Issues," *American Economic Review,* Papers and Proceedings of the Annual Meeting of the American Economic Association, Dec. 1941, p. 7.

[37] One of these plans (at present unpublished) originates from Professor Adolph Lowe, of the New School for Social Research.

that of full employment. This problem will be somewhat moderated by large national and international public investments.

It is impossible to predict under what conditions steel export trade will develop in the transition period. Even on domestic markets one cannot state with any certainty at all what trend steel prices will take. The picture on the export steel market, under the impact of complicated currency, credit, supply and transportation problems, is even more hazy. Absolute scarcity in steel in the first years will probably contract to a minimum sellers' competition even though there is no well-established international cartel. However, one may assume that the buying and selling of steel in the export market will not be done in this period without the intervention of international public agencies.

After the transition period, or probably in its later stages, but surely in the period of ultimate adjustment, marketing agreements between "national steel exporter groups" will enter the international economic scene. In the establishment of an international steel marketing control, the determination of the first quota arrangements will cause particular difficulties because political and economic circumstances on which future steel consumption in import markets depends will be rather unpredictable. In addition, one may assume that the political requirements of full employment in steel-exporting countries all over the world will influence quota negotiations. National steel groups may more stubbornly insist on high quotas than in prewar years. The equilibrium in quota arrangements will be decidedly influenced by the role of the American steel industries in exporting. If, under pressure of employment requirements, the United States should intend to export considerably more steel than it did between 1920 and 1939, and if international credit arrangements do not prepare for a considerable increase in steel consumption in backward areas, the whole quota scheme as compared with 1938-39 will change. One should realize that world steel exports in 1938 did not exceed 12,000,000 net tons. The United States steel capacity in 1942 will probably exceed 88,000,000 net tons.

Even if we assume that there will be international steel marketing controls in the postwar world, these organizations will be adjusted in both structure and operation to new political objectives. Any considerations concerning this future structure and any forecast regarding its operation, would require fundamental reconsideration of the problem of economic competition and of the combination movement from the political, economic and social point of view. Professor J. M. Clark put it, "As a first step, we shall need a revival of objective thinking. It will not do to regard a given action as monopolistic if done by people we do not like, while the same action, if done by people we approve of, becomes an exemplar of 'the democratic process.'"[38] This revival of objective thinking in the contested field of industrial combinations will probably meet many difficulties. It will require the discarding of many slogans. It will equally require a reconsideration of the social responsibilities of entrepreneurs and entrepreneur groups. Political parties will have to adjust their new platforms to the requirements of what is called objective thinking. In the past these platforms often deviated considerably from economic reality, especially in regard to industrial combination problems. The interpretation given to the proverb "My country right or wrong" will decisively influence political thinking and acting in the field of international combinations as well.

Reorientation of the problem of industrial combinations should be based on extensive new research in political science and economics. Modern political and economic literature has not until now discussed substantial problems concerning the future role, or the work of, international industrial combinations.[39] It has limited itself mainly to general statements about the necessity for public control of such institutions. In past literature concerning international cartels, substantial opposition and prejudices were not focused so much against restricting international competition as against the concentration of economic power in private hands and against the possible intrusion of this power on national economic policies. In the future, possible opposition to international cartels may focus primarily on these two

---

[38] J. M. Clark, *op. cit.*, p. 11.

[39] Naturally much valuable material concerning the future role of international commodity controls may be found in general and special treatments of pre-Second World-War combinations. See here e.g. the quoted studies of J. W. F. Rowe, Eugene Staley, and W. Y. Elliott. The International Studies Conference, XII Session, Bergen, Aug. 1939, devoted great attention to the future role of international commodity controls. J. B. Condliff's *The Reconstruction of World Trade* is based on the material presented to the Conference. (See pp. 334-341 regarding international commodity controls.) Dr. Albert Prinzing introduced to the Conference *German Memorandum No. 3,* "Bearing of International Cartel and Control Schemes Upon International Trade Organization." (Mimeogr.) The author emphasized at the very beginning of his paper that ". . . it must be stated with regret that not without reason research on the influence of International Cartels on international commerce has been lacking completely. The author has tried to gauge the influence of international industrial agreements on volume, quality, and direction of international trade by way of statistical inquiries. This attempt had however to remain without success." Mr. Prinzing's study often refers to the structure and operation of the ISC. Several of his generalizations are based mainly on ISC material.

points. However, because opinions about an international cartel structure are considerably influenced by views concerning the domestic cartelization movement, and because there is a certain interrelation between domestic and international cartelization, it may be useful to glance at a representative opinion from a democratic source regarding the future of American cartels.

Mr. A. H. Feller recently stated, "We may safely assume that the fully self-governing cartel on the German model will never be accepted here unless there is a complete reversal in our economic and political ideals." Mr. Feller believes, "that the American cartel, if it comes, will look very much like the N.R.A. code authority, an industrial association exercising police powers over its members with some governmental participation and supervision."[40] Though one could object, in regard to the statement made by Mr. Feller, that the fully self-governing cartel ceased to be the German model many years ago, no doubt his opinion represents the view of many democratic politicians and economists in the United States and elsewhere. As mentioned above, strong government supervision of industrial combinations in the future is almost generally envisaged in the sense that future cartels should not influence the monopolistic position of the modern state in exercising political power, and that they should exercise those social functions which the new welfare society assigns to the entrepreneur. Cartel policies should fit into the general economic and political environment. Thus there is no doubt that future collective marketing controls will have to abide by social standards corresponding to the contemporary general social and moral standards of the community in which they are operating. However, as soon as governments transcend the concept of strong supervision by "participating" in cartel functions, the picture changes. On the one hand participation in cartel policies implies, as emphasized before, new responsibilities on the part of public agencies, on the other it permits the weakening of responsibilities on the part of entrepreneurs.

A more detailed discussion of this point may even reveal that participation in cartel activities by public authorities, either as representatives of publicly owned enterprise, or in some other capacity, may considerably weaken the vigor these same agencies can exercise in supervision. The political consequences of government participation in cartel policies in peacetime economy raises political problems which transcend the scope of this volume. Such measures necessarily

---

[40] See A. H. Feller, *op. cit.,* p. 138.

would require a public policy of fixing wages. The price structure would become subject to political decisions. Probably several entrepreneur groups, subject to great pressure due to full-time employment requirements mentioned before, would find government participation in their responsibilities acceptable. Participation of public agencies in policy-determining activities of collective marketing controls automatically raises the question whether or not such cartels will tolerate outsiders. In the affirmative case the further question arises whether the participation of public agencies in cartel policy will result in a protection or in a more vigorous suppression of outsiders. Every plan and measure regarding cartel policies should most carefully consider the dangerous consequences of restricting outside competition with government support. Even if it is recognized that technical and economic circumstances greatly favor the restriction of competition and the legalization of some form of marketing control for a certain commodity, this should not lead to governmental measures impeding the rise of outsiders who do not want to participate in a collective marketing control. Thus, just as true democracy precludes the concept of a tyrannical majority and provides for balancing the volition of majority and minority groups, so the legalization of cartel structures should essentially provide for the protection of entrepreneurs who do not want to join the cartel organization. The economic diagnosis that an outsider has little hope of faring well in the market of a controlled commodity must not induce governments to cut off by legal means or by administrative practices creative entrepreneurs who intend to challenge such a diagnosis. European cartel legislation furnishes many examples of an institutional instrumentation of such "minority protection."

Considerations concerning the influence by outside forces on the discretion of entrepreneurs in international marketing controls imply an intimate political coöperation by the interested national governments. They also imply that there are ascertainable principles according to which international marketing controls can operate in order to satisfy what is called supranational interest.

As soon as we face the problem of directing international price policy by supranational authorities, we need to analyze the substantial issues which necessarily arise. We have to realize that price and supply decisions of supranational political agencies, without presuming a strong international political government behind them, would be a source of insurmountable political issues. One or two representative opinions concerning the future position of international cartels should be discussed here.

Professor Eugene Staley has said, "It is highly desirable to establish some check over the price and output policies of commodity controls, and to add to their present producer-dominated boards representatives of consuming countries and consumer interests generally. To meet the problem adequately, it will be necessary to create a permanent international economic agency with administrative powers."[41] Professor Percy E. Corbett recommended the establishment of an "International Trade Commission which would supervise the operations of international cartels, which themselves are to be reformed by the introduction of government and consumer representation on their board of direction."[42]

Applying the quoted statements to future international steel marketing controls, i.e., that these agencies include representatives of consuming industries, and of labor, one wonders whether they would advocate prices which are high or low, flexible or rigid, discriminative or equal, and whether export prices below average total unit costs will be admitted. One wonders whether consumer and labor representatives could agree among themselves on a steel price policy to be followed in export markets. One may imagine that labor representatives would find it a sound policy not to make the international cartel a battleground for discussing international labor problems. The question of finding representatives for the community of steel consumers of the world, or labor delegates to represent the common labor interest of steel exporting and steel importing countries, would pose rather an intricate problem.[43] It would be solved probably by conferring

---

[41] "The Economic Organization of Peace," *International Conciliation*, Apr. 1941, p. 413.

[42] *The World's Destiny and the United States* (New York, 1941), p. 142. See also Dr. P. E. Corbett's *Post-War Worlds* (New York, 1942), p. 29. J. B. Condliff (*Agenda for a Post-War World*, New York, 1942, p. 114) considers the creation of great international commodity control institutes and the "incorporation of consumer interests in the machinery of control." Edward Hallett Carr recommends the establishment of a European Planning Authority superimposed upon large international commodity controls. (*Conditions of Peace*, pp. 262-63.)

[43] J. B. Condliff, *The Reconstruction of World Trade*, pp. 339-40, discusses in connection with international marketing controls the economic pressure exerted upon consuming countries. "No great consuming country"—writes the author—"is likely to accept such a situation quietly. . . . Most international commodity control schemes are, in fact, international only in the sense of giving representation to the producing countries, and it cannot be expected that this situation will be accepted gracefully by other countries. . . . The key to the situation may perhaps be found in more effective consumer representation, if possible including consumer countries outside the controlling

the representation of labor upon international labor unions and that of consumers upon the dominant general organization of consumers. Imagining such representation, a guarantee should be provided that marketing decisions would be reached within a reasonable period. Whether or not such a cartel organization may require an arbitration mechanism is a question of detail. This is not to say that in rather simple international raw materials such as tea, rubber, aluminum, copper, sulphur, or tin, the idea of consumer and labor influences on international marketing controls could not be envisaged through intergovernmental agreements. However, a general supervision of combinations by public agencies may include their supervision from the aspect of consumer and labor interests as well. Thus an agent of a future supranational agency may take into account all kinds of public interests having suitable connections with the representatives of those interests.

This author is not acquainted with any pertinent studies in political and economic literature which discuss international price structures that would be equally satisfying to the international community of governments, consumers, and labor. He assumes that such studies should be made with reference to several commodities and their interrelation, this in order to determine whether generally acceptable standards in regard to international supply and prices might exist. Such investigations would also show how far the common interests of consumers, labor, and also of producers of many nations could be expressed in practicable principles.

Even without reference to such case studies, one may safely state that large international commodity marketing controls could be subjected to supranational supervision. This supervision ought to move on a scale that is realizable in the light of present experiences. Its prerequisite is the subjecting of international combinations to an adequate degree of publicity in regard to their structure, interrelationship, and operations. The supervision must see that concentrated economic power does not interfere with international or national politics, especially that this power is not abused in respect to labor. International supervision should inquire whether artificial scarcity is being created in order to increase prices. It should inquire also whether cartel policies are obstructing the technical development of

group." In the opinion of this author the problem of consumer representation in international commodity controls requires several case studies. Concerning supranational control of the oil industry, see Frederick Hausmann, "World Oil Control Past and Future," *Social Research*, Sept. 1942, pp. 334 ff.

their own industries, or of other branches of industries, by self-imposed technical restrictions. If there is established a mechanism supervising international combinations from the point of view of supranational interests, one of the important objectives of such an agency should be to ascertain whether there is a fair possibility for outsiders to operate on the market and by what means the combination fights outsiders, if any. If the political development of the future should lead to something that may be called supranational policies, these policies should vigorously abstain from actively supporting the growth of complete monopolies, though these agencies should not engage in hopeless fights against coöperative international combinations, driving them underground. The very fact that outsiders are not excluded from markets influences cartel policies considerably. If national governments would agree that international combinations, in which their producers or distributors coöperate, participate in international political or economic sanctions, then supranational agencies could direct and supervise this participation. Whether possible national public ownership of large industries would facilitate international supervision of marketing controls cannot be answered unconditionally in the affirmative.

More extended studies concerning the ISC may bring forward valuable conclusions regarding the future role of international steel marketing controls, and regarding the industrial combination problem in general. Such studies should reëxamine the proper position of industrial combinations in what is called a welfare economy.

A few sentences, quoted from A. N. Whitehead, may well conclude this chapter with a somewhat brighter outlook in regard to both the problem of the present world struggle and the equally relevant problem of the economic struggle of the future: "The watchwords of the nineteenth century have been, struggle for existence, competition, class warfare, commercial antagonism between nations, military warfare. The struggle for existence has been construed into the gospel of hate. The full conclusion drawn from a philosophy of evolution is fortunately of a more balanced character. Successful organisms modify their environment. Those organisms are successful which modify their environments so as to assist each other. . . . In the history of the world, the prize has not gone to those species which specialized in methods of violence, or even in defensive armour . . . smaller animals, without external armour, warm-blooded, sensitive, and alert, have cleared monsters off the face of the earth. . . . There is something in the ready use of force which defeats its own object. Its main defect is that it bars coöperation. Every organism requires an environment of friends, partly to shield it from violent changes, and partly to supply it with its wants. The Gospel of Force is incompatible with a social life. . . . Almost equally dangerous is the Gospel of Uniformity. The differences between the nations and races of mankind are required to preserve the conditions under which higher development is possible."[44]

---

[44] "Requisites for Social Progress," in *Science and The Modern World*, Harmondsworth (England), 1938, p. 238.

APPENDICES

APPENDIX I

THE BASIC STRUCTURE OF THE ISC

   I General policy-determining groups
  II National groups
 III Export sales comptoirs

I General policy-determining groups:
   1. International Steel Cartel (ISC)
   2. European Steel Cartel (ESC)
   3. Entente Internationale de l'Acier (EIA)

II National groups
   1. Founder groups
   2. Associated groups
   3. Coöperating groups

III Export sales comptoirs
   1. Directly subordinated to EIA
   2. Closely connected with EIA
   3. Connected with ESC
   4. Coördinating their policy with ISC
   5. Loosely coördinating their policy with ISC

I *General policy-determining groups*
   1. International Steel Cartel (ISC)
      Itinerant unincorporated association. No domicile
      Member units: EIA, United States, Great Britain
      Executive body: Enlarged Joint Co-ordinating Committee
      American-European Commercial Coördinating Agency, London,
         E.C.2, 11, Ironmonger Lane
      Secretarial, routine and statistical services performed "de facto" by
         EIA business office, Luxemburg, ARBED Building
   2. European Steel Cartel (ESC)
      Itinerant unincorporated association. No domicile
      Member units: EIA, Great Britain
      Executive body: Joint Co-ordinating Committee
      Secretarial, routine and statistical services performed "de facto" by
         EIA business office, Luxemburg, ARBED Building

3. Entente Internationale de l'Acier (EIA)
   Unincorporated association
   Domicile: Luxemburg, ARBED Building
   Executive body: Management Committee (Comité de Gérance);
   Chairman: Mr. Aloyse Meyer
   Commercial policy-determining agency: Comptoir Committee;
   Chairman, Mr. Hector Dieudonné
   Secretarial, routine and statistical services performed by business
   office of EIA, Luxemburg, ARBED Building
   Audit and supervision: Schweizerische Treuhandgesellschaft, Basel,
   Switzerland

II *National groups* composing the ISC, participating in general policy
forming

A. Founder groups of EIA
   1. Belgium
   2. France
   3. Germany
   4. Luxemburg

B. Associated groups of EIA
   1. Poland
   2. Czechoslovakia

C. Coöperating groups
   1. Great Britain
   2. United States

D. European Group (ESC)
   1. Belgium
   2. France
   3. Germany
   4. Luxemburg
   5. Poland
   6. Czechoslovakia
   7. Great Britain

E. All national groups (ISC)
   1. Belgium
   2. France
   3. Germany
   4. Luxemburg
   5. Poland
   6. Czechoslovakia
   7. Great Britain
   8. United States

1. *Founder groups* of EIA

    1) Belgian National Group: Groupement des Hauts Fourneaux et Aciéries Belges Société Co-opérative, Brussels, 10 Avenue Galilée; Executive agency: Comptoir de Vente de la Sidérurgie Belge "Cosibel," Brussels, 9, rue de la Chancellerie

    2) French National Group: Comptoir Sidérurgique de France, Société Anonyme, Paris, 1, rue Paul Cézanne

    3) German National Group: Stahlwerks-Verband Aktiengesellschaft, Düsseldorf, Stahlhof, Bastionstrasse 39

    4) Luxemburg National Group: Groupement des Industries Sidérurgiques Luxembourgeoises Société Coopérative, Luxemburg, 31, rue Joseph II; De facto executive agency: "Columeta" Compagnie Luxembourgeoise Métallurgique Société Anonyme, Luxemburg, Avenue de la Liberté

2. *Associated groups* of EIA

    1) Polish National Group: Zwiazek Eksportowy Polskich Hut Zelaznych Sp. Z.O.O. Katowice, Ul. Lompy, 14

    2) Czechoslovakian National Group: Prodejna Sdružených Československých Železáren Akciová Společnost, Prague, Lützovova 55

3. *Coöperating groups*

    1) British National Group: British Iron and Steel Federation, London, Westminster, Steelhouse, Tothill Street; Executive agency: British Iron and Steel Corporation Limited, London, Westminster, Steelhouse, Tothill Street

    2) American National Group: Steel Export Association of America, New York City, 75 West Street, London office: Brettenham House, Strand, 14-15 Lancaster Place

III *Export Sales Comptoirs*

    1. (Category I): *Directly subordinated to EIA*

       Products included: (1) Semifinished steel
       (2) Structural shapes
       (3) Merchant bars
       (4) Thick plates, 3/16 in. and up.
       (5) Medium plates, 1/8 in. to 3/16 in.
       (6) Universal steel, 6 in. and up

    (1) Name: *International Entente for Semifinished Products*
        (Entente Internationale des Demi-Produits, Internationaler Halbzeug-Verband). Unincorporated association
        Domicile: Brussels, 9, rue de la Chancellerie
        Reëstablished: 1933

Chairmanship: Belgian national group
Members: a. Belgium ⎫
 b. France ⎪
 c. Germany ⎬ Founder groups of the Comptoir
 d. Luxemburg ⎭
 e. Poland (associate member with o quota)
 f. Czechoslovakia (agreement only concerning coöperation in general price policy, negotiations in respect
 to quota not terminated)
 g. Great Britain (coöperation according to general and
 sectional agreement)
 h. United States (coöperation according to "heavy steel
 agreement")

(2) Name: *International Entente for Structural Shapes*
 (Entente Internationale des Profilés, Internationaler Formeisen-Ver-
 band.) Unincorporated association
 Domicile: Paris, 5, rue Paul Cézanne
 Reëstablished: 1933
 Chairmanship: French national group
 Members: a. Belgium ⎫
 b. France ⎪
 c. Germany ⎬ Founder groups of the Comptoir
 d. Luxemburg ⎭
 e. Poland ⎫
 f. Czechoslovakia ⎬ Associated groups
 g. Great Britain (coöperation according to general and
 sectional agreement)
 h. United States (coöperation according to "heavy steel
 agreement")

(3) Name: *International Entente for Merchant Bars*
 (Entente Internationale des Laminés Marchands, Internationaler
 Stabeisen-Verband.) Unincorporated association
 Domicile: Luxemburg, 3, rue Joseph II
 Reëstablished: 1933
 Chairmanship: Luxemburg national group
 Members: a. Belgium ⎫
 b. France ⎪
 c. Germany ⎬ Founder groups of the Comptoir
 d. Luxemburg ⎭
 e. Poland ⎫
 f. Czechoslovakia ⎬ Associated groups
 g. Great Britain (coöperation according to general and
 sectional agreement)

h. United States (coöperation according to "heavy steel agreement")

(4) Name: *International Thick Plates Entente*
(Entente Internationale des Tôles fortes, Internationaler Grobblech-Verband.) Unincorporated association
Domicile: Düsseldorf, Stahlhof, Bastionstrasse 39
Reëstablished: 1933
Chairmanship: German national group
Members: a. Belgium ⎫
        b. France ⎪ Founder groups of the Comptoir
        c. Germany ⎬
        d. Luxemburg ⎭
        e. Poland ⎫ Associated groups
        f. Czechoslovakia ⎬
        g. Great Britain (coöperation according to general and sectional agreement)
        h. United States (coöperation according to "heavy steel agreement")
        i. Austria (coöperation according to special sectional agreement)

(5) Name: *International Medium Plates Entente*
(Entente Internationale des Tôles moyennes, Internationaler Mittelblech-Verband.) Unincorporated association
Domicile: Düsseldorf, Stahlhof, Bastionstrasse 39
Established: 1933
Chairmanship: German national group
Members: a. Belgium ⎫
        b. France ⎪ Founder groups of the Comptoir
        c. Germany ⎬
        d. Luxemburg ⎬
        e. Poland ⎬
        f. Czechoslovakia ⎭ Associated groups
        g. Great Britain (coöperation according to general and sectional agreement)
        h. United States (coöperation according to "heavy steel agreement")
        i. Austria (coöperation according to special sectional agreement)

(6) Name: *International Universal Steel Entente*
(Entente Internationale des Large-plats, Internationaler Universaleisen-Verband.) Unincorporated association
Domicile: Düsseldorf, Stahlhof, Bastionstrasse 39
Established: 1933

Chairmanship: German national group
Members: a. Belgium ⎫
       b. France ⎪
       c. Germany ⎬ Founder groups of the Comptoir
       d. Luxemburg ⎭
       e. Poland ⎫
       f. Czechoslovakia ⎬ Associated groups
       g. Great Britain (coöperation according to general and sectional agreement)
       h. United States (coöperation according to "heavy steel agreement")
       i. Austria (coöperation according to special sectional agreement)

    2. (Category II): *Closely connected with EIA*
      Products included: (7) Wire Rods
                     (8) Hot-rolled Bands and Strips
                     (9) Cold-Rolled Bands and Strips
                     (10) Wide-Flange Beams
                     (11) Sheet Piling

(7) Name: *International Wire Rods Entente*
(Entente Internationale du Fil-Machine, Internationaler Walzdraht-Verband.) Unincorporated association
Domicile: Ougrée (Belgium), Société Anonyme Ougrée-Marihaye
Established: 1927
Chairmanship: Belgian national comptoir
Members: a. Belgium ⎫
       b. France ⎪
       c. Germany ⎬ Founder groups of the Comptoir
       d. Luxemburg ⎭
       e. Poland ⎫
       f. Czechoslovakia ⎪
       g. Austria ⎬ Associated groups
       h. Hungary ⎭
       i. Great Britain (coöperation according to general and sectional agreement)
       j. United States (coöperation according to "heavy steel agreement")

(8) Name: *International Hot Rolled Bands and Strips Entente*
(Entente Internationale pour l'Exportation des Feuillards et Bandes à Tubes, Internationale Vereinigung für die Ausfuhr von Bandeisen und Röhrenstreifen.) Unincorporated association
Domicile: Liége (Belgium), 4, Boulevard Piercot
Reëstablished: 1933

Chairmanship: Belgian national comptoir
Members: a. Belgium ⎫
       b. France ⎪
       c. Germany } Founder groups of the Comptoir
       d. Luxemburg ⎬
       e. Poland ⎱
       f. Czechoslovakia } Associated groups
       g. Great Britain (coöperation according to general and sectional agreement)
       h. United States (coöperation according to "sheet agreement")

(9) Name: *International Cold Rolled Bands and Strips Entente*
Domicile: Liége (Belgium), 4, Boulevard Piercot. Unincorporated association
Established: 1939
Chairmanship: Belgian national comptoir
Members: a. Belgium
       b. France
       c. Germany
       d. Luxemburg

(10) Name: *International Wide Flange Beams Entente*
Domicile: Paris, 1, rue Paul Cézanne. Unincorporated association
Established: 1934
Chairmanship: French national group
Members: a. France
       b. Germany
       c. Luxemburg

(11) Name: *International Sheet Piling Association*
Domicile: Düsseldorf, Stahlhof, Bastionstrasse 39
Established: 1936. Unincorporated association
Chairmanship: German national group
Members: a. France
       b. Germany
       c. Luxemburg

3. (Category III): *Connected with ESC*
Products included: (12) Black sheets, less than 1/8 in.
                 (13) Galvanized sheets, less than 1/8 in.

(12) Name: *International Black Sheets Comptoir*
Domicile: London, S.W. 1, 14 Waterloo Place. Unincorporated association
Established: 1936
Chairmanship: British national comptoir

Members: a. Belgium
b. France
c. Germany
d. Luxemburg
e. Poland
f. Czechoslovakia
g. Great Britain
h. United States (coöperating according to "sheet agreement")

(13) Name: *International Galvanized Sheets Comptoir*
Domicile: London, S.W. 1, 14 Waterloo Place
Established: 1936. Unincorporated association
Chairmanship: British national comptoir
Members: a. Belgium
b. France
c. Germany
d. Luxemburg
e. Poland
f. Czechoslovakia
g. Great Britain
h. United States (coöperation according to "sheet agreement")

4. (Category IV): *Coördinating their policy with ISC*
Products included: (14) Heavy rails (36 lbs per yard and more, and accessory material to rails)
(15) Drawn wire and wire products

(14) Name: *International Rail Makers' Association* (IRMA)
Domicile: London, E.C. 2, 11, Ironmonger Lane (Peat, Warwick, Mitchell and Co., Chartered Accountants)
Reëstablished: 1926. Unincorporated association, no permanent chairman
Members: a. Belgium
b. France
c. Germany
d. Luxemburg
e. Poland
f. Czechoslovakia
g. Austria
h. Hungary
i. Italy
j. Great Britain
k. United States

l. Ougrée-Marihaye group

m. Baume and Nimy group

(15) Name: *International Wire Export Company (IWECO), Inc.*
Domicile: Brussels, 54, rue de Namur
Reëstablished: 1932. Incorporated Commercial Company; Independent Chairman
Members: a. Belgium
b. France
c. Germany
d. Czechoslovakia
e. Hungary
f. Poland
g. United States (special agreement)
h. Great Britain (special agreement)
i. Denmark (special agreement)
j. Holland (special agreement)
k. Italy (special agreement)

5. (Category V): *Loosely coördinating their policy with ISC*
Products included: (16) Tubes
(17) Scrap
(18) Tin Plates

(16) Name: *International Tube Convention*
Domicile: Düsseldorf, Hermann Göringstrasse 19
Established: as Continental Cartel 1926, enlarged to International Tube Convention in 1929, dissolved 1935, reëstablished as loose association, 1935. Unincorporated association
Chairmanship: German national comptoir
Members: a. Belgium
b. France
c. Germany
d. Poland
e. Czechoslovakia
f. Hungary
g. Great Britain
h. United States

(17) Name: *International Scrap Convention*
Domicile: London, S.W. 1, Tothill Str., Steel House
Chairmanship: Mr. I. F. L. Elliot
Established: 1937. Unincorporated association
Members: a. Germany
b. Poland
c. Czechoslovakia
d. Austria

    e. Hungary
    f. Italy
    g. Rumania
    h. Sweden
    i. Yugoslavia
    j. Great Britain

(18) Name: *International Tin Plate Association*
    Domicile: London: E.C. 2, 11, Ironmonger Lane (Peat, Warwick, Mitchell and Co., Chartered Accountants)
    Established 1934. Unincorporated association. No permanent chairman
    Members: a. France
             b. Germany
             c. Great Britain
             d. United States
             e. Belgium
             f. Italy (special agreement)
             g. Norway (special agreement)

APPENDIX II

BY-LAWS OF THE BUREAU OF INTERNATIONAL CARTELS

BUREAU OF INTERNATIONAL CARTELS

Founded under the auspices of the International
Chamber of Commerce

June 28, 1938

STATUTES

I. The object of the Bureau of International Cartels is:
  1. To study the international organizations for production and marketing;
  2. To publish:
    (a) The results of its studies in full agreement with its adherents and with the permission of the organizations concerned;
    (b) Releases communicated to the Bureau by the cartels for publication;
    (c) Articles on certain international economic problems concerning the organization of production and marketing;
    (d) Information concerning the legal status of cartels in the different countries as well as on legal problems relating to cartels;
  3. To organize meetings between adherents for the discussion of questions of common interest;
  4. To support international organizations, which already exist or are in process of formation, by lending them material or other suitable collaboration.

II. The Bureau will be supervised by a Managing Committee of not more than 25 members, chosen among its adherents. The President of the International Chamber of Commerce, or his alternate, will be ex-officio member of the Managing Committee.

III. Subject to the approval of the Managing Committee, the following can adhere to the Bureau:
    (a) as active members:
  1. International cartels;
  2. Individual firms entertaining relations with the former;
    (b) as corresponding members:

1. Other international organizations dealings with production and marketing;
2. Business men who are authorities on cartel matters;
3. Other organizations recognized as suitable for membership by decision of the Managing Committee.

IV. The work of the Bureau shall be financed by annual subscriptions from its adherents. These funds shall be administered by the President and Vice-Presidents of the Managing Committee.

V. The seat of the Bureau is in Paris.

VI. The Managing Committee is empowered to complete or amend the above Statutes as necessary.

APPENDIX III

INTERNATIONAL STEEL AGREEMENT[1]

September 30, 1926

Article 1

Each country shall pay 1 dollar monthly into a common fund for each ton of crude steel actually produced.

By the term "crude steel" is meant all the crude steel manufactured in the several countries by the Thomas, Bessemer, Siemens or Martin processes, by the electric, crucible, or any other process. This sum shall be credited to the account of the country in question. The first time, it shall be paid two months after the present Agreement comes into effect in the form of drafts at three months; for subsequent months it shall be paid on the 25th of the month following in the form of a draft at three months.

Should the Government of one of the countries participating in the Agreement object to the transfer of all or any of the sums payable under the present Article, the actual payment might be replaced:

(1) By the guarantee of a bank approved by the Managing Committee; or

(2) By a cash payment into a blocked account at a bank situated in the country in question and approved by the Managing Committee.

Article 2

The administration of the common fund shall be provided for by a Managing Committee of four members appointed respectively by each of the countries Parties to the Agreement, i.e. Germany, Belgium, France, and Luxemburg. Each of these four countries shall also appoint two deputy members to replace the permanent member in the event of his being absent or unable to attend.

The chairmanship of the Managing Committee shall be held for one year by each of the countries concerned in rotation.

In a general way, and in addition to the special provisions laid down in the Articles following, the Managing Committee shall make the neces-

---

[1] Published in *Memorandum on the Iron and Steel Industry,* International Economic Conference (Geneva, 1927), pp. 109 ff. In this publication Articles 12 and 13 were incomplete, and Art. 15 was omitted. In this appendix Art. 12, 13, and the full text of Art. 15 are represented by excerpts from Dr. J. H. Reichert, "Die Festländische Rohstahlgemeinschaft," *Weltwirtschaftliches Archiv,* XXV (1927), 348* ff.

sary arrangements for carrying out the execution of the clauses of the present contract and for exercising the supervision which it entails. It shall also have full powers for the administration, handling, and custody of the monies paid into the common fund or held by it. The number of votes of the Managing Committee shall be allotted in accordance with the quotas.

Article 3

The Managing Committee shall fix the quota of each country for each quarter in accordance with the provisions of Article 4 not later than a fortnight before the beginning of that quarter, by applying coefficients—fixed once for all for each country—to the total tonnage representing the probable demand of the market.

Article 4

The coefficients allotted to the different countries can only be modified by unanimous consent.

The total quarterly tonnage, and accordingly the quotas of each country, shall be fixed by a two-thirds majority of the votes, each country commanding the number of votes proportional to its participation, with the proviso that unanimity of all the countries but one shall constitute a sufficient majority even if this latter country represents more than a quarter of the votes.

The Saar shall never vote individually; its votes shall be divided between France and Germany in their ratios of one-third and two-thirds.

Article 5

Every month each country's actual net production of crude steel during that month shall be ascertained, in relation to the figures indicated by the quotas.

Article 6

If the quarterly production of a country exceeds the quota which was fixed for it, that country shall pay in respect of each ton in excess a fine of 4 dollars, which shall accrue to the common fund, in addition to the payment provided for in Article 1.

Article 7

If the production of any country has been below the quota allotted to it, that country shall receive in compensation from the common fund the sum of 2 dollars per ton.

The tonnage entitling to compensation may not, however, exceed 10 per cent of the quota fixed for the quarter in question. If a shortage of 10 per cent or more below the quota fixed continues during several successive quarters, the tonnage entitling to compensation shall be reduced by two per cent for each successive quarter, so that in the second quarter of such shortage of 10 per cent or more the compensation paid shall not exceed 8 per cent, and in the third quarter it shall not exceed 6 per cent, and so on.

In the event of force majeure, the General Meeting of the several groups shall decide by a majority vote the amount of the compensation payable.

Article 8

The accounts shall be balanced quarterly, the excess contributions and sums due in compensation mentioned in Articles 6 and 7 being payable immediately after the balance of accounts.

At the close of each half-year, the common fund shall be liquidated, after deduction of the general expenses; the remaining balance shall be distributed between the several countries:

(1) in proportion to the actual production during the accounting period, up to the limit of the payments made under Article 1;

(2) And, if any balance remains over from fines, in proportion to the participation figures of the accounting period concerned.

The first liquidation of the common fund shall take place on April 1st, 1927.

Article 9

The present Agreement shall terminate on April 1st, 1931. Up to May 1st, 1929, however, any country shall be entitled to give notice of withdrawal from the Agreement on October 31st, 1929, in which case the other countries shall be released from all obligations of the same date.

Article 10

The present Agreement was concluded on the assumption that throughout its duration the tariff rates applicable to iron and steel products imported into Germany would not be increased. If Germany should proceed to increase the said rates, the present Agreement may be denounced at any time by each of the Contracting Parties at three months' notice, and each of the Parties shall then recover full liberty of action in relation to its Government as regards tariffs.

The present Agreement, however, may be denounced at any time on and after April 1st, 1927, at three-months' notice, if the Government of one of the Contracting Parties objects to it on the ground that, in the absence of a commercial treaty, one of the other countries is applying unfavourable treatment to the products as a whole.

If Germany or France denounces the present Treaty for one of the two reasons mentioned above, they shall also have the right to denounce it as against the other Contracting Parties, who, in turn, shall be entitled to denounce it inter se.

Article 11

Exchange in respect of the quotas of the countries are not allowed in the case of any company or Konzern unless that company or Konzern possesses and operates undertakings in another country. Ownership of at least 40 per cent of the share capital of these undertakings shall constitute possession.

Previous notice of such transfers must be given to the Managing Committee. The transfer cannot take effect until the beginning of the next accounting period, and must apply at least for that period.

Article 12

If on April 1st, 1927, the total consumption has not increased to such an extent that the Luxemburg group shall have obtained a quota of tonnage representing a minimum annual production of 2,360,000 tons and on April 1st, 1929, tonnage representing a minimum annual production of 2,480,000 tons, that group shall be entitled to withdraw from the present Agreement at three months' notice. It shall then be open to the other countries also to withdraw from the present Agreement.

The previous reservations are included in this agreement as a consequence of the following claims:

1. The ARBED Company, beginning from April 1, 1927, shall attain a production transcending its production in the first quarter of 1926 by 50,000 tons quarterly.

2. The Hadir Company, beginning from April 1, 1927, shall attain a production transcending its production in the first quarter of 1926 by 30,000 tons quarterly.

Article 13

Any disputes arising between the Parties as to the interpretation and carrying out of the present Agreement shall be compulsorily settled by arbitration.

The party plaintiff shall appoint its arbiter and communicate the name of the arbiter to the defendant, requiring him in his first communication with the defendant to do the same within a fortnight. If the defendant does not appoint an arbiter within a fortnight and does not communicate the name of the arbiter to the plaintiff, the President of the International Chamber of Commerce shall appoint an arbiter upon the request of the plaintiff. The arbiters then appoint a chairman. If they are unable to agree on the selection of this chairman within a period of one month, the third arbiter shall be appointed by the President of the International Chamber of Commerce which is in Paris. This upon the request of the plaintiff.

Article 14

It shall be open to steel manufacturers in the other European countries to join in the present Agreement.

Admission shall be sanctioned by the General Meeting:

(1) By a majority vote if participation is determined on the basis of the production of the first quarter of 1926.

(2) Unanimously, if admission is granted on some other basis.

If the participation of the participating countries in the total production of the European countries for any one half-year is 5 per cent less than the same participation during the first quarter of 1926, the rescission of the present Agreement may be demanded by any one of the groups Parties to the Agreement, to take effect after three months' notice, which must be given not later than three months after the expiration of the half-year under consideration.

The Agreement may also be rescinded by any one of the countries Parties to the Agreement at three months' notice in the event of the total figure fixed for any one half-year being less than 13,139,000 tons. In this event, the notice of rescission must be given within a month.

Article 15

In all cases of denunciation of this agreement the act of giving notice must be performed by registered letters sent to all participants; in France to the President of the Comité des Forges, in Belgium to an address which will be indicated later, in Luxemburg to the President of the ARBED, and in Germany to the President of the Rohstahlgemeinschaft.

SHARE QUOTAS IN THE INTERNATIONAL STEEL AGREEMENT OF SEPTEMBER 30, 1926[1]

Note transmitted by C. Lammers.

In fixing the share quotas of the individual countries in the International Steel Agreement, the basis taken was that of an aggregate annual production of raw steel of 25,278,000 tons and the annual quotas were fixed on this basis as follows:

	Per cent
Germany	40.45
France	31.89
Belgium	12.57
Luxemburg	8.55
Saar Territory	6.54

These participation figures are changed if the total output rises by 1, 2, 3 or 4 million tons up to 29,278,000 tons. Above this figure the final quotas are as follows:

	Per cent
Germany	43.18
France	31.18
Belgium	11.56
Luxemburg	8.30
Saar Territory	5.78

In the event of any further increase in output, these percentage quotas will remain unchanged. Belgium, however, on joining the International Steel Trust, was granted a fixed quota of 295,000 tons per month irrespective of any restriction which might be imposed on output. As a consequence, the quotas of the other countries were somewhat reduced.

In November 1926, the total output of the International Steel Cartel for the fourth quarter of 1926 was fixed at 29,278,000 tons. In December 1926, by a resolution of the International Steel Cartel, it was decided to reduce the output for the first quarter of 1927 by 1.5 million tons. In March 1927 this reduced output was once more raised by 1.5 million tons for the second quarter of 1927.

At the beginning of 1927, Czechoslovakia, Austria and Hungary joined

---

[1] Published in *Memorandum on the Iron and Steel Industry,* International Economic Conference, Geneva, 1927, p. 113.

in the International Steel Agreement. These three countries together received a share of 7.272 per cent, or 2.14 million tons, annually on the basis of total output by the International Steel Cartel of 27,278,000 tons. These three Central European countries having joined the Cartel as a single unit, the distribution of their quota between them is a matter to be settled by themselves.

APPENDIX IV

MEMORANDUM OF GENERAL AGREEMENT[1]

concluded between

the British Group represented by the British Iron and Steel Federation, London, responsible for the Firms and Companies enumerated in Appendix 1,* and hereinafter called the "Federation" on the one hand and

on the other hand

the French Group represented by the Comptoir Sidérurgique de France, Société Anonyme à Capital Variable, Paris, and responsible for the Firms and Companies enumerated in Appendix I:*

the Belgian Group represented by the Groupement des Hauts Fourneaux et Aciéries Belges Société Co-opérative, Brussels, and responsible for the Firms and Companies enumerated in Appendix I:*

the Luxemburg Group represented by the Groupement des Industries Sidérurgiques Luxembourgeoises, Société Co-opérative, Luxemburg, and responsible for the Firms and Companies enumerated in Appendix I:*

the German Group represented by the Stahlwerks-Verband Aktiengesellschaft, Düsseldorf, and responsible for the Firms and Companies enumerated in Appendix I:*

the aforesaid Groups being represented collectively by the Entente Internationale de l'Acier, Luxemburg, hereinafter called the "E.I.A."

Article I

Object.—The aim and object of this Agreement is to establish collaboration between the Federation and E.I.A. in respect to their general export sales and the protection of their respective interior markets.

It is the intention of the contracting parties to conclude sectional Agreements in respect of iron and steel products other than those enumerated in Article III, as soon as the interested producers are grouped in the different countries.

Article II

Duration.—This Agreement shall come into force on 8th August, 1935, provided that, in the meantime, arrangements shall have been made by the

---

[1] Published as Annex I to the White paper (Cmd. 5201), *Memorandum on Clause 6 of the Finance Bill, 1936,* presented to Parliament, June 1936, London, H. M. S. O. 1936. The permission of the Controller of H.M. Stationery Office in London to reprint parts of Cmd. 5201 is hereby duly acknowledged.

* Not printed.

United Kingdom Government whereby the rate of duty applicable to imports covered by the Agreement may be reduced wherever practicable to not more than 20 per cent ad valorem. This Agreement shall continue subject to the provisions of Article III (a) and Article IV (e) hereof and to any modifications that may be found necessary and agreed between the parties from time to time for a period of five years, but either of the contracting parties shall have the right to terminate the Agreement on the 7th August, 1938, upon giving notice of their intention so to do in writing to the other party not later than the 7th February, 1938.

Article III

Exports.—(a) Sectional Export Agreements—in so far as they are not already concluded—shall be concluded in respect of the following products:

(1) Irma material:
(2) Semis (ingots, blooms, billets, slabs, sheet bars, tinplate bars):
(3) Joists, channels and broad flanged beams:
(4) Merchant bars and sections:
(5) Thick plates (3/16 in. and up):
(6) Medium plates (1/8 in. and less than 3/16 in.):
(7) Large flats or universals (6 in. and up):
(8) Hoops and strip:
(9) Tube strip:
(10) Wire rods, IWECO and other wire products:
(11) Tinplates:
(12) Sheets less than 1/2 in. black and galvanized:

and all sectional Agreements shall be deemed to be an integral part of this Agreement.

The sectional Agreements still to be concluded shall be operated in full from the date of their completion, but in every case the operation of the export quotas for which they provide shall be made to apply from a date not later than the 8th of August, 1935.

In the event of failure to reach a sectional Agreement in respect of any of the aforesaid products by 7th January, 1936, either party may, on giving three months' notice, terminate both this Agreement and such sectional Agreements as have been concluded prior to 7th January, 1936.

(b) The export rights of the contracting parties shall be secured by the application to the total exports in any product of the quotas fixed by the sectional Agreement for that product.

(c) If, during the first year of operation, the total exports of the United Kingdom, Germany, Belgium, France and Luxemburg, under the sectional Agreements enumerated in (a) above exceed the corresponding total of exports for 1934, the following rules shall be applied for the apportionment of the excess:

(i) If the excess is less than or equal to 217,500 tons, it will be divided at the rate of 2/3 for the Federation and 1/3 for the E.I.A. The apportionment of any balance of the said 2/3 remaining to be satisfied after the quotas of all the respective sectional Agreements have been met, shall be applied to the various products so far as practicable in the proportion that they have contributed to the increase of the exported tonnage except that any additional tonnage that would accrue in this way to rails, semis or tinplates shall be taken up in the other products named in (a) above if either party so requires, and on a basis to be mutually agreed:

(ii) If the excess is more than 217,500 tons, the apportionment of a first quantity of 217,500 tons shall be made as stated in (i) above. The division of the tonnage exceeding this first quantity of 217,500 tons shall be made in accordance with the percentages as fixed in the sectional export Agreements.

This special disposition applies only to the first year of operation, and for the following years the apportionment shall be made in accordance with the percentages as fixed in the sectional export Agreements.

Article IV

Importers into the United Kingdom.—(a) The Works situated in the countries represented by the E.I.A. shall be entitled to import into the United Kingdom under the conditions hereinafter provided a total of 670,000 tons made up of the products and quantities as shown hereunder during an initial period of 12 months from 8th August, 1935, and thereafter a total of 525,000 tons per annum as shown hereunder during each of the four periods of 12 months following:

	Imports	
	1935	Each Subsequent Year
Irma material	Nil	Nil
Semis (ingots, blooms, billets, slabs, sheet bars and tinplate bars)	255,329	195,869
Joists, channels and broad flanged beams	97,538	76,432
Merchant bars and sections (including iron bars)	172,948	135,521
Thick plates (3/16 in. and up)		
Medium plates (1/8"-3/16")		
Large flats or universals (6" and up)	35,810	30,635
Black plates and sheets less than 1/8" and galvanised sheets		
Hoops and strips	10,225	8,012

Tube strip	37,500[2]	26,500[2]
Wire rods, IWECO and other wire products:		
(a) Wire rods	39,700	31,081
(b) IWECO products	20,950	20,950
Tinplates	Nil	Nil
Total	670,000	525,000

(b) Inasmuch as both parties are satisfied that the aforesaid importation into the United Kingdom with reduced rates of duty can only be operated satisfactorily and without detriment to the interests of their respective countries by the institution by the United Kingdom of a system of licensing, the Federation undertake to use their best endeavours to secure the institution of such a system for the products named at the earliest possible date.

(c) In order that the coming into force of this Agreement may not be delayed pending the establishment of a system of licensing and the conclusion of the sectional Export Agreements, the Federation will ask their Government to make the reduction of duties referred to in Article II above for a period of five months in the first instance. The E.I.A. undertake that importation from their countries during that period shall not exceed the proper proportion of the respective tonnages prescribed in (a) above, except in so far as exchanges of one category for another may be agreed.

(d) The E.I.A. undertake to consult with the Federation as to prices and destination of sales and deliveries during the aforesaid temporary period of five months, and to consider the conclusion before the expiration of that period of permanent arrangements under which the Federation may, if they so desire, make collective purchase of the agreed importation on a basis that preserves as far as practicable established channels of distribution.

(e) In the event of failure—

    (i) to continue the provision for reduced import duties for the full term of this Agreement: or

    (ii) to institute a system of licensing of imports into the United Kingdom: or

    (iii) to reach agreement in regard to the permanent arrangements referred to in (d) above:

either party may, on giving three months' notice, terminate both this Agreement and the respective sectional Agreements.

---

[2] Subject to verification of the imports of conduit strip in 1933 having been 13,500 tons and not 10,000 tons.

Article V

Co-ordinating Committee—The contracting parties shall establish a Joint Co-ordinating Committee, which shall be responsible for the proper carrying out of this Agreement, and for the general supervision of the various sectional Agreements.

Article VI

Arbitration—In the event of any dispute arising between the contracting parties as to either the interpretation or the application of this Agreement or the sectional Agreements it shall be in the first instance submitted to the Chairman of the Federation and the Chairman of the E.I.A. If no settlement is reached, the dispute shall be referred to arbitration, each Chairman nominating an Arbitrator within one month. If the Arbitrators cannot effect a settlement they shall, within a month, either agree upon an Umpire or request the Chairman of the International Chamber of Commerce to appoint an Umpire. The contracting parties undertake to accept without appeal the verdict passed by the Chairman, the Arbitrators or the Umpire as the case may be.

Article VII

The Agreement is written down both in English and French. It is stipulated that, in case of arbitration, the Arbitrators shall refer to the English text whenever the arbitration is applied for by the Federation and to the French text whenever the arbitration is applied for by the E.I.A.

Signed at London—31st July, 1935.

On behalf of British Iron and Steel Federation: Dudley
Andrew R. Duncan, W. J. Larke
On behalf of Entente Internationale de L'Acier: A. Meyer
Th. Laurent, E. Poensgen, A. D'Heur.

APPENDIX IV A

ANNEX III

to the White paper (Cmd. 5201).
Memorandum on Clause 6 of the Finance Bill, 1936.
Letter from British Iron and Steel Federation to the President of the Board of Trade.

31st March, 1936.

Sir,

At a Meeting of the Council of the British Iron and Steel Federation held here on 19th inst. I explained to them that, in connection with the statutory imposition of a licensing system in respect of importations under our International Agreement there were certain assurances which it would be necessary for the Federation to give to you as President of the Board of Trade.

The Council unanimously agreed to undertake on behalf of the Federation:

(a) to use their best endeavours to secure that adequate supplies of suitable steel are at all times available to meet the reasonable requirements of British consumers, and to make arrangements, if circumstances so require, for the importation of such additional tonnages as the Import Duties Advisory Committee may deem necessary in excess of those fixed by the Cartel Agreement:

(b) To make such arrangements for the disposal of the imports of foreign steel from the Cartel as will secure to the satisfaction of the Import Duties Advisory Committee the equitable distribution of such steel as to quantities, qualities and prices, among all classes of consumers without discrimination as to whether or not they are members of an affiliated Association:

(c) To undertake that membership of affiliated Associations shall be open to all firms who are eligible under their Rules and willing to observe them:

(d) To arrange that the prices of the agreed imports of foreign steel shall not be in excess of the prices charged for corresponding British steel to Members of the Federation; and in this connection to re-affirm the assurance as to the price policy of the Federation given in the Memorandum submitted to the Board of Trade, dated 14th March, 1935.

I have the honour to convey the foregoing assurance to you.

I am, Sir,

Your obedient Servant,

(Sgd.) Andrew R. Duncan

The Rt. Hon. Walter Runciman, M.P.

INTERNATIONAL MERCHANT BAR AGREEMENT[1]

(and decisions of the EIA concerning quota participation)

CONTENTS

---

[1] These documents were printed in German and French. Mr. George H. Hobart translated them into English.

XXII. Settlement of Disputes. Special Committee of Group Presidents of EIA. Language Version to be used in Arbitration Proceedings

Appendices a and b

INTERNATIONAL MERCHANT BAR ENTENTE
(Entente Internationale des Aciers Marchands)
Convention
Between the Undersigned:

1. The STAHLWERKS-VERBAND, Inc. with headquarters in Düsseldorf, acting in its own name and in the name of the following companies, the latter binding their successors in case of change in properties:
[28 German Firms Listed]
Hereafter called "The German Group," and represented by Mr. Ernst Poensgen, Düsseldorf.

2. The COMPTOIR SIDÉRURGIQUE DE FRANCE, Société Anonyme à capital variable, with headquarters in Paris, 1, rue Paul Cézanne, acting in its own name and in the name of the following companies, the latter binding their successors in case of change in properties:
[16 French Firms Listed]
Hereafter called "The French Group," and represented by Mr. Theodore Laurent, Paris.

3. The GROUPEMENT DES HAUTS-FOURNAUX ACIÉRIES BELGES SOCIÉTÉ COOPÉRATIVE, with headquarters in Brussels, 10, Avenue Galilée, acting in its own name and in the name of the following companies, the latter binding their successors in case of change in properties:
[10 Belgian Firms Listed]
Hereafter called "The Belgian Group," and represented by Mr. Jaques Van Hoegaerden, Ougrée.

4. The GROUPEMENT DES INDUSTRIES SIDÉRURGIQUES LUXEMBOURGEOISES, Société Coopérative, with headquarters in Luxemburg, 31, rue Joseph II, acting in its own name and in the name of following companies, the latter binding their successors in case of change in properties:
[4 Luxemburg Firms Listed]
Hereafter called "The Luxemburg Group," and represented by Mr. Aloyse Meyer, Luxemburg.

These groups subscribe to the following agreement:

ARTICLE I

Object

The purpose and object of this agreement is to regulate the export sales of merchant bars and effectively to adjust the supply to the consumer demand by the following means:

1. By determining the share of each group in export deliveries.
2. By centralizing all export sales within the four interested countries in the hands of the four national sales organizations, these national sales organizations to be managed by the contracting companies.
3. By subjecting the sales policy of these four organizations to mutual regulation and control.

ARTICLE II

Nomenclature

This agreement includes quantitatively and without any exception all tonnage of the following products shipped by the four groups outside of their respective domestic markets as defined in Appendix A, whether produced by the Thomas, Bessemer, Siemens-Martin, crucible, electric, or by any other process:

All *Rounds* of 4.76 mm. (3/16″) diameter and over, also all *Squares* of 4.76 mm. (3/16″) or more in width across face, either in bars or coils unless subject to quantity control by the International Wire Rod Entente.

Processed Wire Rods.

All *Concrete Reinforcement Bars,* including round and square corrugated bars.

All *Flats* of sharp or round edges of a width of 8 mm. and over and of 3 mm. or more in thickness, provided they are not subject to quantity control by the International Band and Strip Entente, or by the International Wire Rod Entente, or by the International Universal Steel Entente.

All *Angles,* with equal or unequal legs and with either round or sharp edges.

All *Tees.*

All *Z-bars.*

All *U-bars* and *Channels* of less than 80 mm. in width.

All full *Half-rounds.*

All *Ovals* not controlled by the International Wire Rod Entente.

All *Hexagons, Trapezoids,* or *Conical Bars.*

All *Octagons.*

All *Grate Bars, Standards and Varillas,* of first or inferior grades, for whatever use. "Cobbles" are also to be considered as Merchant Bars.

Exceptions:

A) As to both price and quantity:

1. Rounds used for the fabrication of seamless tubes.
2. Cuttings, waste, and rejects intended for remelting or similar purposes.

B) As to price only:

1. The products designated above, in crucible steel, binaire, or ternaire steel. Copperbearing steel cannot be considered as binaire steel unless it possesses a copper content equal to or greater than 0.70%.
2. The products designated above, by whatever process manufactured (Thomas, Martin, electric, etc.) sold with a minimum surcharge of 30/- (gold shillings) per ton with reference to the normal prices set by the Comptoir for analogous products obtained by the same process (Thomas, Martin, electric, etc.). The Management Committee shall have the power to modify the amount of this surcharge.
3. Bars for shells, steel for springs.
4. All shapes not enumerated above.
5. Products designated above which fall under the special cases provided in Article VI for penetration of domestic markets.

N.B. Shapes for shipbuilding are affected quantitatively, but their prices are fixed by the International Thick Plates Entente.

ARTICLE III

Duration

This Convention shall become effective June 1, 1933 and shall operate for a period of five years.

Any one of the groups directly interested in the agreements enumerated below may denounce the

Convention previous to its expiration by giving 45 days advance notice (provided such notice of termination is not deliberately intended to damage other groups), under the following circumstances:

1) In case the Entente International de l'Acier expires or is not renewed;

2) In case the association called "CONTINGENT LORRAIN-LUXEMBOURGEOIS" expires or is not renewed.

3) In case of expiration or non-renewment of the French-Belgian-Luxemburg Agreement concluded between the French Group on the one hand and the Belgian and Luxemburg Groups on the other, for the importation of products either for the Belgian-Luxemburg domestic market or for the French domestic market;

4) In case the political or economic status of the Saar territory is changed and new arrangements satisfactory to the contractual participants cannot be concluded between the interested groups;

5) In case of expiration or the rupture of the arrangement in regard to the Saar Contingent concluded between the French group and the Saar plants;

6) In case of the expiration or the rupture of the arrangement between the Stahlwerks-Verband and the Saar plants;

7) In case of the expiration or the rupture of the Belgian-German Entente concluded between the Belgian Group on the one hand and the German Group on the other for the importation of products either for the Belgian domestic market or for the German domestic market;

8) In case the international agreements actually existing relative to wire rods or bands are dissolved.

The right of denunciation applicable to any one of the above cases may not be invoked if not made use of within three months following the date on which the circumstances making possible this denunciation become known.

ARTICLE IV

Outsiders

This arrangement, agreed to by the German, French, and Luxemburg groups, has not as yet been subscribed to by the Belgian group, which reserves its compliance thereto until a satisfactory understanding shall have been reached with the re-rollers in its territory

The groups assume for the present and future outsiders in their countries, the engagements which the groups have made for themselves. The groups shall be charged with the export tonnage of these outsiders, but shall not incur the sanctions provided for infraction if they can prove that the outsiders have been supplied with raw material by plants other than those listed in the preamble to this Convention as belonging to their group. If the re-rollers in question have been supplied with raw materials by other groups which have subscribed to this Convention, these other member groups shall be entirely responsible for the offending exports.

If in the meantime there should appear in the domestic market of a group participant a new outside producer whose deliveries during three consecutive months exceed 3% of the three-month average of total deliveries (domestic and export) made by the interested group during the last twelve months preceding the notice given by this group to the respective international comptoir, the Management Committee (provided by Article VII) shall first deliberate, during a period of not more than one month, as to what steps are to be taken. If the decision made by the Management Committee does not satisfy the interested group, this group may, within a period of one month, serve notice of withdrawal from the Convention after the expiration of a 45 day notice.

This right of denunciation cannot be invoked later if advantage of the opportunity has not been taken during the three months following the date on which the circumstances making possible the denunciation become known.

ARTICLE V

Denunciation

In case of denunciation of the present Convention or at its expiration, the contracting groups shall recover their freedom of action thirty days before the end of the operation of the Convention, but only for deliveries to be effected after the expiration date. In every case, deliveries made during the months which follow the end of the agreement shall enter into the calculation of excess and deficit for the last period of accounting, whatever may be the booking date of the corresponding orders.

ARTICLE VI

Territorial Protection

This agreement includes the obligation on the part of all groups and affecting all products subject to their export control, that the groups will not deliver these products, nor offer them for sale, nor sell for delivery on the domestic market, of other groups (cf. Appendix A). To this end, the Management Committee shall require the groups to insert in their bids and confirmation of orders—even on the domestic market—penalties and other stipulations effectively to prevent merchandise sold for delivery to their own domestic market or to any other specified destination, from being diverted to other countries in violation of the terms of the contract.

In case of infraction of the terms of this article, the terms of Article XIX shall become applicable. In addition, the tonnage originally sold to the domestic market of the delivering group which has been diverted to another destination contrary to the terms of the Convention, shall be charged quantitatively as exportations of the said group.

The only exceptions to the principle of the protection of the domestic market are such special agreements as exist between certain groups at the time of signature of this Convention, as modified or renewed during its continuance, including:

a) The Lorrain-Luxemburg quota agreement, concluded between the French and Luxemburg Groups on the one hand, and the German Group on the other;

b) The French-Belgian-Luxemburg agreement, concluded between the French Group on the one hand and the Belgian and Luxemburg Groups on the other, for the importation of products, either for the Belgian-Luxemburg domestic market, or for the French domestic market;

c) The agreement as to the Saar Contingent, concluded between the French Group and the Saar plants;

d) The agreement concluded between the Belgian and German Groups as to the importation of products either on the Begian domestic market or on the German domestic market.

ARTICLE VII

Management Committee

Composition—Fulfillment of this Convention shall be effected through a Management Committee to consist of one titular delegate from each of the participating groups. In addition to the titular delegate, each group shall appoint two substitute delegates.

Powers

In order to insure fulfillment of this Convention, the Management Committee shall have the widest powers. It may delegate all or part of its powers to such committees as it may appoint, and whose jurisdiction it shall control.

Chairmanship

The Management Committee shall appoint each year by unanimous vote a chairman and a vice-chairman. The vice-chairman shall act in the chairman's place when the need arises. Both chairman and vice-chairman shall be eligible for reappointment.

Voting

In all decisions made by the Management Committee, each group shall have one vote, and, unless otherwise specified by the regulations, all decisions shall require a majority vote.

Calling of Meetings

The Management Committee shall meet as often as necessary. Members shall be notified by the chairman or vice-chairman at least eight days before the dates set for meetings. However, in case of urgent necessity the members shall be notified by telegraph three full days in advance of the meetings.

The order of business for each meeting shall be explicitly formulated in advance and new matters not included therein shall not be discussed except by unanimous agreement of the Committee, all groups being represented.

If any one group so requests, the Management Committee shall call a meeting to be held within eight days following the date of such request.

ARTICLE VIII

Central Bureau

The Management Committee shall create under the authority of its chairman a Central Bureau, whose main duty shall be to collect and to supply all statistics necessary for the functioning of the Convention.

As soon as possible after the end of each month, and not later than the tenth of the month following, the Central Bureau shall supply all the groups with the following:

1) A table containing the tonnages shipped during the preceding months, and showing the status of each group as to excess or deficit, according to the quotas as specified in Article IX.

2) A list of tonnages sold during the preceding month.

3) A list of undelivered quantities on order as of the last day of the preceding month, taking into consideration the provisions for deliveries to be made by the interested groups under the authority of the special territorial penetration agreements defined in Article VI.

Each group agrees to supply punctually to the Central Bureau after the end of each month and not later than the 8th of the following month, all the information necessary for the compilation of general statistics for the month, as well as all the statistical information requested from it at any time and covering any period whatever.

Every quarter the expenses of the Central Bureau shall be divided among all the groups in proportion to their effective deliveries.

ARTICLE IX

Quotas

The share of each group in the total export deliveries made by all the contracting groups is determined by the "Protocol of decisions arrived at during the meetings of April 25 and May 5, 1933," promulgated at Luxemburg on May 5, 1933, abstract of which is appended to this agreement (Appendix B).

All the figures shall be subject to revision at such times as the results of a check-up of the period to which they refer shall be established.

ARTICLE X

Transfer of Quota Rights

Quota rights may be transferred from one group to another, provided such transfers in no way damage the interests of other groups.

The transfer of quotas between plants belonging to the same concern is authorized insofar as such transfers do not damage the rights of the groups to which the plants belong. A list of plants recognized as belonging to a concern shall be attached to this agreement.

Should objections arise in regard to quota transfers, such transfers cannot be invalidated except by a three-fourths vote of a special committee composed of the chairmen of the groups belonging to the EIA.

Such transfers of quotas as are above contemplated shall be announced before the beginning of the quarter to which they are to apply, and notice of such transfer shall be given:

1) to the Central Bureau, which will then notify the groups.

2) to the Central Bureau of the EIA in order that the corresponding transfer of crude steel may be made.

Transfers of tonnages for rolling among plants belonging to the same concern are authorized, provided that they may be considered by the respective comptoirs and by the EIA as the exclusive deliveries of the transferring group. Notification of these transfers shall be given to the interested groups, who may communicate their opinions as to whether or not their interests have been damaged.

ARTICLE XI

Tonnage Program

In order to furnish the contracting groups with schedules which will provide a basis for the regulation of their sales, the Management Committee shall proceed, before the end of the second month of each quarter to establish the provisional amount of tonnage which each group shall be authorized to sell and to deliver during the following quarter.

For this purpose, the Management Committee shall first of all establish the program of tonnage which can be supplied by all the contracting groups combined, taking into consideration on the one hand, the average shipments made during the previous quarter and on the other hand, any changes which may have occurred meanwhile in export markets or new competition which may have arisen. The tonnage program applicable to each group shall next be established by the application of the allotted quotas provided in Article IX, to the global tonnage program, with due consideration of the provisional excesses and deficits which remain to be corrected at the end of the current quarter.

The Management Committee shall at all times have the right to correct the tonnage program which it has provisionally established, whether such changes relate to the provisional reckoning of global exports or to the particular quotas of those groups whose status as to excesses or deficits could not be originally estimated in a sufficiently exact manner.

ARTICLE XII

Excess and Deficits— Charging of Quota Accounts. Equalization of Excess and Deficits

The Management Committee shall attempt to equalize as exactly as possible the status of excess and deficits of the different groups by employing for this purpose all measures which it may judge necessary, especially:

1) Requiring the group or groups which have exceeded their allotments to turn over certain orders to groups in deficit, under conditions which the Committee shall establish, and provided that in principle and in the absence of a decision to the contrary, the group which relinquishes the order shall guarantee payment (del credere).

2) Requiring the group or groups in excess to quote protective prices;

3) Requiring the group or groups in excess to withdraw partly or wholly from the market.

In order to facilitate the application of these different measures, the Management Committee shall also require the groups in excess to insert in certain contracts a clause which shall reserve the right of the selling group to transfer to another group all or part of the contracted tonnage, provided that the terms of delivery shall be fulfilled by the group which benefits from the tonnage transfer. In such cases, the deliveries shall be made for the account and risk of the group which effectively makes delivery, except for the provision above cited in respect to payment guarantee (del credere).

If a group which is in deficit shall refuse an order which it is obliged to accept by virtue of this article, the tonnage thus refused shall be provisionally charged against its quota share. Such charge shall become definitive if at the end of the month for which it is made, the interested group is still in deficit as to its delivery allotment; otherwise the charge shall be canceled.

The excess and deficits which appear at the end of each month and at the end of each quarter according to the shipment statistics compiled by the Central Bureau shall be reported each month and each quarter in order that the Management Committee may accomplish so far as possible the effective application of tonnage participation under the conditions provided by Article XI and the arrangements above specified.

At the end of each twelve month period, or at the date which shall result from the application of Article V, the excess and deficits in deliveries of all the groups shall be canceled by the payment to the groups in deficit by the groups in excess, of an equalization payment consisting of an assessment on each ton of excess at the rate of 20/- gold shillings, such equalization payments to become due and payable within thirty days after the statistical information has been communicated.

These groups whose shipments during this quarter are less than the alloted quotas, shall receive for each ton in deficit the amount specified in Article XII, provided sufficient payments have been made by those groups which exceeded their quotas. If the payments of the groups in excess are insufficient to cover the amount due to the groups in tonnage-deficit, the payments to the latter groups shall be reduced proportionately. The tonnage deficits shall be canceled in all cases.

AMENDMENT TO ARTICLE XII OF THE REGULATIONS

(Decision of the Management Committee of the EIA, dated January 10, 1935)

The Management Committee of each Comptoir shall, before the 15th of the first month of each quarter, determine the tonnage to be shipped by the 4 groups during the following quarter. In setting the tonnage program it shall take into account the shipments of preceding months and of such information in regard to market conditions as may be indicated by the record of orders booked. Whenever a decision is made without a unanimous vote, each group shall have the right of appeal to the Committee of Directors of the EIA which shall render a final decision.

The tonnage program thus determined may be modified by the unanimous agreement of the four groups before the end of the period to which it applies.

The amount of tonnage to be allowed each group for delivery during the quarter under consideration shall be determined by the application to the tonnage program of each group's quantum percentage, the tonnage thus obtained being increased or diminished by the amount of excess or deficit shown on the last day of the preceding quarter.

Any groups whose booked orders are insufficient to complete the delivery tonnage allowed to them, shall request the transfer of orders to them. If he deems the requests legitimate, the chairman of the Management Committee shall order the transfers to be made, and compliance with the chairman's orders shall be deemed imperative and enforceable through the imposition of compulsory debiting of the quota accounts. Should a group fail to deliver within the time specified any order which it has accepted or which has been transferred to it by order of the chairman, the amount of such undelivered tonnage shall be officially charged against its tonnage quota.

Groups which have exceeded their quotas during the preceding quarter according to the above methods of calculation, shall be penalized for each ton in excess, the amount specified by Article XII of the regulations and the excess shall be canceled by the payment specified.

ARTICLE XIII

Organized Markets

The Management Committee shall establish an appropriate organization of the distributors in all export markets which are particularly important. Such organizations shall in the first place aim to exclude entirely competition among the local agents of the four groups on the export market, and in the second place, to assist in supplying compensatory tonnages for the purpose of balancing conditions of excess and deficit.

ARTICLE XIV

Price Fixing

The Management Committee shall fix prices and shall also as far as possible, determine minimum prices "cif" ocean ports, or free frontiers of the countries of destination.

It shall take into consideration, if necessary, the different rates of customs duties affecting the groups as to imports into certain countries. It shall specify both the classifications and the conditions of sale, and shall determine to what extent and under what conditions both agents and jobbers may operate in executing these business transactions.

Strict observance of minimum prices and conditions of sale fixed by the Management Committee is obligatory for all groups. Any reduction or discount in prices or alleviation of sale conditions, in any form whatsoever, is absolutely forbidden.

ARTICLE XV

*Meeting
Price
Competition*

When, for the purpose of fighting competition, the Management Committee shall authorize bids and sales with respect to certain tonnages at prices appreciably below normal prices, each group shall, in principle, share a portion of the sacrifice involved, according to the conditions which the Management Committee shall specify at the opportune time.

ARTICLE XVI

*Business
Booked in
Advance of this
Agreement*

All the groups agree to make known within fifteen days following the date at which this Convention becomes effective all deliveries for which they have contracted previous to this date, and to supply all details (including selling prices and delivery details).

All tonnage shipped on such contracts from this date forward shall be charged against the quotas of those interested groups whose duty it is to make delivery, provided always that such delivery is completed within the first three months of the operation of this agreement.

After these first three months, the Management Committee shall have the right to require, under conditions which it shall specify, that business booked in advance of this agreement shall become the object of tonnage transfers provided in Article XII, unless the measures indicated in this article as applicable to new orders shall be sufficient to accomplish a rapid equalization of conditions of excess and deficit.

It shall become the duty of the groups which are parties to the sales contracts to obtain the approval of their purchasing clientele with respect to the tonnage transfers thus required by the Management Committee at the end of the third month. Should the contracting buyers formally object to such tonnage transfers, the selling group which is party to the contract shall continue to make deliveries, but on orders originating previous to this Convention, all shipments made after the beginning of the fourth month shall be charged against the quota at double the tonnage involved, provided the group's tonnage quota status is in excess at the time. All delivery agreements which extend over more than three months shall be declared with all details before the signature of this Convention.

ARTICLE XVII

Compensation Under Exceptional Circumstances

If any one of the groups shall during a specified accounting period meet with conditions especially severe as a result of circumstances entirely beyond its control (force majeur), the Management Committee, after examination of the case, shall have the power to decide by unanimous vote whether and in what measure it is desirable to accord a more favorable treatment to such group.

ARTICLE XVIII

Supervision

All groups assume the responsibility of continuous and efficacious supervision over the operations of their members, their agents, and their sales organizations, in order to guarantee that the provisions of this Convention shall be strictly observed by all. Each group shall send to the Central Bureau a complete list of its agents and sales organizations. This list shall be carefully kept up-to-date.

In addition, the Management Committee shall organize in as short time as possible an international audit (supervision) entrusted either to an independent organization which it shall designate, or, by unanimous decision, to a supervising body established by its own members. The method of operation and the measures to be used by the international supervisory body shall be determined by the Management Committee.

All the groups undertake, without reservation, to

facilitate in the most comprehensive manner the investigations of the international supervisory agency. The groups shall be responsible for any infraction whatever of the provisions of this Convention, whether by themselves, their members, their agents or their sales organizations.

ARTICLE XIX

Infractions

For each infraction of the provisions of this Convention, the Management Committee shall have the power to impose upon the group which is at fault penalties of not over 50/- gold shillings per metric ton applying to all tonnage involved in the infraction (but at a minimum rate of 20/- gold shillings per ton in case of a violation of regulations concerning the protection of the domestic markets).

Whenever the interested group shall judge the Management Committee's decision inequitable, it shall have the right of appeal to a special committee composed of the chairmen of the groups of the Entente Internationale de l'Acier, which committee shall make final decision by not less than a three-fourths vote.

The Management Committee shall decide upon the disposition of the amount received from the penalties which have been finally levied. Those penalties which result from a violation of regulations concerning protection of domestic markets shall be paid to the group which has suffered from the violation.

ARTICLE XX

Payments and Guaranties

The Management Committee shall, whenever it deems necessary, call upon the groups for contributions proportional to their quotas, to provide for or to participate in the general expenses or other funds disbursed in the common interest.

The deposits intended to insure the orderly performance of obligations assumed by the groups under the EIA agreement shall be used equally to insure performance of obligations resulting from this Convention.

ARTICLE XXI

New Members and Amendment of Regulations

Producers in other countries may not be admitted to membership in this international association, nor may the regulations be amended except by unanimous decision.

ARTICLE XXII

Settlement of Disputes

All disputes which may arise between groups in regard to the interpretation or the execution of this Convention shall without exception be first brought before a special committee consisting of the chairmen of the groups of the EIA, whose decisions shall require a three-fourths vote.

If the decision of the special committee composed of the chairmen of the groups of the EIA is not accepted, it shall be compulsory to obtain a ruling on the case through the medium of arbitration. In such case each of the parties shall, within a period of one month, appoint an arbiter and the two arbiters so appointed shall choose a third. If these two arbiters are unable to agree in the selection of a third within the period of one month, this third arbiter shall be appointed by the president of the International Chamber of Commerce.

The board of arbitration shall render its decision by a majority vote and shall likewise by majority vote decide who shall assume the arbitration expenses. Its decisions shall not be subject to appeal. All groups signatory to this Convention obligate themselves to conform to the decisions of the board of arbitration and they expressly renounce any recourse to legal proceedings.

The text of this Convention is printed simultaneously in both French and German. It is hereby specified that in all cases under arbitration the board of arbitration shall be guided by the German text if the arbitration has been requested by the German group, and by the French text if the arbitration has been requested by one of the other three groups.

The groups sign this Convention with the reservation that an agreement shall be concluded with the Belgian re-rollers.

Brussels, the 18th day of July, 1933.

Al. Meyer
J. Van Hoegaerden
Th. Laurent
Poensgen

APPENDIX V A

DEFINITION OF DOMESTIC MARKETS

The following shall be regarded as domestic markets:

a. For the German group:

The territory of the German Reich (including the free ports). The territory of Danzig, provided that special agreements shall be made with the other groups.

b. For the Belgian and Luxemburg groups:

Belgium, Luxemburg, and the Belgian Congo.

c. For the French group:

France proper, the Saar Territory, Algiers, Martinique, Guadeloupe and its dependencies, French Guiana, Reunion Island, Indo-China, New Caledonia, the Island of Madagascar and its dependencies, the former Gabon, Senegal, Guinea, the French Sudan (the Upper Senegal and Niger), Mauretania, the French possessions in Oceania, the Islands of St. Pierre and Miquelon, Tunis, the French Congo, the Ivory Coast, Dahomey, Oubanghi, Chari-Tchad, French Somaliland, and the French possession in India.

The French Protectorate of Morocco, provided that there shall be concluded separate quota-agreements with the other groups based on the reference period.

APPENDIX V B

EXTRACT

From the Minutes of the Decisions Taken in the Meetings [of the Management Committee of the EIA] of April 25 and May 5, 1933

The quota-shares fixed for the first year, that is, from June 1, 1933, to May 31, 1934, are as follows:

	Per Cent
Germany and the Saar	24.500
France	37.644
Belgium	16.213
Luxemburg	21.643
	100.000

These quotas were established, taking into account on the one hand the German and French [quota] sales:

	Per Cent
Germany and the Saar	3.000
France	4.016

On the other hand the following quota renunciations of the four groups:

	Per Cent
Germany and the Saar	0.159
France	0.072
Belgium	0.168
Luxemburg	0.168

The quota-shares fixed for the second year, that is, from June 1, 1934, to May 31, 1935, are as follows:

	Per Cent
Germany and the Saar	25.750
France	39.317
Belgium	14.961
Luxemburg	19.972
	100.000

These quotas were established, taking into account the German and French [quota] sales:

	Per Cent
Germany and the Saar	1.750
France	2.343

and the voluntary renunciations of the Belgian and Luxemburg groups:

	Per Cent
Belgium	1.252
Luxemburg	1.671

For the following years the quotas of the German and the French groups will be the following:

	Per Cent
Germany and the Saar	27.500
France	41.660
Belgium and Luxemburg	30.840
	100.000

It is agreed upon that the Belgian and Luxemburg quotas mentioned above will be adjusted according to specific agreements concluded between these two groups.

Rates Under Which Quota-shares Are Sold

It is agreed that the German and French Groups receive for the quota-sales effected by them 11/- gold shillings per ton for finished products ceded by them. This amount will be paid to the German and French Groups through a common fund composed of the payments of all groups proportionately to their deliveries within the framework of the EIA agreement.

Quota-shares of the German and the Belgian Groups for the Second Year and the Following Years

When sales of quota-shares agreed upon for the first year cease in part, or entirely, those quota-shares which were not sold, are to be charged to the Belgian and Luxemburg groups.

The distribution of the shares of the Belgian and Luxemburg groups will be made according to their quota-shares in the respective comptoirs.

SPECIAL TREATMENT ACCORDED TO THE LUXEMBURG GROUP FOR THE ENTIRE DURATION OF THE AGREEMENT

In each quarter in which the total exportation of this group is less than 1,700,000 tons, the Luxemburg group will be entitled to exceed its quota in each product up to 0.5% of the whole quantum without paying penalties. The special commission of the EIA shall find an appropriate method to administer this regulation in the most practical way.

SPECIAL REGULATIONS RELATING TO THE THIRD AND TO THE FOLLOWING YEARS

Three months before the end of the second year, the Belgian and Luxemburg Groups shall have the right to denounce the Convention effective at the end of the second year if according to the known results of the six last months, the total exportation of crude steel remained less than 4,000,000 tons.

The same right of renunciation shall belong to the same groups under the same conditions at the beginning of the third year and six months later.

This right of denunciation belongs to all groups at the beginnings of the fourth and fifth years if within the last six months of which the results are at that time known the total export of crude steel remains less than 4,000,000 tons.

Taking into account several observations made, it is agreed upon by all groups:

If after twenty-one months, the total exported tonnage reaches 2,000,000 tons per quarter, upon the request of one group the quota-shares in all six comptoirs (semifinished steel, structural shapes, merchant bars, thick plates, medium plates, universal steel) shall be revised. The newly established quotas shall be effective at the beginning of the third year.

This revision should provide that the several groups should attain a position which makes it possible for them to realize their quota-shares in crude steel.

Thus, for instance, the quotas of the Belgian Group should be adjusted in such a way as to put the Belgian Group in a position to realize their quota-shares within the EIA, and especially to attain 26% of the exported total tonnage if this tonnage reached 11,000,000 tons. This 26% includes the figures realized by the Belgian Group during the 22 months in addition to those quantities which result from the augmentation of the Belgian share by the EIA agreement from February, 1933. This later quantity is distributed on the one hand among the six fundamental products of the EIA and on the other hand among those which are outside of the EIA.

If this later distribution should cause disputes, the possibility of arbitration should be considered.

In case no accord can be reached as to the establishment of new quotas, the six comptoirs shall terminate three months after the introduction of such a request.

Luxemburg, May 5, 1933.

Signed: Al. Meyer, J. Van Hoegaerden, Th. Laurent, Poensgen.

APPENDIX VI

WORLD STEEL PRODUCTION 1868-1940, IN MILLIONS OF LONG TONS

Year	United Kingdom	Germany	Saar	Luxemburg	France	Belgium	U.S.S.R.	Poland	Sweden	Spain	Austria	Hungary	Czecho-slovakia	Italy	U.S.A.	Canada	Australia	India	Japan	Other Countries	Total
1868.	0.11	0.09			0.07		0.01		0.01			0.01									0.30
1870.	0.22	0.13			0.08		0.01		0.01			0.02			0.04						0.51
1875.	0.71	0.32			0.21	0.05	0.01		0.02			0.09			0.38						1.79
1876.	0.83	0.37			0.19	0.08	0.01		0.02			0.09			0.55						2.14
1877.	0.89	0.39			0.25	0.10	0.05		0.02			0.10			0.60						2.40
1878.	0.98	0.46			0.28	0.12	0.10		0.02			0.09			0.73						2.78
1879.	1.01	0.51			0.33	0.11	0.20		0.03			0.09			0.94						3.21
1880.	1.29	0.69			0.38	0.13	0.29		0.05			0.12			1.25						4.18
1881.	1.78	0.90			0.42	0.14	0.29		0.06			0.13		0.09	1.59						5.30
1882.	2.11	1.07			0.45	0.18	0.24		0.06			0.15		0.13	1.74						6.09
1883.	2.01	1.06			0.52	0.18	0.22		0.07			0.16		0.12	1.67						6.01
1884.	1.77	1.14			0.50	0.18	0.21		0.08			0.31		0.14	1.55						5.85
1885.	1.89	1.20			0.55	0.15	0.19		0.08			0.28		0.18	1.71						6.19
1886.	2.26	1.29			0.43	0.16	0.24		0.11			0.26		0.24	2.56						7.48
1887.	3.04	1.65			0.49	0.23	0.22		0.11			0.30		0.29	3.34						9.68
1888.	3.30	1.76		0.02	0.58	0.24	0.26		0.13			0.39		0.33	2.90						9.86
1889.	3.57	1.96		0.06	0.62	0.26	0.38		0.17			0.42		0.28	3.39						11.04
1890.	3.58	2.10		0.07	0.67	0.22	0.43		0.17			0.50		0.22	4.28						12.28
1891.	3.16	2.41		0.10	0.73	0.24	0.50		0.16			0.48		0.21	3.90						11.85
1892.	2.92	2.61		0.10	0.81	0.26	0.62		0.16			0.50		0.19	4.93						12.97
1893.	2.95	2.98		0.11	0.78	0.27	0.71		0.16			0.56		0.21	4.02						12.68
1894.	3.11	3.56		0.13	0.80	0.40	0.86		0.19			0.65		0.20	4.41						14.12
1895.	3.26	3.83		0.13	0.86	0.45	1.00		0.25			0.73		0.21	6.11						16.65
1896.	4.13	4.63		0.13	1.16	0.59	1.19		0.26	0.10		0.87		0.20	5.28	0.02					18.36
1897.	4.49	4.81		0.14	1.30	0.61	1.58		0.27	0.10		0.92		0.21	7.16	0.02					21.22
1898.	4.57	5.19		0.17	1.41	0.64	1.85		0.29	0.11		1.05		0.25	8.93	0.02					24.18
1899.	4.86	5.78		0.16	1.47	0.72	2.16		0.26	0.11		1.11		0.30	10.64	0.02					27.29
1900.	4.90	6.36		0.18	1.54	0.63	2.18		0.27	0.12		1.14		0.30	10.19	0.02					27.83
1901.	4.90	6.04		0.25	1.40	0.51	2.13		0.29	0.15		1.07		0.30	13.47	0.02					30.56
1902.	4.91	7.34		0.31	1.54	0.76	2.13		0.28	0.16		1.13		0.27	14.95	0.03					33.96
1903.	5.03	8.29		0.37	1.81	0.95	2.38		0.31	0.20		1.11					0.18					

Year	(1)	(2)	(3)	(4)	(5)	(6)	(7)	(8)	(9)	(10)	(11)	(12)	(13)	(14)	(15)	Total
1906	6.40	10.53		0.43	2.41	1.37	2.43	0.39	0.29			0.59	23.36	0.65		52.13
1907	6.52	11.43		0.44	2.72	1.44	2.60	0.41	0.29			?	?	0.51		?
1908	5.30	10.56		0.45	2.68	1.18	2.63	0.43	0.30			0.73	14.02	0.51		40.75
1909	5.88	11.32		0.53	2.99	1.55	3.07	0.31	0.30			0.88	23.96	0.68		53.38
1910	6.37	12.89		0.59	3.36	1.91	3.48	0.46	0.31			1.01	26.09	0.74		59.33
1911	6.46	14.08		0.70	3.78	2.15	3.87	0.46	0.32			0.99	23.68	0.79		59.57
1912	6.80	16.09		0.93	4.36	2.47	4.42	0.51	0.33			0.97	31.25	0.85		71.62
1913	7.66	17.32		1.31	4.61	?	4.75	0.58	0.30			0.92	31.30	1.04		75.15
1914	7.84	13.59		1.12	2.61	?	4.66	0.50	?			0.90	23.51	0.74		59.49
1915	8.55	12.09		0.97	1.07	0.10	4.82	0.59	?			0.99	32.15	0.91		65.57
1916	8.99	14.64		1.29	1.92	0.10	?	0.60	?			1.25	42.77	1.29		77.01
1917	9.72	15.26		1.07	2.20	0.01	?	0.57	?			1.31	45.06	1.56		80.76
1918	9.54	13.87		0.87	1.78	0.01	?	0.54	?			0.98	44.46	1.70		75.99
1919	7.89	7.72		0.36	2.15	0.33	?	0.48	0.25			0.72	34.67	0.93		57.56
1920	9.07	8.40	0.73	0.57	3.00	1.23	0.16	0.26	0.19	0.04	0.96	0.76	42.13	1.11		71.30
1921	3.70	8.93	0.91	0.74	3.05	0.78	0.18	0.35	0.34	0.09	0.84	0.69	19.78	0.67		43.51
1922	5.88	11.53	1.24	1.37	4.46	1.54	0.31	0.31	0.48	0.31	0.98	0.97	35.60	0.48		67.66
1923	8.48	6.20	0.98	1.18	5.03	2.26	0.59	0.27	0.50	0.28	1.11	1.12	44.94	0.88		76.93
1924	8.20	9.68	1.45	1.86	6.79	2.83	0.98	0.53	0.37	0.24	0.67	1.34	37.93	0.66		77.23
1925	7.39	12.00	1.55	2.05	7.33	2.51	1.84	0.57	0.46	0.23	0.77	1.76	45.39	0.76		88.93
1926	3.60	12.15	1.71	2.21	8.30	3.32	2.86	0.60	0.47	0.24	0.78	1.75	48.29	0.78		91.79
1927	8.10	16.06	1.86	2.43	8.18	3.62	3.53	0.49	0.55	0.42	1.23	1.93	44.94	0.92		100.13
1928	8.52	14.29	2.04	2.53	9.35	3.84	4.09	0.65	0.63	0.46	1.41	1.97	51.54	1.24		107.86
1929	9.64	15.99	2.17	2.66	9.55	4.04	4.65	0.76	0.63	0.48	1.36	2.11	56.43	1.39		118.37
1930	7.33	11.36	1.91	2.24	9.33	3.30	5.46	0.86	0.47	0.50	1.22	1.72	40.70	1.01		93.10
1931	5.20	8.16	1.51	2.00	7.70	3.06	5.53	0.53	0.31	0.30	1.02	1.39	35.95	0.67		68.41
1932	5.26	5.68	1.44	1.93	5.55	2.75	5.83	0.52	0.20	0.25	1.54	1.37	13.68	0.34		49.90
1933	7.02	7.49	1.65	1.82	6.43	2.69	6.73	0.62	0.22	0.22	0.80	1.74	23.23	0.40		66.73
1934	8.85	11.73	1.92	1.90	6.08	2.90	9.54	0.85	0.30	0.31	0.84	1.80	26.06	0.74		80.81
1935	9.86	16.19		1.81	6.18	2.98	12.32	0.88	0.36	0.44	0.93	2.18	34.09	0.92	4.63	97.86
1936	11.78	18.91		1.95	6.60	3.12	16.08	0.96	0.41	0.46	1.12	1.99	47.77	1.08	5.28	122.10
1937	12.98	19.54		2.47	7.80	3.81	17.55	1.09	0.64	0.60	1.43	2.05	50.57	1.35	5.72	133.28
1938	10.40	22.89		1.41	6.08	2.25	17.80	0.96		0.60	1.52	2.29	27.74	1.16	5.80	?
1939	13.50	?		1.80	8.47	3.06	18.65	1.10		0.75	?	2.70	47.15	1.35	6.34	?
1940	13.48	?		?	?	?	?	?		?	?	?	59.64	1.94	?	?

Source: Primarily *Statistics of the Iron and Steel Industries for 1937*, published by the British Iron and Steel Federation. This table covers as far as possible the total production of crude steel (ingots and castings). Several countries include, others exclude from their steel production figures for crucible and electric steel. Lorraine is included with Germany until 1918, and with France from 1919 onwards. The Spanish statistics for 1937 and 1938 include the production of Biscay only, representing approximately 75% of the total for all Spain in 1935.

APPENDIX VII

Foreign Trade in Steel Products—1936—Net Tons

Country	Production	Imports	Exports	Consumption
Albania......................	....	5,005	....	5,005
Algeria......................	....	147,072	....	147,072
Argentina....................	....	692,134	....	692,134
Australia....................	783,587	207,874	58,792	932,669
Austria.....................	322,662	50,268	171,277	201,653
Baltic States................	....	121,222	....	121,222
Belgian Congo...............	....	14,227	....	14,227
Belgium-Luxemburg	4,208,438	455,957	3,318,627	1,345,768
Bolivia......................	....	8,170	....	8,170
Brazil.......................	....	369,698	....	369,698
British East Africa..........	....	46,662	....	46,662
British West Africa.........	....	73,174	....	73,174
British Malaya..............	....	123,352	....	123,352
Bulgaria.....................	....	87,332	....	87,332
Canada.....................	937,878	517,871	304,123	1,151,626
Canary Islands..............	....	2,178	....	2,178
Other Central America......	....	43,413	....	43,413
Ceylon......................	....	29,518	....	29,518
Chile.......................	....	123,209	....	123,209
China.......................	....	683,380	....	683,380
Colombia....................	....	83,075	....	83,075
Cuba.......................	....	64,649	....	64,649
Cyprus......................	....	341	....	341
Czechoslovakia..............	1,221,920	48,968	358,417	912,471
Denmark....................	....	571,018	....	571,018
Ecuador....................	....	12,779	....	12,779
Egypt.......................	....	196,940	....	196,940
France......................	5,245,180	181,662	1,789,731	3,637,111
Finland.....................	....	267,377	....	267,377
French Indo-China..........	....	48,284	....	48,284
French West Africa.........	....	37,914	....	37,914
Germany....................	15,023,887	706,709	4,053,575	11,677,021
Great Britain...............	9,574,432	1,538,653	2,287,131	8,825,954
Greece......................	....	152,734	....	152,734
The Guianas.................	....	560	....	560
Hungary....................	....	73,477	....	73,477
Iceland.....................	....	4,315	....	4,315
India.......................	668,193	557,671	586,441	639,423
Irak........................	....	1,251	....	1,251
Iran........................	....	107,094	....	107,094
Ireland.....................	....	112,525	....	112,525
Italian East Africa.........	....	27,302	....	27,302
Italy.......................	1,587,267	235,906	78,531	1,744,642
Japan.......................	4,873,780	1,499,053	88,559	6,284,274
Jugoslavia..................	....	112,690	....	112,690
Liberia.....................	....	1,158	....	1,158
Libya.......................	....	10,028	....	10,028
Madagascar.................	....	6,907	....	6,907
Mexico.....................	....	172,228	....	172,228
Netherlands.................	....	1,028,223	300,936	727,287
Netherlands Indies.........	....	197,071	....	197,071
New Zealand................	....	194,122	....	194,122

Country	Production	Imports	Exports	Consumption
Norway..................	....	355,647	....	355,647
Palestine.................	....	73,684	....	73,684
Panama..................	....	24,496	....	24,496
Paraguay.................	....	3,830	....	3,830
Peru.....................	....	48,894	....	48,894
Philippines...............	....	102,768	....	102,768
Poland and Danzig........	924,728	60,362	313,871	671,219
Port. East Africa..........	....	46,227	....	46,227
Port. West Africa.........	....	3,150	....	3,150
Portugal.................	....	165,828	....	165,828
Rhodesia.................	....	3,522	....	3,522
Rumania.................	....	185,767	....	185,767
Siam....................	....	26,722	....	26,722
Spain....................	401,242	35,796	....	437,038
Sweden..................	754,596	774,245	413,709	1,115,132
Switzerland..............	....	419,068	....	419,068
Syria....................	....	32,874	....	32,874
Tangiers and Morocco.....	....	51,169	....	51,169
Tunisia..................	....	48,468	....	48,468
Turkey..................	....	174,199	....	174,199
Union South Africa........	247,968	738,717	....	986,685
United States.............	37,857,544	626,986	1,372,796	37,111,734
U. S. S. R...............	13,758,752	312,628	783,503	13,287,877
Uruguay.................	....	47,935	....	47,935
Venezuela................	....	98,042	....	98,042
Other West Indies Islands..	....	82,649	....	82,649
TOTAL.............	98,392,054	16,598,073	16,280,019	98,710,108

These figures compiled by the American Iron and Steel Institute give an approximate picture of the foreign trade in finished steel products for 1936. As mentioned several times in this study trade statistics about iron and steel products are often blurred by a rather hazy terminology on the one hand, by cumulative publication of figures for iron and steel products on the other. In addition, the trade in scrap iron and steel is not always separated from other iron and steel. For instance, in the above listed figures the exports of steel products of the Soviet Union are listed as 783,503 net tons. According to the foreign trade statistics of the U. S. Department of Commerce the exports of the Soviet Union in 1936 included 700,000 long tons of pig iron, and 73,000 long tons of other iron and steel products. According to the *Annual Report for 1938 of the Stahlwerks-Verband*, the iron and steel exports of the Soviet Union for 1936 amounted to 782,000 metric tons, and this figure includes 710,000 metric tons of pig iron. The figures published in the annual statistics for 1937 of the British Iron and Steel Federation are the following: Total iron and steel exports of the Soviet Union in 1936, 814,149 long tons: this figure includes 761,621 long tons of pig iron and ferro-alloys, the rest is made of several kinds of steel products.

APPENDIX VIII

UNITED KINGDOM
TOTAL EXPORTS OF IRON AND STEEL AND MANUFACTURES THEREOF, 1867-1938

Year	EXPORTS Quantity—long tons	EXPORTS Value—£	Year	EXPORTS Quantity—long tons	EXPORTS Value—£
1867	1,920,740	17,374,915	1910	4,588,009	42,976,671
1870	2,718,826	23,536,554	1911	4,515,905	43,730,292
1875	2,435,696	26,664,434	1912	4,807,523	48,597,677
1880	3,549,380	27,225,247	1913	4,969,225	55,350,747
1884	3,428,850	24,272,643	1914	3,884,153	41,677,830
1885	3,045,466	21,449,303	1915	3,196,983	40,406,196
1886	3,243,634	21,479,230	1916	3,294,624	56,673,705
1887	3,853,716	21,164,559	1917	2,328,030	44,828,253
1888	3,821,591	26,019,685	1918	1,608,103	36,843,078
1889	4,039,463	28,709,954	1919	2,232,843	64,423,510
1890	3,851,528	31,063,114	1920	3,251,225	128,907,361
1891	3,129,078	26,522,631	1921	1,696,889	63,603,550
1892	2,632,791	21,438,152	1922	3,397,185	60,861,674
1893	2,738,052	20,258,303	1923	4,317,537	76,155,978
1894	2,566,742	18,467,447	1924	3,851,435	74,534,129
1895	2,738,441	19,428,383	1925	3,731,366	68,178,462
1896	3,422,974	23,462,793	1926	2,987,930	55,060,875
1897	3,599,273	24,405,374	1927	4,196,206	69,383,416
1898	3,159,548	22,391,711	1928	4,260,462	66,789,184
1899	3,601,454	27,712,727	1929	4,379,531	68,002,782
1900	3,446,752	31,623,353	1930	3,159,661	51,261,119
1901	2,812,523	25,008,757	1931	1,978,958	30,375,155
1902	3,473,645	28,877,337	1932	1,887,295	28,040,810
1903	3,564,601	30,399,261	1933	1,921,794	29,879,132
1904	3,262,842	28,066,671	1934	2,250,176	35,078,385
1905	3,721,382	31,826,438	1935	2,368,659	37,056,744
1906	4,682,200	39,840,595	1936	2,234,372	36,678,170
1907	5,152,227	46,563,386	1937	2,607,043	49,191,075
1908	4,096,521	37,406,028	1938	1,961,951	42,791,626
1909	4,210,799	38,192,142			

Source: *Statistics of the Iron and Steel Industries*, published by the British Iron and Steel Federation.

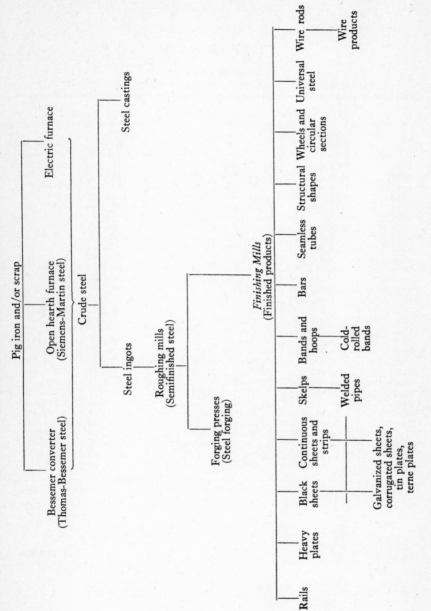

SIMPLIFIED DIAGRAM OF STEELMAKING

Pig iron and/or scrap

Bessemer converter
(Thomas-Bessemer steel)

Open hearth furnace
(Siemens-Martin steel)

Electric furnace

Crude steel

Steel castings

Steel ingots

Roughing mills
(Semifinished steel)

Forging presses
(Steel forging)

Finishing Mills
(Finished products)

Rails

Heavy plates

Black sheets

Continuous sheets and strips

Galvanized sheets, corrugated sheets, tin plates, terne plates

Skelps

Welded pipes

Bands and hoops

Cold-rolled bands

Bars

Seamless tubes

Structural shapes

Wheels and circular sections

Universal steel

Wire rods

Wire products

Index